American Work Values

SUNY series in The Sociology of Work
Richard H. Hall, editor

AMERICAN WORK VALUES

Their Origin and Development

Paul Bernstein

State University of New York Press

Published by
State University of New York Press, Albany

For information, address State University of New York Press,
State University Plaza, Albany, NY 12246

Production by Cynthia Tenace Lassonde
Marketing by Terry Abad Swierzowski

Library of Congress Cataloging-in-Publication Data

Bernstein, Paul, 1927–
    American work values : their origin and development / by Paul
Bernstein.
        p.   cm. — (SUNY series in the sociology of work)
    Includes bibliographical references and index.
    ISBN 0-7914-3215-7 (hardcover : acid-free paper). — ISBN
0-7914-3216-5 (pbk. : acid-free paper)
    1. Work ethic—United States—History.   2. Industrialization—
United States—History.   3. Public welfare—United States—History.
I. Title.   II. Series
HD8066.B45   1997
306.3′613′0973—dc20

96-21982
CIP

10 9 8 7 6 5 4 3 2 1

To Irma

Contents

Acknowledgments

I would like to offer my deep appreciation to the many members of the Rochester Institute of Technology library staff for their invaluable assistance. Over the last four years they rendered a level of support that made my research far less difficult. Special thanks are due Margaret Bartlett, Sheila Simmons, and Wendy Di Matteo for their close attention to numerous requests for books, articles, microfilm, and interlibrary loans.

I also want to extent my thanks to all at SUNY Press who made this publication a pleasant task. In particular, I want to acknowledge the efforts of Chris Worden and Dick Hall who have seen this work through from the very beginning.

But above all, I want to thank my wife, Irma Bernstein, for the many hours spent proofreading and offering numerous ideas that improved both the writing and organization of the book. Her valuable observations and questions materially enhanced the manuscript and helped the author avoid more than a few pitfalls.

INTRODUCTION

Throughout history work has been the constant companion of the human race. It has been seen as an obligation to God, a source of livelihood and opportunity, and of late, a promise of self-fulfillment. But in all its hues and gradations, work has continued to intrigue its participants. To early churchmen like Luther, it formed the base of life. For the faithful, he saw labor as a station from which none should deviate. Luther demanded that everyone maintain themselves in a calling so they would not be a burden to society. And in doing that, they would fulfill their earthly obligations to God and their communities. For Luther, work existed in a context that favored physical labor. He lauded the toil of peasant and artisan, and denigrated the efforts of merchants who produced neither goods nor food. But even in his circumscribed approval of work, Luther inadvertently opened the door to the entrepreneurial types he despised.

For Calvinists and Puritans, the God-centered universe of Luther remained the central feature of their worldview. Wealth earned by hard work and intelligence was permitted, but never for personal pleasure or self-aggrandizement. The saintly souls of Geneva and Boston viewed work as a worldly way-station that staved off temptation, and possibly paved the path to election. One could never be sure of salvation, but for Calvinists and their Puritan offshoots obedience to God in one's general calling was a *sine qua non*. To be industrious in a personal calling was a secondary but increasingly necessary adjunct. But all of this was done in God's name. Accumulated riches could be donated for community betterment. They might even be reinvested, but could not be used for material self-improvement. Yet even within this strict

1

prescription, the Puritans were gradually but inexorably overwhelmed by the commercial tide that first swept over the globe after 1450. During the course of the sixteenth and seventeenth centuries, their outlook underwent a change that more and more supported diligence and the wealth that flowed from it. One only has to scan the sermons and admonitions of William Perkins and the later Cotton Mather to see how they tried to cope with this shift in work values. But within this ideological transformation, other forces were operative. During the three centuries after the beginning of the Commercial Revolution, the Tudor enclosures forced many from the land in England. They moved to small workshops, and were severed from their traditional agricultural base except for tiny plots near their cottages. Impersonal market forces soon became the arbiter of their existence, although their limited landholdings provided a small shield from the irregular work doled out by merchants through the domestic system. By the sixteenth century a growing number of factories could be found in both the public and private sectors. They provided badly needed work, but also subjected the growing industrial workforce to the job insecurity of the market system.

For those who possessed neither cottages nor work in the newly emerging industries of the sixteenth century, the open road beckoned. Many became wanderers, vagrants, or vagabonds, the displaced poor who struck fear into village and town as they wended their way on the road to nowhere. They were assumed to be idlers, and some were. But the bitter distaste with which they were regarded did not take into account the enormous population growth of sixteenth-century Europe which made work exceedingly scarce despite the growth of industry. And when considered along with the terrible inflation and new market forces that also came into play after 1500, these wandering vagabonds were not a good indication of a declining work ethic. More likely, they could be described as a socially displaced proletariat weighed down by a lack of jobs. But to Luther and Perkins these unfortunates were little more than dangerous idlers. In colonial America the Connecticut minister Thomas Hooker continued this attack on vagrants. In his 1659 *The Application of Redemption*, he urged that vagabonds come "under the eye of authority" so they would not live "idly or unprofitably" (Dorfman, 1:43). In the 1770s the town of Fairfield,

Connecticut signalled the wandering unemployed that they would not maintain new arrivals who became dependent, while Virginia statutes of 1672 and 1723 applied English laws against able-bodied persons who were idle(Handlin and Handlin, 9; Morris, *Government and Labor*, 6). Thus, in both England and America those without work were seen as a dissolute remnant that defied God and man in their willingness to avoid labor and seek public largesse.

At the time there was little understanding that thousands had been torn from their traditional agricultural roots, that they were subject to unseen and misunderstood market forces. Moreover, they had no place to turn until the Poor Law of 1601 was passed in England and then supplemented by workhouses on both shores of the Atlantic. It was true that many artisans and laborers took advantage of the numerous saints days, feasts, and wakes to absent themselves from work. Saint Monday became a standing complaint among masters, and was noticed with some pain by Franklin. And while time and work discipline would continue to trouble employers for centuries to come, it should not obscure the fact that the new eighteenth-century factory hands were making a great socioeconomic leap into the unknown.

On the industrial front, Britain entered into a period of great economic expansion after 1730. This far outstripped the growth described by John Nef for the period 1540–1640, and was many decades ahead of the American colonies, which remained a pre-industrial region until at least the 1840s. Rapid progress was made in the British woollen, cotton, mining, and iron industries, among many others. But continued absenteeism made efficient production in the factories of Arkwright and Wedgwood difficult. The new managers tried such inducements as liquor, cash bonuses, long-term contracts, and a gift of some of goods produced. All worked to some degree, but there was a long road to travel before the irregular work habits of the traditional past could be modified. A similar pattern prevailed in colonial America. Poor work habits were cited by Innes in the Springfield, Massachusetts of 1682 (Innes, *Labor in a New Land*, 104). It was no better in early Jamestown, and the Massachusetts General Court found it necessary in 1633 to threaten punishment for the idle (Bruchey, *Colonial Merchant*, 101). That the new factory work with its division of labor required the coordinated effort of many people was not perceived by laborers as their problem. Factories were able to "coax" agricultural laborers through their portals by superior wages. In this regard both Perkin and Mantoux viewed improved compensation as a decisive factor (Perkin, 128–29; Mantoux, 421–24). Beyond this, job security would have been a positive, but in most establishments the fluctuations of the market did not permit it. Thus, the tedium of repetitive work and its chancy availability reenforced the absenteeism and lateness of many English workers. And when these problems were exacerbated by layoffs due to poor market conditions or weather that disrupted the flow of materials, the traditional irregularity of the workers was given an added impetus. Many of the same problems were to be played out on the North American side of the Atlantic, but in a context of greater opportunity and a stronger entrepreneurial ethic. But even here poverty could be an unpleasant companion. Poor relief in Philadelphia increased sharply between 1700 and 1775 as almshouses and hospitals were often overwhelmed by a floodtide of immigrants from Scotland and Ireland (Nash, "Franklin's Philadelphia," 170). By 1750 virtually every city on the Atlantic coast had an almshouse, while rural areas like Albemarle County, Virginia used overseers of the poor to deal with unemployment and idleness (Bruchey, *Roots*, 58–59).

For those who would work, labor in the New World could be as rigorous in Massachusetts as in the Midlands. North America offered new immigrants abundant work, opportunities for their children, and a society less beholden to a prideful gentry. Few mills had appeared in North America prior to 1776, but for the artisans and laborers who migrated across the Atlantic work was available at good pay. There was as Bernard Bailyn pointed out a "powerful American magnet" from 1695 to 1801 that drew off twenty percent of the natural increase of population of England. For these bookbinders, goldsmiths, glassblowers, and carpenters, North America offered challenge and opportunity. And for the very ambitious who were willing to endure the rigors of the Appalachian frontier, there was land to be had at little cost. Work on the frontier was not easy, but compared to what was available in England or the Germanies, it offered more promise for the future. Bailyn's example of John Harrower who fled the Shetlands in 1773 is an excellent case study of the opportunity ethic that drove so many to the New World (Bailyn, *Peopling*, 41–43).

For slaves who were forcibly removed from Africa from the seventeenth century onward, opportunity was an unknown concept. In place of what white settlers enjoyed was a "racial subordination" attached to a paternalistic social structure. In the plantation world of the South, paternalism was integral to the socioeconomic bargain that defined slave labor "as a legitimate return" to the master class for its "protection and direction." But in its acceptance slaveowners became partners in an pact of mutual obligation. Within this value system, the slaveowners of the antebellum South recognized their need for the productive capacity of slave labor, but they placed little emphasis on the humanity of its participants (Genovese, 3–5).

But for European immigrants the open continent offered opportunity and challenge for those who would grasp it. Among those who did were the Moravians of Pennsylvania and North Carolina, the Quakers of Philadelphia, the farmers of the Connecticut valley, and the tobacco planters of Virginia. Their life styles and attitudes were based on work values transported to America with the Puritans, Anglicans, and various German sects. Most came from an England that was largely pre-industrial before 1730, and the values they brought reflected a belief system that prized faith in God, work, and thrift.

But within both Britain and its colonies the tide of a powerful market economy was also enveloping and enervating these older values. It was a current that had been growing before the Tudor reign, and had jumped the gap from Britain to America. The American ministerial elite worried in both sermon and script that a communitarian and God-centered universe was being undermined by a spirit of self-interest and entrepreneurial drive. Worldly gain through competition had become the new justification for hard work. The spirit of self-improvement and belief in an opportunity ethic was subtly pushing God into the background. In this situation, the new entrepreneurial types in America were not to be denied. Men like Thomas Breedon, Richard Wharton, and Stephen Girard would not be held off by the theology of the past. Toil had to lead to riches or the risk was not worth taking. And to their great delight, the new continent offered the perfect milieu for their venturesome spirit. Social mobility, availability of land, and a can-do outlook drove the new leaders to earn all they could. America was a frontier society that enabled energetic farmers, artisans, and businessmen to work for personal success in a world devoid of British class strictures. Yes, there were patroons and proprietors, but the opportunities in the New World were so great that they were but isolated and momentary barriers.

Stephen Innes has argued that English workers lacked a "possessive individualism and economic rationality" (Innes, *Labor in a New Land*, 75–77). This would suggest that those who came to America were among a select group that grasped the opportunity ethic and were able to sense the possibilities inherent in the new continent. This did not mean that North America was a problem-free zone. There was poverty in the urban centers along the Atlantic during the early eighteenth century, and attempts to alleviate it included European-style workhouses as well as the more high-minded Quaker "bettering houses." Moreover, it does not suggest that every immigrant was of sterling character. Some who came to Maryland and Georgia were convicts, while others brought with them the English traditions of hard drinking and the idleness of Saint Monday.

But it does indicate that by the 1730s the traditional God-centered work values had undergone a fundamental change. For the next century and a half, work would increasingly be viewed as opportunity, but this optimistic outlook would be modified by the unpleasant and repetitive labor needed in the mills of Lynn and Lowell. Setting the tone for the nineteenth-century emphasis on diligent effort in America were the new industrial magnates, politicians, and publicists. But with the advent of the twentieth century, the proponents of scientific management seized the initiative by defining a new systematic nature of work and how people should be rewarded for its repetitive labor. Following them, but not necessarily building on their structure of time-and-motion studies, were a new cadre of social scientists. Men like Elton Mayo initiated an interest in human relations in the 1920s, while researchers such as Kurt Lewin and the Tavistock investigators began significant work with groups in the workplace. By the 1960s the focus had shifted to workers as a valuable human resource, to their need for participation in decision-making and their desire for self-fulfillment.

With this in mind, it is important to underscore that the dominant work themes of nineteenth-century America emphasized hard work, punctuality, and reliability. Horace Mann could tell Americans that "we are an industrious and frugal people," while the young American politician Lewis Cass dangled the prospect of opportunity and riches to Americans if only they would strive to succeed. The McGuffey readers, the Peter Parley books, and the Horatio Alger stories taught generations of children that labor, time-discipline, and steadiness were virtues worth emulating. Later Andrew Carnegie, the banker Henry Clews, and advocates such as Richard Nixon and Ray Kroc of McDonald's rounded out a more recent cast of cheerleaders.

Despite this adulation of labor, the workers themselves had not fully put the irregular habits of the past behind them. Not only was the problem of a shortened work-week due to the ravages of Saint Monday still a problem in industrializing America, but heavy drinking on the job inhibited efficiency. Some nineteenth-century American workers absented themselves to hunt, "frolic," or attend election day and Independence Day celebrations. Others left to harvest crops at their homesteads. All of this caused American employers to seek female employees, and in some cases children, since they proved to be more compliant. Still, these more leisurely carryovers of an agricultural past lingered. Not until the more rational methodology of the Tayloristic timekeepers was introduced late in the nineteenth century were the surviving remnants of ancient work values expunged.

Yet there were other matters to consider in looking at work in its broadest context during the nineteenth and twentieth centuries. Of great importance was the opportunity factor. In the United States this "opportunity ethic" was far more powerful than in the class-driven upstairs-downstairs society of Britain. The idea of getting ahead was preached with vigor in the McGuffey readers, from the lips of Andrew Carnegie, and by the success of current leaders such as William Gates of Microsoft and Steve Jobs of Apple Computer and Next. Foreign observers like the British visitor Frederick Marryat in the 1830s noted that in America "there is room for all . . . and all may receive the reward due for their labor." And Michel Chevalier observed during the same decade that an American is "brought up with the idea that he will have some particular occupation . . . that if he is active and intelligent he will make a fortune." The cult of the "self-made man" was alive and would survive into the twentieth century as part of the mythology of the American business world.

In the United States attitudes of deep concern over the mechanization of factories also emerged in the first half of the nineteenth century. These could be seen in the writings of the New England worker-poet Lucy Larcom and the ideas of Albert Brisbane when he spoke to the Lowell workers in 1846. But they also appeared in an 1881 publication of George Beard, an early pioneer in psychosomatic medicine, who saw the use of clocks and watches in plants as a cause of "nervousness." Resistance to rationalization and regularity continued into the twentieth century, and even during World War I large American plants reported 10 percent absenteeism.

Edward Bellamy in *Looking Backward 2000–1887* sought the solution to the problem of rationally organized facilities by his advocacy of centralized control. Industrialists like Henry Frick and Andrew Carnegie were also smitten by the idea of scientific efficiency, and while unionists could sing "Solidarity Forever" after 1912, this new theme of control, rationalization, and efficiency swept over them in the early years of the twentieth century. These ideas were most effectively advocated by Frederick Taylor who was ably reenforced by the Gilbreths and Gantt. His impact was so profound that even today more than a few plants and service industries employ variations of his methods. Taylor's advocacy of time studies, later supplemented by Frank Gilbreth to become time-and-motion studies, was an attempt to find the most efficient movements needed to complete a job in the shortest time. Planners and production managers, the new bureaucratic-managerial elite, would then control, coordinate, and monitor the work. To prevent malingering on the job, Taylor recommended a piece-work system that would provide the incentive needed for work-intensification. Because he felt that workers were primarily "economic men," such an approach was certain to result in greater output. However, workers saw the possibilities of a speed-up in this new scientific management, and responded with anger, threats, and passive resistance to the men with stop-watches.

The new managerial elites who increasingly ran American industry after the 1860s were subject to other important influences that shaped their thinking about work. The social Darwinism of both Herbert Spencer and William Graham Sumner helped shift their value systems to accept business as a battlefield where only the strongest would survive. Managers came to see themselves as forward-looking and knowledgeable leaders who were ready to battle the American Federation of Labor and other unions in a bitter open shop campaign in the 1890s and the decade beyond. They had no intention of sharing control nor were most alert to the need for worker cooperation as a way of improving productivity.

Blending in nicely with these views on administrative direction and control were the ideas of the sociologist Max Weber. His publications stressed the need for managers to push for precision and speed and purge the personal and emotional elements out of work. Henri Fayol added to this support of management by control in his influential *General and Industrial Management* (1916). Not only did he suggest a division of labor so important to managers and the advocates of scientific management, but he argued that managers must organize, plan, command, coordinate, and control. In the following year E. H. Fish suggested a "human engineering" approach. He believed that if one constructed an appropriate work environment employee behavior could be redirected into productive channels. Incentives and penalties could also be used to get the desired results. There was no discussion of what motivated employees to perform, only how the physical conditions of labor could be changed to make work more palatable.

By the 1920s work values based on control, authority, and oversight had become the touchstones of American management. Workers were not capable of contributing their ideas. Their bodies would do. In fact, the "rabble hypothesis" that was prevalent among managers saw society as a loose collection of unorganized individuals who looked only to their self-interest. This thesis was attacked by the Australian social scientist Elton Mayo during a 1923 study of Philadelphia mule spinners. It marked an important milestone that would lead him to the famous Hawthorne experiments, and of equal importance, signalled the emergence of behavioral scientists as the leading thinkers in the redefinition of what people wanted from work. The theological period of work values based on ministerial direction and hopes for salvation was long gone. A second phase that offered its participants both opportunity and alienation was still strongly in place, and it would now fall to the social scientists of Hawthorne, Tavistock, and men like Kurt Lewin to lead the way into the era of human relations, sociotechnical studies, and the use of autonomous work groups.

The Hawthorne experiments, beginning in 1924, proved to be the beginning of a new mind-set about work, work values, and the motivation needed to enable employees to perform at peak levels. Beginning with the Illumination experiments and including the Relay Test Room and Bank Wiring efforts, Mayo and his colleagues noted that things other than the physical conditions of work might be of value in determining work output. Paying attention to employees by making them participants in the experiments seemed to be important, as was the influence of informal groups in the factory. These groups could and did restrict output in the Bank Wiring experiment to what they felt was a fair day's work. Other efforts suggested the importance of good social relations in the workplace. Beyond this, many felt that the primary group to which employees were attached did much to shape their values and goals. The power of the group could also be seen in a study done in Britain in 1931 by S. B. Matthewson in which non-union workers restricted productivity to avoid speed-ups.

During the decades of the thirties and forties the Human Relations Movement gained strength. Managers who treated employees badly were seen as the cause of low-quality work and poor morale. Workers wanted to be viewed as "cooperators" rather than servants. Thus, it was the job of the manager to develop systems that would lead to a mutuality of effort by everyone in the business. Chester Barnard urged not only cooperation between managers and employees, but the need for better *upward* communication. He went as far as to say that organizations should no longer be based on coercion and stressed the importance of "natural groups."

But it was left to Kurt Lewin to illuminate the importance of the work group. In his research at the University of Iowa and Massachusetts Institute of Technology, Lewin's work on group dynamics called attention to the fact that the group could modify individual work values impeding change in the workplace.

Through this process Lewin believed each group member could learn to participate in decision-making that in itself would become an important source of motivation. In the late forties the Tavistock Institute of Human Relations in London also studied the significance of work groups in the newly nationalized British coal industry. Their work underscored the centrality of group norms, and showed the importance of both social and technical factors in work. This sociotechnical approach was later to prove of great value in the 1962 Industrial Democracy project in Norway where Eric Trist worked closely with Einar Thorsrud and his colleagues. Here the use of autonomous work groups resulted in increased output in most of the experiments, and at Norsk Hydro, led to decreased absenteeism and lower costs.

Business leaders were also active in redefining the role of the employee. In the late forties and early fifties men like Alexander Heron of Crown Zellerbach attacked Taylorism because it confined thinking to managers and engineers, while James C. Worthy of Sears, Roebuck argued that scientific management failed to secure the participation of workers and had thus diminished their "creative relationship with work." The Guest-Walker study of the assembly line in a 1952 auto plant offered yet another appeal to replace the Tayloristic division of labor.

Social scientists like Abraham Maslow added to the voices that sought to understand the needs that motivated human beings. His concept of self-fulfillment, while not supported by conclusive empirical evidence, still provided a powerful stepping-stone for later investigators. Douglas McGregor reenforced Maslow's thinking in 1960 when he argued for more positive managerial assumptions about the work capacity of employees in his Theory Y approach. Openness and trust rather than control and punishment gradually entered the lexicon of business in the Sixties. In 1966 Frederick Herzberg added to this thinking by stressing the importance of work content as the key to employee motivation. Critical to his theory were the positive roles of challenge, achievement, responsibility and advancement. To this Two-Factor (Motivation-Hygiene) theory, Richard Walton suggested in 1975 that Quality of Worklife (QWL) programs offered employers the opportunity to increase productivity by treating employees as valued human resources. To do this, employees needed job security and opportunities to develop their capacity.

For the future it seems clear that a modern work ethic will need to enlist the loyalty and skills of employees. In many occupations requiring advanced education and personal initiative empowerment and trust will become the *sine qua non* of industrial progress. Even in more standardized work, employee initiative will continue to be a necessity. As Paul Adler noted in his 1993 publication "Time and Motion Regained," Tayloristic work of a repetitive nature can still be made challenging if the work teams themselves are holding the stop-watches. For many managers, Adler's analysis of the GM-Toyota venture in Fremont, California may be of more than passing interest.

Attention also must be given to a very different series of work values that have emerged in the last three decades. Because women in the nineties comprised 46 percent of the labor force, employers have had to institute a variety of flexible work options. In addition to such changes as the use of home work and job sharing, firms such as Stride Rite of Cambridge, Massachusetts have set up child-care facilities. GE Silicones of Waterford, New York has initiated a program through which employees can get a leave if a child or elderly relative is ill. Critical to these programs of the 1990s is the desire of many firms to retain the services of their female workers by accommodating to the needs of a new age.

Newer work values, as well as Title VII of the Civil Rights Act of 1964, have moved business a substantial distance along the path of diversity in the workplace. And while these have helped increase minority and female participation, the new affirmative action programs used to implement Title VII have spawned more than a little tension. Improved support for poor families through programs such as Aid to Families with Dependent Children have also led to a great public debate on work and welfare, particularly since the 1994 congressional elections. Interestingly, much of the welfare debate in America centered around the centuries-old concept of the deserving and undeserving poor. It harked back to Luther's denunciation of those who would not work and English statutes between 1597 and 1601 which underscored the obligation to help only those who would labor. Many in colonial America also believed the undeserving poor deserved little more than detention in a workhouse. To support loiterers would only undermine diligence and encourage beggary. It was an outlook that continued to dominate American thinking until the Great Society programs of the 1960s. Only then did the concept of entitlement emerge to compete with the old values that saw work as an obligation to family and community. Whether these antithetical values can be blended remains a heated policy issue of the nineties.

Not to be overlooked has been the quiet but persistent demand for a better balance between work and life. This new work value stressed the need to blend the demands of job and family, and by implication, suggested that work was less than a central aspect of existence. But this new concept had to contend with the ancient quest for job security. It was a problem that settled on the European world of the late fifteenth century with the emergence of a market economy. For the ensuing five hundred years stability of employment continued to be most consistent and elusive work expectation of workers in Europe and America. In our own time, it was exemplified by widespread downsizing to make American industry more competitive with its global rivals. In the context of the mid-nineties, it has lessened loyalty to employers as companies such as Eastman Kodak and IBM have dropped the security blanket that once clothed their employees. Now, as firms search for new markets, lower costs, and improved productivity, their persistent restructuring may diminish the effectiveness of many empowerment efforts. Increasingly, employees may come to see participative management as a sweet but temporary palliative if their livelihood is held hostage by short product life-cycles and competition from distant shores. For the future workers can expect little more than relative job security, and even that will be based on the vagaries of the market and a willingness to learn and grow.

PROLOGUE

This study proposes to evaluate the evolution of American work values during the past five centuries through the prism of historical continuities and discontinuities. For the earliest era, Work as a Sign of Salvation (c. 1450–1730), clergy emerged as the great arbiters of public values. Virtually all saw toil as a service to the community, and many looked to diligent labor as a possible sign of eternal reward. Luther in particular gave work in a calling an early blessing. He extolled Christ the carpenter, and as early as 1530 urged his own son to work hard and walk in the way of the godly. For Luther man's ideal role on earth was to labor in a fixed calling and avoid wordly aggrandizement.

This outlook was modified by the later Calvinists and Puritans. Like Luther, Calvin laid great stress on the calling, but differed by urging that what individuals did through their vocation was of fundamental importance. And while this perspective left the door open to upward mobility, this was not Calvin's intention. Later ministers such as William Perkins and Cotton Mather spoke of a God-ordained duty to toil as part of a personal calling. It was a diligence that demonstrated individual devotion to family and society and might prepare individuals for possible entry into the Elysian fields. In no case was work depicted as an avenue for personal betterment. It was not a road to opportunity nor was it conceived as a vehicle for social improvement.

Significant deviations from these perspectives developed by the initial third of the more secular eighteenth century. In terms of work values, this important *discontinuity* was a phase that can be described in terms of Work as Alienation and Opportunity (c. 1730s–1930s). In colonial America the personal calling was modi-

15

fied to reflect the worldly values of opportunity and self-improvement. Belief in a calling remained, but it was a vocation more often viewed in secular terms of artisanal skill and professional commitment. Salvation was not forgotten, but became a footnote to opportunity and success. With the help of publicists like Franklin and the examples of successful businessmen such as Thomas Hancock, Girard, Carnegie, and Rockefeller, the new ethic of "getting ahead" became the anthem of an industrializing society. It filled the McGuffey readers and offered hope for a better tomorrow through the stories of Horatio Alger.

But in the brave new universe of factories and mines, time-discipline and Taylorism became the industrial passwords to profitability for owners and alienated labor for workers. Employees were forced to abandon a work life defined by the seasons and tides. Their craft-oriented world was replaced by the deskilled factory jobs of the nineteenth and twentieth centuries. They were robbed of pride in product, and reacted to this alienated setting by seeking refuge in the collective work values of unionization. Only under the leadership of Samuel Gompers and the AFL did unions begin to accord American workers a small measure of improved material benefits. But this did nothing to alleviate the on-going problem of job security.

African-Americans, on the other hand, were shunned from the ranks of the AFL except for the United Mine Workers and the cigar makers. Combined with a background of abduction from Africa, slavery in the South, and numerous race riots in cities like Philadelphia, New York, and Detroit, blacks were pushed far more in the direction of alienation than opportunity. Not until the moderately successful push for better positions in defense industries during World War II, the 1954 *Brown* decision, and the programs of the Great Society, did the doors of opportunity budge.

Despite the bittersweet legacy of alienation and opportunity during the two centuries after 1730, important improvements followed. Labor during this *second period of historical discontinuity* could be characterized by the more optimistic description of Work as Self-Fulfillment (c. 1930s–present). Unlike the past, its focus was centered on the worker. For the first time a growing number of employers seemed aware that their operatives had needs, human as well as economic. The more enlightened began to understand that rewards and motivation might yield better results than threats and punishment. With this in mind, industrialists like Pullman, Patterson, and Rockefeller promoted welfare capitalism during the four decades after 1880. Because of their initiatives welfare capitalism helped advance some industries from the twilight zone of alienation to an industrial world that would ultimately accord employees a measure of challenge and autonomy. As yet, it was almost a century away from the world of self-fulfillment that emerged in the 1970s, but it was an attempt to enlist the support of the workforce through model communities and a system of substantial benefits. Managers believed that these would win the loyalty of their semi-skilled operatives and link them to managerial objectives. Company housing, medical facilities, libraries, and schools were the bait. Employees might even make their views known through company unions, but in most cases welfare capitalism failed to win their confidence even as they appreciated some of its benefits. Nevertheless, it was the key that unlocked the door to the Human Relations Movement which emerged as a somewhat more substantial attempt to make Work as Self-Fulfillment a reality.

Many of the ideas of the Human Relations Movement can be traced to the work of Elton Mayo and Mary Parker Follett. Like welfare capitalism, it tried to win the cooperation of employees in the pursuit of improved productivity. During the period from 1924 to 1932 its foundation was established by the celebrated Hawthorne experiments. Taken as a group, these experiments (Relay Test Room, Bank Wiring Room, etc.) under Mayo and his colleagues suggested to enlightened employers that the key to worker cooperation lay in areas beyond the physical conditions of work. Yes, ergonomic matters were relevant, but unless the commitment of the workforce could be tapped, "stretch goals" would not be achieved. It was necessary to motivate workers, a concept rarely found in the history of human labor. From Mayo through George Homans and William F. Whyte, social scientists argued that good human relations would produce results. Be nice to employees, offer good benefits, and even consult with them from time to time. But despite these fond hopes and the support of industrial leaders like Chester Barnard, results were meager. By the sixties the Human Relations Movement was dead.

Despite the very limited progress made toward viewing employees as valuable and participating human *resources*, both welfare capitalism and the Human Relations Movement offered some hope. By the sixties it was no longer possible for engineers and employers to extol the virtues of fractionalized labor without serious questioning by social scientists. In addition, the upheavals of that decade caused many to question all forms of authority. More and more workers now wanted a chance to be included in decision-making, to have jobs that would enable them to grow and learn. The Tayloristic practices of industrial engineers now incurred resistance among the younger and spunkier baby boomers. Nowhere was this more evident than at the Lordstown, Ohio plant of General Motors, where slowdowns and sabotage reigned in the early seventies. It was from these sources that the Human Resources Movement surfaced. Now the drive for good work was cloaked in aspirations for employee empowerment. To just have a job might be sufficient for the heirs of the Great Depression, but for boomers work had to have meaning and challenge.

In this new era of self-fulfillment managers also had to deal with the career aspirations of African-Americans. For blacks the policies of the Great Society formed a cornerstone of hope. Affirmative action programs in both the workplace and campus began to open the doors of opportunity, although court decisions became increasingly unfavorable in the eighties. By the mid-nineties tension over affirmative action and welfare led to major battles in Congress. These centered on questions of fairness and whether existing laws fostered dependency rather than opportunity. How all of this will end is still unclear, but if affirmative action is curtailed it may ultimately affect the upward mobility of blacks.

For women, the feminist movement of the sixties offered a sense of empowerment that had been the exclusive domain of men. In this milieu women made more progress than blacks. They had been seen as adjuncts to the careers of their husbands, or as part-timers whose salaries were ancillary to those of the key breadwinner. But by the 1990s women had won a legitimacy in the workplace not known to their grandmothers. Many firms adopted flexible working hours or provided in-house day care. A few businesses even offered some assistance in elder care, and a growing number of females were moving into managerial positions. And while much more ground had to be covered, it appeared that women had made some headway since the sixties.

But for Americans in general the great discontinuity that was reflected in the desire for self-fulfillment in work went beyond a neat behavioral concept. Rather, it was a desire to find the "good work" advocated by E. L. Schumacher. Increasingly, workers saw themselves as singular individuals, almost as "sacred objects" who required involvement in their tasks. In short, these citizens, mothers and fathers, viewed themselves as more than their job. Their work values were far removed from the God-centered injunctions of Calvin and Mather, nor were they willing to accept the time-discipline and scientific management of an era that produced more than its fair share of alienation. But given the right motivational tools, these post-sixties employees could become paragons of productivity.

Side by side with the *discontinuities* in work values that spanned the five centuries from Work as a Sign of Salvation to Work as Self-fulfillment, four important *continuities* emerged. Among the most important was the search for job security. No work value assumed greater importance since the mid-fifteenth century, and none proved more elusive. This absence of stable employment made its negative presence felt during the advent of a market economy after 1450. Fluctuations in distant demand, changes in taste, and the effects of war, weather, and demographics all made work chancy. These unpredictable events offered early modern Europe its first spectre of widespread unemployment and homelessness. It caused men like Luther to see hordes of urban vagrants as outdoor loafers. But in time it led to the introduction of municipal relief and workhouses in both Europe and America. The problem did not cease with the advent of the Industrial Revolution in Britain, and followed opportunity-seekers to the New World. Here, despite an abundance of land and a shortage of skilled labor, heavy tides of immigration often made work scarce in Boston, New York, and Philadelphia. Even with the vast industrialization that occurred in the United States during the nineteenth and twentieth centuries, a boom-and-bust economy became a permanent feature of the employment world. Beginning with the early Panic of 1819 and continuing to 1990-91,

unemployment continued to reflect the problems of an industrializing nation lodged in a global economy.

Yet another continuity of great importance was the belief in
opportunity. In Renaissance Italy the desire to do well was
personified by the banking houses of Bardi, Pitti, and Datini. Later
businessmen like Jakob Fugger and Jacques Coeur continued the
trend. In England their efforts were emulated by Thomas Gresham
who developed a money market and later industrialists like
Boulton and Arkwright. But opportunity took on a wider meaning
with the opening of the New World. Here much larger numbers
could escape the class-ridden confines of Europe and become
landowners. In an age where property was the prime source of
wealth and prestige this was a powerful attraction. In addition,
artisans in America found themselves in demand, and in many
cities like Philadelphia and New York, became successful merchant-
entrepreneurs. Beyond this, early swashbucklers like Richard
Wharton, Thomas Breedon, and Stephen Girard set the stage for
the business moguls of the nineteenth century. Even if workers
could not participate in the wealth-accumulation of the Gilded Age
or the Roaring Twenties, studies such as those by Thernstrom on
Newburyport, Massachusetts suggested that their view of opportunity might be fulfilled by moving up within the working class.
Bodnar and his colleagues found a similar situation in early-
twentieth-century Pittsburgh, and for a short time during the nineteenth century African-Americans also enjoyed this experience in
Detroit and Cleveland. During the twenties and thirties, the idea of
success was pushed by publicists like Babson, Barton, and Dale
Carnegie, while later in the century Peale offered a renewed theological formula in support of enterprise. But if most today could
not become a Bill Gates or Andrew Grove, their example still
inspired many to seek success in software development, computers,
and health care. Clearly, the belief in opportunity was still alive.

Perhaps the best known of the continuities is that of the work
ethic. If it is defined in its classical sense as a commitment to hard
work, it clearly was given enormous support by the early ministerial elite. Whether one cites Calvin, Perkins, Hooker, or Cotton
Mather, diligence was seen as a possible signal of salvation and
was revered as service to family and community. The work ethic
was often tied to a fixed calling from which none should deviate.

This personal calling, however, was paired with a general calling in which the faithful might earn additional merit by living a Christian life. But with the coming of workshop and factory, hard work took on a new meaning. Punctuality and steadiness in work became the norm if expensive new machinery was to be made profitable. Workers could not absent themselves for drunken weekends only to work at a furious pace between Tuesday and Saturday. Now the clock became the arbiter of men and women, and time-discipline their measure. In the new global market economy the work ethic increasingly came to mean labor that was systematized and measured. Now men like Frederick Winslow Taylor formulated a methodology to match men and machines in an ergonomic dance. Work was timed and body movements prescribed. Skill was drawn out of labor, and the new meaning of hard work came to be repetitive effort under the watchful eyes of foremen and the stop-watches of industrial engineers. By the early years of the twentieth century the old artisanal order was gone. For those who toiled in factory and mine, efforts by businessmen and publicists to win their allegiance to hard work went largely unheeded by an alienated army of the semi-skilled.

Not until the 1960s did the work ethic take on a quite different meaning. Some began to refer to it as a "worth ethic" to explain the greater work expectations of a generation of baby boomers. These men and women reflected the anti-authoritarian values of the time, and their work ethic called for jobs that offered challenge and autonomy. Still, a dedication to hard work in itself had not passed from the scene. A 1983 Yankelovich and Immerwahr survey showed that 52 percent of American respondents endorsed the classical concept compared to only 17 percent in Britain. And while the ancient view of the calling was gone, the New Calling reflected the secular expectation of empowerment in work. Such a calling had to provide opportunities to learn and grow in a context of career development. Clearly, the work ethic of today had to tap the inner commitment of employees if it was to be successful.

The last of the major continuities centered on the centuries-old issue of work and welfare. This debate has raged since Elizabethan times and focussed on the nature of community obligation to those involuntarily out of work as well as the elderly and infirm. Both then and now it was frequently framed in terms of the deserving and undeserving poor, words calculated to raise passionate debate in Elizabethan England, colonial America, and the political precincts of Washington in the mid-1990s. Then as now there was a search to help those seen as truly in need as compared to persons who preferred to live off the system. Over the centuries taxpayers were incensed by those too willing to accept public largesse. In Britain attempts to find a better way through the Poor Law of 1601, the Speenhamland System, and the Poor Law Amendment of 1834 did not yield stellar results. Workhouses were used to supplement public philanthropy, but they yielded no permanent solution in Britain or the United States during the nineteenth century. More recently problems of the work and welfare in the United States were compounded by high rates of illegitimacy, substance abuse, and inferior educational preparation for work. From the public perspective of the 1990s, these were often seen as insufficient explanations for families that had been on welfare for generations. But for those on welfare, public assistance seemed to be the minimal monthly payments that kept them alive. It was a debate that has ranged across the centuries and will not likely be resolved in our time.

In terms of these continuities and discontinuities we can better understand the work values of the past five hundred years. They describe the historical threads that crossed the centuries along with the great divides that ushered in new belief systems. Taken together, they offer an insight into what people wanted from their work and the symbolic meaning that work had in their lives.

This discussion would not be complete without some commentary on the historiography of work values. Because so much of the literature feeds off the ideas of Max Weber's *Protestant Ethic and the Spirit of Capitalism* (1904–05), his thoughts on how the Reformation influenced modern work values are a necessary introduction. Weber believed that Luther first consecrated labor for modern man by his emphasis on work in a calling as an "outward expression of brotherly love." In this context Luther looked to toil as the fulfillment of earthly obligations and the best way to serve God. For Weber, Luther's advocacy of "worldly activity" was a key outcome of the Reformation (Weber, 81). To these Lutheran beginnings, Weber added the contributions of Calvin and the Puritans who extolled work so long as its profits did not lead to gluttony, fancy clothes, or splendid homes. Earthly striving that might yield success was for the Calvinist a possible sign of election and not a warrant to consume. But in their zeal to define a new moral standard for man they unintentionally gave diligence in commerce a moral sanctification. By the eighteenth century, Weber asserted, men like Franklin were able to secularize the Calvinist-Puritan belief system and give work a utilitarian blessing (Weber, 89–90, 109, 112, 114–15, 52–53).

This study, of course, does not deal with Weber's hotly debated thesis that the Protestant Reformation (particularly its Calvinist offshoots) was the springboard to modern capitalism. Nevertheless, it is important to note that Tawney's *Religion and the Rise of Capitalism* (1926) took up the Weberian view that the Calvinists had established a heavenly city in which a "new scale of moral values" and a fresh "ideal of social conduct" was offered as the avenue to salvation (Tawney, 98–99). A far wider range of views on the Weberian thesis and the work values inherent in it became available in Robert Green's 1959 book of readings on *Protestantism and Capitalism* (Green, *Protestantism and Capitalism* vii–xii). Eight years later S. N. Eisenstadt published an additional set of articles on the Weber thesis in *The Protestant Ethic and Modernization*, and as in the case of the Green compendium, presented considerable material on the work values of early Protestantism (Eisenstadt, 3–45). By comparison, the behavioral scientist William H. Whyte, Jr. in *The Organization Man* (1956) cared little whether the Protestant Ethic preceded modern capitalism or emerged as a result. What was more important was the fact that it linked how people wanted to act with how they believed "they *ought* to behave." It also gave entrepreneurs a shield against those who would object to their acquisitive values, and provided their consciences with a moral justification for the continual pursuit of wealth. By the early years of the twentieth century, however, Whyte believed a Social Ethic had developed in the United States. Within this belief system, writers and reformers such as Charles Beard, William James, and the Muckrakers asserted a public need to curb individual excesses that were shielded by the values of the Protestant Ethic (Whyte, 16, 20, 22).

By contrast, J. E. Crowley made an important contribution in his well-researched analysis of the secularization of work values in eighteenth century America. In *This Sheba Self* (1974) he showed that by the 1730s the old Calvinist values of industry and thrift had been transformed into secular criteria for toil and life. Hard work and frugality now were lifted out of the realm of religious prescription and given a place of honor in a new earthly order. And while Americans still tried to measure the worth of work by social and moral standards to at least the 1760s, by the end of the century the economic value of labor had become paramount (Crowley, 75–79, 153–54, 156). Later historians such as Irving Wyllie, John Cawelti, and Moses Rischin, Christopher Lasch, and Richard Hofstadter (see bibliography to part I) took up the inter-related nineteenth-century themes of the gospel of success and the ideal of the self-made man. In sermons, addresses, essays, and children's literature, Rischin painted an intriguing picture of the honor accorded success from the early nineteenth century. Wyllie, Cawelti, Lasch, and Hofstadter, on the other hand, depicted the self-made man as a paragon of enterprise who related his success to good character, hard work, frugality, and self-discipline. For these makers of a new world, formal education was not as important as moderation and the ability to overcome obstacles by personal struggle. That these rough-and-tumble types received the support of many Congregationalist ministers suggests how profoundly the old Calvinist values had changed.

For Reinhard Bendix, however, the ideology of the new nineteenth-century managers held a particular interest. In his *Work and Authority in Industry* (1956) he suggested that American managers believed their superior ability justified their authority. Those who worked for them were by nature destined to be subordinates, although there was a chance they might advance through hard work. Bendix challenged this view. He argued that it supported the values of those already in authority who believed there was an "identity of virtue and success." And he questioned the validity of the success theme's basic premise that wealth was the proper goal for all, that business and Christianity were closely intertwined, and that the businessman as an ideal type was worthy of emulation (Bendix, 2–3, 256–59).

For Daniel Rodgers, dedication to the work ethic was particularly strong in pre-industrial America among the self-employed, craft workers, and those engaged in agriculture. But he asserted that the appearance of the factory system by the 1850s weakened the old ties to hard work. Pride in craft, industry, and individual accomplishment were diminished by the regimentation of factory labor as repetitive work, time-discipline, and wage labor all combined to sever the tie between "work and godly virtue." Who, then, continued to embrace the work values of the Calvinist-Puritan past during the period from 1850 to 1920 that Rodgers analyzed in his *Work Ethic in Industrial America* (1978)? To this question, Rodgers looked to the "Northern, Protestant, propertied classes" as the carriers of the old faith. But for most in both Europe and America he claimed dedication to diligence was limited to the era between the "manors and the factories." As such, it emerged as the basic work value of pre-industrial America but had a declining influence thereafter (Rodgers, *Work Ethic*, xi–xiii; Rodgers, "No's to the Grindstone," A27). Paul Bernstein, on the other hand, saw the work ethic under constant pressure during the five centuries after Luther gave labor his blessing. On both sides of the Atlantic workers clung to the ill-defined work habits of the pre-industrial world with its numerous holidays and festivals, including Saint Monday. Many continued this resistance during the factory era as a reaction to deskilled wage work and Taylorism. Not until the twentieth century was there a modicum of change as managers finally perceived their workforce as valuable human resources (P. Bernstein, *Work Ethic*, 19-24). Likewise, Herbert Gutman in his *Work, Culture, and Society in Industrializing America* (1977) believed that in both pre-industrial and industrial America there was a continuous resistance to the work ethic. In numerous examples, Gutman showed how pervasive this resistance was among native Americans and immigrants who came to the United States in such large numbers after 1880. Both had to be socialized to accept hard work, punctuality, and factory discipline, but they remained alienated from the Tayloristic labor that characterized industrial America. Despite this, the work ethic retained a powerful symbolism for many Americans long therafter (Gutman, *Work, Culture and Society*, 3–7, 80).

By contrast Christopher Lasch provided a broad analysis of the evolution of work values since the sixteenth century. In his *Culture of Narcissism* (1979), Lasch suggested that seventeenth-century work values centered on devotion to a calling in a framework of social responsibility. But by the eighteenth century a "Yankee ethic" had emerged. It encouraged self-improvement, self-discipline, and supported the acquisition of wealth as preconditions for moral and intellectual improvement. By the nineteenth century, Lasch contended, these values were replaced by a "cult of compulsive industry." Now the chief goal of labor was worldly success in which competition did not emerge as a key value until the turn of the century. Only then did the nineteenth-century belief that achievement should be measured against the concepts of self-discipline and self-denial weaken in favor of a more competitive spirit among ambitious corporate managers (Lasch, *Narcissism*, 108–9, 111–14). While Lasch's view that competition was less important prior to 1900 remains open to question, his analysis of twentieth-century work values is important. In this setting Lasch argued that work had ceased to be a "moral obligation" and now represented the effort needed to enjoy the material benefits of society. For twentieth-century workers ideologies that supported the postponement of gratification were neutralized in favor of work as an avenue to consumption. In short, the "ethic of pleasure . . . replaced the ethic of achievement" (ibid., 125, 138–39).

What Lasch called the "cult of compulsive industry" (ibid., 111) already had been suggested by Adriano Tilgher in *Homo Faber: Work Through the Ages* (1930). In an eloquent volume that deserves more attention than it has received, Tilgher suggested that the "religion of work" in twentieth-century America had produced a society devoted to amusement and consumption (Tilgher, 142). It was a view endorsed by Riesman (1960), who found the twentieth-century middle class had lost their zeal for the old work ethic in their race for momentary gratification (Riesman, "Sociability, Permissiveness, and Equality," 334–36). Likewise, in *The Cultural Contradictions off Capitalism* (1976), Daniel Bell argued that the old religious emphasis on restraint, self-control, and guilt had been submerged by a hedonistic consumerism that could be traced to the "new capitalism" of the twenties. And so business continued to press for diligence in the workplace (as sanctified by Protestant Ethic) even as it encouraged consumption in private life. What Bell saw lacking in the United States was a new belief system to replace this "disjunction" of values (Bell, *Cultural Contradictions*, 55, 72-75).

Richard Huber's *American Idea of Success* (1971) offered an interesting interpretation of nineteenth and twentieth-century work values centered on the character ethic, mind power, and the personality ethic. Huber argued that the character ethic could be traced to ministers like Cotton Mather and secular publicists such as Franklin who believed that "personal virtues" such as hard work, self-reliance, and thrift were the keys to success. It was an outlook that de-emphasized heredity and environment, and suggested opportunity was always at hand for virtuous individuals. Neither wealth nor formal education were as important as such personal qualities as diligence and self-discipline. This value system remained strong during the century after the 1820s, and was supplemented by the mind power school from the 1880s to the 1920s. Huber suggested that through advocates such as Elizabeth Towne, self-help through mental concentration and personal determination offered an avenue to wealth for the meek and those worried about the moral aspects of money-making. In addition, he traced the emergence of the personality ethic during the twenties and thirties through such books as B. C. Forbes' *Keys to Success* and Dale Carnegie's *How to Win Friends and Influence People* (1936). Through winning ways and the manipulation of people it suggested a pathway to success that was light years away from the old character ethic (Huber, 95–96, 165–66, 172–75, 226–28, 502–3).

Finally, Cherrington's *Work Ethic* (1980) added little to earlier research. He suggested there were six important justifications for the work ethic up to the middle of the twentieth century. According to Cherrington, the religious principle supported work because it was ordained by God, while the success ethic viewed diligence a *sine qua non* for attainment. In addition, the work ethic was given support for its character-building attributes, its improvement of health, and its motivational capacity to help workers learn and achieve. Cherrington also believed that the work ethic won considerable approval because it encouraged cooperative effort and provided a nation of workers with an economic stimulus (Cherrington, 83-86).

By contrast, the author has suggested a five-century overview of how work values have changed from Luther to Norman Vincent Peale. Within this broad framework, modern work values

emerged as a necessary precondition to salvation that was transmuted into a bittersweet amalgam of opportunity and alienation
in nineteenth-century America. But it was not until our own time
that managers moved from their concentration on rationality and
control to a recognition that employees were valuable human
resources essential to proper performance in a knowlege society.
In this sense, the author has gone beyond earlier contributions
that have concentrated on interpretations over relatively restricted
periods of time, and has offered a five-hundred-year overview
that reaches the present. This approach links the findings of
modern social science to earlier historical analysis so that scholars
can perceive the discontinuities that led to work values prizing
empowerment and participation. It is left to the reader to determine whether this mode of analysis has made for a useful addition to the literature on American work values.

Part I
Work as a Sign of Salvation

Chapter 1

LUTHER OPENS THE DOOR

On the twenty-second of August in the year 1530 Martin Luther wrote a letter to his son Hans in which he instructed the boy to "work hard, pray well, and be good" (Bainton, 303). The former Augustinian monk could also have quoted his spiritual mentor, St. Augustine, who warned that "those who want to be spiritual only and not labor with the body, reveal their indolence." And like St. Augustine, Luther threw his support to work in the handicrafts, agriculture, and manual labor in general (Hyma, 100). But in his condemnation of idleness, Luther drew on a well-established medieval tradition that was wholly Catholic. Thomas Aquinas (1225–74) had urged the faithful to labor diligently in a permanent niche, a point Luther was to later reaffirm. And Antoninus Pierozzi, later St. Antonine of Florence (1389-1459), condemned laziness and urged his parishioners to lead a busy and active life if they wished to serve God and their community. The medieval Schoolmen also attacked idleness; all should work, but should not make their livings by taking interest (Sombart, "Capitalist Spirit," 31–34; D'Entrèves, 171–75).

But despite the rationalist thinking of Aquinas and the medieval scholastics who unknowingly helped provide the intellectual base for expanded business activity after 1450, precapitalist work traditions only supported labor that enabled the worker to live in his accustomed station. As Max Weber noted, medieval man did not live to amass ever-increasing wealth, or to work with growing intensity (Weber, 60). It was this older tradition that Luther embodied and continued. If men had to work in order to serve God, then it was to be on the land or in the craftshops. Work was to maintain oneself in a calling (*Beruf*), a permanent station (*Stand*) through which both God and community could be served

(Althaus, 36–38). In this context, the labor of a peasant or weaver was akin to that of a priest. Trade was permissible, said the wary Luther, but should be limited to the exchange of necessary goods and services. And the seller should ask no more than the minimum amount needed to pay for labor and risk. Above all, idleness was to be avoided, and vagrants should be banished or forced to work. Luther urged that each town should make provision for the "honest poor" (Tawney, 83). This may have led the burghers of Amsterdam to establish the first workhouse in Amsterdam in 1596. It may have also triggered other means of social support to help the unemployed like the general funds that were set up in Nuremberg and Lyons, the *gemeine Kasten* and the *aumône générale* (Garraty, 44–45, 24).

But while Luther remained tied to the medieval conception of good work, that is, the labor of the peasant and the craftsman (Sombart, "Capitalist Spirit," 34), he did give God's blessing to toil. Of Christ himself Luther said:

> I can just imagine the people of Nazareth at the judgment day. They will come up to the Master and say, "Lord, didn't you build my house? How did you come to this honor?" (Bainton, 233–34)

Luther thereby gave work the strongest possible support. If Christ labored as a carpenter and Peter toiled as a fisherman, then work could be an ennobling way of life for the peasants and artisans of the sixteenth century. Luther went on to urge the faithful to work hard in his November, 1520 *On the Freedom of the Christian Man*:

> Plainly then faith is enough for the Christian man. . . .
> But he is not therefore to be lazy or loose. Good works
> do not make a man good, but a good man does good
> works. (Bainton, 230–31)

In this task, Luther had considerable support in his own time. Hugh Latimer (?1484–1555), the English Protestant bishop, also cited Christ's manual labor as a justification for work. And like other Puritans, Robert Crowley emphasized honesty in work in his 1550 tract *Voice of the Last Trumpet. . . . Calling All Estates of Men to the Right Path of Their Vocation* (Hyma, 106). But while all of these divines praised hard work in one's vocation, they steadfastly opposed the growing commercialism of their times. Richard Baxter was to do the same in the seventeenth century, and it was not until the eighteenth century that business activity won a measure of support among Puritans (Fanfani, 92). Only then was the door to work fully open.

How, then, did the new entrepreneurial work values so alien to Luther emerge? To understand this we must remember that Luther was born in 1483, a child of the late medieval world. His world embraced the very early years of modernity, and stood at the end of five centuries of growing business life. Braudel and Hartwell have suggested that there was a general economic awakening in Europe beginning in the eleventh century. From this time, the needs of "everyday life" forced Europeans to gradually reverse their negative attitudes to hard work and risk-taking. Diligence that maximized profit tied an increasing element of the community to the marketplace (Braudel, *Wheels of Commerce*, 555; Hartwell, 24, 26). But the work values of the medieval order— those of the Schoolmen—could not adjust to the world of trade. Nor could they appreciate the growth of urban economies that were linked to the market, and "all the elements created by a new, nonfeudal development." Luther was to a large degree part of this medieval ethos. Because of this he saw urban business and finance as sinful, for it was gain without real work (Lüthy, 105-6). Particularly bothersome to Luther were huge profits made in a short span of time. In this connection, he attacked the banking house of his contemporary, Jakob Fugger, and urged that "we must put the bit in the mouth of the Fuggers and similar companies" (Althaus, 110). For the "medieval" Luther, work had to be tangible. Agriculture, fishing, and manual toil all fit. But the world of finance produced profits devoid of ostensible labor, and the buying and selling of products without the added value of artisanry was sinful. Luther was at home with the ideas of the medieval founder of canon law, Gratian, who wrote in his *Decretum* around 1140:

Whosoever buys a thing, not that he may sell it whole and unchanged, but that it may be a material for fashioning something, he is no merchant. But the man who buys it in order that he may gain by selling it again unchanged and as he bought it, that man is of the buyers and sellers who are cast forth from God's temple. (Tawney, 37)

But this was no longer the prevailing view of his time, and Luther found himself fighting the tide of economic history even as he tried to establish a Protestant beachhead in Germany.

The changes that engulfed Luther first emerged in Western Europe after the reappearance of urban communities in the eleventh century. With this invigorated city life came blacksmiths, tailors, shoemakers, and butchers who began to sell in open markets. Their modest economic activity was supplemented by fairs in all parts of Europe; those at Troyes and Lyons even dated from Roman times, while the Leipzig and Champagne marts were famous throughout Europe. It was at these fairs that money could be changed and accounts balanced off against each other. In addition, money markets developed in Italy, Germany, and the Netherlands during the thirteenth century. These aided capital accumulation, yielded the bill of exchange, produced the first public-debt bonds, and supported investment in industrial or craft work, shipbuilding, and long-distance voyages (Braudel, *Wheels of Commerce*, 62–67, 82–83; Braudel, *Structures of Life*, 90–91; 472, 113–14). In addition, double-entry bookkeeping may have been used as early as the thirteenth century in Florence, and was employed extensively in Italy after 1450. From here it was introduced into Flanders by Ympym in 1543, and was employed by the famous Jakob Fugger in Augsburg. French and English businessmen also adopted this system during the sixteenth century, so that much of Europe was using a systematic method of recording the results of trade (Robertson, "Max Weber," 81; R. Davis, *Atlantic Economies*, 244).

What would have been even more disturbing to Luther was the emergence of stock markets. One of the earliest was the 1328 Florentine exchange. Genoa could later boast of an active bourse in the Casa di San Giorgio, while Bruges and Antwerp established exchanges in 1409 and 1460, respectively. But because Luther felt that stock exchanges strongly symbolized profit-making without "labor," they caught his particular fury. When Luther was offered mining shares by the Elector of Saxony so that he would have an income of 300 gulden, Luther rejected the gift summarily: "I want no shares! This is speculative money and I will not make this kind of money multiply." (Braudel, *Wheels of Commerce*, 456).

Luther thus gave his wholehearted support to work, but at the same time was horrified by the entrepreneurial spirit that encouraged labor. His medieval perspective led him to approve of traditional toil in the field or workshop, but compelled him to oppose the new capitalist "spirit" that seemed to undermine all that he cherished. His particular dislike of merchants and bankers stemmed from their desire to be successful in this world, to "climb out of the place where God had put them." Not only did Luther want everyone to be content with their present station, but he argued that difficulty was an integral aspect of Christian life— "suffering, suffering, cross, cross" (Marius, 229–30). Work on the land was his ideal, for this effort would help the faithful avoid the degrading practices of the commercial world. Money could not be accumulated without bodily toil. Yet Italian bankers like the Bardi, Pitti, and Datini earned huge profits in Renaissance Italy, and in Luther's own time, the Amsterdam exchange had over 1,000 brokers. As Braudel pointed out, the exchange had become a permanent fair. Here everything could be bought and sold: currencies, shares, maritime insurance, and commodities. And in Venice banks had been issuing notes that circulated like currency even before Luther's birth (Braudel, *Wheels of Commerce*, 99–100, 473). It was this "capitalist spirit" and not work itself that angered Luther. He saw about him a rapidly changing world with questionable values. It was a universe disrupted by the desire for ever more gain, a world of systematic record keeping, numbers, and fiercely energetic businessmen whose work ethic was "more." He abhorred their rational worldliness, and fought for the stable past that was slipping away.

In this sense, Luther was enveloped by the paradox of "progress." He wanted everyone to work, but it had to be labor of a specific character. Bankers and merchants did not toil, but used their efforts to exploit. He failed to see that the new businessmen created the very work he applauded because he was so at war with their goals. Luther also failed to distinguish between the work values of the entrepreneurs and the new laboring class they were beginning to create. To the new businessmen, no amount of time and energy was too great for the profitable task at hand. But for the new laborers and apprentices, fresh from the farm, the practice of taking some fifty to sixty religious holidays annually in addition to fifty-two Sundays seemed perfectly normal. Luther also failed to appreciate that farmers turned industrial workers riled against the systematic industrial labor that required punctuality, routine, and precision. In addition, Luther overlooked the short time-horizons of the new proletariat. They engaged in the precarious practice of living day to day in the new market economy where the only certainty was uncertainty. For the new workers, "the opportunity of earning more was less attractive than that of working less" (Weber, 60). They failed to see, like Luther, that their increasing dependence on distant markets in textiles and other products required a time and work discipline not expected of them as they worked in land and craft. And yet Luther approved of their traditional bent because he neither understood nor approved of the massive economic changes that were welling up around him. He did not see the new capitalist work effort as opportunity for work, growth, and a better standard of living, but attacked its emphasis on profit, interest, and rationalized production. The function of work was to support one's family and community, but above all, to serve God. Not to do so was clearly a defect in character, a fault that could lead to the sin of beggary or vagrancy (Bainton, 237–38).

This, then, was the paradox of "progress" that dogged Luther. And it should not be surprising. How could a former Augustinian monk see the connection between the money markets of Amsterdam and Antwerp and the creation of needed work that he fervently supported? Luther seemed more at home with the fourteenth-century Schoolman Henry of Langenstein, who argued that

> He who has enough to satisfy his wants and nevertheless ceaselessly labors to acquire riches, either in order to obtain a higher social position, or that subsequently he have enough to live without labor. . . .—all such are incited by a damnable avarice, sensuality, or pride. (Tawney, 38)

Unlimited worldly striving and the spirit of enterprise was hateful to the Protestant reformer. He particularly detested the calculating nature and rationality of the bourgeois ethos (Sombart, *Moderne Kapitalismus*, 1:327–29). And despite the fact that the new entrepreneurial world created the work that Luther cherished, it simultaneously brought forth a greed and rationality he could not abide. Ernst Troeltsch succinctly describes what troubled Luther when he noted that "this [capitalist] spirit displays an untiring activity, a boundlessness of grasp. . . . [I]t makes work and gain an end in themselves, and makes men the slaves of work for work's sake" (Troeltsch, *Protestantism and Progress*, 133–34).

In short, the new man of business would never accept the "satisfaction of fixed needs," the static ideal of the medieval village economy (Sombart, *Moderne Kapitalismus*, 1:13–15). He set aside the ideal of St. Antonine (1389–1459), who had warned merchants and financiers that "riches exist for man, not man for riches." And despite the great authority of the sixteenth-century clergy on the socioeconomic thinking of the time, the new entrepreneurs persisted (Tawney, 35, 229). It was not likely that Luther contributed to the new "capitalist spirit," although his strong advocacy of work was an unintentional boost for the profit motive. In *The Sermon on Good Works* written in May 1520, Luther extended the idea of a divine calling to all work he considered worthy (Bainton, 233). Good work disciplines man, helps him to control his desires, and offers the reward of patience. Labor in itself is a beneficial act, and offers the worker independence and the ability to help those in need. But above all, work was a key aspect of God's creation. Even in paradise, Luther noted, God gave Adam "work to do, that is [to] plant the garden, cultivate, and look after it" (Althaus, 101–2). But Luther was quick to warn those on earth that "no one is so heavily burdened with work that he cannot speak with God in his heart at the same time." By this reasoning, Luther's advocacy of work in a calling never diminished the central purpose of existence: work was God's offering to man through which he could express his love for his fellow human beings (Boehmer, 314). Luther opened the door to work, but never in an earthly or economic sense, We can appreciate this through Luther's sermon on John 21 at Kemberg on 27 December 1519

> Everyone should remain in the natural calling to which
> divine Providence has appointed him. This calling of
> his is the place in which he can and should serve God
> and his neighbor. Anyone who neglects the duties of his
> calling will not be helped at all by fasting . . . and such
> other "good works" as there may be. (Boehmer, 302)

For Luther the calling was a way to serve God "by humbly
and cheerfully acquiescing in that lot in life to which God had
assigned him." This was a step away from the Catholic view of
the calling that posited a path apart from this world. But for
Luther, the greatest good was to live the secular life religiously by
serving God in a vocation. Calvin later built upon Luther's conceptualization: what counted was what the individual could do
"through his calling" (*per vocationem*). This provided the sixteenth-
century businessmen and their successors with an intellectual
opening to anoint work and the profitability that could flow from
it (Fullerton, 10). When Calvin amended Luther's injunction to
remain in the position to which one was called, this new mobility of
employment was a further support for the new market economy.
Calvin was quick to warn that this should not be done for material
gain, only for the glory of God. This more flexible view of the
calling opened the door to gainful employment for a later generation of Calvinists (McNeill, 221; Bouwsma, 199).

The concept of the calling also migrated to England. As on
the continent, it gave the work of ordinary folk a "positive moral
value," and won wide acclaim among English Protestants. The
calling recognized the individuality of each worker, but tied him
to God: all were defined by the spiritual and worldly parameters
imposed by the Almighty (Crowley, 53–54). The Puritan leader
Robert Crowley was very influential in spreading the idea of the
calling. He urged the faithful to "fyrste walke in thy vocation
and do not seke thy lotte to chaunge; for through wycked ambition, many mens fortune hath ben straynge." For Crowley, as
Luther, the calling was a lifelong commitment. But it was not to
be used to gain riches or to seek societal elevation (Robertson,
"Max Weber," 70).

Hugh Latimer, a contemporary of Luther, agreed with his
fellow Protestant leaders in the approval of all vocations. In the

sixth sermon he preached before King Edward VI (1547–53), Latimer stated

> Therefore let no man disdain or think scorn to follow him [Christ] in a mean living, a mean vocation, or a common calling and occupation. For as he blessed our nature with taking upon him the shape of man, so in his doing he blessed all occupations and arts. (Robertson, "Max Weber," 70)

Some four decades later the great teacher of theology at Cambridge University, William Perkins (1558–1602), argued that the secular aspects of vocation were meaningless outside a more General Calling that committed the individual to a Christian life. And like Calvin and Luther before him, every calling had to contribute to the betterment of society (Crowley, 54). Still later the Presbyterian minister Richard Baxter (1615–91) passionately argued that "if you have a necessity of labouring in your callings, you have no necessity of loving the world or caring inordinately, or of being discontented with your estate" (Robertson, "Max Weber," 72).

Luther's emphasis on the calling was written about and sermonized on by many later British and American religious leaders. In terms of work values, it remained the keystone of Christian thinking about work until well into the eighteenth century. Even as late as 1693 J. Jeffrey urged that every person who was diligent in his calling was "a benefactor to mankind" (Cunningham, 38-39). But beyond all of this we must look at Martin Luther's contribution to work in its broadest perspective. Luther opened the door to traditional labor, but was not willing to bless workers who left their assigned place in the world. Upward mobility or an improved status were not in Luther's frame of reference. And in this matter he worried about the power and effect of the growing business establishment. He viewed the power and wealth of the great commercial centers like Antwerp with concern, and had only disdain for wealth created by investment rather than physical labor. If, as Adriano Tilgher noted in 1930, "Luther placed a crown on the sweaty forehead of labor," he did so in a most conditional sense (Tilgher, 50). It would be left to Calvin and his successors to further shape society's attitudes toward work. But as with Luther, these ministers were in a race with the work values of the growing market economy. It was a race they were destined to lose.

Chapter 2

THE DEMOGRAPHIC AND ECONOMIC IMPACT ON WORK VALUES

If Luther and his contemporaries offered the European world a conditional approval of work, they also mounted fierce and continuous attacks on the beggars and vagrants that plagued their world. These miscreants simply avoided labor, and were not to be confused with the deserving poor who wished employment but found it unobtainable. To combat this lack of a work ethic, city gates were often locked at night after the vagrants had been cleared out. And if one of them had so much as stolen a loaf of bread, his eyeless and bloody head stump could be found on a stake (Huppert, 16–17). A not-so-innocent rhyme of the time sums up how many felt about the unemployed beggars who flooded the towns of sixteenth-century Europe

> Hark hark the dogs do bark,
> The beggars are coming to town
> (Minchinton, 2:154)

If lesser penalties for vagrancy were deemed necessary, labor on chain gangs, whipping, the use of stocks, and branding could be entertained. The fundamental problem was the great increase in beggary during the sixteenth century and the public attention that concern clearly received. Even in England where begging was legal until 1536, an act of Henry VIII required justices of the peace to issue begging licenses only to the aged and deserving beggars (Garraty, 28). And a statute of 1530–31 limited begging to specific districts. If done outside these areas, offenders could be taken "to the nearest market town" where they were tied to a cart, naked, and repeatedly beaten as it moved through. After this, they were to be returned to their place of birth (Coulton, 380). If this were not sufficient, a law of the 1580s called for branding vagrants with a "V" on their chests (Ribton-Turner, 50–51). But it was Thomas More (1478–1535) who came closest to the mark when he noted in the *Utopia* that it was the enclosures that chased people off the land and cast them into an undesired idleness. Many became "tramps and beggars" and were "put into prison for being idle—when nobody will give them a job, however much they want one" (More, 47).

But beyond England where there was no enclosure movement the problem was equally serious. Fanucci, writing in Rome in 1601 noted: "In Rome one sees only beggars, and they are so numerous that it is impossible to walk the streets without having them around." The same was true of Venice (Cipolla, *Industrial Revolution*, 14). A 1578 report from the Amiens law courts spoke of five to six thousand laborers "living on the charity of prosperous citizens." In Germany, a book on the increasing number of vagabonds appeared in 1514, and over fifty regulations regarding the poor and beggars (often thought of as one and the same) appeared in Brandenburg and Prussian edicts between 1565 and 1735. Landowners in Germany also issued edicts against the beggars and poverty-stricken like the 20 October 1599 document attacking "unemployed vagrants, imposters and idlers" (Abel, 133–34).

But Luther and his ministerial brethren had little sympathy for those without work. In *A Treatise on Christian Liberty*, Luther denied the possibility that a person could not have work: "Therefore, it is impossible that he should ever in this life be idle and without works toward his neighbors" (Kerr, 182). And yet the poor existed. In Hamburg their number was estimated at 20 percent in the year 1500 (Cipolla, *Industrial Revolution*, 18–19). Additionally, Holborn noted one of the many problems that the ministerial elite overlooked in Germany: the guilds could not absorb the numerous new workers supplied by the fast-growing population. In this situation, few could become masters. This gave rise to a growing class of journeymen, but because work was scarce, these men were forced to seek employment as toll collectors, gate wardens, and street hawkers. In effect, the journeymen became laborers, but only when they could find employment (Holborn, 70–71).

Added to this was the role of the emerging merchants and financiers. These businessmen often bypassed the guilds and allotted work directly to people in their homes. But even if they placed orders with the guilds themselves, a separation of the direct producer from the market had occurred. Much work now had to be funneled through this new group of middlemen who "produced" nothing but controlled much. By 1500 most of the high-quality textiles made in Western Europe were produced by this "putting out" or domestic system (R. Davis, *Atlantic Economies*, 21). Even in the German mining and metallurgical industries, many princes gave concessions to entrepreneurs like the Fuggers who made loans to Emperors Maximilian and Charles V (Tawney, 72). The new owners now viewed the miners as employees which resulted in a loss of status and job security that contributed to the Peasants' War that erupted in Germany in 1525. Much of the power behind this rebellion came from unhappy Saxon and Thuringian workers (Holborn, 71–72) who saw their world being turned on its axis.

But so ingrained was the belief that idleness resulted from a desire to remain outside the world of work, that Luther could not be dissuaded from attacking beggary. His continuing assumption was to equate any form of idleness with a desire to avoid labor. Thus, Luther continued to argue in his *Liber Vagatorum* (1528) that "sturdy beggars and vagabonds were the villains." In this he was joined by Pope Sixtus V (1521–90) who denounced vagabonds feigning poverty so they could live off the community without labor (Garraty, 27–28).

Martin Bucer (1491–1551), the German Protestant reformer, also rose to the occasion from his new home in England. In his book *De regno Christi*, Bucer urged that those who refused to work should be excommunicated by their church and disciplined by the civil authorities (Tawney, 122). The matter took on greater urgency when some beggars boasted they could get more in alms in a day than a laborer could earn in a year. Other vagrants confided to an English doctor in 1555 that they preferred to be idle and ill rather than work "with great payne and labour." It is little wonder that an English chronicler attacked them as "lousey leuterars" who avoided their societal obligation to work (Garraty, 27–28). Much of the community frustration with idleness that seemed to be the *cause* of poverty was thus codified in the 1563 Statute of Artificers.

This law posited the principle that every person had an obligation to work, and was based on the belief that a job was available to anyone who would claim it (Garraty, 30).

It may be that the existence of many holidays led contemporaries to the conclusion that employment could be had for the asking. How else could so many people be on the streets during working hours for so many days each year? In Paris, for example, some 103 holidays were celebrated in 1660, while they were so numerous in Carinthia during the seventeenth century that the local iron industry could operate only 100 eight-hour shifts each year (Minchinton, 2:98). Luther was not unmindful of this problem. In his analysis of the Third Commandment, he demanded a large decrease in the number of holidays because they were too often used for carousing, idleness, gambling, and gluttony (Boehmer, 309). The key to understanding the "problem" of these holidays and feast days was to see them as a traditional carryover from the world of the Middle Ages. During the Middle Ages, the Church designated over 25 percent of the year as sacred time. This period was augmented by local saints' festivals and a day in which each craft honored its patron saint. In all, the number of the days in which the mills ran in Narbonne was reduced to 265 days annually; in Toulouse it was 281, while church construction in Paris in the year 1320 encompassed only 275 working days (Thrupp, 1:253–54).

But despite the many holidays that existed, the scarcity of work was widespread in Western Europe. It was a situation in which the traditional irregularity of work existed side by side with a dearth of employment. The older lack of work intensity may have been peculiar to some laborers, while others desperately sought work that was often unavailable. But in the world of modernity, work which had been defined by events such as the seasons and tides was now circumscribed by a time element, "a sort of chronological net" (Le Goff, *Time, Work and Culture*, 48) that often embraced an unwilling workforce. It is not likely that the theological elite understood this shift in work values, but we can see from their many comments on the idle that their focus was on the results of the transition rather than the cause. Put another way, Luther, Zwingli, and Bucer sought to maintain the old traditions of work on the land and the craftshop by anointing work, and requiring laborers to stay in the place to which they were called. In a very real sense it was an attempt to at once consecrate labor and simultaneously invest it with the traditional values that were under attack in the new mercantile ethos based on rationality, numbers, and profit.

Luther and his contemporaries were also unaware of the impact of the major economic and demographic trends of the sixteenth century. Their view that a feckless coterie of vagrants were endangering society by a disregard of the work ethic is open to considerable doubt. Yet this does not seem so strange if the priestly attacks on willful idlers is examined in the context of the sixteenth century, for it was from this point in history that their theological thrusts were launched in the absence of demographic data and economic understanding (P. Bernstein, *Work Ethic*, 10–11). In short, Luther and his contemporaries saw their world through a religious prism. They did not appreciate the power of the new market forces to dislocate so many workmen, nor did they understand that the population explosion all about them placed more people in the marketplace than could be absorbed. And yet their eyes and ears told them of vagrants who besieged European cities from Bristol to Brescia. Beyond this, the ministers also failed to grasp that growing numbers of people were competing for a limited supply of tillable land. In this situation, landlords did not hesitate to increase rents. When combined with the lack of capital to open up new lands, many laborers were forced into vagrancy (Koenigsberger and Mosse, 31).

So great was the population increase in western Europe from 1500 to 1600 that some have estimated its growth at from eighty to one hundred ten million (Mols, 2:38–39). Others have suggested that the population doubled during the sixteenth century (R. Davis, *Atlantic Economies*, 18; Garraty, 32). An Erfurt observer of 1483 noted that many couples were having eight to ten children, and that death due to disease was small. But during the sixteenth century the urban population of western Europe grew rapidly as huge increases were recorded in Venice, Antwerp, and Lyons (Ball, 13–14). Cologne, the largest city in Luther's Germany, had about 20,000 souls in the fifteenth century, but by the early sixteenth century its population grew to between 40,000 and 60,000 (Braudel, *Structures of Life*, 51; Mols, 2:43). For all of Germany, the population grew from twelve to fifteen millions during the sixteenth century (Mols, 2:38), and in the area Luther could observe most closely, certain urban laborers and farm workers saw their wages, expressed in terms of "corn value," drop by over one-third in Augsburg, Wurzburg, Frankfurt-am-Main, Munich, and Göttingen (Abel, 135–36). The problem might be traced to the fact that German grain production did not grow fast enough to meet the need of a population that rose by three million. Germany also had a rural-urban population ratio of 10:1 which left a much smaller surplus available to feed the cities. It is little wonder that prices rose more quickly for food than industrial products (Braudel, *Structures of Life*, 51; Koenigsberger and Mosse, 36).

These problems were made even worse by the increase in life expectancy during the sixteenth century (Mols, 2:68–69). This European-wide problem of increased population, food scarcity (Sella, 2:366), and price increases combined to create a class of seemingly worthless idlers who, in reality, were people without prospects and hope. What the theologians who blessed work clearly missed was that many of the "idle" had come into the new capitalist economy as a result of a "biological revolution" that had created a labor surplus in western Europe. For Germany alone, the population was growing at the rapid rate of 0.71 percent per year during the decade 1520–30, the period when Luther was at the height of his power. An anonymous writer from Saxony reported in 1531 that "this country is more crowded than it ever was in the time of our forefathers." And the Zimmer family chronicler said of Swabia in 1550 that "in our day the people in Swabia, as indeed in other lands, have greatly increased and multiplied." Sebastian Franck in his *Deutschen Chronik* of 1538 noted that while huge numbers died during the Peasants' War of 1525, "there were so many people everywhere, no one can move" (Abel, 99–100).

Increases in population were proportionally greater in the British Isles (4.4 to 6.8 millions) as well as Italy, but they were substantial in France and Spain as well. The population of the great commercial center of Lyons rose from 30,000 in 1500 to between 40,000 and 50,000 in the 1530s. It attracted poor peasants from rural France, and artisans from Flanders and Italy. So many came that there were not enough jobs for all. This helped bring on the *Grande Rebeine*, a bloody riot of 1529 in which mobs broke into the city granary and vandalized the homes of the wealthy (Garraty, 25). The uprising was essentially a protest against the rising price of bread which hit urban dwellers throughout Western Europe in the sixteenth century. Even in accessible ports like Antwerp, the price of rye fluctuated wildly, so that townspeople ate poorly even in good years (Cipolla, *Industrial Revolution*, 29–31).

Because of the sizable increase in the population of Europe during the sixteenth century, many employers were able to keep a lid on wages. In turn, landlords kept dues and rents relatively high for rural tenants. These problems were only magnified when land for the production of wheat, corn, and rye was pulled out of cultivation so that more profitable wool, flax, and dyestuffs could be grown for the luxury trade. The resulting increase in the price of cereals only exacerbated the problems of overpopulation, unemployment, and low wages until after 1550 when more land was shifted to corn. Still, it was corn imports from the Baltic that probably kept much of western and southern Europe fed during the latter half of the sixteenth century (R. Davis, *Atlantic Economies*, 20, 116). Matters were not helped by the cool and humid summers between 1500 and 1550. And when food prices rose more rapidly than industrial goods the "common folk" were placed in jeopardy (Spitz, 360).

If this were not enough, the problems of religious and political warfare devastated the urban and rural economies of many areas. Luther's Germany was no exception. But it was the vast expansion of commercial enterprise that changed the economic face of Europe. Business was no longer largely local in character, and financial power was increasingly concentrated among the financiers and merchants in Antwerp, Amsterdam, Frankfurt, and London. The new European monarchs often allied themselves with these emerging businessmen, and gave enterprise a national (if mercantilist) direction. International trading companies such as the Muscovy and Virginia firms emerged, and with them came a large expansion of global business. A good example was the growth of English cloth exports which increased by fifteen times between 1500 and 1730 (Langton, 174–75). John Nef even argued that a first industrial revolution occurred in England from 1540 and 1640, and gave rise to considerable growth in mining and manufacturing in such areas as coal, salt, glass, ships, alum, soap, and metal goods.

New technical processes also powered this early industrial growth, and whether it can be compared to its better known successor or not, it strongly suggested the importance of the world of enterprise at the time of Luther (Nef, *Progress of Technology*, 4, 16–17; R. Davis, *Atlantic Economies*, 22).

In addition, important international trade patterns were also developing within Europe and between European centers and the world beyond. London and Hamburg, St. Malo and Cadiz, Lisbon and Amsterdam, and London and the Chesapeake area were only a few that emerged by the early seventeenth century (R. Davis, *Atlantic Economies*, 235). And not to be overlooked was the pre-eminent position of Antwerp as a financial center and a port until 1560. It became the "soul" of the new capitalist world and hence the repository of all that Luther found wrong because it turned men away from God even as it moved their hands and minds to labor. It was the antithesis of the medieval spirit of localism and guild privilege, of a set world order based on farm and craft (Tawney, 69).

The net result of this commercial revolution for the everyday laborer was an increasing capitalist control of new manufacturing establishments that led to low wages, a lack of upward mobility, and quick fluctuations in demand and output. The workers in these businesses had little security, and were frequently thrown out of work when demand in distant lands ebbed (Garraty, 32). An example of this precarious labor situation can be seen in the northern French city of Beauvais. This textile center had to sell its high quality linen and cloth in central Europe and the Mediterranean regions, since there was an inadequate local market for its goods. It also had to import wool from England, Flanders, and Spain. So if the new faraway markets dried up, workers faced unemployment and poverty. And since wages were paid only for days actually worked, many who appeared to be idle were in reality unemployed because of the vagaries of the international marketplace (Huppert, 27).

To these factors that were largely overlooked by the ministerial opinion-makers of the time, must be added the inflationary impact of the influx of silver from Mexico and Peru. This caused an enormous increase in the money supply as Inca loot began to enter Europe after 1535. Imports reached seven million ounces per year after 1590, but substantial increases were recorded during the four decades after 1552. The inflationary impact of poor harvests around 1530 and the mid-1590s added to the problem by raising the price of corn. The debasement of the English currency around 1550 did not help. And as Davis has noted "those who had nothing to offer but their labour suffered nearly everywhere, if in greatly varying degrees." Many landless peasants throughout western Europe were forced into the cities between 1550 and 1575 only to become the paupers that attracted the ire of ministers and citizens alike (R. Davis, *Atlantic Economies*, 96–101). For the century as a whole, inflation may have risen by two to three per cent annually, but it was more pervasive after 1550. Grain prices in particular rose by 386 percent during the course of the sixteenth century, an annual average of 4.3 percent. It varied from 255% in the German states to 651% in France (Abel, 116–17). The outcry over the impact of inflation in the German states was largely directed against the Fuggers, but merchants in general were the recipients of both theological and secular wrath (Koenigsberger and Mosse, 23). It was not until about 1650 that this inflationary spiral began to abate. Only then did food prices drop and wages stabilize (Mols, 2:96).

So serious were the problems of unemployment and poverty that many who denounced idlers and vagrants were forced to confront the realities of starvation. The poor lived with hunger as a constant companion, and often spent 60–80 percent of their meagre income on food. Little was left for housing or heat, and large numbers, often over 70, were often forced to share a single dwelling. Plague and other diseases spread with ease (Cipolla, *Industrial Revolution*, 31–34), and those who survived had little energy to work with so little food at hand. In Pavia, for example, a study showed that in 1555 two per cent of the families had 45% of the private grain reserves. 60% of the families had no reserves whatsoever. And a 1545 survey of Lyons noted that 10% of the population had 53% of the wealth (ibid., 10–11). Since many lived at the subsistence level, had no savings, and could not look to social agencies for help, charity was the only escape. It was clear that an "industrial proletariat" had emerged that had only its labor to sell. It was a group that lived from hand to mouth, and who created fear among their more prosperous brethren (Garraty, 22–23).

What, then, was to be done? Looked at in the context of economics and demography, it is clear that the sixteenth-century men of God brought a relatively narrow focus to the problem of unemployment and poverty. Neither the ministers nor their secular counterparts distinguished between the poor and the unemployed, and in many instances identified both with beggary (Cipolla, *Industrial Revolution*, 19). Yet there was a hint from Luther that the deserving poor ought not be allowed to starve. We can almost hear Luther thunder in his "Epistle Sermon, Sunday after Ascension Day,"

> So, too, it is today incumbent upon Christians to pro-
> vide for the really poor—not lazy beggars, or vaga-
> bonds—the outdoor pensioners, so called.

Luther went on to argue that no Christian should be allowed to beg, that "every city could support its own poor, and if it were too small, the people in the surrounding villages also should be exhorted to contribute" (Kerr, 183; Ozment, *Age of Reform*, 266). On the other hand, the Swiss Protestant leader, Ulrich Zwingli (1484–1531), could also cite the moral dangers of idleness as he attacked begging. Like Luther, he endorsed the incentive to work and urged all to support themselves because labor was a heavenly act

> With labor will no man now support himself. . . . And
> yet labor is a thing so good and godlike . . . that makes
> the body hale and strong and cures the sicknesses
> produced by idleness. . . . In the things of this life, the
> laborer is most like to God. (Tawney, 101)

Yet both preachers saw the need for some action on behalf of those without work. This they did in the form of municipal ordinances in the 1520s which were among the earliest poor relief laws to be administered by lay authorities.

Catholic thinkers such as Juan Luis Vives also supported secular efforts to provide poor relief in his 1526 tract *De Subventione Pauperum*. Three years later a rebellion of poor peasants and artisans in the city of Lyons led to a poor relief system run by eight unpaid rectors. These officials visited applicants in their homes, and if they were found in need, allowed them to receive food and money weekly. The Lyons authorities also tried to create employment through a new silk establishment, but they were adamant in their opposition to begging. Those who did could be jailed or forced to do hard labor (Garraty, 25–26). In Calvinist Geneva the ordinances of 1576 ordained that the poor be taken care of by the community. Under the direction of Theodore Beza (1519–1605), a "Hospital well ordered for the support of the poor" was made available. In addition, the ordinances required the establishment of a "certain rule and order of living, by which each man may be able to understand the duties of his position." No chance was being taken that relief was to be given without the obligation to seek work in a calling (Tawney, 103). Poor relief was also instituted in Ypres, although its system had to withstand a challenge from the town's mendicant friars (Garraty, 27). Help for the needy also became a state obligation in England in 1572; in Scotland, it was begun under church authority seven years later (Tawney, 111).

Nevertheless, the first true workhouse was founded in Amsterdam in 1596 as a "house of correction" to teach its inmates weaving and other trades. Hard work in this establishment was deemed good for its residents. Paris followed with a "general hospital" in 1611 for beggars and vagrants, with Toulouse, Marseilles, and Lyons not far behind. Instructive was the earlier use of Bridewell Prison in London which was founded in 1555 to put "idle and lewd people to work" (Garraty, 44–45). Through all of this ran a common thread. To be without work was to be an idler, a person of poor character, an ingrate of the first order. Unemployment (a term not used at this time), poverty, and vagrancy were of the same cloth. Not to work was a willful misuse of time, a denial of effort that would damage both the individual and the community. In short, a tinge of evil equated with the absence of paid labor.

It seems clear that the sixteenth-century men of religion missed many of the economic and demographic changes of their time. They spoke strongly about the need to work, and believed that such labor cast an economic shield over family and community even as it glorified God. But if work had become "the base and key to life" for Luther (Mills, *White Collar*, 216), the secular activity he seemed to support never included an awareness of the powerful market forces he so disliked in commercial bastions like Antwerp and Amsterdam. He wanted work without greed and effort without profit. It was a selfless spirit that was forever lost in the medieval past, if it ever really existed then. When the financier Jakob Fugger was urged by his nephew Georg Thurzo to retire from business and attend to family matters, he rebuked him by stating that he "had quite another disposition, he would make money as long as he could" (Robertson, "Max Weber," 66).

It was the confluence of the Reformation and the commercial revolution that redefined the work values of the sixteenth-century theologians. In this maelstrom of change, capitalism strongly influenced the economic message of both Protestantism and Catholicism. As business activity expanded after 1500, the Dutch and English in particular had less and less interest in the religious parameters placed on business (Hyma, 101). Other forces also supported the individualism and commercialism inherent in the new world order. The influence of humanism under men like Erasmus played no small role. Additionally, the Copernican revolution helped many to view the universe in a different way, and offered a perspective that made change more palatable. The discovery of new continents by Da Gama, Columbus, Cabral, and Cartier widened the consciousness of Europeans, and forever ended a world centered on the Mediterranean and North Seas (Lüthy, 91).

In this rapidly changing world the work values of yesteryear were under attack. The ministerial phalanx from Luther to Cotton Mather (1663–1728) were left to fight a rear guard action against the forces of the marketplace. Here they were trying to keep back the encroachments of bankers and merchants and stymie the influence of stock exchanges. But they could not deter the precision of commerce and science that made exactitude a greater virtue than godliness. Labor now had to be organized rationally (Weber, 21–26). Everything had to be weighed, measured, and counted. In essence, it was the combined forces of science and business that the theologians were attempting to repel. It is a credit to their zealousness and tenacity that they held out so long.

Chapter 3

CALVIN AND THE CALLING

When Calvin was recalled from exile to Geneva on the second of September in the year 1541, the town council complied with his demand for a set of *Ecclesiastical Ordinances* that would bring every aspect of city life under theological scrutiny. But even in his moment of victory, Calvin realized that his Geneva of 10,000 souls was an important commercial center that could not be divorced from an international economy centered in Antwerp and Venice. He came to accept the new mercantile economy far more than Luther, but continuously concerned himself with the potential pitfalls of wealth. It was necessary to save the souls of its citizenry and provide for the welfare of the poor, but always within the parameters of a society that regulated business for the good of the commonweal (Bouwsma, 24, 196, 202).

This more "worldly" Calvin gave labor its strongest endorsement to date when he lectured "that men were created for activity" so they would not "sink into laziness." He went on to tell his congregation: "We are born to work," and in doing so we can fulfill the calling for which we were destined (ibid., 199).

Nevertheless, Calvin's strong support of a calling for all men would be hedged by admonitions against greed and the display of finery. Hard work and the wealth that flowed from it could be used to support the poor, but gain at a neighbor's expense "to satisfy our greed or to spend on superfluity" was forbidden (Fanfani, 89). The aim of life was the glorification of God as the basis of labor in one's calling. If this created a more "intensified mood for work," the worldly outcomes had to be kept in check through "systematic self-control" (Fullerton, 15).

This Calvinistic definition of work and its limitations did not settle out in a vacuum. It was affected by the commercial and scientific revolutions that preceded, accompanied, and followed the theocracy that unfolded in Geneva. Together these evolutionary changes provided a context of cultural change that had a significant role in shaping life and work in the sixteenth century. Calvin was influenced by these twin heralds of modernity, and in turn, unintentionally added to their weight through the rationalism and systemization that flowed from his encouragement of hard work and self-discipline. To these forces Calvin appended his "guarded permission" to change vocation and charge interest, two decisions that helped establish an environment of "industrious altruism" along Lake Leman (McNeill, 222).

Calvin himself provided a living example of incessant labor. His contemporary, Nicholas Colladon, commented that "he never failed to be ready for his work and the exercises of his office." And while he worked on his books, correspondence, and public activities (nothing was done in Geneva unless he was consulted), Calvin "was always ready at the hour to go into the pulpit" (T. H. L. Parker, 104). So concerned was Calvin with steady labor that he had a rule promulgated in June 1537 limiting festivals to Sunday, the day of Resurrection:

> Here it is said that some people are celebrating festivals, and it is ordered that each ought to work as has already been proclaimed without celebrating festivals except on Sunday. (W. F. Graham, *Calvin*, 128)

Calvin went on to urge the life of Christ as an example for all to follow. Christ's role as a workman of "humble origins" who led a "thrifty and frugal life" was underscored as a beacon to the faithful. And while "the work in which men now engage is a punishment for sin"—even Adam was "placed in a garden in order to tend it"—life's labor should not lead workmen to "torment and weaken themselves in vain when they busy themselves more than their calling permits or requires" (Bouwsma, 196, 200, 199).

In a very real sense Calvin was looking for a "golden mean" between work as a godly and communal duty and labor that did not consume the laborer. He was concerned with the businessman who devoted his entire being to profit, but was equalled worried by those who loafed (Calvin, 1:721). How to deal with this difficult problem became a serious matter for Calvin and the Genevan theocracy. Here the role of the Venerable Company and the Consistory was important (Littell, 83), as the Calvinist emphasis on "methodical endeavor and self-control" became the dual guidelines for human activity. Through the definition of these parameters, Calvinism offered significant support for the "systematic work in shops, offices, and factories" that was essential to a modern market economy. If affection and intimacy were missing, the saints of Geneva hoped that work would provide "a sense of vocation and discipline which would free people from sinfulness and the fear of disorder" (Walzer, 113–14). That all of this was a perfect platform for modern business activity was an outcome not foreseen by Calvin, but there is little doubt that it provided the rationale for orderly work under the aegis of a watchful God. The faithful were urged to live in this world but to avoid its materialistic pitfalls. God was to be hallowed through the calling, but His glorification was to remain "the supreme and absorbing motive of all human endeavor" (Fullerton, 13). But despite these warnings and qualifications, Calvinism did open the door wider to the more intense work required in the expanding world of commerce. What Luther had begun, Calvin strengthened. Neither intended their endorsement of labor to be a vote of confidence in the new market economy. Neither supported the goal of profit maximization. But both inadvertently pushed forward the frontiers of modern business, and stoked the engine of capitalistic activity that was destined to change the world of work in ways neither could imagine.

In doing this, the Calvinist view of labor moved leagues away from the ideas of the medieval Schoolmen. The Schoolmen had viewed pauperism and poverty as normal aspects of a natural order "willed by God upon a sinful world." In this setting, unemployment was to be countered by alms-giving. But the later Calvinists avoided pity and grace, and saw this life as a "workhouse" in which the inmates acknowledged labor and discipline as their portion (Lüthy, 106–7). But even in this edifice of toil, Calvin commanded his flock to see labor as a gift of God, and like other things in life, a "fallen good" (W. F. Graham, *Calvin*, 80). So if the "spirit of the calling" demanded thrift, hard work, and frugality, it was to exist without "creature worship" and become part of a systematized laboriousness in which toil as a heavenly offering was its own reward (Troeltsch, *Protestantism and Progress*, 23–24, 136).

If Calvin and his followers allowed work and entrepreneurial activity a guarded approval, it was uncompromising in its in its attacks on laziness. In 1564, Calvin's successor, Theodore Beza, attacked "idleness, foolish extravagance, foolish sins, and law suits." The Consistory should appoint censors "to see that all children of ten to twelve are taught some useful trade" (Tawney, 106). Calvin himself attacked idleness in uncompromising terms when he observed that there was "nothing more disgraceful than a lazy good-for-nothing who is of no use either to himself or to others but seems to have been born only to eat and drink" (Bouwsma, 199). But unlike Luther who preferred agricultural employment to business (Luther, 106–8), Calvin believed all work had value. His support of commercial effort was clear when he wrote that "the life of the godly is justly compared to trading" (W. F. Graham, *Calvin*, 77).

But the matter of how to deal with unemployment, fair pay, and job security bedeviled him. For a city crowded with Protestant refugees from France and beyond in 1545, the Genevan Council ordered that the unemployed be set to work building defensive ramparts. This form of public relief was repeated in 1554 when 400 new families arrived as a group and were offered employment digging ditches (ibid., 108). But if Calvin urged the church authorities to visit every home to see if its family was idle or drunk (Tawney, 101), he and his colleagues promulgated an edict in 1559 limiting pay to masons, hat-makers, and other workers to six sous a day. A similar measure for farm wages was passed two years later (W. F. Graham, *Calvin*, 129–30). In both cases, Calvin did not appreciate that the influx of gold and silver from the Americas had caused a raging inflation in Western Europe that undoubtedly had an effect on wages in Geneva. But Calvin did understand the benefits of labor in another sense all too well when he stated that "it is by his own undeserved favor, and not by the value of our work, that God is induced to reward it" (ibid., 83).

Yet Calvin could be both supportive and reassuring about job security. He argued that since workers have only their labor, "when they are deprived of necessary means, it is as if one cut their throat. . . . He has ordained that we work. But, is work denied someone? Behold, the man's life is stamped out" (ibid., 82). To this Calvin added a warning to employers:

> When the poor whom you have employed at work, and who put their work, their sweat, and their blood for you, have not been paid as is right . . . . if they demand vengeance from God against you, who will be your lawyer, or your advocate, so that you will be able to escape? (ibid., 86)

It was a warning that Calvin reiterated in the *Institutes* so that none would forget the potential eternal punishment that awaited transgressors: "For all are not created in equal condition; rather, eternal life is foreordained for some, eternal damnation for others" (Calvin, 2:926).

If Calvin saw all labor in one's vocation as "highly important in the sight of God" (Michaelsen, 318), he warned employers in particular and the wealthy in general that they had a special obligation to their community. While "each one will have his station," Calvin stated, it was with the warning that "no one may be exempted from the community so that he can say, I will live for myself alone." He continued: "It is too great a cruelty on our part if we see a poor and afflicted man and do not try to help him" (Bouwsma, 201). Calvin excluded monks because they "fatten themselves at the expense of others without working." Beggars were to be put to work. But for the poor who would labor if it were available, those with either earned or inherited means were obligated to relieve the needs of the "brethren" (W. F. Graham, *Calvin*, 81, 68). In this sense the wealth of the successful was not condemned. But they were compelled to realize that those who survived on a "scanty diet" required the rich to live "temperately" and thus have the means to help those in need. Heaven was open to all who used their resources in a communal spirit or "endured poverty patiently" (Bouwsma, 196-97).

Calvin also endorsed a division of labor through which the interdependence of the community could be validated. Each would follow his own calling, and in doing so assist his neighbors by not attempting too many lines of work (ibid., 201). For Calvin this may have been a momentary lapse into medieval thinking, an endorsement of a static society in which all had a fixed place. But it more likely was a desire for order and control, and when coupled with Calvin's other messages, did not weaken his support for a limited movement from one type of job into another. And in no way did it decrease his demand for hard work and community responsibility. Yet Calvin never wavered from his strong belief that one worked for the glorification of God, not personal enhancement:

> Work, then, should be discharged in this spirit of glorification, of duty, and of service to Him through service to fellow men, but never as a means to a person's self-enhancement. (Michaelsen, 317)

From Calvin's perspective worldly goods were given only in temporary stewardship. All that we possessed, including ourselves, belonged to God (McNeill, 221).

Calvin, of course, had much more to say about one's devotion to a calling. To his way of thinking, everyone was bound "in all of life's actions to look to his calling." This was essential so that the "fickleness" of man not lead him "hither and thither" and try to do too many things at one time. To avoid lapsing into a maze of indirection, Calvin assured his followers that God "has appointed duties for every man in his particular way of life." So that none would go beyond what God has ordained for them, "he has named these various kinds of living callings" which serve "as a sort of sentry post" so that men do not live a disorganized existence. Calvin concluded this theme by again underscoring the vital importance of the calling:

> It is enough if we know that the Lord's calling is in everything the beginning and foundation of well-doing. And if there is anyone who will not direct himself to it, he will never hold to the straight path in his duties. (Calvin, 1:724)

Calvin also warned that heavy drinking would seriously impede the faithful from both their religious duties and work in their vocation (ibid., 1:721). He urged his followers to avoid "wickedness," greed, and "evil arts" as they pursued their labors, for nothing must "lead us away from innocence" (ibid., 1:699). Calvin also made it clear that even the lowliest form of toil was a joy to God. To this he added a "guarded permission" for a change in vocation, and by his ardent support for conscientious labor offered an unintended but very real foundation for the tireless efforts required in modern enterprise (McNeill, 221). His caution that the limitless acquisition of wealth was to be subordinated to the "blessing" of God (Calvin, 1:698–99) was somehow lost in translation over the succeeding centuries. Clearly, men took from his teachings what they found congenial at a given point in time.

Most important was Calvin's tenuous connection of the calling and election. The calling, he urged, was a potential sign of election, and could only be contemplated through an "internal illumination of the spirit by means of which *he knows* the reality of the objective fact" (Michaelsen, 316). In even more direct terms Calvin spoke of the linkage between the calling and ultimate election:

> Now among the elect we regard the call as a testimony of election. Then we hold justification another sign of its manifestation, until they come into glory in which the fulfillment of that election lies. (Calvin, 2:931)

Whether this stimulated Calvin's followers to dedicated labor is an open question. But since many of his parishioners were city folk who already demonstrated the motivation, thrift, and entrepreneurial skill needed to succeed in the new market economy, they could not help but be attracted by this endorsement of their efforts. As Henri Sée observed "it is also possible that precisely those individuals who were the most energetic and independent embraced the Calvinist cause." In other words, while Weber and Tawney looked to *Protestantism* as the root cause of dedicated work in the calling, Sée suggested the reverse: it was the entrepreneurial class which had *earlier* projected a passion for precision, punctuality, and profit who now accepted the tenets of the Geneva saints. Put another way, those who approached work in a methodical and orderly manner, who valued time-discipline and the importance of contract, were the very people who would find these aspects of Calvinist thinking in conformity with the entrepreneurial life they were already leading. It is no accident that these urban merchants, bankers, and artisans were among the earliest and most fervent supporters of Calvinism (Sée, 63–64). They found in this faith a reenforcing rationale for their belief in hard work and enterprise. In this sense, the Calvinist calling may have offered them a "rationalization of conduct within this world, but for the sake of the world beyond" (Weber, 154). But more importantly, it attracted those who already accepted hard work and rationality in business as a way of life. These people saw in the new religion a validation of their lives, and accepted the faith despite its tight behavioral parameters (Fanfani, 93–94).

Those who accepted the calling in Calvin's time also had the weight of history behind them. Their systematic pursuit of profit and careful use of time was not a recent innovation of sixteenth-century man. Three centuries earlier a rudimentary market economy was already well-established. Government securities were being traded in Florence as early as 1328, while shares in German mines could be bought and sold at the Leipzig fairs in the early fifteenth century. There is evidence of a forward market in Verona as early as 1318, while commodity exchanges proliferated throughout the Mediterranean from Venice to Barcelona in the fourteenth century. Bills of exchange were in general use during the thirteenth century, and by 1410 the earliest endorsement of one of these instruments could be verified (Braudel, *Structures of Life*, 472; Braudel, *Wheels of Commerce*, 99–100). Also significant was the use of double-entry bookkeeping by the Florentine house of Peruzzi before it went bankrupt in 1343 (Ball, 26–27). Added to all of this were early forms of a systematic division of labor in the medieval cloth industries of Florence and Flanders. In fourteenth-century Florence, its 30,000 textile workers employed twenty-six different operations to make a piece of cloth (Gimpel, 104), while Flemish textile regulations led to a similar division of labor (Thrupp, 1:250–251).

In short, Western Europe embraced the business practices, systemization, and time-discipline of a mercantile economy long before Calvin offered his concept of the calling to the burghers of Geneva. His ideas strengthened and validated the existing predilection toward methodical work, precision, and rationality, and provided additional momentum to a powerful trend that had much history behind it. They offered his followers a religious basis for the methodical lifestyle required in their work. In doing that, Calvinist thinking built upon an existing line of history, and without intending it, reenforced the entrepreneurial and individualistic tendencies that had been gaining strength over the preceding three hundred years.

Viewed from another perspective, Calvinist work values required that the faithful labor fruitfully in this world but be not of it. All were to engage in "sustained and systematic work," but were to avoid "the lust for acquisition and gain." Work was good, but it had to be practiced within the parameters of a "worldly asceticism" that denied the energetic the full fruits of their successful activity (Walzer, 114–15). Work, but do not enjoy. Be orderly, methodical, and watchful of time. But do not forget that all earthly blessings came from God. Above all, the faithful were to remember that worldly considerations were of secondary importance (Calvin, 1:41). But it was precisely these that led later Calvinists to give labor and profit a greater place in their pantheon of values. Even in mid-sixteenth-century Geneva, Calvin had the difficult duty of dealing with such temporal problems as usury, unemployment, and private property. Business conditions forced him to allow interest rates to rise, while unemployment required the creation of public projects for the unemployed. Calvin also felt the need to give private property his endorsement (Bouwsma, 197). It became increasingly clear that his "worldly asceticism" was under pressure even during his own lifetime. A Calvin could continue to walk the fine line between the needs of this world and the requirements to enter the next, but within a century after his death, the secularist trend evident since the early Renaissance was to shave wide corners around his belief-system.

While Calvin continued to urge that hard work and a circumscribed success was a gift of God, his advocacy of a "rational methodising of life" offered considerable intellectual support for nose-to-the-grindstone businessmen (Robertson, 66). As a by-product, it also provided a moral context for the labor and industrial organization that were essential ingredients of the new mercantile order. But some have suggested that the habit of motivated work was the result of a long period of economic development, that Calvinism was at best a consolidating force rather than an originator (Robertson, "Max Weber," 48–49). In this sense, Calvinism provided a validation for past capitalist activity that was grounded on an intensification of work. Yet Protestantism by its very nature underscored the individuality so vital to work and business by its "insistence that each believer should look inward to his own heart" (Hill, *Change and Continuity*, 84–85). This Protestant individualism offered its followers the inner confidence to deal with the new commercial order that saddled the world with hitherto unknown economic fluctuations. Calvinism in particular gave its adherents "a magnificent bond of unity and strength." Its members saw themselves as the vanguard of a new world, and believed that because God was with them no obstacles could stand in their way (ibid., 92). Thus, John Calvin assured his flock that "to have faith is . . . to possess some certainty and complete security of mind, to have whereon to rest and fix your foot." Calvinism also offered its faithful a positive context for diligence. Here Thomas Taylor stressed "that only Doers shall be saved, and by their doing though not for their doing" (ibid., 89).

All of this makes it evident that the Calvinist sanctification of work in the new market economy of the sixteenth century should not be underestimated. But it must also be placed in its proper historical context. If this is done, the Calvinist contribution to diligence in craft and business can be seen as the outcome of a long series of earlier events that it drew upon without offering them a footnote. Succinctly stated, it must be asked if there were "Calvinists" before Calvin, that is, those who internalized the work ethic without reference to the later theology of the saint of Lake Leman. The great medieval Italian banking houses of Bardi, Datini, and Peruzzi all personified the "Calvinist" commandments of hard work, thrift, and contract, while the many participants of the great medieval fairs of Champagne, Leipzig, and Piacenza demonstrated how influential enterprise had become (Braudel, *Wheels of Commerce*, 82–92). Added to this was the wide business reach of the Hanseatic League from Scandinavia to the Steelyard for the two centuries after its founding in 1241 (Bernard, 298). Of further importance to the methodical functioning of business was the use of bills of exchange as early as the thirteenth century. Later, money markets emerged in Italy, Germany, and the

Netherlands (Braudel, *Wheels of Commerce*, 51) accompanied by the rapid growth of great international commercial centers at Bruges and Antwerp (Bernard, 301). Could anything be more rational, more orderly, more "Calvinist"? Even in this medieval setting, Schoolmen of the fourteenth and fifteenth centuries such as Thomas Aquinas and Albertus Magnus gave an unwitting assist to orderly work and enterprise by developing a "highly rational system of ethics which fostered rational habits of mind and had as its corollary a rational methodizing of life" (Hudson, "Weber Thesis," 89). Beyond this, the men of the Quattrocento added to the secular support for striving, labor, and worldly gain (Baron, 1:73).

There were still other intellectual and commercial influences that paved the path to the rational heritage of sixteenth-century Calvinist strictures on work and business. Noteworthy were the contributions to algebra, arithmetic, and the use of Arabic numerals by Leonardo Fibonacci (c. 1170–1240) in his *Liber Abbaci* (Berton, A1, A9). To this must be added Luca Pacioli's *Summa de Arithmetica, Geometria, Proportioni, et Proporcionalita* of 1494, which spread the knowledge of double-entry bookkeeping throughout much of Western Europe, and served as yet another example of an emerging culture that was both systematic and mathematically oriented (Braudel, *Wheels of Commerce*, 555; Luzzato, 118). Additionally, the use of reckoning masters and reckoning schools increased the employment of computational mathematics in business. The number of reckoning schools grew rapidly after six were established in Florence in 1338; by 1613, Nuremberg had forty-eight. A further impetus in this direction was the appearance of the first printed commercial arithmetic book in the north Italian city of Treviso in 1478 (Swetz, 15–17, 24–25). Even more significant was the development of the modern clock. Could anything have had a greater impact on the precision and time-discipline prized by Calvin? As early as 1309, the Church of St. Eustorgio in Milan had an iron clock, and by 1335 Milan's Church of St. Gothard possessed a time piece with a clapper that struck its bell twenty-four times to reflect the total number of hours each day and night. Early astronomers and navigators also used these new clocks to chart their longitude "and the right ascension of the stars" (Cipolla, *Clocks and Culture*, 40, 57). So important were these early timepieces to life and work that one historian stated that "the clock did not create an interest in time measurement; the interest in time measurement created the clock" (Landes, 58). Thus "people became very conscious of time, and, in the long run, punctuality became . . . a need, a virtue, and an obsession" (Cipolla, *Clocks and Culture*, 104).

Not to be ignored was the key impact that science and mathematics had on the order and method inherent in the Calvinist outlook. The Calvinist John Napier (1550–1617), a contemporary of Genevan leader, first discovered logarithms which had an important impact on every science using calculations. In addition, his introduction of the decimal point (Nef, *War and Human Progress*, 57–59) was of incalculable value to the business world of which Geneva was an integral part. It is also reasonable to assume that the humanist demand for accuracy and precision in the translation and interpretation of old texts by Ptolemy, Galen, Archimedes, and Averroës had some effect on the well-educated Calvin. Nor should the possible influence of contemporaries such as Copernicus, Galileo, and Da Vinci be underweighted. Of necessity, they required order, method, and mathematical accuracy in their work (Gilmore, 252–53), and offered a contemporary example of a broad trend that had it origins in earlier times. Even the later Puritans, Baptists, and Pietists remained partial to both mathematics and physics as they sought "from empirical knowledge of the divine laws of nature to ascend to a grasp of the essence of the world" (Weber, 249).

For all of these reasons and more, the European economy was expanding rapidly by the year 1500. Its international component still did not equal the volume of local trade, but it was growing vigorously. The new economic order leaned on the merchant-trader who was a key to the growth of cloth manufacture in Western Europe. He was seconded by travelling businessmen (Everitt, 468–73) who frequented the fairs, and the exporting merchants who sent goods abroad for sale. All of these entrepreneurs became intermediaries for craftsmen and other producers who came to depend on distant markets beyond their control. In time, many smaller producers were destined to become either cogs in the wheel of a far-flung putting-out system, or wage-laborers who lived and died by the beneficence of the marketplace (R. Davis, *Atlantic Economies*, 25–26). This new world of impersonal and systematic industrial methods began to supersede the ways of the craftsmen. As early as the fifteenth century, Fugger capital enabled German engineers to bring many eastern and central European mines under "central management," and integrated them with smelting operations (Thrupp, 1:257). In northern Europe and England iron establishments shifted from goods desired for their beauty to those wanted for their utility. Pots, pans, locks, keys, and strong boxes were now made in rationally organized factories and were sold in a wide variety of markets (Nef, *Cultural Foundations*, 50–53). The use of blast furnaces in the Liège area and eastern France after 1500, and the new organization of the English coal pits using twenty to thirty laborers each also typified the beginning of a move away from the age of the artisan to the time of large, systematized industries employing wage earners (R. Davis, *Atlantic Economies*, 22). By the end of the sixteenth century, industry was spreading throughout Western Europe from its old concentrations in Italy and the Netherlands (Braudel, *Wheels of Commerce*, 309). It was accompanied by an increase in the use of money payments in business transactions due to a rising price structure, the wealth English merchants drew from abroad, and new needs following the Renaissance (Postan, 130, 134).

While it would be inaccurate to suggest that Calvinism alone promoted the rationalization and expansion of the industry in the sixteenth century, it would not be unreasonable to argue that it offered men of commerce a favorable context within which they could operate. If the Calvinist endorsement of hard work, time-discipline, and order is accepted as the last link in an chain of historical events, then it is important to look "to the internal transformative capacities of Protestantism" and to its "impact on the transformation of the modern world" (Eisenstadt, 7–8). While desperately opposing the grossest forms of commercial greed and aggrandizement, Luther was willing to praise manual work in the calling. Ever suspicious of "unearned" wealth and financial speculation, Luther budged only slightly from his medieval mind-set of a working world peopled by peasants and artisans who labored long and hard from fixed social positions. But he did move.

But it was Calvin who permitted a conditional mobility of employment and a carefully circumscribed sanction of profit (S. Parker, *Future of Work*, 35). Yet he did warn in his lecture *On*

Job, 21:7 that "it is much more dangerous to be rich than poor" (McNeill, 222). Again, the preacher of Geneva was only willing to support the accumulation of wealth on a very conditional basis, for success was a possible sign of God's pleasure, not a certainty. Wealth and good conscience were thereby given a tenuous reconciliation. With it came the clear admonition that hard labor was valued only for the glory of God and the preservation of one's soul. And so Calvin could say:

> No man will be so unhappy but that he may every day make some progress however small. Therefore, let us not cease to strive, that we may be incessantly advancing in the way of the Lord, nor let us despair on account of the smallness of our success; for however our success may not correspond to our wishes, yet our labor is not lost, when this day surpasses the preceding one; provided that with sincere simplicity we keep our end in view and press forward to the goal, not practicing self-adulation, nor indulging our own evil propensities, but perpetually exerting our endeavors . . . till we shall have arrived at a perfection of goodness. (Calvin, 1:775–76)

Still, Calvin allowed for some "use of the creatures" but only "what is absolutely necessary." But he warned that men are but stewards of their success, and for this they must eventually render an account to God (ibid., 1:723). In the meantime, the populace was cautioned to do their duty to God and the community (Tawney, 104). But no matter how hard Calvin tried to combine an internal and external discipline that would lead Genevans on the right path, his guidelines on work ultimately, if unintentionally, pointed more and more men in the direction of worldly success.

Some evidence of the "worldly" Calvin could be seen in Geneva's introduction of a watch industry to replace the cloth and velvet enterprises edged out by Lyons. Calvin also pushed a state loan to support industries that offered work to the poor and the unemployed. In fact, Calvin's letters abound with references to business, a fact that was tied to Geneva's role as a mercantile center of some importance (Troeltsch, "Economic Ethic of Calvinism," 21–22). But these secular ventures did not deter Calvin from warning successful businessman that they were temporary recipients of God's generosity. The merchant and financier had a duty to increase their wealth, but more importantly, "were to utilize it for the good of Society as a whole." This was a major step beyond the life of a fixed "natural existence" inherent in the medieval and Lutheran worlds (ibid., 25). In this new setting, contemplation was replaced by sanctioned activity. And within a century after the passing of Calvin, that activity was to be accepted as the legitimate avenue by which the needs and wants of the individual could be satisfied.

Some have argued that both Luther and Calvin were compelled to tolerate a certain level of individuality simply because they split off from "an established church." Calvin's emphasis "of the littleness of man in the face of the awfulness of God" may have increased the importance of the individual, because only as an individual could man reach "an awareness of God" (Brinton, 77). This loosened the "concrete frame of reference" inherited from the "static feudal social system" (Fromm, 110). Individuals now "stood alone before God" as they were soon destined to live as socially separated entities (Ruitenbeek, 48) who sought their own destiny through work, thrift, and punctuality.

The emerging mercantile and industrial world "required profound changes in human motivation and personality" (Albee, 153–57) if work was to attain its highest level of efficiency. Inherent in the new values promulgated by Calvin was an emphasis on self-control and methodical behavior that helped prepare people for toil in the workshops, factories, and counting-houses. Attention to detail and the need to forego afternoon naps and saint's days were crucial elements of the new order. Contractual relationships among men became paramount as work was now offered for wages in increasingly impersonal settings (Walzer, 113). But above all, the new capitalism went far beyond the medieval conception of satisfying fixed needs. The new acquisitive "value attitudes" (*Wirtschaftsgesinnung*) reflected a fundamental change from the traditional to the rational (Sombart, *Moderne Kapitalismus*, 1, 13–15). Here Calvin acted as a bridge between the medieval and modern conceptions of work and life. He gave his utmost efforts to reconcile the "old economics of the soil . . . where money was weak and man's dependence on nature strong, and the new denatured money economics." To make matters more difficult, Calvin had to "wrestle with the Word as well as the world" (W. F. Graham, *Calvin*, 93–94). Here he tread a narrow path. By support of diligence in one's vocation, Calvin inadvertently encouraged a "dynamic, tradition-denying, forward-looking" view of the world" (ibid., 195) that within the next 150 years altered its values in a way Calvin would not have accepted. On the one hand, Calvin could sermonize that "we are born to work," but then quickly warn that wealth could impede our progress "toward the kingdom of heaven" (Bouwsma, 198–99). He seemed to be torn between what he felt men had to do in this world and dangers of doing it so well that they would suffer eternally for their success.

Calvin's most lasting contribution to the evolution of work values was the added momentum he gave to an already well-established entrepreneurial trend. He enlarged on Luther's limited approval of labor, and unlike the Wittenberg monk, endorsed the work of merchants. To be sure, this support was conditional, and required businessmen to be honest in their dealings and offer charity to the poor. But it was a clear step beyond where Luther had gone. His demand that all good Christians work hard, be thrifty, and follow their calling with precision was advice to the converted. But his flock was required to accept the whole sermon: it was vital to work with energy and skill, but this was to be done in God's name and in a spirit of communal responsibility. Success was to be sought in God's grace rather than the counting-house. It was a severe standard to demand worldly effort without worldly enjoyment. To a degree it could be enforced in Geneva, but after Calvin's death in 1564, the tide of enterprise could no longer be contained. Within the next century and a half, Calvinist restraint would gradually be overwhelmed by continuing growth of secular activity and the values it came to represent. It was to be a victory of this world over the next. Luckily for Calvin, he did not live to see the domination of success over virtue.

Chapter 4

THE PURITAN INFLUENCE

To assess the Puritan impact on the work values of the sixteenth and seventeenth centuries is to observe a sea-change in the belief-system of this new faith. So great was the shift from the Calvinist orientation that offered worldly labor a circumscribed approval, that by the time of the Restoration Puritans would more often be seen as solid supporters of business in a well-established entre-preneurial world order.

Based on the individual conscience elevated by Luther and Calvin, Puritanism consistently heaped praise on diligent labor. Puritan theologians like Thomas Taylor and Richard Sibbes made it clear that while those who worked might be saved, it would only be "by their doing not for their doing" (Hill, *Change and Continuity*, 89). A theological standard such as this became the daily fare of influential seventeenth-century Puritan clergymen (Laslett, 9–10) like William Perkins, Nicholas Bownde, John Preston, and Richard Baxter. And through them, Puritan ideas on work and life reached a circle of pre-1688 contemporaries that went beyond the sphere of the faithful (Hill, *Society and Puritanism*, 30).

Who, then, were these godly souls so addicted to toil? The earliest Puritan thinking emerged shortly after the beginning of the Tudor reign through the teachings of men like William Tyndale and John Hooper (Trinterud, 57). These early preachers began to attract the numerous small masters who continued to practice their craft between 1500 and 1700. To them could be added the many country yeomen who served in Cromwell's armies as well as the more radical Levellers of mid-seventeenth-century England. They also could be found in considerable numbers among the merchant-bourgeois groups that were important to the commercial life of England, France, and the Low Countries (Sée, 63–64). Tawney viewed the Puritans as important among

> those classes of society which combined economic independence, education and a certain decent pride in their status, revealed at once in a determination to live their own lives, without truckling to earthly superiors, and in a somewhat arrogant contempt for those who, either through weakness of character or through economic helplessness, were less resolute, less vigorous and masterful, than themselves. (Tawney, 168)

The early Puritans saw themselves as reformers within the Church of England, but by the 1590s Anglican authorities put an end to their zealous pressures to "purify" the practices of the establishment (Ziff, 32–33). In essence, the Puritans were an "out" party that vigorously criticized the Anglican "in" group. As Archbishop John Whitgift noted "the name Puritan is very aptly given to these men; not because they be pure . . . but because they think themselves to be . . . 'more pure than others'" (George and George, *Protestant Mind*, 399–400, 407).

But the key to all their teachings on worldly labor was to put boundaries around the enjoyment of what one had earned in favor of "vocation as serving transcendent ends." Yet Puritans and other Protestants were to find satisfaction in earthly work and came to see toil as "an expression of salvation." Work was a form of prayer for both the godly and the ungodly, and became a *sine qua non* for inclusion in the saintly circle (ibid., 142). The Puritan preachers even allowed the faithful to accumulate wealth, but it could not lead to greed or an obsession with money-making. The widely read *Decades* of Henry Bullinger urged heavy toil on the saints for "the Lord mislikes the yawning mouth and folded arms." John Preston pushed work as a duty to God and community, but like the earlier Calvinists, warned that earnings from labor was not an end in itself but a bequest from God. The greatest of all the early Puritan preachers, William Perkins, demanded stricter guidelines when he warned his followers that one should "not desire and seek for goods more than necessary, for if he doth, he sinneth" (Hill, *Change and Continuity*, 95–96). But it must be asked whether many of the faithful who accepted permission to acquire wealth through work went on to ignore the theological warnings about its dangers. Evidently, the Puritan minister Thomas Adams thought so when he said: "They are very hot for the Gospel. . . . [T]hey love the Gospel: who but they? Not because they believe it, but because they feel it: the wealth, peace, liberty that ariseth by it" (ibid., 96).

In their "conversionist" zeal, the Puritans tried to evangelize all of Europe and North America with their gospel of work. They "urged parishioners to glorify God in their own fields of endeavor" (Eusden, 22), but true to their Calvinist traditions, warned the holy to "seek riches not for themselves but for God." If these admonitions were not enough, the Puritan minister Thomas Adams added: "We teach you not to cast away the bag, but covetousness" (Hill, *Change and Continuity*, 96). To this the preachers Dod and Cleaver appended that God would want business "to proceed from love" rather than greed. Even a market price could be acceptable to God and the "brethren," said Richard Greenham, if it was genuine and came from the heart. The distinction between avarice and usury on the one hand and a fair business arrangement on the other all emanated from the internal motivation of the individual (ibid., 97).

But for Protestants in general and the Puritans in particular, the artisan, farmer, and merchant were given their highest regard. In contrast to the Catholic hierarchy of vocations which placed these callings in the "Six Lower Orders" (George and George, *Protestant Mind*, 143). William Perkins exemplified the shift in values when he argued that work in industry "is as good as land, because land may be lost; but skill and labour in a good occupation is profitable to the end, because it will helpe at neede, when land and all things faile" (Hill, *Puritanism and Revolution*, 227). Perkins also told his parishioners that a good Christian could accumulate wealth through his labor, for these gifts of God were not to be condemned in themselves. Riches did not make a man good or bad, explained Lancelot Andrewes. But because "he may do good with them they are good" (George and George, *Protestant Mind*, 123–24). Joseph Hall confirmed the new bias toward earned wealth when he told his flock: "O ye rich citizens we tell you from Him, whose title is Rich in Mercy, that ye may be at once rich and holy" (Hill, *Change and Continuity*, 97). Thomas Adams offered additional evidence that the Puritan divines were leaning more and more toward support of wealth through work when he stated:

> Riches are the staires whereby men climbe up into the height of dignitie; the fortification that defends it; the food it lives upon. (George and George, "Protestantism and Capitalism," 161)

From these declamations it became clear that even in the early seventeenth century Puritan thinking was moving toward acceptance of the realities of the world. The commercialization of the world that both Luther and Calvin had tried to keep under a semblance of control continued its unabated growth in the century and a half after the decline of Antwerp in the 1560s. Northwestern Europe became the industrial heartland of the continent, and drew raw materials such as timber and iron from the Baltic, wine and oil from the Mediterranean, and silver and sugar from Spanish America (R. Davis, *Atlantic Economies*, 88–90). England in particular was finding its industrial legs, and during the seventeenth century expanded its growth at the expense of the Dutch and French. Seaports such as Bristol, London, Hull, and Southampton gave the English a window to all the seas, and they used these harbors to extend their commercial reach (Bernard, 299). Woollen exports, for example, grew so rapidly between 1600 and 1650 that they accounted for 80 percent of all goods sold abroad. The decline of Antwerp during the 1560s saw English goods continue to pour into Western Europe through German and Dutch ports such as Hamburg and Amsterdam. In addition, the English established trade links with India and Indonesia after 1600, and imported tobacco, furs, and sugar from the Americas. By 1688 there was such an excess of Asian and colonial goods in England that re-exports accounted for 25 percent of all goods sold abroad (R. Davis, *Atlantic Economies*, 206–7). Business enterprise was also strengthened by the emergence of modern stock exchanges in Amsterdam and London. Amsterdam became the center of frenzied trading in shares among the Dutch at the beginning of the seventeenth century; in London, a Royal Exchange in Change Alley emerged in 1695 (Braudel, *Wheels of Commerce*, 100–103, 106–7).

Beyond all of this business expansion, coal production in England increased enormously by the early seventeenth century. From but 50,000 tons annually in 1550, output from the Lower Tyne reached 800,000 tons in the first years of the next century. Coal mining had become so important by the early seventeenth century that the parson at Cole Orton in West Leicestershire observed the blessing of the crops at Rogationtide (Plough Monday) was sparsely attended because so many of the men were now employed in the pits (Hoskins, *Plunder*, 50). Of this growing production some 75 percent went to London (Langton, 178), which was rapidly becoming the heart of an integrated English economy. The vast requirements of this new metropolitan economy was in the process of changing "an amalgam of separate, cellular marketing areas into a cumulating cascade of flows toward the capital." In this respect, the northeastern coal industry and its satellite manufacturing enterprises were tied to demand from the London market. London merchants also acquired large quantities of other raw materials, turned them into finished products, and then reexported these more valuable goods at a profit (ibid., 193–94). Finally, the very considerable growth of iron production between 1540 and 1620 saw output in England increase between five and six times (Nef, *War and Human Progress*, 10–11).

In short, while England still remained a pre-industrial society until at least the 1730s, its great business enterprise was forcing a transformation of work values even as it changed the industrial landscape. The circumstances of the world now pressed in on the English saints and their Scottish and American counterparts, and faced them with an implacable problem that required accommodation. It was this accommodative path that the Puritan fathers were ultimately compelled to follow, but it was all done in the name of useful work for community benefit and as a token of God's esteem. It was at best a compromise with reality, a nod to the inevitable. And by the early eighteenth century the secular world had so engulfed the Puritans that even their lessened opposition to work for wealth and ostentation appeared to be an archaic remnant of past principles.

This gradual adjustment to the growing power of the business world has already been noted in the writings of Thomas Adams, Richard Greenham, and Joseph Hall. These early-seventeenth-century voices made a valiant effort "to adapt Christian morality to the needs of a population which was being steadily driven from its old feudal status into the untried conditions of competition between man and man in an increasingly commercial and industrial society under a money economy" (Haller, 116–17). And while it is true that entrepreneurs were given increasing praise by the clergy, it was largely for their role as productive workers. Their ambition and endless search for riches and display continued to attract the fire of the Puritan ministers. In his 1634 book entitled *A Three-Fold Treatise*, Robert Bolton went even further by his denunciation of the newly rich because of such anti-social practices as usury, rack-renting, and enclosures (George and George, *Protestant Mind*, 150, 171). Richard Baxter told the faithful to "labour hard in your callings," but signalled that such business was secondary to "the more immediate service of God" (Weber, 262). He warned his readers that "you have no necessity of loving the world." Work to do the most good and to escape sin, not to "be most Rich or Honourable in the world" (Robertson, "Max Weber," 72). Baxter went on to urge that one could work to be "rich for God, though not for the flesh and sin" (Sombart, "Capitalist Spirit," 38), but in his *Christian Directory* he somewhat tempered this admonition when he said:

> It is a sin to desire Riches as worldlings and sensualists do . . . but it is no sin, but a duty, to labour not only for labour's sake . . . but for that honest increase and pro-vision, which is the end of our labour. (Michaelsen, 333)

John Robinson, who did exceptional work among the Puritans when they were in Leyden, added that "we must then mingle our sweat with faith to make a sweet odor withal to God" (George and George, *Protestant Mind*, 131).

What appears to be increasingly evident is the dichotomy of the Calvinist-Puritan message. On the one hand, there was a con-sistent need to concentrate on prayer, meditation, and church-going. It was vital to be at one with God. But the second message, the one that most appealed to the many businessmen in the Puritan fold, was the demand for diligence within one's personal calling. As the sixteenth century wore on it was this latter emphasis

on worldly effort and its secular rewards that more closely paralleled the lives of the faithful. Some even came to believe that
efficient labor might "induce God's mercy" (Eusden, 22). Such
wanderings were not acceptable in sixteenth century Scotland
(Sombart, "Capitalist Spirit," 35), but the Reverend Richard Steele
of London in his 1684 *The Tradesman's Calling* required businessmen to be up early and continue to labor steadfastly as long as the
sun shone:

> You should indeavour to be as much in your Shop,
> Warehouses, or places where your most constant Busi-
> ness is, as possibly you can; yea, ye ought to delight to
> be there . . . and to be restless when you are necessitated
> thence, until you return thereunto. (Michaelsen, 330)

But an earlier Puritan minister, William Perkins, reflected the
staunch resistance to work for wealth. He maintained this stance
even if the resources earned went to help the poor. But only a few
years after Perkins' death in 1602, John Downame took the oppo-
site position in his 1616 tract *The Plea of the Poore*. A century later
Samuel Willard's argument in favor of wealth was clear evidence
of the transformation of the early Puritan stance: "Riches are
consistent with *Godliness*, and the more a Man hath the more
Advantage he hath to do Good with it" (Foster, 111). Richard
Baxter concurred. All of God's servants were to exert their best
efforts to improve their financial position. If this were not done,
warned Baxter, "you cross one of the ends of your calling, and
you refuse to be God's steward, and to accept His gifts and use
them for Him when He requireth it" (Weber, 162). The Puritan
pamphleteer R. Younge added to chorus of wealth-approving
saints in his 1654 publication entitled *The Poores Advocate*: "No
question but it [riches] should be the portion of the godly than of
the wicked, were it good for them; for godliness hath the promises
of this life as well as of the life to come" (Tawney, 221). Baxter put
the final touches on the changes that were occurring among the
faithful during the seventeenth century when he called for effort
and performance. He went on to remind his followers that "it is
for action that God maintaineth us and our activities. Work is the
moral as well as the natural end of power" (Fullerton, 16). But

within this message was the implicit concern with poverty as an end result of willful idleness, the view that "distress is a proof of demerit" (Tawney, 221). It was to be a theme of the times, and would reoccur consistently. Poverty, so the belief went, was equated with a lack of goodness. It had to be dealt with firmly or the idle would drain the resources of the diligent under the guise of hunger and disease. Unemployment, a synonym for destitution, was a sign that a meaner station on earth was a portent of a gloomier reception in the world to come.

Thus, it was no accident that many in Tudor and Stuart England had such antipathy for vagrants. These "sturdy rogues" were depicted as the undeserving poor, and chasing them back to their home parishes for support (Youings, 254) seemed more just than seeking an explanation for unemployment. Few if any contemporary observers saw the likely causes of unemployment in the cumulative effect of business gyrations in the new market economy, the population explosion of the sixteenth century, and the Tudor enclosures. It is little wonder that the Puritans, so addicted to labor, could but scorn the poor and blame them for their poverty. That this perception was shared by the prosperous classes in general suggested a value system that lauded the successful even as it denigrated its victims. As Christopher Hill noted "poverty . . . ceased to be a holy state" and became "presumptive evidence of wickedness" (Hill, *Puritanism and Revolution*, 218). The poor came to be viewed as the permanent sinners of successive generations, the lazy residue who rested on the backs of the industrious. And so men like the minister Richard Baxter could condemn idleness and urge the deserving poor to be like the "bees" who "labour to replenish their hive" (Perry, 307), but he could not tell them where to find employment. Too often the Puritans assumed they were of the elect by virtue of their worldly success, and saw those who were less enterprising as a feckless crew to be condemned for moral weakness (Tawney, 191–92). The ultimate sting came from the hand of the same Richard Baxter who advised all to avoid more sleep than was necessary, take cold baths, and eat a moderate vegetable diet (Weber, 157–59). How the wandering poor could take any type of bath or be selective enough to eat only vegetables suggests this stoic message was for the more substantial persons in his congregation.

While it is true that the seventeenth century English workers enjoyed a reputation for assiduously avoiding labor if we are to believe a 1647 pamphlet to this effect as well as the remarks of a French visitor in 1694 (Hill, *Change and Continuity*, 235), those who could not find work would have been repelled by Baxter's demand to "work hard in your calling" (ibid., 159). Many of these unfortunates had been forced off the land, and were unable to adjust to the vagaries of the market. An example of the existing job insecurity could be found in the English cloth industry, the dominant manufacturing business during the sixteenth and seventeenth centuries. While prosperity reigned in this sector during the 1580s in southwestern England and East Anglia, a decade later disaster struck. Unemployment in the 1590s was compounded by high food prices, and brought on such a severe crisis that it was a major factor in the passage of the Poor Law of 1601. The situation improved until 1614 only to have war on the continent in the 1620s disrupt the demand for English broadcloth and "new draperies." Misery among many cloth workers followed, since few had financial reserves to cope with sudden unemployment. Compounding the problems of the new workforce were famines in 1597–99 and again in 1623 coupled with outbreaks of bubonic plague in the 1620s (Wrightson, 143–45).

To those without work, Baxter's maxims were messages to the forlorn. His warning that sloth and idleness were "destroyers of grace" fell gently on the ears of the Puritan faithful, for they believed it was intended for the less industrious sort. It was more a message of congratulation for the good thoughts and wise habits already in evidence among the diligent. In short, Baxter was chastising those who could not comply with his strictures even as he elevated those who were already living the Puritan life of rational laboriousness. But the portrait of the undeserving poor would remain as a legacy of the protestant past.

A more positive gift of the Puritan saints was their emphasis on order and rationality. This may have been an attempt "to regain control of a changing world" by providing parameters for secular life coupled with strenuous religious obligations. Method, order, and discipline became the reigning watchwords (Walzer, 126–27). Later Puritan ministers who looked to accommodate the faith with the new realities of commerce urged businessmen to be "as wary . . . of Time as of Money. . . . Hours have wings, and every moment flies up to the Author of Time, and carries notice of our usage of it" (Michaelsen, 330). In his 1693 book entitled *On Industry*, the mathematician-theologian Isaac Barrow urged rational self-regulation when he said "we should check our inclinations, curb our appetites and compose our passions" (Sombart, "Capitalist Spirit," 36). Baxter believed that Christians were capable of more "*orderly*" work, that others would be in a state of "continual confusion" (Michaelsen, 331). Two and a half centuries later Tawney offered a succinct summation of Puritan constancy and order when he said they were

> an earnest, zealous, godly generation, scorning delights, punctual in labor, constant in prayer, thrifty and thriving, filled with a decent pride in themselves and their calling, assured that strenuous toil is acceptable to Heaven. (Tawney, 175)

Systematic work became the byword of the faith. It gave profit a quiet nudge forward, and offered a philosophy that shaped English and American work values for generations to come. Puritanism supplied a rationale for getting a disciplined workforce into the mills and mines even as it offered the faithful a rational way "to live on earth" as a waystation to the Elysian fields (Hill, *Society and Puritanism*, 495). Within its demand for systematic effort, Puritan doctrine required less consumption and unremitting effort. That these elements pointed in the direction of profitability and the accumulation of capital gave modern business the rational framework needed for competitive success. Puritan rationality also gave its mercantile adherents the weapons needed to challenge the fixed socioeconomic order of Stuart England. By the onset of the 1688 revolution, its imprint assured the success of the new "commercial civilization" (Tawney, 192–93).

   Among the more important elements inherent in the triumph of Puritan rationality was their devotion to time-discipline. Aided by the widespread use of modern watches and clocks thanks to the improvement of the pendulum clock and invention of the balance spring by Christiann Huygens (1629–95), Englishmen such as Hubin and Butterfield were able to produce fine timepieces. English watchmakers became so proficient (Sir George Clark, *Seventeenth Century*, 19) that pocketwatches and other timepieces became far more common. Undoubtedly, it assisted the Puritan preachers when they insisted that sufficient time be allocated for religious obligations and work. To be sure, these "masters of regimentation" left little room for leisure. But by the seventeenth century the clock helped make industrial rationalization an emerging reality. It influenced "counting house and shop," and "reduced life to a careful, uninterrupted routine" (Mumford, 42). The Puritans in particular worried much about the waste of time, a passion that helped the saints "concentrate effort" and "focus attention on detail." It also prepared them and their less willing neighbors "for the rhythms of an industrial society, our society of the alarm clock and factory whistle" (Hill, *Society and Puritanism*, 127). Clocks divided the working day into identifiable parcels and made careful use of every minute a reality. All of this underscored the belief that "every second counts," (Arnold, 28) and time had a money value. In his *Christian Directory*, Baxter made the point with precision when he noted that the faithful must so order their daily routine that every aspect of their lives "should be . . . as the parts of a Clock or other Engine, which must be all conjunct, and each rightly placed" (E. P. Thompson, "Time and Work-Discipline," 87nl02). This became so important that seventeenth-century rural employers and eighteenth century industrialists made every effort to see that worker time was used efficiently. The new watchword was "time is now currency: it is not passed but spent" (ibid.,61). Time now was viewed "as a precious commodity, because it alone made possible the production of all other commodities" (I. Bernstein, "Time and Work," 5). The fiery Puritan minister Robert Bolton (1572–1631) made this point well when he stated:

> Time is short. Time is precious. . . . Wee must bee countable for time. . . . At the dreadfull Barre of that last Tribunall . . . must wee . . . give up a strict account for the expence of every moment of time. (George and George, *Protestant Mind*, 133–34)

If this were not enough, we find that one Richard Palmer of Wokingham left a bequest in 1664 that bells be rung (many church clocks noted the hour but did not ring) at four each morning and at eight every evening from the tenth of September to the eleventh of March. This, he said, would insure that all would be up each morning so they could attend to their "labours and duties of their several callings" (Thompson, "Time and Work-Discipline," 63). It was clear the Puritan devotion to time-thrift had strengthened a lifestyle that had been gaining momentum since the later Middle Ages. Leisurely "agrarian rhythms" now yielded more and more to a time-based "exactitude" (Le Goff, "Labor Time," 44). The nonconformist minister Matthew Henry, author of the *Worth of the Soul*, could add that "those who are prodigal of their time despise their own souls" (O'Brien, 118). For the Puritans and other members of the emerging business class productivity based on the rational use of time, labor, space, and materials was the new standard. But of these time was the great regulator.

Linked to the Puritan obsession with rationality and the frugal use of time was the sabbatarian issue. It surfaced during the sixteenth and seventeenth centuries, and became a defining divide as England moved away from the traditional-agrarian medieval world to the bustling commercial-industrial era that followed. In the course of this change, a intense conflict between "two modes of life" took place. Many rural inhabitants who were wedded to the old tradition of Sunday sports fought the Puritan demand that Sunday be devoted to prayer and meditation.

The Puritan position on this issue probably can be "dated" from the 1595 book by Nicholas Bownde entitled *Doctrine of the Sabbath* (Hill, *Society and Puritanism*, 163). It stemmed from the desire to have those who labored fastidiously in their callings during the week be able to labor for God on the Lord's day. If this were done, said the Puritan minister Arthur Hildersam, the faithful could avoid being "glued to the world." And while even the Puritans permitted a little labor on Sunday such as dressing of meat, it was an "activist" day in which all were to devote their energies to spiritual effort. In this sense, even Sunday was a working day (George and George, *Protestant Mind*, 140). It is true that Calvin played bowls on Sunday, but Puritans before Bownde had pushed hard to free that day from earthly toil. While at Cambridge in 1578, just fourteen years after Calvin's death, Lancelot Andrewes advocated that no work or play be allowed on Sunday.

Richard Greenham looked to Sunday as a day of meditation in a 1592 publication called *Treatise of the Sabbath*. And while it would appear that the Puritans were more Calvinist than Calvin on this issue, the Laudians applauded sports on Sunday. Like Calvin, the Laudian bishops also played bowls on the Lord's day (Hill, *Society and Puritanism*, 164–65). Nevertheless, the saints were able to turn their sabbatarian values into law when the parliamentary government passed legislation in 1645 endorsing Sunday sabbath. Perhaps there was more at stake for the Puritans than the prohibition of Sunday sports. Could it be that many of the faithful saw Sunday meditation as a relief from the demanding worldly labor of the week? If we listen to the preachers this was not so. They insisted that Sunday be a day of strenuous (everything was strenuous for the Puritans) religious activity, that each person use the time as an investment in faith. But many of the Puritans were substantial businessmen and yeomen, and their interest in workless Sundays could well have been a response to the intensified demands of commercial activity that characterized England in the seventeenth century. Again the question must be raised: was the growing mercantile ethos continuing to shape the Calvinist-Puritan outlook, or were the saints molding a new capitalistic universe? It seems that the impact of the centuries pressed heavily on the faithful even as their work values, in turn, left more than a passing imprint on the world. In any event, the sabbatarian issue was ample testimony to the long-range impact of Puritan principles (ibid., 170, 201–2). Only in the twentieth century was sport and labor on Sunday to make inroads.

No where was the Puritan desire to fulfill a fundamental aspect of their philosophy more evident than in their commentaries on idleness. In the influential *Homily Against Idleness*, it was strongly advocated that children be taught a trade to avoid sloth. "Serving men" were to make themselves ready to serve their employers rather than to spend their time in idleness (Hill, *Society and Puritanism*, 126). The *Homily* even attacked the wealthy who did not labor, since God had commanded all to work (ibid., 135). For the Puritans, the fact of work was more important than the nature of the toil. Idleness not only made the wealthy and the undeserving poor the drones of the earth, but gave them time for unseemly temptations. There was to be no rest in this world.

Activity became the *sine qua non* of religiosity, the most likely avenue to heaven. It was a doctrine that served the Puritans on earth even as it paved a possible path to eternal grace.

If William Perkins struck at the idle rich in England (Morgan, "Puritan Ethic and American Revolution," 4) and Elizabeth Joceline urged English children to avoid the life of a drone in her *Mothers Legacie to her unborne Childe* (1632), Puritans in the American colonies took up the cause with equal fervor (Hill, *Society and Puritanism*, 121). John Cotton (1584–1652), one of the founders of the Congregational Church in New England, attacked idleness in a catechism for children in 1646 when he advised that "the Idle *Fool* is whipped at school." This appeared in the very influential *New England Primer* for children under the title "Milk for Babes." The Primer went through nine editions during the latter half of the seventeenth century, and had a great impact on several generations of colonial youngsters (B. Labaree, *Colonial Massachusetts*, 79). Idleness was actually made a legal offense in Massachusetts in 1648, and Robert Cushman, in his well-known *Discourse* of 1622, asserted that "idle drones are intolerable in a settled commonwealth" (Hill, *Society and Puritanism*, 137–38). The New England theocracy advocated whipping for idlers (Tawney, 112), while the Boston First Church records for 1657 show that the Puritan clergy excommunicated a woman who insisted that Christ told her "to remain idle" (Oberholzer, 152). It is little wonder that the New England Puritans sent those who did not use their time well to the local magistrate. On the thirteenth of January in the year 1699 the Selectmen of Woburn "reproved" one John Carter, Jr. for idleness and warned him to find a productive use for his hours or be punished (Wertenbaker, *Puritan Oligarchy*, 165–66). Clearly, the Puritan strictures on the wastage of time had crossed the Atlantic. Much more was to follow.

Possibly the most important Puritan contribution to the changing work values of early modern Europe was their interpretation of the calling. While the concept of the calling can be found in the Catholic *Vulgate* (c. 383–405) of St. Jerome, the ideas of St. Paul, and implicitly in the Benedictine and Augustinian rules (Robertson, "Max Weber," 68–69), it was through the ideas of Martin Luther that this concept received its first "modern" endorsement. Luther's support of vocation was carefully tailored to avoid validating the growing commercial spirit of his time. Of all forms of labor, Luther most loved agriculture. He despised businessmen and their commercial practices, and did not attribute the calling to their efforts because they exploited peasant and craftsman. Yet he did give labor a push forward by his guarded support for toil in the calling (Bainton, 233–34), and left it to Calvin and his Puritan successors to wrestle with the further implications of vocation. They, in turn, leaned toward a concept of the calling that had two linked parts: the personal and general callings. To the ministerial elite, both were important. They operated in a theological tandem, and reenforced good behavior in this existence while preparing the saintly for the hereafter. But during the century and a half after the death of Calvin, the faithful were to increasingly participate in the ascendancy of the personal calling. More and more work for profit became an allowable activity. The merchant was no longer the devil incarnate. And ambition took on a sweet smell. Here the comment of the non-conformist minister, George Swinnock, is indicative:

> [The] true Christian is like the good merchant whose mind is always on his business. Whenever he makes a visit, such a merchant inquires about prices and commodities, always seeking new opportunities for profit. (Michaelsen, 333–34)

How, then, did the calling undergo such a metamorphosis? Early Puritans such as William Perkins followed the Calvinist tradition of giving labor in the personal calling circumscribed approval. In his *A Treatise of the Vocations, or Callings of Men*, Perkins required all to have a personal calling in which they labored diligently and thereby were "profitable to society." It was essential that workers "rise early to their businesse, lest night overtake them." None were to emulate the wandering vagrants or idle rich, for they had forsaken their obligations to God, community, and family (Hill, *Puritanism and Revolution*, 226). Above all, those who served in a particular calling had to avoid covetousness and seek no greater return from labor than what was required for their basic needs. It was crucial to be diligent in one's vocation, and to remember that the personal calling was subordinate to the general calling which obligated all to lead a holy life. If one gave God their full heart, then the personal calling could find its proper niche (Michaelsen, 319–23). But unless a person had a general calling no amount of excellence in their particular vocation could point a person to possible election. Man's general calling was paramount, said Perkins, "whereby a man is called out of this world to be a child of God" (Foster, 99). And like Luther, Perkins urged that all stay with the particular vocation "in which God had placed him" (ibid., 103). This may have reflected the desire of many in early Tudor England to retain the status quo in a world that was being buffeted by theological, commercial, scientific, and geographical change. But it placed Perkins at some distance from Calvin and quite close to Luther in his demand that all remain in the occupation to which they had been originally called (Morgan, *Puritan Political Ideals*, 43–44). Perkins particularly objected to ambition, envy, and impatience in the calling, for these personal attributes could only make individuals unhappy with their present station and lead them to seek a "higher place, and a better estate" (George and George, *Protestant Mind*, 135). What a man did mattered little. The key to the Christian fulfillment of the personal calling was in "the heart of the worker." For Perkins, the work of the shepherd was equivalent to that of the magistrate for "the meannesse of the calling, doth not abase the goodnesse of the worke" (ibid., 138). Perkins also demanded that good Christians integrate their worldly work into their general calling for "both callings must be joyned, as bodie and soule are joyned in a living man" (ibid., 136).

The more conservative thinking of Perkins on the issue of callings initially had a powerful influence on the Puritan ministers who followed. These men were the opinion-makers of the time, and for much of the early seventeenth century hewed to the line taken by Perkins. But even here there were deviations, and as the power of the commercial culture grew, so did the deviations.

It is not surprising that early in the Tudor reign John Hooper (c. 1495–1555) reflected the same opposition to a change in vocation as Perkins did fifty years later. He opposed those who "transgresseth his vocation," and likened them to Jonas (W. Jones, 98). More indicative was Richard Sibbes (1577–1635), who demanded in his 1639 *Bowels Opened* that all must work hard in their calling, but view honors and riches as "but secondary things." What matters in the calling is how it enables each person to serve society (George and George, *Protestant Mind*, 167). Thomas Adams, the Rector of St. Bennett's Church in London, also supported the ideas of Perkins in *The Works* (1629) when he urged all to work hard so that they "may eate the labours of [their] owne hands." But he also urged that every worker stay in "that station, wherein God hath disposed us" (ibid., 131–32).

Later in the century Richard Baxter (1615–91) returned to the theme that workers should not let the duties of their personal calling detract them from their religious obligations:

> [C]hoose a calling which so exerciseth the body as not to overwhelm you with cares and labor and deprive you of all leisure for the holy and noble employments of the mind. (Hudson, "Puritanism," 60)

But, said Baxter, all were to work. No one was to live like a "drone" off the labor of others (Fullerton, 16–17), a shot at the idle rich whom the Puritans despised as much as the feckless vagabonds. And just as Theodore Beza had suppressed Wednesday as a traditional holiday in Geneva in 1561, the Puritan minister Nicholas Bownde urged that the number of holy days be reduced in England "lest thereby men should be hindered from the necessary works of their callings." In 1624 James Howell noted that Spain lost five months each year from work due to the many holy days or festivals. In France, the mercantilist Colbert reduced saints' days to a mere nintey-two so more time for work could be available, and by 1697 the English economist, H. Pollexfen, estimated that every holiday cost England 50,000 pounds in lost labor. We can see that from both Puritan and non-Puritan sources the support for steady work was increasingly seen as a national necessity (Hill, *Society and Puritanism*, 144–45).

If the Puritans helped to shape modern work values through the personal calling, they themselves were shaped by an encroaching entrepreneurial culture that required diligence, punctuality, and everyday presence. They helped, intentionally or not, to push forward capitalist endeavor even as they espoused an ordered life, steadiness in a calling, and the need to live in a Christian spirit

(W. Jones, 97, 100). This the Puritans did by their continued approval of work as a good in itself. Labor in one's personal calling, said the poet-preacher John Donne (1572–1631), was meant "to mend and improve, to enlarge ourselves, and spread, even in worldly things." Man could increase his possessions and "take dominion" over the world, said Donne, and in this way give God his portion and continue to work "industriously in an honest calling" (H. Alford, 3:284–85). The Puritan minister of Suffolk, John Carter, gave added credence to the religious character of the particular calling when he told the story of finding a tanner who apologized for being caught in the midst of his labors. Carter replied "let Christ when He comes find me so doing" (Clarke, *Eminent Divines*, 11).

But it is when we look to the teachings of the nonconformist minister George Swinnock in the 1660s that we can observe the circle of change. Swinnock moved sharply away from Perkins' earlier position on the calling and gave it a mercantile twist that his Calvinist predecessors would have found unacceptable. But the world was changing, and it had caught Swinnock, Petty, Steele in its net as we can see from Swinnock's statement:

> Thy duty is, reader, to mind thy general in thy particular calling, and to drive a trade in heaven, whilst thou art following thy trade on earth. (Michaelsen, 333)

More change was to follow in both England and North America. In time, the Puritan influence might be seen as a quaint and rigid legacy of a bygone age. But to look at their contribution in this narrow light would be to ignore Puritan contributions that gave work the additional blessing it needed to support the new business culture.

To further assess the Puritan contribution to work intensification, punctuality, and pride in product, an evaluation of their efforts in North America is in order. For mainly religious reasons between 1629 and 1642, over 20,000 Puritans came to New England during the Great Migration. Additionally, many of the 45,000 migrants to Virginia and the West Indies at this time were also Puritans (R. Davis, *Atlantic Economies*, 131). But it was in New England that they were to have their greatest impact on both colonial work values and faith as a total way of life. Benjamin Labaree noted that for both Pilgrim and Puritan crossing the Atlantic itself was tantamount to a religious experience. It could be equated with the passage across Sinai, for beyond that desert lay the challenge of Canaan, "the promised land." The passage across the sea confirmed to the faithful that they were God's chosen people (B. Labaree, *Colonial Massachusetts*, 33). Like their forebears in England, the Puritan society in the New World prized order in all walks of life. And in line with their Calvinist heritage, the Puritans looked to Scripture to learn what God had planned for His people. The Cambridge Platform of 1648 was drawn up by Richard Mather (1596–1669), a Lancashire minister who embraced Puritanism before coming to Boston. It quickly became the Puritan guide to church organization and government (ibid., 70, 72–73, 77). Both Richard Mather and his son, Increase Mather (1639–1723), hewed to the English Puritan tradition that required Bible study, church attendance, and constant vigilance against personal or communal sin. Despite the fact that few would receive God's grace, a "doctrine of preparation" was needed. Through it, a small number might achieve election, but it was necessary to be ready for the possibility (ibid., 68–69).

A section of Increase Mather's diary for the years 1663–67, reveals his concern that too many of his comrades were addicted to laziness and the things of this world, a matter that paralleled the worries of his English contemporaries (Murdock, 89–90). In his *The Doctrine of Divine Providence* published in 1684, Increase Mather told of a worker who was cutting wood. When asked what he was doing, the worker replied that "I am cutting wood for God." Mather commented that one could buy and sell, build and fashion, or engage in any other worldly labor, but it was of little consequence unless it was done for the "glory of God" (Middlekauff, 394, 170). The preacher John Higginson put it more trenchantly in a sermon before the General Court of Massachusetts on the twenty-seventh of May in the year 1663:

> My Fathers and Brethren, this is never to be forgotten, that *New-England is originally* a plantation of Religion, not a plantation of Trade. (Bruchey, *Colonial Merchant*, 112)

John Cotton (1584–1652), a Puritan clergyman at St. Botolph's Church in Boston, Lincolnshire, looked to the New World as a theocracy in which the ministerial elite had the right to dictate to their parishioners. He founded the Congregational Church with this in mind and set the tone for his son Increase and grandson Cotton Mather (1663–1728). In a 1646 catechism for children entitled "Milk for Babes," John Cotton set the standard for life among the faithful. He left no room for idleness, greed, or the accumulation of wealth when he defined the church as

> a congregation of saints joined together in the bond of the Covenant to worship the Lord and to edify one another in all His holy ordinances. (F. P. Cole, *Mather Books*, 18)

For the Puritan, life itself was a constant struggle between good and evil, "an eternal conflict with the flesh" (Murdock, 101). It was a battle that had to be won if men were to escape eternal torment (Boas, 55). To avoid temptation and evil doing, Puritans were required to espouse the "gospel of work" and make it a central element of their belief system (Wright, *American Colonies*, 24). Such an endorsement would keep their people linked to God because He demanded diligence and frugality as a sign of faith. Hard work was their keystone, but this marker had within it the possibility of offending wealth if one were too enterprising. And even if abundance was a gift of God and used for the community rather than personal betterment, it contained within it snares that at best allowed the saints to give it only a cautious acceptance (Morgan, "Puritan Ethic and American Revolution," 5).

This led the Puritans as well as Quakers to warn the successful against the snares of achievement. Idleness was to be avoided, but so were the excesses of wealth that flowed from diligence and frugality (Bruchey, *Colonial Merchant*, 91). For early Puritans like Thomas Hooker (1586–1647) of Connecticut, the faithful had to guard against "the fallibility of material existence." All had to remember "that the world will pass" and it was therefore incumbent upon believers to stay close to the commandments of the Lord (Miller and Johnson, 1:287). Still, Hooker demanded that his flock be "effectual" in their callings (Dorfman, 1:37–38).

Even when the Puritans were in Holland, the Dutch admired their devotion to work as well as their honesty and steadiness (Bradford, *History of Plimouth Plantation*, 26–27). This was reconfirmed by Thomas Dudley in a November, 1642 letter in which he stated "that every man ought . . . to serve God in such a way whereto he hath best fitted him by nature, education, or gifts" (Foster, 100). Above all, said Cotton Mather, idleness had to be avoided because it was "the most *concealed*, and yet the most *violent*, of all our passions" (C. Mather, *Bonifacius*, 9). Work had to be orderly, said Benjamin Colman (1673–1747), like "the *Wheels* of a *Clock*." The minister at Boston's Brattle Street Church went on to urge his parishioners to strive and persevere in their work (B. Colman, *Sermon*, 12–13).

But the saints continued to worry that riches resulting from their diligence would corrupt them. The minister John Danforth stated that hard work could ultimately lead to "sinful vanity" and "fewer works of Piety & Charity" (J. Danforth, *Vile Profanations*, 40). In this matter the merchants were the lightning rod that caught the wrath of the ministers. Clerical attacks centered on traders who maintained high prices during periods of scarcity. Even the good Calvinist Robert Keayne, a Boston merchant, was brought before both secular and religious courts for overcharging on such necessities as nails and thread. He could not understand why he was convicted, for as a good Christian, he had not led "an idle, laxie, or dronish life." But he had put self-interest above the common good, and had charged a market price when Puritan parameters demanded that he ask less in a time of troubles (Bruchey, *Colonial Merchant*, 103; Bailyn, *New England Merchants*, 43). And while even the highly respected John Cotton had allowed businessmen to fix a higher price if scarcity was God's doing rather than that of man, the concept of charging what the market would bear continued to appear as oppressive (Bailyn, *New England Merchants*, 20–21).

Within this Puritan concern about merchants and markets was their deep disapproval of energetic entrepreneurial activity. Men such as Thomas Breedon who arrived in Boston in 1648 lived only for business, not Puritan principles. Richard Wharton who followed in the 1650s and became a major player in both real estate and commerce, was an early prototype of the nineteenth-century American risk-taker. Along with men like Andrew Belcher, Breedon and Wharton typified values that were anathema to the early Puritans (ibid., 110–11). These tireless businessmen did not take kindly to admonitions like those of Thomas Shepard (1605–49), who urged that in addition to a prohibition on ships setting sail on the sabbath there be no buying or selling. However, Shepard's *Theses Sabbaticae* did make a small concession: fires were permitted in iron furnaces on Sundays (Morison, *Bay Colony*, 129). Still, businessmen increasingly ignored the advice of a John Cotton who warned that "we are never more apt to forget God then when he prospers us" (Cotton, *Way of Life*, 455–57). Nor would his admonition that "we are never to desire more than we have good use of" strike a responsive chord (Dorfman, 1:42). To the emerging entrepreneurs, wealth was a good in itself. Earning more could improve their estate on earth rather than require them to await an uncertain return in heaven. They could, however, accept Cotton's demand that all work hard within their calling (Cotton, *Way of Life*, 449; Cotton, *True Constitution*, 3), but they shunned his advice that success in a calling be accepted with "moderation" (P. Miller, *American Puritans*, 179). Never would these bold businessmen agree that all were to look to heaven before they contemplated the world, nor did more than a few accept the maxim that by serving men they served God (ibid., 177–78). Increasingly they felt that work that enriched the individual was an appropriate end in itself, that material happiness in this existence could be a pinnacle of attainment. There was no need for "deadness to the world" as John Cotton had advocated. What became paramount was "diligence in worldly business." The Calvinist-Puritan world view was not as yet dead, but it was teetering under the weight of centuries of materialistic erosion.

The last of the great Puritan preachers in early America, Cotton Mather (1663–1728), continued the familiar refrain of diligence in a vocation. But within this call to labor was a more favorable reference to business, an accommodation with the inevitable:

> I tell you, with *Diligence* a man may do marvallous [sic] things. *Young* man, work hard while you are *Young*: You'l Reap the effects of it when you are Old. Yea, How

can you Ordinarily enjoy any Rest at *Night*, if you have
not been well at work in the *Day*? Let your *Business*
engross the most of your time (C. Mather, *Two Brief Discourses*, 48)

Mather continued by urging that if a person were to succeed in
the business world he had to "*Rise* to his Business." Yet the old
message remained: God could be glorified by labor in business
and the "doing of Good for others" (ibid., 48, 38). Mather also
attacked idle drones (C. Mather, *Christian at his Calling*, 42–43), and
suggested in his 1695 *Durable Riches* that starvation was a proper
fate for those who would not work (Hill, *Society and Puritanism*,
277). All should be "*serviceable*" (Silverman, *The Life and Times of
Cotton Mather*, 236) in labor, and should "let the baneful *thoughts of
idleness* be chased out of our minds" (C. Mather, *Bonifacius*, 40).
Such diligence, Mather argued, could cure "economic depression"
and serve as a way of dealing with "masturbation" (Foster, 107).
Work, indeed, had benefits that most never imagined before
reading Mather's instructions on the calling.

But to understand the changing tone of Cotton Mather's
underlying message, it is necessary to appreciate the growing
commercial character of the Boston in which he matured. The city
of 7,000 soaked up huge imports of fish, firewood, charcoal, sugar,
and molasses. Its harbor was filled with ships from Manhattan,
the West Indies, Gloucester, and Salem. Commerce and manufacturing abounded as hundreds of carpenters, blacksmiths, rope-
makers, tanners, shoemakers, and butchers all added to the mercantile din of the city. It was in this milieu that Mather grew up
(Boas, 14–15), and it helped to shape the values he enunciated
from book and pulpit. In 1714, for example, he took an active role
in urging that a bank be established in Boston to deal with the
shortage of currency. To this end he wrote to Ashurst, Governor of
the New England Company, urging that something be done:

Our country grows full of people and full of business.
But a medium of trade almost wholly failing among us,
we find ourselves plunged into inexpressible difficulties.
(Silverman, *Selected Letters of Cotton Mather*, 157)

Yet Mather continued to urge the old principles of work for social betterment, the proper use of time, and "service to God" (C. Mather, *Christian at His Calling*, 23; Michaelsen, 330; C. Mather, *Bonifacius*, 107–8). In his essay on "Home and Neighborhood," he required those responsible for the welfare of families to teach the principles of "*obedience, honesty, industry,* and *piety.*" And if there were idle in the neighborhood, do not give them help for this will but "harden" them in their idleness. The true solution was to "find 'em *work*, set 'em to *work*; keep 'em to *work*" (C. Mather, *Bonifacius*, 56, 60). To this he added the demand for pride in craft. All workers, he advocated, should "be well instructed in, and well acquainted with, all the mysteries of his *Occupation*. Be a master of your trade; count it a disgrace to be no workman" (C. Mather, *Two Brief Discourses*, 53). But in all these things acknowledge the Lord— "work for God," for "*it is He that gives thee Power to get Wealth*" (C. Mather, *Small Offers*, 19; *Sober Sentiments*, 25). Nevertheless, Mather saw the near impossibility of distinguishing between the reasonable desire to do well through hard work and the temptation of greed that could be the outcome of diligence. And so he warned all in his 1707 book, *A Very Needful Caution*, to be diligent in business but avoid "Covetous Inclination" (Bushman, *Puritan to Yankee*, 25-27).

With the passing of Cotton Mather in America and the waning Puritan influence in England after the Stuart Restoration, more and more people came to see their world in secular hues. Pleasure and profit seemed more important than finding a surer way to heaven. Making money disturbed fewer consciences (Davidson, *Jonathan Edwards*, 47), and as Nathaniel Clap noted in 1720, "persons may be Diligent about their Business, without being real Christians." Yet he added that "they cannot be Real Christians, that have no Care about their Business" (Crowley, 55–56). From Pennsylvania northward the calling continued to be a strong element in the work values of Anglicans, Congregationalists, and Quakers (Breen, "Non-Existent Controversy," 273–87), but by the 1730s colonists would increasingly view their business as beyond the purview of God and preacher. The idea of vocation, industry, and frugality became more a matter of personal ethics rather than religious prescription. This "ethical secularization" of society allowed people to see sloth and extravagance as offenses against "oneself and society" rather than sins against God. Work continued to be judged by "standards of justice" and"economic performance," while the old values of hard work and thrift were more often used to "apply" a traditional value system to the new economic realities in England and North America (Crowley, 56, 75–76).

If all of this could be seen by John Wise of Connecticut in 1721 when he said that "a thriving trade animates the Farmer" and "Reconciles him to all his hard labour, and makes him look Fat and Chearful" (Bushman, *Puritan to Yankee*, 27), Puritan ministers like Peter Thatcher, writing in 1729, still worried that New Englanders had abandoned the old virtues. Fifteen years later the Reverend Andrew Eliot budged a bit when he said there was no "evil" in desiring worldly gain so long as it is "subordinate to our Love of God." But by 1752 the minister Charles Chauncy could pronounce that "we are made for Business" (Cochran, *Business in American Life*, 37–38). There is little doubt that the growing commercialization in England after 1700 plus the rapid expansion of industry as the century wore on was eroding the old Calvinist-Puritan message (Lemon, "Spatial Order," 100–101). The expanding economy of colonial America was also creating a mercantile milieu that enabled its citizens to pursue profit "with an avidity dangerously close to avarice." And while the old order still had some vitality even as late as 1765, Puritans found it more difficult to distinguish between worthy work and worldly addiction. People now sought a new frame of reference within which they could place work, thrift, and commitment (Bushman, *Puritan to Yankee*, x). Above all, it was clear that the clergy, Puritans and non-Puritans alike, had lost the battle to direct their flocks to work intensely in the here and now while seeking a reward in the world to come. Businessmen found this new outlook congenial to their needs, for the values that exalted the virtues of labor, individuality, and commitment could easily be turned to support their vision of a world of rational relationships.

In this mid-seventeenth-century setting, the Puritans and their contemporaries came to accept vocation as a means of accumulating wealth. There developed among them a differentiation between this world and the next that replaced their fixation on the primacy of the general calling. Earlier Puritans like William Perkins and John Cotton demanded all work be dedicated to God, that gains from labor be seen as His gifts. But the later Puritans, sensing the battle had been lost, concentrated their efforts in denouncing temptation rather than greed. They even accepted the notion that God rewarded the decent with prosperity, that poverty was the punishment visited upon the "bad" children of the earth. Individuals were free to drive their own destiny, and through a new-found mobility, be free from the bondage of sin and guilt (Michaelsen, 334–35). If, as Tawney has commented, "Puritanism helped to mould the social order . . . it was . . . itself increasingly moulded by it" (Tawney, 9). Perhaps the Puritan legacy to modern work values might best be characterized by the biblical injunction: "Seest thou a man diligent in his business? He shall stand before kings" (Proverbs 22.29). It was this belief that was to encompass the non-Puritan world of Tudor-Stuart England as well.

Chapter 5

WORK AND WELFARE: THE TUDOR-STUART LEGACY TO AMERICA

During the two centuries after the accession of Henry VII to the Tudor throne in 1485, the tide of economic individualism gradually overcame the stubborn resistance of the ministerial elite. Puritan, Anglican and nonconformist clergymen were overwhelmed by the secular trend, and by the end of the Stuart reign prosperity through diligence was a well-established work value among merchants and professionals. For them success was the great motivator. Now nobles and yeomen vied for wealth and upward mobility rather than spiritual merit.

But these entrepreneurial values had little attraction for the many unemployed who were buffeted by the fluctuations of the marketplace and the effects of enclosures (W. Jones, 115–16). Those who could not deal with the new realities were relegated to almshouses established by municipalities or wealthy merchants. That this was done for the betterment of the recipient rather than the elevation of the giver (Jordan, 370) did not reduce the stigma that accompanied welfare. This badge of dishonor reflected a *continuity* of the earlier work values of Luther and Calvin which now flowed to America with the tide of British immigration. In the New World as the old, unemployment and poverty became a badge of humiliation, and the workhouse emerged as a penitentiary for the poor. From Newport to Virginia almshouses appeared in parallel with those in Tudor-Stuart England (Youings, 257, 260–61; Morgan, *American Slavery*, 67, 326–27, 338–39). On both shores of the Atlantic the authorities hoped to set the poor to work so they might avoid dependency even as ratepayers escaped increased taxation. But this would prove to be an unattainable goal. Then as now remedies for unemployment and poverty remained beyond the grasp of society. But the belief that unemployment and poverty were manifestations of intentional idleness and moral degradation remained as the dominant Tudor legacy to American policymakers of the twentieth century. It was a great *continuity* in the history of work values except for the color of the targets.

To better understand the development of work values at this time it is important to understand how the general population lived in the sixteenth century. Most still earned their sustinence from the land, although many were forced into unemployment and vagrancy by the enclosure movement (Youings, 27). Nevertheless, about 75% continued to live in rural areas (Clark and Slack, 1). Here continued attachment to meager holdings made "persistent poverty" their on-going portion, although Englishmen generally fared better than their continental counterparts (Clarkson, 10). Still, a cold, damp one room cottage with an earthen floor was home to most. All family members worked either in a nearby plot or in household labor under a putting-out regime (Bridenbaugh, *Vexed and Troubled Englishmen*, 84). In poorer households, children toiled as early as age six or seven, for the span of working life was very short. More significantly, most poor English families had a low level of life expectations (Briggs, *Social History*, 122). But in this setting every person had a place. Families looked after those too old or too ill to work in sixteenth century towns like Norwich, Bristol, Exeter, and York. Flimsy as this support might be, all had an anchor (Hoskins, *Plunder*, 48–49). But it was soon to be pulled up by fluctuating market demand, poor harvests, and the displacement due to enclosures. Now for the first time communities would be forced to offer their reluctant support to the jobless. For the deserving poor there might be some minimal aid; for vagrants, every legal device and public pressure would be used to shift expenses to the rate-payers of their home parish.

Events abroad could also lead to increased unemployment and poverty in England. An upward valuation of the currency in 1554 and 1560 wrecked England's price advantage on the continent, and a Dutch embargo against English goods in 1563 added to a job insecurity that was already a common feature of English life. Not until 1614 when cloth export reached 127,000 pieces did the industry recover (Ball, 152, 156). Changing styles contributed to fluctuations in textile employment. The late sixteenth century introduction of cheaper "New Draperies" was a boon, since these lighter low quality cloths could be marketed effectively among southern European consumers. Additionally, the west of England producers tried to capture the high quality "Spanish cloth" market by using wools imported from the south of Europe (Clarkson, 109–10). But in both cases producers and workers became the servants of fashion and the slaves of the marketplace. With the exception of those who sought opportunity in America or participated in the expanding economy, England remained home to a large reserve army of jobless men and women.

But Tudor businessmen saw the sixteenth century world of affairs through the prism of rationality. They needed to accumulate capital for further expansion which, in their minds, justified their take-it-or-leave-it offers of low wages to a workforce that had few options. If their employees would not accept this, they were free to better themselves elsewhere. No feudal bond tied them to tenants, for in the new world of unfettered business all were thrown into the cauldron of the free market. The new Tudor entrepreneurs felt little social responsibility for poor relief, since poverty seemed to be an intractable problem of the ages. Disciplined toil was the true path, the only regime that could deal with both joblessness and industrial growth (Hill, *Puritanism and Revolution*, 220–21). How this was to be done in a society weighed down with unemployed workers and desperate vagrants was answered with the ingenious reply that those who *really* wanted work could find it.

For those in the lower orders who could find employment work remained a socially sanctioned activity. Under the influence of Luther, William Tyndale argued that all callings have the same weight in the eyes of God. And in *The Parable of the Wicked Mammon* (1527) he urged that every man should serve his master faithfully "not as a man, but as Christ himself" (Wright, *Elizabethan England*, 171n7). Two years later, Simon Fish also exhorted servants to work diligently in his *The Summe of the Holy Scrypture* (W. Jones, 101). Thomas Becon (1542–43) used his *Early Works* to argue on behalf of hard work (ibid., 99), while Hugh Latimer offered a Christmas day sermon in 1552 to persuade the faithful that strenuous labor in their occupation would bring "everlasting life" (Wright, *Elizabethan England*, 173). Robert Crowley, on the other hand, seemed aware of the poor state of many Englishmen, but he, too, pushed the idea that all ought to "live on their labors, as beseemeth a Christian" (*Tudor Economic Documents*, 3:406). Others such as Bishop James Pilkington worried that laboring men wasted much of the working day by arriving late, taking a long rest after noon, and quickly leaving their work at the end of day even if a task was left partially undone (K. Thomas, "Work and Leisure," 61). Excessive drinking also contributed to lax work discipline. In 1547 the city of Coventry's leet (a criminal court for the punishment of small offenses) ordered that laborers, apprentices, and journeymen be barred from inns during the working day. A 1603 *Survey of London* by J. A. Stow further confirmed the excessive use of beer and ale by working men (Hoskins, *Plunder*, 51).

These exhortations to work hard and drink less overlooked the fundamental reasons for the plight of the poor. The key question that contemporary ministers, political leaders, economists, and writers never seemed to ask was whether there was sufficient stable employment. They assumed that those without work were idle by design. And while some were, they never asked if unemployment, the lack of future prospects, and separation from their native agriculture created a state of mind that saw drink and vagrancy as the logical outcome of hopelessness. A possible insight into the scarcity of jobs can be seen in the pitched battles fought by gangs of cartmen for "the right to work in certain lucrative areas" of London (Hodges, 10).

Richard Hakluyt (?1552–1616), the Oxford geographer, noted that employment was so scarce in England that many, including landless sons, had to seek a livelihood in the American colonies (R. Davis, *Atlantic Economies*, 140-41). So high was the poverty level in the 1520s and 1540s that tax exemptions in Coventry, Exeter, and Leicester included from one-third to one-half the population (Clarkson, 233). From 1500 to 1550 the per capita income probably did not increase at all, while the population grew by about 25 percent, enough to outrun farm output and thus raise prices. Poor harvests hurt terribly. They struck in 1545, 1549, 1550, 1551, 1555, and 1556, which led to appreciable price increases. Again, population growth from the 1570s onward overtook food production, and caused an increase in grain prices from 1585 to

1600 that were 50 percent higher than for 1575–85. Poor harvests in 1586 and 1594–97 caused additional suffering, and led one researcher to conclude that wage earners in 1600 were worse off than a century earlier (ibid., 211–12; Wrigley, "Growth of Population," 122). To this should be added the effect of irregular employment due to a poorly organized economy that was still pre-industrial. Poor weather often made employment chancy, especially in construction and maritime work. During periods of drought work in textile operations was frequently curtailed by lack of water (Hoskins, *Plunder*, 111). The net result was unexpected unemployment. When added to joblessness caused by fluctuating market demand and changes in fashion, life became precarious for those in the putting-out system and the new workshops.

High inflation due to the influx of precious metal from Mexico and Peru also hurt wage-earners as the cost of living rose by 300 percent in the two generations beginning in the 1540s (ibid., 49). By 1556, a famine year, grain prices were already 550 percent higher than in 1500. The price of cattle had also risen appreciably during this period. Both of these events were due in part to Henry VIII's debasement of the coinage in 1544, but the net result of all of these factors was an additional burden on those who were unemployed, underemployed, or poorly paid (Youings, 143–49). Pay levels in 1600 were so low that one researcher estimates that few workers in London earned more than one shilling per day; the average weekly wage for England as a whole was about five shillings per *week* (Hibbert, 234). It is little wonder that the plight of the poor in late-sixteenth-century England was described in such dire terms:

> From pillar to post the poor man he was tossed: I mean the labouring man, I mean the ploughman, I mean the handycraft man, I mean the victualling man and also the good yeoman. (Briggs, *Social History*, 114)

In Exeter alone poverty was so severe that an estimated 50 percent of the population was affected. Children were put to work early to help family survival (Hill, *Society and Puritanism*, 266, 223). To deal with the problems of unemployment and underemployment, the Tudor governments pressed employers to retain workers and servants for a minimum period of one year. Day labor was discouraged, since it was believed that it led to "the great depauperization of other labourers" (Morgan, "Jamestown," 604).

Additionally, the effect of diet on the ability to work hard was not understood. The high inflation after the 1540s, many poor harvests, and the low wage levels (Ashley, *People of England*, 87) may have left many workers with diets so meager that they could not perform their duties with sufficient energy. Despite the fact that 90 percent of worker income went for food and drink, diet was tied "precariously" to the size of the annual harvest. Thus, the pace of work was often slow, since many workers did not have the caloric intake to work the prescribed sixty-three hour week from 6 September to 25 March, nor could they effectively produce during the 75 hour weekly regime required for the remainder of the year (Hoskins, *Plunder*, 116–17, 109). Even if these lengthy hours were not observed in toto, regular meals were not the rule, and an estimated 25–50 percent of the total population lived below the level of poverty (Coleman, 295). In this situation low productivity may have caused some contemporary observers to see the Tudor workforce as lazy and unreliable.

To the catalog of low wages, poor diet, high prices, and irregular employment, the negative effect of the Tudor enclosures on unemployment and vagrancy must be added. While the earliest enclosures can be dated from the Statutes of 1235 and 1285, it was those of the Tudor era which first encompassed large tracts of land. By 1500, considerable tracts in England had been enclosed, including much of Essex and Kent (Yelling, 153). Authorities disagree on the extent of Tudor enclosures after 1500, but the net effect was that large numbers were thrown off the land to seek sustinence elsewhere. Edwin F. Gay observed that on the basis of official inquiries in 1517, 1519, 1548, 1566, and 1607 no more than 516,000 acres were enclosed during the sixteenth century. In central England, most of the open fields were given over to grass for more profitable sheep-raising. However, R. H. Tawney argued that peasant revolts and the on-going concern over enclosures suggested the problem was more pervasive (Mantoux, 153n1). Even contemporary supporters of enclosure like Anthony Fitzherbert and Thomas Tusser worried about what would happen to the new poor now that they had been forced off the land (W. Jones,

160). Writing in 1549, John Hales shared their concern: "These inclosures doe undoe us all . . . . all is taken up for pastures, either for shepe or for grasinge of cattell . . . whereas xl persons had theire lyvinges, now one man and his shepard hathe all . . . . for by theise inclosures men doe lacke lyvinges and be idle" (Hales, 15). Still, both Youings and Hoskins argued that most of the damage was done prior to 1486 (Youings, 59; Hoskins, *Plunder*, 68).

To the problem of enclosures must be added the loss of employment due to the Statute of Liveries in 1504. This denied lords the right to be served by a body of liveried retainers which threw thousands into vagrancy. The later dissolution of the monasteries by Henry VIII in 1536 put servants and dependents of the monks on the road, for their services were seldom required by the new secular owners of confiscated church property (Hibbert, 178–79).

Whatever the extent, the effect of the Statute of 1504, the seizure of church lands in 1536, and the result of the Tudor enclosures added to the problems of joblessness and vagrancy caused by changing markets. Men and women accustomed to daily labor found themselves subject to forces they neither understood nor could control. Their old world had faded away and was replaced by the righteous admonitions of the clergy, the indifference of the merchant class, and the sometimes vengeful hand of the state.

It never occurred to the more substantial classes that there was no connection between these new conditions and the alleged moral weakness of the unemployed. It was easier to believe the mass of wandering beggars after the 1520s was a social menace to law-abiding citizens (Aydelotte, 17). A proclamation of 1530 noted the increasing number of vagabonds and spoke of the thefts and murders they ostensibly committed. Justices of the peace were told to have no pity. All should be returned to their home parish for support. In 1531, an interesting statute suggested that a differentiation be drawn between those who were out of work involuntarily and beggars vigorous enough to labor. The former could be granted licenses to beg, but if the latter were outside their home parish, they were to be whipped, given a "punishment certificate," and sent to their legal residence (W. Jones, 129). Since many of these vagrants were concentrated in urban areas, cities like Gloucester, York, and London began to issue begging licenses.

Later in the sixteenth century, London, Norwich, and York were forced to use a compulsory tax to handle vagrants and the sick (Youings, 261–62). But within this restricted circle of generosity, there remained a deep fear of vagrants. Thomas Harman described some as dirty, ragged wretches who left a trail of havoc as they crossed the byways of England. Many feigned illness or insanity ("Bedlam beggars"), while others were well-dressed tricksters known in the trade as "conny-catchers" (Hibbert, 179–80). Beggar children were not exempt from legislative action. Statutes of 1536, 1547, 1549, 1572, and 1597 dealt with this aspect of vagrancy through corporal punishment and apprenticeship (Beier, "Vagrants," 9). Women adjudged to be "rogues" were whipped and then returned to their parish of origin (Bridenbaugh, *Vexed and Troubled Englishmen*, 51).

Beier estimated that the number of vagrants in the later Tudor period at no more than 2 percent of the population, probably less than 80,000 persons. Nevertheless, the rhetoric and actions taken by Tudor authorities indicate that this unemployed mass conjured up a deep-seated fear. Probably the most important reason was the Tudor view that everyone had a set place, function, and master. In this paternalistic hierarchy, there was no role for masterless vagabonds. They might be dangerous persons per se, or supporters of Mary Queen of Scots, Anabaptists, or peasant revolutionaries (Beier, "Vagrants," 5–6, 26–27). The East Anglian disorders of 1526 due to unemployment and hunger were remembered as was Ket's Rebellion of 1549 (W. Jones, 51–53). Even Edward VI noted in a 1552 *Treatise* that those prone to begging were "given and bent to all mischief" (Hill, *Society and Puritanism*, 264). And while a substantial minority worked hard at avoiding employment, unskilled laborers had an increasingly difficult time finding work after 1540 (Youings, 279). But all except the deserving poor were seen as carriers of wickedness, and as Perkins put it, "a cursed generation" (Hill, *Society and Puritanism*, 274). How the poor survived the stings of poverty and social attack is still hard to fathom (Ogg, 1:85).

To deal with this widespread socioeconomic disaster, the Tudor authorities resorted to a series of sixteenth statutes that were codified in the Poor Law of 1601. There clearly was much public support for these enactments among the protestant clergy (Cranmer, Ridley, and Lever) and people of means who dominated Parliament, the courts, and the bureaucracy. This led to the so-called Beggars Act of 1536 which required vagrants to work or be whipped. If this did not have the desired result, a part of one ear could be severed. It did empower local officials to collect alms on behalf of the vagrants, but pushed work as the leading alternative. It may be that the real objective was cheap help for work on Dover harbor (W. Jones, 130; Youings, 281; Goldwin Smith, *Legal History*, 300). But this legislation did not solve the problem. A proclamation of 1545 indicated that vagabonds might even be sent to the galleys; two years later the relatively moderate Duke of Somerset allowed enactment of laws that permitted healthy vagrants to be branded with the letter V. Forced labor and slavery were also held out as possible punishments, and men under the age of twenty-four might be required to enter an apprenticeship. In practice, however, the act proved unenforceable and was repealed in 1549 (W. Jones, 131).

By 1572 Parliament felt impelled to deal with the problem of vagrancy once again, possibly due to concerns that a new insurrection might follow the 1569 Northern Rebellion of the Catholic earls. In the Act of 1572 "rogues, vagabonds, and sturdy beggars" were defined to include the idle, minstrels, and those engaged in palmistry. It specifically attacked those "refusing to work for such reasonable wages as is taxed and commonly given," and required the unemployed or poor who had not lived in a parish for three years to be sent back to the parish of their birth (G. W. Prothero, 68–71; *Tudor Economic Documents*, 2:328–31). In 1576 Parliament again tried to legislate their way out of a socio-economic problem, but this time it acknowledged that work might not be available to all who wanted it. Justices of the peace were to deliver into the homes of the unemployed wool, hemp, and flax. "Collectors and Governors of the Poor" would then collect the finished goods. For those who refused this arrangement or other work, a stay in the local House of Correction, a kind of penal institution, was required so that the offenders be "straightly kept, as well in diet as in work." York and Winchester had little success with this approach, but Ipswich found it worked well. The basic problem was poor quality and a surplus of goods in the market (Youings, 287–88; *Tudor Economic Documents*, 2:331–34).

Despite this additional law, vagrancy and poverty continued to plague England. While children and cripples were often given aid, it was single men who most frequently were whipped and sent on their way. Vagrants did know the roads of England well, but of those studied in Sussex, Sheffield, and Salisbury, it was evident that their movements were generally limited to an area within forty miles of their birth place. Most vagrants travelled in ones or twos, but records suggest that about half were single men and one-quarter single women (Slack, "Vagrants," 366–68). In this situation cruel treatment of the unemployed and vagrants continued. Whipping and branding by the Middlesex Quarter Sessions Court in the autumn of 1590 proceeded at the rate of one person a day (Hill, *Society and Puritanism*, 277). Discipline and order became the watchwords of the 1590s, particularly among the influential Puritans (Walzer, 122-23), which led Robert Allen to note in 1603 that "men are so busy in examining the poor about their estate . . . that they can find no leisure to open their purses or relieve their wants" (George and George, *Protestant Mind*, 158). Sir Thomas Browne added that aid to the poor was "but moral charity, an act that owest more to passion than to reason" (Hill, *Society and Puritanism*, 281). And a 1596 letter to William Cecil, Lord Burghley, noted that the unwillingness of rogues to labor was because "their sinews are so benumbed and stiff through idleness" (Hill, *Puritanism and Revolution*, 222).

Despite these continued moral reservations about the jobless and the vagrants, circumstances forced the Elizabethan government to act. Except for the very serious famine of 1556, the poor harvests of 1594–97 proved to be the worst since 1482 and 1527. Along with Essex's rebellion and the problems in Ireland, the famines led to even more vagabondage and poverty (K. O. Morgan, *Oxford Illustrated History*, 276; Slack, "Vagrants," 370). Parliament thus moved to legislate once again in 1597–98 in line with the existing work values of Tudor England: the idlers of the realm constituted a criminal presence against God and society, and those deemed to be sturdy beggars had to be set to work. All recognized that cities such as Coventry, York, Norwich, and London were flooded by the poor. They had already established hospitals for the sick, workhouses for those who would work, and "houses of correction" for the idle. But the "terror of the tramp" persisted, and Parliament felt some action was needed (Bindoff, 291–93). The Act of 1597 repeated the litany of earlier legislation which demanded that the poor be set to work. Those who refused to labor for "reasonable wages" were to be whipped and returned to their home parish (*Tudor Economic Documents*, 2:355–56). The poor relief Act of 1598, later extended by the 1601 Poor Law, fixed a compulsory poor rate to support the indigent. The "Overseers of the Poor" (churchwardens and substantial householders) were to build places of abode for the "impotent poor," and provide them with materials so they could be put to work. Houses of correction were designated as the proper destination of idlers and vagabonds. Children of the poor were to be placed as apprentices so they might learn some useful craft (Clarkson, 171; Goldwin Smith, *Legal History*, 300; G. W. Prothero, 96).

The 1601 Poor Law codified and extended existing legislation, and remained the primary avenue by which parishes could deal with joblessness and poverty. Although it kept many alive and occupied, it did not strike at the underlying causes of unemployment. That the Poor Law of 1601 was not working well could be seen by the need to enact yet another law two years later which provided that "incorrigible" rogues be branded on the shoulder with a large R (Garraty, 33, 35). In 1608 the town of Maidstone forbade its citizens to house strangers for fear that the idle and disorderly would descend on the parish en masse (Bridenbaugh, *Vexed and Troubled Englishmen*, 381). Such actions did not prevent large numbers of "idle and loose persons" from plaguing London in the 1620s. In rural areas, gangs terrorized Radborne, Sawbridgeworth, Gilston, and Widford during the 1620s and 1640s (ibid., 386–87). Private philanthropy attempted to alleviate the problem during the first four decades of the seventeenth century (Jordan, 370), but over one thousand vagrants were admitted annually to Bridewell during the same period (Clark and Slack, 89). The later Stuart "Political Arithmeticians" attacked the Poor Law of 1601, which they blamed for the crisis. Most of the destitute, they argued, would prefer to sponge on their parish rather than seek gainful employment (Tawney, 222). But despite the existence of the Poor Law of 1601 and the attacks of the affluent, the problem of joblessness did not disappear. In fact, the number of workhouses to care for the unemployed grew rapidly in the eighteenth century and numbered almost 2,000 by 1776 (Briggs, *Social History*, 176).

In this harsh setting, Stuart opinion-makers lent their support to the Tudor outlook that idleness was equated with sin. In the village of Terling, thirty-eight miles northwest of London, Henry Smith was determined that charity dispensed in the year 1626 was to be given only to the deserving poor. No help would be given to vagrants or other "idle persons" (Wrightson and Levine, 179). An English pamphleteer of 1646 noted that "the generall rule of all England is to whip and punish the wandring beggars." And although the House of Commons in 1649 ordered county authorities to give the poor materials with which they could earn a living, little came of this old concept (Tawney, 219). In Warwickshire, for example, only four of the four hundred forty-seven who became idle during the period 1649–60 were kept at work by the distribution of raw materials as stipulated by the Poor Law of 1601 (Beier, "Warwickshire," 80–82). The earlier Stuart attachment to charity for the destitute was replaced by the Tudor view that the innate wickedness of the downtrodden was responsible for their low estate. It may be that this uncharitable view stemmed in part to the demobilization following the civil war when an estimated 80,000 vagrants swarmed over the country. In 1655 the town clerk of London attacked these people as "vermine" who infested the city by seeking help at the doors of private homes and churches (Garraty, 34).

In view of the persistent vagrancy, parliament felt impelled to pass the 1662 Act of Settlement. It established barriers to the free movement of people by permitting local authorities to forcibly return individuals to their home parish if they were likely to become a burden through a lack of work or unwillingness to labor (Deane, 145; Plucknett, 688–89). Only the more business-oriented Act of 1697 permitted labor mobility, since the older legislation was seen as inhibiting industry (Hill, *Century of Revolution*, 268). In this way, the 1697 legislation typified the new values that now consecrated money-making. Whether one looks to the actions of government or the writings of Petty and Defoe, unemployment and poverty were now viewed as the vice of the idle (Sée, 64). Earlier Stuart efforts to reduce joblessness by controlling the use of new machines or prevailing on employers to keep unneeded personnel on the payroll (Sir George Clark, *Seventeenth Century*, 64–65; Hill, *Century of Revolution*, 29) were set aside in the floodtide of laissez-faire enthusiasm toward the end of the seventeenth century.

By the end of the Stuart reign unemployment and poverty had become established in the public mind as the outcomes of idleness. Only those who refused a job or worked sporadically would find themselves without means. These undeserving poor did not merit the support of ratepayers, for they took sustinence from the deserving souls whose poverty was involuntary. Attempts to return vagrants to their home parish did not have the desired effect, and workhouses that meted out harsh labor along with a bed and meals also failed to push the idle to work. Even the deserving poor often were unable to make the transition to a market economy because of the vagaries of trade, war, weather, and demographics. So serious was the concern over vagrancy that both James I and John Donne suggested the idle be sent to Virginia (Garraty, 35–36; Andrews, 1:61).

All of these problems found their way to colonial America. Particularly important was the *continuity* that distinguished the deserving and undeserving poor. In terms reminiscent of those used in Tudor-Stuart England, the editor of the *New York Minerva* in 1797 felt compelled to speak out about the numerous paupers that had come from Ireland: "We shall have the refuse of all the corrupt parts of society poured in upon our country. . . . We shall be over-run with vagabonds" (Mohl, 17). Poor relief also burdened the taxpayers of Philadelphia. Between 1760 and 1775 an estimated 10 percent of the population "suffered impoverishment." The number on poor relief rose dramatically during the eighteenth century from about 5 to 8 per thousand persons between 1700 and 1750 to 28 to 30 from 1765 to 1775 (Nash, "Franklin's Philadelphia," 170). Almshouses appeared all along the East Coast by 1750 (Bruchey, *Roots*, 58–59) as numerous poor immigrants, market cycles, and currency depreciation made America less than a land of opportunity for some (Morris, *Government and Labor*, 47). Attempts to employ the poor in Boston and Philadelphia linen mills failed, and by 1776 Philadelphia had 220 paupers in its almshouse (Nash, "Pre-Revolutionary Philadelphia," 14). The popular notion that the poor could be put to work profitably in workhouses proved erroneous (Greene, *Pursuits of Happiness*, 73). Beyond this, the destitute continued to be held in such low esteem that they were thrown together with criminals in the early Boston workhouse (Bridenbaugh, *Cities in the Wilderness*,

82). New York City even converted part of its prison to a work-house in 1767 which prompted the *New York Gazette* to observe that this was "a proper receptacle for the abandoned miscreants that infest this city" (Sachs and Hoogenboom, 125). And as in England, Newport, New York, and Philadelphia authorized the expulsion of nonresidents and strangers (Bridenbaugh, *Cities in the Wilderness*, 392–393), a *continuity* of no small importance.

In short, colonial Americans mirrored the English disdain for idleness. Rhode Island aped Elizabethan laws and openly denounced beggars and vagrants. And throughout the colonies poverty continued to be stigmatized as a character defect. New Jersey even forced paupers to wear a large blue or red P on the right shoulder. But it was left to Cotton Mather to sum up the prevailing American wisdom on the unemployed when he said "Let them starve" (Dorfman, 1:57).

Part II
Work as Alienation and Opportunity

Chapter 6

WORK VALUES IN COLONIAL AMERICA

The history of colonial America encompassed the work values of two very different eras and served as a bridge between the belief systems of John Cotton and Benjamin Franklin. For early America, Cotton, Hooker, and Mather represented the last bastion of God-centered work values. They strived to beat off the precepts of a strengthening market economy, but were overwhelmed by the 1730s. Opportunity and success now emerged as the dominant guideposts of a mercantile society. Thrust into a background were the beliefs of an older order (Work as a Sign of Salvation, (c. 1450-1730) that were gradually undermined by a world of rational relationships. From the 1730s to the 1930s this new universe of alienation and opportunity emerged as the first major *discontinuity* from an earlier time. In this era the last four decades of colonial American history formed a stepping-stone into a secular-commercial universe in which a God-ordained calling was transmuted into systematized work for wages.

But even as this major discontinuity in work values became apparent, four major *continuities* flowed from the era of salvation to the world of alienation and opportunity. Among the most significant was the continued belief in hard work. In the ministerial epoch from Calvin to Cotton Mather labor was expressed in terms of a calling, a station in life through which God's gifts could be expressed. It encompassed the worker's obligations to family and community, and offered a vocation by which all could serve God on earth and possibly earn heavenly merit. As John Cotton (1584–1652) pointed out *"cursed is He that doth the worke of the Lord negligently, and the work of his calling is, the worke of the Lord"* (Foster, 104). But although the calling gave work a moral value, Edward Reyner warned in 1641 that it was important to live in this world but keep its snares at arms length (Miller and Johnson,

289). And as late as 1710 Cotton Mather thundered that while life had to be both useful and holy "the chief end of man is to *glorify God*" (Mather, *Bonifacius*, xi-xii). But by the early eighteenth century this view was under increasing pressure. Congregationalist, Anglican, and Quaker ministers found themselves fighting a powerful commercial tide. The old relationship between the general and personal calling faded as "personal autonomy displaced the previous stress on divine omnipotence" (Crowley, 55). By the 1730s some intellectual space separated work and calling. Diligence was now seen as a sign of independence and less often commanded godly overtones. More often dedicated labor was viewed as an ethical prescription rather than a heavenly command, a way in which people could fulfill their obligations to society (Breen, "Non-Existent Controversy," 273–87; Crowley, 55–56). In this sense hard work remained as a *continuity* that linked the worlds of Luther and Franklin, but it now took on worldly overtones that would not be shed.

Thus, during the eleven decades after the Pilgrim passage to North America in 1620 the ministerial elite of the Old and New Worlds lost the battle against the work values of an increasingly entrepreneurial world. It was a period during which commitment to work in a calling was superceded by a quest for opportunity. Puritans had tried to differentiate "laudable industry" and "reprehensible worldliness" (Bushman, *Puritan to Yankee*, x), but the power of the market economy made this distinction irrelevant. The shift was clearly reflected in the remarks of ministers like Charles Chauncy who summed up the new outlook in 1752 when he stated that "We are made for Business" (Cochran, *Business in American Life*, 37–38). Work as a Sign of Salvation had yielded to the realm of opportunity, but it had only done so after a ministerial phalanx that stretched from Martin Luther to Cotton Mather had been set aside. Opportunity thus remained as a *second continuity*, but with a far stronger base of support than it formerly enjoyed. It now offered poor immigrants a new chance to succeed on an open frontier. Skilled artisans could easily find work. And most important, its hopeful aura went beyond the more spectacular successes of individuals like Thomas Breedon in early Massachusetts and Stephen Girard in later Philadelphia. Now it was a promise to the multitude.

But this promising secular terrain would also bring with it a continual job insecurity. By the 1840s the workshops of New York City and the textile mills of Philadelphia and New England would not seem like the promised land to those who fled from Europe. For many the cyclical downturns that commenced in 1819 and 1837 now led to unemployment and poverty. These periods of boom and bust made work the chancy plaything of the marketplace, and put the new semi-skilled factory workers of America on an economic rollercoaster. In this situation the lack of job security became a *third continuity* that had started in early modern Europe and was destined to remain a boon-companion of the unemployed to the 1990s.

A *fourth continuity* that passed from the Age of Luther to the entrepreneurial world of the eighteenth century was the public distinction between the deserving and undeserving poor. Even with the vast opportunities offered by an open frontier in North America, the harsh Elizabethan evaluation of its homeless vagrants came to America on the same ships that took many to a better life. If the unemployed and poor were chased back to their home parishes in England, they were treated no better in colonial Newport and New York. On both sides of the Atlantic poverty was thought of as a character flaw. Many believed the unemployed could work if only they would rouse themselves to make a concerted effort. That this moralizing outlook ignored the fluctuations of market demand, the ravages of war, and huge waves of immigration made little difference. The view persisted that many did not make a real effort to obtain work. These undeserving poor merited little more than the harsh confines of the workhouse, while their more deserving brethren were worthy of whatever assistance private or public charity could provide. This distinction not only flowed over into the era of alienation and opportunity, but survived into the 1990s to flavor our current debate on work and welfare.

It is with these historical discontinuities and continuities in mind that we can place the North American context of alienation and opportunity in its appropriate context. While war, poverty, and religious strife *pushed* many to cross the sea, others were *drawn* to North America by opportunity, social mobility, and personal freedom. Perhaps the most salient values of this transatlantic civilization was its emphasis on hard work, wealth accumulation, and a disdain for idleness and vagrancy. But it also tendered a growing endorsement of the marketplace and the objective values it placed on both human and economic relationships. This gave added impetus to those who strived to better their lives through diligence and enterprise, but it left behind a remainder who could not compete or temporarily became surplus labor. Despite these stark alternatives, thousands braved the hazards of the Atlantic and the risks of a primitive environment.

Among the more important reasons for abandoning the Old World was the poor economic situation in early- and mid-seventeenth century England. This drove many laborers to leave as indentured servants during the thirty years from 1630 to 1660, and when this emigration dropped between 1670 and 1690, the gap was filled by Irish and German immigrants (Dunn, 162; Slack, "Vagrants," 364–68; Abbott Smith, *Colonists in Bondage*, 309). Still, Wrigley and Schofield have shown that 69 percent of the total natural increase in England emigrated to North America in the 1640–99 period, a number that dropped to a not inconsiderable 20 percent between 1695 and 1801 (Wrigley and Schofield, 175).

The many Germans who came to North America were driven from their homes by the atrocities of the Thirty Years War (1618–48) and the depredations of the French under Louis XIV. While these made life, labor, and practice of their faith a dangerous enterprise (Kuhns, 85), many refrained from signing articles of indenture like their British counterparts. Instead a considerable number became redemptioners after 1700, and as such tried to borrow the cost of their passage within a few weeks of their arrival in America. If unsuccessful, they could be sold as indentured servants; in some cases one or two family members of a redemptioner group could be put into service to pay the travel costs for all. It is estimated that about two-thirds of the 65,000 to 75,000 Germans who came to Philadelphia from 1727 to 1776 were redemptioners (Simmons, 184). Thus, whether the indentured servant or redemptioner route was chosen by those who came to North America, the lure of opportunity caused many to accept a temporarily unfree status for the hope of a better tomorrow. America had become a "magnet" for some and a "last resort" for others (Cochran, *Business in American Life*, 13; Bailyn, *Peopling*,

42–43). They were not unlike the three young foreigners who founded AST Research with little money in 1983, and who now employ 1,500 Californians, nor do they substantially differ from the many thousands of immigrants who took the first step up the economic ladder in southern California's large manufacturing sector (Louis Uchitelle, "The New Faces of U.S. Manufacturing," *New York Times*, 3 July 1994, 6F).

Other negatives such as enclosures contributed to the exodus from England. The demand for wool for home use or export caused Tudor landowners to acquire large tracts to pasture sheep. This led contemporaries like Thomas Tusser and Anthony Fitzherbert to express concern for the new poor who had been forced off their land (Youings, 57–59; W. Jones, 160–61). Added to this was the high inflation in England from 1550 to 1650, which depressed wages by 50 percent and forced many to accept indentured servant status in the colonies. About half of the 350,000 white laborers who came to America from Britain and continental Europe during the colonial period came as servants (Dunn, 159, 161). These burdens were compounded by the persistent vagrancy in England between 1598 and 1638. The numbers peaked every April and October, and as grain prices rose, so did vagrancy (Slack, "Vagrants," 370). Dunn estimates that 50,000 vagabonds, convicts, and political prisoners were sent to North America between 1607 and 1775, while Garraty attributes the pressure of vagrants in England to the demobilization following the English Civil War (Dunn, 159; Garraty, 34).

Also contributing to the emigration from England was the low esteem accorded wage-laborers. Those who worked for others were thought to have lost their freedom of economic action, and were held in poor repute. The 1563 Statute of Apprentices contributed to this loss of status, since a laborer could not change jobs without his employer's permission (Notestein, 186–87; Malcolmson, 14). The later statutes of 1597, 1598, and 1601 did establish parish relief for the poor, but the prevailing belief maintained that those without work lived in "able-bodied idleness." If one was in good health and was not employed it was done out of choice. In 1618 James I (1603–25) ordered that "idle young people" be sent to Virginia, while Richard Eburne in his 1624 tract *A Plaine Path-way to Plantations* suggested that two people from each parish be sent to America to rid the country of vagrants, criminals, and other "superflous" types. John Locke seconded this sentiment, whereas John Donne saw the virtue of settling undersirables in Virginia as a way to "sweep your streets, and wash your doors from idle persons" (Garraty, 36-38; Andrews, 1:61–63).

Few understood how market forces affected the availability of work, for it was easier to impute bad motives to the umemployed than seek economic reasons for their degradation. That even the "new poor" could easily be caught up in poverty could be seen from the 1597 situation in New Romney where those who had recently supported the destitute now found themselves in need of aid (Youings, 278, 270–71). But even to work as an independent craftsman in Britain from about 1590 to 1650 was extremely difficult due to the debilitating depressions of 1620-24. Economic stagnation and bad harvests between 1646 and 1651 added to the woes of many workers (K. Thomas, 63; Hill, *Century of Revolution*, 321), and may have led some to respond to the 1648 Puritan poem *Good News from New-England* which suggested that those with small earnings should "venter to this new-found world, and make amends for all" (Innes, *Work and Labor*, 6).

That the situation in Britain did not improve can be seen by the prevalence of tenancy in the seventeenth century and the fact that as late as 1775 half the British workers were wage-laborers. Only 20 percent of the American colonists were in this category at that time (Lemon, "Spatial Order," 102; Clarkson, 61–68). In addition, freeholders in Britain held only 30 percent of the land in 1750, while the rest was controlled by the upper classes. In North America the numbers were reversed (Henretta, "Wealth and Social Structure," 45; C. Williamson, 75). But two sets of seventeenth century records, the Bristol list for 1654–85 and the London list of 1683–84, indicate that many who left those ports for America were farmers or skilled workers, not landless laborers. Those who crossed the ocean as indentured servants looked for change and upward mobility, and, except for debtors sent to Georgia and felons who were packed off to Maryland, did not represent the lowest rungs of British society. In addition, some of the emigrants who left in the seventeenth century had sought work in London, Liverpool, and Bristol without success. From these ports more than a few were willing to cast their destiny in the Chesapeake during the servant emigration of the seventeenth century (Horn, 94–95).

But few gentry came except for men like the West brothers and Lord de la Warr (Campbell, 66–71).

Added to the negative reasons that forced so many to leave Britain was the lack of agricultural innovation prior to the eighteenth century changes that increased productivity and made England a food exporter. Complacency seemed to be the rule as explained by W. Folkingham in 1610: "Wee are too wise, holding it ridiculous to innovate, nay to imitate, anything not approoved by continual practise" (Kerridge, 326). Risk-taking was not part of the English agricultural outlook, and her workers lacked a "possessive individualism and economic rationality" that would inspire the hard work needed to activate ambition and mobility. In addition, Britain was not a frontier society that offered presented a vista of open acreage. Thus, few laborers could realistically hope to become freeholders which contrasted unfavorably with the situation in settled areas like Springfield, Massachusetts or Virginia (Innes, *Labor in a New Land*, 75–77). In short, there was a vision of hope in America that did not touch the majority in Britain, and despite the dominance of values such as wealth-accumulation by the late seventeenth century, most Britons elected to stay with what they had.

Heading the list of the attractive forces that brought so many to America was the hunger for land and shortage of labor that provided openings for craftsmen and laborers. The "promise of the land," as Jack Greene has put it, drew multitudes from Europe who sensed the openness of society and the prevalence of opportunity. While they could not know that colonial America would enjoy a high growth rate of about three and a half per cent annually from 1650 to 1770, there was a belief that they were coming to a society of possibilities (Greene, *Settlements to Society*, 260–67; McCusker and Menard, 51, 57; Bailyn, *Voyagers to West*, 26). In America they would no longer have to bow and scrape before a landed aristocracy that relegated them to perpetual tenancy (Wertenbaker, *Puritan Oligarchy*, 184).

Of those who made the journey to the New World, the extremely poor and the gentry accounted for relatively few migrants. Small craftsmen, laborers, textile workers, indentured servants, and tenants displaced by enclosures accounted for many of the 155,000 who came from the British Isles before 1700. Most important were the 350,000 to 375,000 white indentured servants who came to the various American colonies between 1580 and 1775. They made up almost two-thirds of all the whites who came from both Britain and Europe during this period (Innes, *Work and Labor*, 7; McCusker and Menard, 238, 242). In New England and the northern colonies free families dominated the labor force, but indentured servants were important in Pennsylvania, western New Jersey, and Delaware and had an initial importance to Chesapeake planters (Greene, *Pursuits of Happiness*, 131–34; Vickers, 49–51). Later in the seventeenth century, slave labor tended to supplant the use of servants in the Chesapeake region. Thus, while the opportunity factor was absent for slaves, indentured servants who came to Maryland and Virginia in the seventeenth century could receive their "freedom dues" if they survived the hard labor and disease during their period of service. Like their British counterparts, the Chesapeake planters saw their servants as "idle, lazy, simple people" (Henretta and Nobles, *Evolution*, 42). Still, they gave Maryland servants a fifty acre tract along with their freedom until 1681 (Carr and Menard, "Immigration and Opportunity," 206–7). Only after this time did the southern masters come to rely on a growing slave population that reached 175,000 in British North America by 1760 (Carr and Walsh, 157, 147; Curtin, 137).

Yet another attraction to the New World was the colonial shortage of labor. Skilled artisans were in particular demand and were able to command high wages from John Pynchon of Springfield in the 1660s. He also needed considerable numbers of men to clear, stub, plow, and reap in addition to those with canoes who could transport his goods (Innes, *Labor in a New Land*, 72–73). Edward Johnson confirmed this great need for workers, while in 1660 Governor Leete of Connecticut noted that labor was dear and few needed "relief." A 1699 Maryland report confirmed the trend: the "Province wants workmen, workmen want not work; here are no beggars." Additional confirmation came from Peter Arundle in Virginia in 1622 and John Bolzius of Georgia as late as 1743 (E. Johnson, 114; Morris, *Government and Labor*, 45; R. Davis, *Atlantic Economies*, 269; Dunn, 161). That opportunity beckoned for the skillful and productive could be seen by colonial advertisments for Sheffield hammer-men, forge-men, and saw-makers in the *New York Journal* of 8 October 1767. Three years later the owners of a china factory in Philadelphia advertised in Europe for skilled craftsmen (Morris, *Government and Labor*, 27–28), while a 1769 Boston paper sought six young apprentices to "learn the Art of Hackling Flax and Weaving Linen" (Bridenbaugh, *Colonial Craftsmen*, 132). Added to this was the influx of many Scotch-Irish linen workers who came to America in large numbers between 1771 and 1774. In Paisley, Scotland weavers went on strike in 1773 holding the threat of emigration to America over the heads of employers (Bailyn, *Peopling*, 38). Beyond the scarcity factor was the matter of greater colonial productivity. This provided the base for the greater remuneration that led many artisans to flock to North America. Germans, in particular, were prominent in the glass and iron industries of Pennsylvania, Spottswood's Virginia furnaces, and potteries in many of the colonies. Amsterdam sent the colonies her first paper-makers, while Switzerland and Ireland added to the eighteenth-century influx. Nevertheless, many colonial enterprises failed for lack of skilled labor even as the transatlantic masses settled the land and pushed settlement to the west (Victor Clark, *Manufactures*, 1:154–56; Bailyn, *Voyagers to the West*, 25). Despite this, the frontier formed the classic setting for opportunity that energized thousands of Europeans to challenge the Atlantic and the Appalachians.

If the idea of opportunity brought so many to the shores of America it had within it the hope of socioeconomic mobility. This had its origins in the British Isles where short-distance moves and regional-mobility patterns eventually led to national emigration. Centered on the key ports of London and Bristol, it was the backdrop of a great exodus from Britain. Many like the Puritans, unemployed west-country workers, and settlers from East Anglia all came to the New World to seek better prospects. Religion, of course, played a significant role in propelling the Puritans on their Great Migration (Bailyn, *Peopling*, 21–28; E. E. Rich, 247–65; Coleman, 291), but the driving force that led so many to travel so far and risk so much was the hope of economic improvement (Bailyn, *Voyagers to the West*, 92, 193–97). In fact, many Puritans elected to remain in England to protect their economic base and stayed on to outfight the Cavaliers. Of those who did come for religious reasons, the mobility motive was far from absent for "commerce was central to colonial economic life" (P. Miller, *Wilderness*, 4; McCusker and Menard, 71; Greene, *Pursuits of Happiness*, 61).

In Connecticut mobility was considerable. It was estimated that from 12 to 14 percent of the men in each generation changed occupations. That Connecticut was an "open society" was reflected in the choice of wives from the "middling sort" by its leaders (J. T. Main, *Colonial Connecticut*, 370, 374). Upward mobility remained strong in both New England and the Chesapeake during the seventeenth century, but in the succeeding hundred years it was weakened from the Chesapeake to Georgia as the Byrds, Lees, Pinckneys, and others became dominant (Richard Brown, *Modernization*, 57; Jedrey, 5–6, 7, 10). In Philadelphia some 20% were able to rise to the middle third of society, while 10% elevated themselves to the top 40% of the social structure. Jackson Turner Main also suggested that many improved their situation by learning a trade. Others could reasonably aspire to becoming property owners (Nash, "Franklin's Philadelphia," 172–73; J. T. Main, *Revolutionary America*, 185–86, 194–95). Virginia offered yeomen land and freedom, but they could not elevate themselves to the postion of gentlemen unless they owned slaves (Isaac, *Virginia*, 132). For the commercial gentry of South Carolina and Georgia their great wealth enabled them to maintain opulent homes in Charleston and Savannah as well as comfortable plantations in their rural domains. They not only aspired to to an "anglicized lifestyle," in America but also maintained fifty South Carolinian proprietors in London (Greene, *Pursuits of Happiness*, 147–48). Thus, with the exception of the lower South during the eighteenth century, "social fluidity" flourished in the "competitive environment" of North America, and "position in the new society became primarily a function of direct economic activity, not of birth or privilege" (Campbell, 65; Diamond, "Values," 570; Iorweth Prothero, *Artisans and Politics*, 26). It is little wonder that this more open society beckoned to many in the stratified and class-conscious European world (Cochran, *200 Years*, 5–6, 9); B. G. Smith, "Death and Life," 373–75).

Further interest in the opportunities of North America was kindled by the depiction of New England as a paradise, the Land of Cockayne. The voyages of John Frobisher who sought the Northwest Passage in 1570, Sir Humphrey Gilbert's later attempt at colonization, the accounts of Walter Raleigh, and the propaganda of the younger Richard Hakluyt raised the hopes of many in England. The hope of emulating Spanish success in finding gold and silver played no small role in attracting greedy adventurers (Hill, *Change and Continuity*, 222; Simmons, 9–11; Wright, *Elizabethans' America*, 9–12). During the early years of the Plymouth Colony, William Bradford added to the attractiveness of North American settlement by supporting individual ownership to insure "industrious" behavior (Bradford, *Of Plymouth Plantation*, 120–21). Zealous colonial recruiters also snared many destitute people who straggled in English port towns, while the English Board of Trade and Plantations encouraged emigration to help assure the home country of a supply of raw materials that it otherwise would have to buy from Holland, Spain, or France (Bridenbaugh, *Vexed and Troubled Englishmen*, 355–56; Wright, *Dream of Prosperity*, 63–64).

But it was in the aftermath of Britain's victory over France in 1763 that a huge territory stretching from Nova Scotia to Florida was opened to settlement. A wave of land speculation, Coleridge's depiction of Florida as the mysterious land of Xanadu, and John Bartram's travels in East Florida that added a sense of adventure to the hope for economic elevation (Bailyn, *Peopling*, 75–76). But there was more. While land passed to the eldest son in England, greater opportunity for other family members was available in the colonies because of the American practice of partible inheritance. That an abundance of land made this possible can be seen through the New England clan of Moses Cleaveland (1624–1702) and the declarations of an "honest farmer" in the *Pennsylvania Packet* of 1786 (Morris, *American Law*, 77–78; Jedrey, 15; S. W. Fletcher, 315). When local hierarchies tried to undercut this desire for property and social mobility, agrarian upheaval ensued along the Hudson in 1766, among Ethan Allen's Green Mountain boys, and in the 1770 Regulator Movement in North Carolina (Shalhope, 18–25). Taken together, all of this offered the promise of a better tomorrow.

Once in North America the opportunity ethic did not prove a disappointment for most who came. Francis Higginson wrote to his friends in Leicester in 1629 that New England was a healthful haven whose plentiful land and forests offered an independent life to those willing to work hard (E. Emerson, 36–37; Cochran and Brewer, 24–25). John Winthrop (1588–1649) wondered why anyone would struggle over a few acres in Europe when an abundance of land was available across the Atlantic (Morison, *Winthrop Papers*, 2:138–39). Fishermen from the west country ports of Britain also found prosperity in the seacoast towns north of Boston, while other newcomers did well in fur trapping and logging. It is not surprising that exports from this area expanded greatly from 1660 to 1760 (McCusker and Menard, 310–11, 108).

New Jersey also offered work for all who desired it. "Class barriers" were no difficulty for the ambitious, as most Jerseymen looked to better the lives of their family. Still 10% owned one-third of the land, and 30% of the families had no farm of their own (Pomfret, 217; Cochran, *Business in American Life*, 14–15). But the remaining 60 percent had some level of land ownership, the key to success in that colony. Nearby Pennsylvania offered "a sense of remarkable opportunity" during the period from 1681 to the 1740s. Here "movement off the bottom" was more important than "ascent to the top." Thus, the tanners and shoemakers of Philadelphia noted in 1779 that they were content "to live decently without acquiring wealth." Nevertheless, men like Lionel Brittain could begin as a blacksmith and become a merchant by 1720. Thomas Coates made his way from brickmaking to an import-export business, while both John Palmer and John Warder elevated themselves from craftsmen to merchants (Nash, "Franklin's Philadelphia," 167–68). Testimony of what was available to the industrious in 1756 was recorded by the German immigrant Gottlieb Mittelberger: "All trades and professions bring in good money. No beggars are to be seen; for every township feeds and takes care of its poor" (Mittelberger, 51).

To the south, Maryland's tobacco culture attracted between 9,000 to 10,100 people during the 1630–40 decade, and despite the later decline in tobacco prices, received almost 16,000 in the last decade of the seventeenth century (G. Main, *Tobacco Colony*, 10). In 1656 John Hammond extolled the opportunities in Maryland when he noted that the country offered "imployments both for the learned and the laborer," and gave settlers the chance to discard the "lewd and idle" ways of England (Greene, *Settlements to Society*, 51–52; Hawke, *Everyday Life*, 122–23). More recent research has confirmed the validity of this optimistic outlook. Seventeenth-century court records indicate little concern about paupers or vagrants, a point underscored by the Maryland assembly which stated that the province needed workers who would not lack for employment. That the demand for labor was real can be seen by the growth of tobacco exports from a negligible 2,500 pounds in 1616 to 21 million by 1700. When coupled with brief life spans and a shortage of women, freedmen could strike attractive bargains for wages or a share of their produce (Carr and Menard, 216, 207–9, 212–13).

Virginia tried to encourage emigration by offering those who came and paid their own passage fifty acres of land per person. Indentured servants received no land as a rule, but were rewarded with "freedom dues" (Bruchey, *Enterprise*, 36; Diamond, "Virginia in Seventeenth Century," 21–22) and the later opportunity to prosper (Wright, *Atlantic Frontier*, 64). But by 1700 many freedmen fled the Carolinas, Pennsylvania, and Jerseys to escape low tobacco prices and a scarcity of land in eastern Virginia. The exodus continued between 1700 and 1740, but only those with capital could succeed on the Potomac frontier (Carr and Menard, 234–36; Kulikoff, 92, 97–98; Bruchey, *Enterprise*, 37). Land was the key ingredient (Hawke, *Colonial Experience*, 71) that had drawn so many from Europe, and when it was no longer available, many moved on to more promising horizons.

But for the slaves who were forcibly removed from Africa neither Europe nor the New World held the heady scent of opportunity. Both the Portuguese and Spanish had brought African slaves to Europe in sizable numbers in the mid-sixteenth century and rationalized their servitude by the opportunity to embrace Christianity. But Europe could absorb only a few slaves in its shipyards and businesses as ample numbers of poor whites were available to claim these jobs (J. H. Franklin, 32–33). It was to North America and the West Indies that large numbers of slaves were diverted beginning in the early 1680s as poor whites increasingly refused to indenture themselves and Indian enslavement failed because of inhumane treatment. By 1760 blacks made up 60% of South Carolina's population and 40% of that in Virginia (Bailyn, *Voyagers to West*, 25; Sheridan, 45–46). To fill this labor gap in the southern colonies, slavers looked for healthy Africans who could toil in rice, cotton, tobacco, and indigo. Selling them profitably was their main concern (Heyward, 53), although Southern buyers often preferred slaves from Senegambia (Littlefield, 100–103).

For blacks in the southern colonies the doctrine of the calling was meaningless. Slaves could not accept the idea of "work as duty," and despite their miserable condition, were inclined to "joy in life" whenever such meager opportunities presented themselves. Beyond this lack of connection to a Calvinistic worldly asceticism, neither slaves nor their masters were part of the rational and systematic labor world that had won the support of the English middle class by the seventeenth century. By contrast, the slave society of the South was set in nature. In place of a time-discipline that was pushed with increasing vigor in British factories, slaves worked in spurts with duty particularly heavy at harvest time. Steady and systematic work in the mode suggested by Samuel Smiles in the nineteenth century could not be imposed easily, and this left blacks poorly prepared for the rationalized industrial society they had to enter after 1865 (Genovese, 287, 290–91). Instead, paternalism defined the relationship between master and slave. In return for servile labor, masters could somewhat soothe their souls by extending both "protection and direction." And while this forced masters to recognize the humanity of their slaves, it could not mask the fact that they forcibly took the labor of their chattels (ibid., 5–6). By comparison, the early nineteenth century paternalism of the British factory owner Robert Owen also carried with it the power to "control, reward, and punish" in return for obedient work, but his workers retained their personal freedom and could abandon their employment (Anthony, 74–76). Nevertheless, David Brion Davis argued that there was some similarity between the textile factories of Richard Arkwright in Derby in 1773 where women and children worked long hours and the slave labor on colonial plantations (D. B. Davis, *Slavery*, 437; Genovese, 61–62). Adam Smith, on the other hand, believed that slaveowners lacked the "magnanimity" of their slaves, and attacked the institution of slavery in his *Theory of Moral Sentiments* (1759) because it "stifled initiative" (D. B. Davis, *Slavery*, 440, 434).

Some researchers have suggested that blacks were not passive onlookers to their servitude. They brought knowledge of rice cultivation from Africa and won the respect of overseers for their expertise. In addition, some whites even took on the work patterns of their slaves. Washington complained that his slave overseer, one Mr. Bloxham, often abandoned English methods of farming and adopted the ideas of his slaves (Littlefield, 97–101; Piersen, 177–79). Blacks, both free men and slaves, were also employed in the colonial iron industry. Here they worked in the charcoal pits as well as on the forges and furnaces, all jobs that were dirty and dangerous. It was, wrote William Eddis from Maryland in 1770, labor delegated "to worthless servants" (Bailyn, *Voyagers to West*, 250; Oblinger, 97). But there was an element of competition between black and white workers in a few cities like Charleston and Savannah because of a labor shortage, but in Williamsburg craftsmen of both races seem to have labored with "no sense of racial competition" (Genovese, 403–4). But despite these very few exceptions the opportunity ethic was largely closed to blacks whether slave or free. It remained a value reserved for the white population of North America.

For those who could elevate themselves by the opportunities of the New World, a burgeoning market economy proved to be an additional bastion of support. During the colonial era its values of enterprise, competition, and hard work dominated the trans-atlantic world, and from them consumption emerged as a common currency. Even the ministerial elite gradually accommodated to the new world and its values. In 1701 Cotton Mather argued that in business a man can glorify God by the "doing of Good for others" (Mather, *Two Brief Discourses*, 38). Later Puritans became more concerned with the sins of the flesh than money-making, and came to believe that God endowed the decent with prosperity. Money-making was further blessed if it was used for good purposes and its owners were sensitive to the social effects of entrepreneurial activity (Michaelsen, 334–35; Sachs and Hoogenboom, 53). While some ministers like Jonathan Marsh of Connecticut continued to lament the ascendancy of money over salvation (Bushman, "Great Awakening," 303), Jonathan Edwards (1703–58) argued that when God "decrees diligence and industry, he decrees riches and prosperity; when he decrees prudence, he often decrees success." It was a plea for harmony between worldly work and the requirements of salvation (R. Perry, 103), and signaled a subtle recognition of change. By the 1730s the secular calling had become widely accepted among Anglicans, Congregationalists, and Quakers in the middle colonies and New England, and while still important to a shrinking coterie, the old religious prohibitions against excessive wealth and worldliness were giving ground to the desire for a better life through profitable work (Farnie, 212–13; Wertenbaker,

Puritan Oligarchy, 202; Hacker, 120). Countinghouse had triumphed over church, and men sought their destiny in earthly accumulation rather than heavenly reward. Work in the world was not only acceptable, but became the touchstone of success and the visible manifestation of goodness.

If money-making now became "the mystic common denominator of all values," (Namier, 13), its daily manifestations could be found in every corner of the colonies. The commercial spirit was particularly strong among New England merchants and farmers after the 1670s. By 1687 Boston had over 500 skilled artisans and 500 additional shopkeepers, merchants, and masters in a population of only 7,000 (Henretta, "Colonial Boston," 79). This emphasis on enterprise and private ownership also flourished in the smaller ports north of Boston. Typical was the Parsons family of Gloucester, but counterparts could be found in other towns such as Newbury and Falmouth. The presence of considerable commercial traffic in Boston, Northampton and Kent, Connecticut underscored the spread of the New England market economy and the wealth values that accompanied it (Bailyn, *New England Merchants*, 139–42; Heyrman, 53, 62–63; Boydston, 23; Handlin and Handlin, *Restless People*, 11–13). In this commercial setting, prosperity replaced religiosity and material success became the new community hallmark.

Work lives were also "tethered to the market" among the wheat farmers of Pennsylvania and the meat producers of Connecticut. It also embraced the tobacco planters of the Chesapeake, and the cultivaters of rice and indigo in the Carolina-Georgia lowlands (Innes, *Work and Labor*, 35; Henretta, "Families and Farms," 16–17; Bushman, *Puritan to Yankee*, 107–43). The Philadelphia merchant Thomas Willing and his New England counterparts amassed fortunes in the carrying trade (McCusker and Menard, 71–73, 111), while Pennsylvania farmers were so ensconced in the market economy that they were virtual "agents of capitalism" (Lemon, "Spatial Order," 102). Even "frontier communities quickly integrated themselves into market networks" and responded to "commercial incentives" as well as the new consumerism (Appleby, "Value and Society," 309). It was this consumerism that helped break down the "ascetic tradition," and made the shopkeeper not only the seller of goods but the purveyor of "new values to all who spent more and more time in the new activity of shopping" (Farnie, 212). In addition, the great expansion of agriculture by 2–3 percent annually from 1700 to 1770 and enormous growth of foreign trade with Britain, Africa, the West Indies, and coastal America put the final seal on the victory of the market and the values it represented (Greene, *Pursuits of Happiness*, 126, 129; Breen, "An Empire of Goods," 485; McCusker and Menard, 53–55; Shalhope, 11–12; R. Davis, *Atlantic Economies*, 274, 307; Egnal, 192–93, 198; Sachs and Hoogenboom, 27). By the mid-eighteenth century "the Atlantic became the busiest ocean highway in the world" (Farnie, 213).

The great economic leap forward had many partisans. The anonymous 1731 tract published by *Amicus Republicae* in Boston strongly argued that none would work without a "foresight of profit." Everything depended on diligent labor, the writer argued, but this would come to naught "without the advantage & encouragement of profitable *Commerce*" (Greene, *Settlements to Society*, 270–71). In a 1754 letter to Franklin, Richard Jackson extolled the virtues of commerce and industry as beneficial to society (L. Labaree and Bell, 5:244), while many Harvard professors openly encouraged money-making (Dorfman, 1:120). Others noted the preoccupation with wealth during the two centuries after Jamestown, among them Roger Williams, James Logan, and Cadwallader Colden (Nash, "Franklin's Philadelphia," 166–67; Bruchey, *Roots*, 194–95). But few could surpass the competitive and acquisitive spirit exhibited by the planters of the south and Caribbean (Clemens, 19–20; Greene, *Pursuits of Happiness*, 36).

In the wake of this vast emphasis on material improvement as a key life objective, privatism emerged as a permanent feature of American values. For now and the foreseeable future its "essence" lay in the individual's search for wealth and upward mobility. Increasingly, the community was viewed as an agglomeration of "money-making, accumulating families" which offered its members a setting for success (Warner, 3–4). Intellectual support for such enterprise was readily available from the pen of Adam Smith (1723–90) and the Scottish historians. For Smith, efforts to improve one's material condition were depicted in terms of "natural" and "insatiable wants" that pushed a society of individuals to "industry." Their diligent labor was portrayed in terms of self-interest, which would bring about the greatest good if emulated by society as a whole (Smith, *Wealth of Nations,* 29–31, 118–19). Hume (1711–76) and Locke (1632–1704) added to the philosophical support for private values. They extolled enterprise, property rights, and hard work in the pursuit of self-interest (Laird, 247–49; Locke, 131), and together with Smith, provided an ideological justification for striving and diligence within a market economy.

Given the long term trend toward a powerful market economy since the Middle Ages and the victory of its values by the late seventeenth century, it is no surprise that many entrepreneurs emerged in colonial America. Not only did politicians and publicists extol enterprise and the hard work it represented, but businessmen began to develop a consciousness that they were "a distinct social group" (Bridenbaugh, *Cities in the Wilderness,* 340; Bushman, "Great Awakening," 303; Sachs and Hoogenboom, 43–44). Urban areas in particular witnessed a substantial growth of entrepreneurial endeavor during the eighteenth century. Here achievement took precedence over inherited position and individualism superceded communitarian values (Nash, "Social Development," 248–50). Schemes involving land speculation and town development also absorbed a good deal of early enterprise. Sir Robert Montgomery's promises of a paradise in Georgia and Alabama (Azilia) (Wright, *Dream of Prosperity,* 77–79) and the activity of New England promoters such as Richard Wharton, Humphrey Atherton, John Winthrop, Jr. and the Wentworths of New Hampshire typified this free-wheeling effort (J. F. Martin, 28–31, 46–48, 54, 63; L. Mayo, *John Wentworth,* 21–22; Bailyn, *Peopling,* 269).

Other restless businessmen like Thomas Breedon and Andrew Belcher gave early Puritan ministers more than a little distress (Bailyn, *New England Merchants,* 110–11; 192–94), but the value structure of New England was already moving in the direction of Yankee enterprise. Even the Boston Puritan John Hull became a prosperous merchant and mint-master, while Thomas Hancock elevated himself socially on Beacon Hill by 1735. Other New England merchants such as Thomas Amory and Peter Faneuil left large estates (Ziff, 41–42, 150; Wright, *American Colonies,* 31–32; B. Labaree, *Colonial Massachusetts,* 164–65; Baxter, 27, 29, 37, 39; Hacker, 138) which led John Adams to question the values of those who sought only "a living and a fortune" (Butterfield, Garrett, and

Sprague, 1:53). But the views of the rich Boston merchant Ezra Collins in 1773 demonstrated that the new money-oriented values were a permanent fixture: "'Tis profit, the prospect of reward that stimulates people" (Sachs and Hoogenboom, 80).

Whether one looks at Colonel William Pepperell of New Hampshire, the aristocratic Philip Livingston of New York, or Stephen Girard and Jonathan Dickinson of Philadelphia, the common denominator that linked these entrepreneurs was their willingness to take risks. In this regard, they exceeded their British counterparts and emerged as a "scrappy and innovative" lot (Wright, *American Colonies*, 38–42; Doerflinger, 159–60). Some like Auguste Jay and Frederick Philipse of New York mixed their legitimate business with a bit of smuggling and piracy (Beard, 2:48–50), while the suceess of Robert Livingston led to the establishment of a commercial dynasty (Kammen, 134–36). The meteoric rise of Thomas Clifford in Philadelphia, on the other hand, seemed to typify that city as home to an unusually large number of "vigorous" businessmen during the latter half of the eighteenth century (Doerflinger, 14–15, 153–54, 17; Warner, 5–6). To the south planter-entrepreneurs flourished in the Chesapeake. Maryland families like the Carrolls and Ridgelys rivaled the elitist landowners of the Hudson Valley, and such hard-driving and profit-seeking men like William Byrd II, William Fitzhugh, and Edward Dixon thrived in Virginia (Bruchey, *Enterprise*, 147; Clemens, 121; Perkins, 83–85; R. Brown, *Modernization*, 40, 45). Enterprise in South Carolina was distinguished by a large number of French Huguenot families, among them the Manigaults, Hugers, Mottes, Legendres, and Legares who did well as merchants and then rode the path of upward mobility by purchasing coats-of-arms and plantations (Beard, 2:52; Wright, *Atlantic Frontier*, 285–86; Bridenbaugh, *Cities in the Wilderness*, 339).

But business endeavor did not flourish without criticism. Deceit in business dealings and the cornering of markets to raise prices drew vehement denunciation. Some argued that social and moral obligations superceded profit, and urged cooperation in the context of Christian values. They saw the energy devoted to business as futile, for it led the successful to pursue an endless quest for even greater achievement that never led to fulfillment (Crowley, 102, 105, 109). Other colonists deplored the selfishness inherent in rational economic relationships. They wanted to preserve their "social wholeness," and overcome the uneasiness they felt as commercialization changed the nature and meaning of work. A 1721 letter in *Colonial Currency Reprints* relative to the South Sea stock scandal argued that life in a market economy was a strain on both social ties and moral values, for people in competition were people in conflict. The Dorchester minister John Danforth identified the "wicked self" of New Englanders with Sheba, Queen of the Sabeans, who was known for her great wealth. Like Sheba, the economic inclinations of the colonists was leading them into sin and away from the more wholesome ideals of hard work and frugality. Samuel Davies, a renowned Presbyterian minister in Virginia, believed that striving for luxury goods and craftiness in business would weaken society, while a 1753 sermon from Thomas Barnard looked for a socially oriented business environment that could maintain traditional values (ibid., 12, 3–4, 104–6).

During the Great Awakening ministers quarreled about the role of work and business in society. While Benjamin Colman and Jonathan Mayhew supported the concepts of self-interest and entrepreneurial activity, "radical awakeners" like Gilbert Tennent had serious qualms about acquisitiveness and the accumulation of great wealth (Nash, *Urban Crucible*, 217; Bushman, "Great Awakening, 303, 305–6). Later Federalists like Thomas Green Fessenden (1771–1837) so feared for the end of the old system that he urged every American to "be contented with his station" (Rossiter, 116). For those who saw the great increase in private wealth (Alice H. Jones, 298–300, 341) and economic activity as a concern, work for personal success now challenged the social outlook of the individual. To be part of this new rational economic order each person would be obliged to fend for themselves in a milieu of profit maximization. But despite the persistence of these nagging concerns about social stability, colonists gradually came to accept economic individualism as a work value (Crowley, 96–97, 12). It was a situation that induced colonists to attack "the consequence of progress but never progress itself." The new commercial world based on hard work, the desire to get ahead, and aggressive business relationships was accepted, but along with it came the threat that it would destroy the old communitarian values (Miller,

"Bible Commonwealth," 68). This fundamental ambivalence has lingered on to torment the American conscience.

Work itself, however, never raised such doubts. The rationalist minister John Wise (1652–1725) and Benjamin Franklin (1706–90) both played important roles in shifting the Puritan emphasis on labor to a worldly justification of toil (Miller, *American Puritans*, 172). But it was Franklin who wielded the greatest influence on the secularization of work in America. In his famous "Way to Wealth," a preface to "Poor Richard Improved for 1758," Franklin noted that "he that hath a trade hath an estate; and he that hath a calling, hath an office of profit and honor." He went on to advise that "leisure is time for doing something useful" (Greene, *Settlement to Society*, 255–56), that "God never encourages Idleness" and does not look down upon those who toil in even the "meanest Employments." And in typical Franklin prose he cautioned that "idleness is the Dead Sea, that swallows all Virtues." Therefore, "be active in Business, that Temptation may miss her Aim." And finally he cautioned his fellow colonists to avoid sloth: "The Bird that sits, is easily shot" (L. Labaree and Bell., 6:326, 7:83). Franklin went on to advise his compatriots to avoid the wastage of Saint Monday, and added an admonition against alcohol as injurious to the pursuit of trade (Smyth, 5:122–27). Time, he argued, was the "Bullion of the Day," and as such was too precious to idle away. "Remember," he said, "that time is money" (L. Labaree and Bell., 4:86–87; Fleming, 82). Franklin also provided the ideological support for the making of more and more money, even beyond that required for basic needs (Weber, 53–54). In this and his other maxims he supplied even the most reluctant colonists with a philosophy that justified success and upward mobility. Franklin's ideas continued to have a powerful influence during the next two centuries, and constituted the most notable American intellectual legacy in support of hard work and enterprise.

Franklin, of course, was not alone in his advocacy of diligent work, opportunity, and the importance of "push" in business. Support for these values came from a growing middle class in the Middle Colonies and New England who saw success as the end result of hard work, thrift, and drive (Wright, *Atlantic Frontier*, 323–24). In this matter children were of great concern to the colonists. Massachusetts in 1648 and Connecticut in 1673 both required fathers to see that their children were instructed "in some honest lawful calling." Some years later in a 1712 tract entitled *The Well-Ordered Family* Benjamin Wadsworth deplored the substitution of children's play for earnest labor, while the jurist Samuel Sewall requested materials for his young daughters so they could work on curtains and chairs and avoid idleness (Morgan, *Puritan Family*, 66–67). The memoirs of the missionaries David and John Brainerd reflected that the same work ethic was required of them as boys on their Connecticut farm: "laziness was the worst form of original sin" (Earle, 307–8). In addition, many colonial children were required to repeatedly write the Biblical admonition "by the sweat of thy brow thou shalt eat thy bread (Kiefer, 5). The Reverend Samuel Willard told parents in 1726 to see that children apply themselves diligently to both school and labor, while Franklin's 1753 tract on *The Value of a Child* warned that "idleness is a sort of non-existence" (Cochran, *Business in American Life*, 30). In the early 1760s the Anglican minister Samuel Johnson (1696–1772) added that it was "indispensably necessary that they [children] be inured to industry and diligence" (Greene, *Settlements to Society*, 307), a point Jefferson made in letters to his daughters in 1787 (Boyd, 11:250, 349). It is little wonder that young John Cleaveland was inured to heavy labor on his father's New England farm until he left for Yale (Jedrey, 16).

For the community at large such admonitions flowed from pen and pulpit. Ministers like Benjamin Colman of Boston offered the view that "*All Nature is Industrious and every Creature about us diligent in their proper Work* (Colman, 14). John Pynchon of Springfield, Massachusetts was careful in the hiring of tenants and workers, for he had no time for those with poor work habits (Innes, *Labor in a New Land*, 41). The almanacs of Nathaniel Ames and his son of Dedham, Massachusetts also extolled the virtues of labor by exclaiming that "the Law of Nature so ordains, *Toil, and be Strong*" (Morris, *Government and Labor*, 5). Another almanac writer, Theophilus Grew, used his *Virginia Almanack* of 1753 to advocate that "industry will make thee wealthy," while Abigail Adams offered to make cloth with her own hands to encourage nonimportation of British goods in 1774 (Crowley, 122; Morgan, "Puritan Ethic and American Revolution," 12). Her husband, John Adams (1735–1826), urged that all members of society "would be obliged in

Conscience to temperance and frugality and industry" (Butterfield, 1:9). The work ethic also had strong support among many other prominent colonial leaders. Presbyterians and Congregationalists like Benjamin Rush and Samuel Adams exemplified this tendency as did Henry Laurens and Richard Henry Lee who were Anglicans. To this group could be added the Deist Thomas Jefferson (Morgan, "Puritan Ethic and American Revolution," 6–7). That these views were winning support could be seen in the observations of an eighteenth century traveler from Maryland, Dr. Alexander Hamilton. He remembered from his journeys to Philadelphia, Chester, and Albany that people everywhere were consumed with business, work, and a frugal way of life. Profit took precedence over everything, and there was little time for small talk or good manners (Bridenbaugh, *Gentleman's Progress*, 23, 73, 193). The colonial press also took time to shower praise on labor and frugality as can be seen in the *Virginia Gazette* out of Williamsburg in 1771 (Morgan, "Puritan Ethic and American Revolution," 6). Even the Norman-French visitor Crèvecoeur who came to the colonies around 1760 and lived in Orange County, New York noted that new arrivals to America sensed the opportunity that was available to them if they were "honest, sober and industrious" (Bourdin, *Crèvecoeur*, 90–91).

Within this tendency toward toil was a growing emphasis on time-discipline in work. For those who worked outside their home a sunrise to sunset routine was normal, but those artisans who labored at home could take time to chat with customers or stop for a drink at a nearby tavern (Warner, 7–8). As in England, a twelve-and-a-half-hour day was routine for farm laborers in seventeenth century Springfield, Massachusetts. But in Springfield, the farm laborer Francis Pepper was not allowed a midday nap like his English counterparts (Thompson, "Time and Work-Discipline," 113–15; Innes, *Labor in a New Land*, 113–16). More leisurely English work customs prevailed in the Chesapeake during the seventeenth century, but things tightened thereafter (Hammond, "Leah and Rachael," 290). Beyond this, other voices called for the responsible use of time. Samuel Sewall, Chief Justice of the Massachusetts Superior Court, sent the schoolmaster Ezekiel Cheever a letter in 1708 urging him to inculcate the habit of time thrift in his students. Thomas Shepard forwarded the same message to his son at Harvard in 1672: "Abhor therefore one hour of idleness as you would be ashamed of one hour of drunkenness." Connecticut even resorted to a 1715 regulation to encourage sobriety and keep the poor away from taverns where they would waste "precious time needlessly." Others felt it was useless to help those who led a bad life, and advocated workhouses to insure they labored with regularity—attitudes similar to those in England (Wright, *American Colonies*, 25–26). Still, workers like the shoemaker George Hewes (1742–1840) spoke of a life dedicated to hard work and the careful use of time (Gutman and Bell, 18–20). John Adams underscored the need to conserve time by berating himself for arising as late as eight in the morning: "God grant me . . . every Opportunity . . . to save, with the Parsimony of a Miser, every moment of my Time" (Butterfield, 1:132). In this vein, a Baltimore merchant deplored the time laxity in answering commercial correspondence (Bruchey, *Roots*, 48–49). Clearly, there was a tendency toward a more efficient use of time by the end of the eighteenth century, but this trend was still burdened with the more leisurely work habits of time past. Only in the nineteenth century would the emerging workshops and factories begin to impose a time-discipline that signaled a break with traditional practices.

Idleness, on the other hand, was attacked with great ferocity. Generally, only children under eight, the aged, and the ill were exempt from labor. All others were required to produce. In this sense, British North America in its first century had one of the smallest leisure classes in early modern history. The colonies did not have a "distinct" aristocracy nor did they possess clerical and courtly classes, and men and women of the middle ranks often labored at tasks that would have been considered "vulgar" in Britain (Innes, *Work and Labor*, 20). A good example was set by Governor John Winthrop of Massachusetts. No sooner had he come to Massachusetts than he went into the fields to work (E. Emerson, 52). And while many of the early Puritans brought servants with them, there was a trend for them to "disperse" (Breen and Foster, 194; Vickers, 55). Even among the Chesapeake planters masters and servants shared the work during the seventeenth century. Half the white women in early Maryland also worked in the tobacco fields (Carr and Walsh, 149, 152–54; G. Main, *Tobacco Colony*, 108–9). Virginia presented a similar picture, according to Jaspar Dankers who traveled through that colony around 1679–80

(James and Jameson, 133). While this situation changed radically in the Chesapeake and the southern colonies in the eighteenth century, most colonists had difficulty accepting idleness, luxury, and ostantatiousness. American colonists who visited England decried the pomp and lack of industry they observed (Morgan, "Puritan Ethic and American Revolution," 14–15), but even at home many of the successful tried to emulate the good living of the English counterparts even as they continued to strive and produce. The beautiful home of Thomas Hancock on Beacon Hill and those along "Tory Row" in Cambridge (B. Labaree, *Colonial Massachusetts*, 164–65) could be matched by the town houses and country seats of Philadelphians like Robert Morris, William Bingham, and John Nicholson (Doerflinger, 162–63). Likewise, the early Virginian Samuel Matthews built a manor in Newport News and married off his daughter to a titled Englishman (Wright, *Atlantic Frontier*, 68–71, 93). Nevertheless, these men and many others continued to work diligently. Except for some of the southern leaders in the later colonial period, these merchants and planters combined the spirit of enterprise with a luxurious lifestyle.

But from the earliest of times, idleness was attacked by the many even as it was practiced by the few. The Jamestown colonists presented an exception to this generalization, but within this experiment there was much to be learned. As John Smith described his work program in 1612, labor spanned a four hour period daily with the remainder of the time available for "pastimes and merry exercise." Even when faced with starvation many did not exert themselves, probably because all worked for the Virginia Company which took the reponsibility for feeding them. It is also likely that these settlers brought the worst of English work values with them, and waited in vain for the Indians of King Powhatan to do their work. In addition, the Jamestown group included many "gentlemen" who disdained physical labor. Only the later prospect of acquiring land changed the work habits of the early Virginians (Morgan, "Jamestown," 596–600). To supplement this, the 1619 Virginia General Assembly, "in detestation of idleness," required those seen as idlers to be attached to a master until they demonstrated "apparent signs of amendment" (Appleby, *Materialism and Morality*, 15). The Virginia Company was also forced to import skilled workers from Sweden, France, Holland and Poland (Hill,

Society and Puritanism, 126). Elsewhere in the colonies the disdain for idleness held sway.

A shortage of labor in America undoubtedly contributed to the detestation for laziness which in 1633 led Massachusetts to require "that all workmen shall work the whole day, allowing convenient time for food and rest." No man was to "spend his time idly or unprofitably" under pain of punishment by the court (Bruchey, *Colonial Merchant*, 101). This scarcity of workers probably placed a greater valuation on female labor. And while the work of women was largely "gender prescribed," they had to be productive within this format. The Puritan minister John Cotton even described a woman's toil as "her trade" (Boydston, 19–20, 5–6).

The Massachusetts General Court also tried to fix wages at a lower level, for the lack of labor had raised them to a point that some felt encouraged idleness. Attempts to fix wages betweeen 1633 and 1675 failed (Dorfman, 1:44–46; Morris, *Government and Labor*, 58–60, 70–71), but it did little to change the general unhappiness with those who would not work steadily. A report adopted by the town of Boston in 1769 viewed idleness as "the parent of all vices," while the early records of Providence, Rhode Island denounced beggars, masterless men, and vagabonds, an indication that Elizabethan values had traversed the Atlantic. Additionally, the Connecticut minister and lawgiver Thomas Hooker, in his 1659 tract *The Application of Redemption*, argued that vagabonds had to come under the eye of authority so they would not live "idly or unprofitably" (Dorfman, 1:43). By the 1770s the selectmen of Fairfield, Connecticut began to prosecute idle strangers and pushed vagrants out of town by serving notice they would not maintain a new arrival who became dependent. In Pennsylvania, Penn's *Frame of Government* provided that that all children aged twelve should be taught "some useful trade or skill to the end none may be idle." To discourage poor work attendance, Philadelphia even forbade theatrical performances during the eighteenth century (Handlin and Handlin, 9; Dorfman, 1:8–9; Morris, *Government and Labor*, 4). In New Jersey, the English practice of requiring paupers to wear a large red or blue "P" on the right shoulder was used to make idleness so unpleasant that work would become a preferable alternative (Wright, *American Colonies*,

27). To the south, Virginia passed the Statute of 1672 legislating "against vagrant, idle and dissolute persons." A later 1723 act directed that the English Poor Law of 1601 be used against vagabonds who were fit to work but were found to be "loitering" and otherwise failing to maintain themselves (Morris, *Government and Labor*, 6; Morgan, *American Slavery*, 339). Colonial Virginians and North Carolinians went so far as to exchange broadsides against each other's leisurely work habits (Beverly, 319, 351; Marambaud, 122, 231), while South Carolinians like the minister Josiah Smith saw idleness as the "Bane of Society." The editor of the *South Carolina Gazette*, Peter Timothy, was so disgusted with apprentices addicted to "Drink, Play and Scandalous Company," that he fired his "villanous Apprentice" (Crowley, 80; Bridenbaugh, *Colonial Craftsman*, 137).

The reactions to idleness in early colonial America could take an ugly turn. Plymouth Colony records for 1639, 1658, and 1661–63, Connecticut public records for 1650 and 1718, and Rhode Island materials for 1702 all indicate that whipping and fines were often imposed (Morris, *Government and Labor*, 5). As mentioned earlier, Cotton Mather's solution for those without work was to "let them starve." He argued that for the poor who can work and refuse to do so, the best course was to "*make* them" labor. He further cautioned that society had to be hard in this matter and should not "misapply" their charity (Dorfman, 1:57). But within this charge lay the distinction that both colonial Americans and their English forbears both drew: the differences between the "deserving poor" and "sturdy beggars." The second group deserved nothing beyond the workhouse to correct their evil proclivities, for poverty was due to laxity or improvidence. To tax the diligent in support of worthless loiterers was to decrease the assets of the productive and increase the incidence of beggary (Sachs and Hoogenboom, 83–84).

To deal with this problem, various colonial communities resorted to the establishment of almshouses, workhouses, and "bettering houses." By 1650 Boston, Newport, and New Amsterdam accepted the concept that the community had some responsibility for the idle and destitute. This led to the establishment of an almshouse in virtually every Atlantic seaport by the 1730s. In Virginia paupers looked to the county government for help, and the Albemarle County Court provided for the election of overseers of the poor (Bruchey, *American Economic Growth*, 58–59).

During the eighteenth century poverty increased in colonial America, and if Philadelphia can be used as an example, the problem led to the erection of a Quaker almshouse in 1717 and a public counterpart fifteen years later. Attempts to absorb the growing number of immigrants from Germany, Ireland, Acadia, and Holland eventually failed, and by 1766 the almshouse had 220 paupers. While some historians like Billy Smith placed the number of poor in Philadelphia at between one-quarter and one-third of the population, Nash suggested the number approximated 11 percent of the taxable population between 1760 and 1775. Perkins, however, argued that by European standards very few were "destitute" in the colonies (Nash, "Franklin's Philadelphia," 170; Nash, "Pre-Revolutionary Philadelphia," 4–6, 14; B. G. Smith, "Laboring Philadelphians," 201–2; Perkins, 11–12). But the cost of maintaining the poor rose after 1763 when many soldiers and sailors were discharged after the end of the French and Indian War. Many repectable citizens feared this as an accretion to "The Mob," and rebelled at the thought of taxing themselves on behalf of the poor. Despite this, Boston was compelled to spend about 24 percent of its budget in 1763 on poor relief, an amount that increased substantially by 1770. By comparison, expenditures for poor relief in New York City rose from 700 pounds in 1750 to 4,000 just prior to the revolution (Sachs and Hoogenboom, 123–24). Twenty years later, the New York City almshouse commissioners were still grappling with the problem of poverty. They noted in February 1795 that 44 percent of its paupers were immigrants which led the editor of the *New York Minerva* to declare in 1797 that "we shall be overrun with vagabonds." However, the city's ministers responded to this by citing the Calvinist concept of stewardship: those with means had a responsibility to care for their less fortunate brethren (Mohl, 17, 160–61).

If almshouses provided less than an ideal solution to the problems of idleness and poverty, workhouses on the English model might drive the lazy to labor. Here the unemployed could at least pay for some of their upkeep, and not expect those with resources to support them. In this sense, the workhouse was built for the improvement of vagrants, and the Quakers in particular referred to some of their insitutions as "bettering houses." A recession in the 1760s saw the Philadelphia Quakers erect such an establishment to both reduce poor relief costs and dismantle the ineffective out-relief system. This 1767 institution was probably modeled after John Bellers' "colleges of industry" where the poor could work as a group and attain self-sufficiency (Nash, "Pre-Revolutionary Philadelphia," 14–16; Nash, *Urban Crucible*, 327–31; Polanyi, 105–6; S. V. James, 212; Porter, 315). In Boston a 1685 type of workhouse threw together the poor and criminals, people who lived in "idlenesse & tipplinge with great neglect of their callings." While Greene estimates that the New England population getting poor relief in the eighteenth century never rose above 5–7 percent, Boston had both an almshouse and a workhouse by 1739 (Bridenbaugh, *Cities in the Wilderness*, 82, 393; Greene, *Pursuits of Happiness*, 73– 74). However, because so many were seeking work in Boston in April, 1769, local merchants provided funds to train children and buy equipment and thereby "habituate the People to Industry, and preserve their Morals instead of their continuing a burden to society" (Morris, *Government and Labor*, 13). Like Boston, New York City found the high cost of "outdoor relief" so burdensome that it erected a workhouse in 1736. The output of its inmates saved the city little money. Still, in 1767 the local authorities converted parts of its prison to a workhouse so its inmates could be set to work (Handlin and Handlin, 51; Sachs and Hoogenboom, 125). Both Boston and Newport also "warned" vagrants and indigents out of town so they could deal with the heavy immigration between 1720 and 1742. Philadelphia and New York City also drove off immigrant vagrants at the wharf in order to cope with the problem of unemployment in the 1760s (Bridenbaugh, *Cities in Wilderness*, 392-93; Sachs and Hoogenboom, 124).

Whether communities resorted to almshouses, workhouses, or "bettering houses," the problem of those without work remained. Colonial responses were similar to those afloat in Britain and reflected the moral indignation against idleness as well as an community reluctance to support those who did not support themselves. This distaste for the undeserving poor would remain an American dilemma for the next two centuries with solutions no closer in the self-fulfillment world of the 1990s than they were in the more Calvinistic ethos of the 1690s. But the pervasive colonial support of diligence, thrift, and striving all contributed to an opportunity ethic that enshrined enterprise and gave those who did work considerable social approval. In this sense, the belief system that emerged by the end of the colonial period formed a core of work values that became a key part of the mainstream of American thought and practice. It was a context that endured during the growth of the factory culture, and continued in post-industrial attitudes toward work.

Chapter 7

WORK VALUES IN MODERN AMERICA

During the nearly two centuries that followed the conclusion of the War of 1812 work values in America underwent a revolutionary change. They continued to reflect Poor Richard's enthusiasm for work, perseverance, and thrift, but unashamedly elevated success and opportunity in the American belief system. Added to this was a "boundless belief in progress" encouraged by fluid class and craft lines and the presence of an open frontier. Within this value system great emphasis was placed on "personal advancement" and the drive to accumulate wealth (Sawyer, 376). It made the nineteenth century the pantheon of self-made men in which entrepreneurship was idolized in every precinct from the pulpit to the political podium.

Children's literature strongly supported these goals. It stressed self-discipline, diligence, and integrity as avenues to the Promised Land, and projected the development of good character as the prerequisite of a successful life. To this social conditioning some Protestant ministers added a heavenly blessing to the search for success (Wyllie, 183, 57–59). But the drumbeat of success gained its greatest acceptance within the growing middle class. It was this group in particular that internalized these values and socialized their children to drink at the fountain of opportunity. During the twentieth century the widely read books of Coué, Carnegie, and Peale offered the upwardly mobile "positive thinking" as a new path to worldly goals. Businessmen like Roger Babson and Bruce Barton extolled initiative and industry, and publisher B. C. Forbes added personality as a key element in getting ahead when he suggested that "success in business, if not in life itself, is simply the art of pleasing" (Forbes, 75).

Despite this middle-class enthusiasm for progress and artful ways to move along the road of opportunity, many craftsmen and factory operatives viewed the evolving industrial world in a more somber light. As nineteenth-century employment gradually shifted from small establishments run by a master craftsman to larger workshops and mechanized factories under a new managerial class, workers saw relatively few chances to elevate themselves. More and more artisans were separated from control of their time and tools, and with exception of a "labor aristocracy" that would parallel British practice in the nineteenth century, were increasingly relegated to semi-skilled factory wage-work. This downward slide combined the acrid taste of alienation and limited opportunity, and offered workers a Faustian bargain of repetitive wage-labor for an uneven measure of security. Talk of self-made men and a world of opportunity based on hard work and perseverance was meaningless for the operatives of textile mills and steel factories. Even the late nineteenth century immigrants who sought a better life for their families in the manufactories of Paterson and the mills of Pittsburgh came to see the controlled environment of the factory as less than utopian. To this baleful situation workers were also compelled to contend with a new form of control by the Tayloristic time and motion experts (Haber, ix; F. W. Taylor, *Principles*, 7) which robbed them of their former independence. They knew the success literature of Orison Swett Marden (Huber, 155–56) was not meant for their children, that their best hopes lay in a modicum of security that might be won by improved compensation.

From this perspective there emerged a pattern of collective values that were formalized during the development of early nineteenth century unions in Lynn, Philadelphia, and New York City. What workers could not achieve as individuals they now tried to accomplish as a group. Success would not come through business enterprise, and upward mobility remained a vision of the middle class. And while it was true that some craftsmen such as typographers, potters, puddlers, hatters, and miners retained a measure of control over their work (Montgomery, "Workers' Control," 487; Cumbler, *Trenton*, 31–32; Montgomery, *House of Labor*, 29–30; Bensman, "Workers' Control, 129–30, 133–34; Bensman, *Solidarity*, 43–44; Dubofsky, 5; Corbin, 38), Gompers' emphasis on pay and benefits (Kerr et al., 210) became the keystone of union values in the late nineteenth century. If workers could not share in the American dream of opportunity and success, then they were determined to rely on ever-increasing consumption as compensation for alienated labor and circumscribed vistas. As wage workers (only 20% were self-employed in 1920 as compared to 50% in 1865), the problem of job insecurity hit with particular fury during the depressions that wracked America in the six decades after Appomattox (Dubofsky, 3, 23). To this was added the deterioration of personal relations between employers and employees, a point underscored with great poignancy by the *Frostburg Mining Journal* of 25 November 1876 (Gutman, *Power & Culture*, 77).

Given this combination of alienated labor, job insecurity, poor pay, and exclusion from the opportunity culture, it is not surprising that three decades of industrial strife followed the great railroad strikes of 1877. The 1880s alone witnessed some 10,000 labor actions, and while these slackened during the recession of 1893–97, mechanization, bureaucratization, and the large scale of business activity "diminished the worker and cut him down to fit the productive system" (Trachtenberg, 89–92; Dubofsky, 45–52; Gordon, Edwards, and Reich, 122, 97–99; Perlman, 84; Brody, *Industrial America*, 13).

James Kitson, a British visitor to Pittsburgh around 1907, commented on how foremen pushed American operatives to produce: "The bosses drive the men to an extent that employers would never dream of in this country [England] getting the maximum work out of them, and the men do not have the inclination or the power to resist the pressure" (Bodnar, Simon, and Weber, 18). It is little wonder that by 1912 the collective values of the American workforce were accurately reflected in the labor song "Solidarity Forever." Within it lay no dreams of self-made men nor the virtues of success, but of laborers who proclaimed "the Union makes us strong" (Bird et al., 221–22, 146). For those who could not leave the station on the train of success only the Holy Grail of consumption remained.

But any form of union activity was bound to clash with the values that placed complete control of the workplace in the hands of a managerial class that emerged in the 1850s and 1860s. These administrators first surfaced in the railroad and telegraph industries, but during the early twentieth century spread to such mass distribution firms as Sears, Roebuck (Chandler and Tedlow, 396, 398–99). Managers at firms such as Pullman and National Cash Register showed a willingness to mollify their workers by the palliatives of "welfare capitalism," but improvements in safety, health, and recreation did not address the collective aspiration for union recognition as a measure of self-respect and security. Above all, the new managers demanded control. Thus, while the brass ring was momentarily grasped by a few workmen like the artisans of Poughkeepsie in the three decades after 1850 (Blumin, 120), it was an unfulfilled fantasy for the vast multitude of factory operatives. For them upward mobility was a dream postponed until the consumption boom after the Second World War. Only then were workers in "low-prestige occupations" able to increase their earnings enough to send their children to college, the rite of passage to upward mobility (Lipset and Bendix, 273–74; Duncan and Blau, 286). By the Sixties the old drive for "more" had been tempered by a generation of baby boomers who added self-fulfillment in work to the old agenda of consumption.

What, then, was the nature of the industrial platform on which this medley of work values emerged after 1815? In colonial America industrialization had made good progress during the eighteenth century, but most enterprises remained small (Morris, *Government and Labor*, 38). Still, by 1775 the colonies had eighty-two charcoal-fueled furnaces, and could boast of more forges and furnaces than in England and Wales (McCusker and Menard, 326; Bining, 27–30). The shoemakers of Lynn were producing 80,000 shoes by 1767, and eight years later 30 percent of all ships used in British commerce had been built in the colonies (Gutman and Bell, 20; Gipson, 15). Germantown, Pennsylvania had become a woollen center, and Franklin himself observed an abundance of sawmills near Philadelphia (Jernegan, 368–69). In Boston, William Molineux developed a proto-textile factory before his death in 1774, while the a linen manufactory was established in New York City as early as 1767 (Victor Clark, *Manufactures*, 1:189–90). But while most businesses were of modest size in this pre-industrial world, a strong commercial and industrial base had been laid. There is little question that the capitalist spirit that beat so strongly in the breasts of the Morrises, the Livingstons, the Carrolls (East, 19), the

Hancocks, and the Manigaults had laid a strong foundation for an expansion of an opportunity culture.

To this was added a growing support for business enterprise during the quarter century after the adoption of the new constitution. Washington himself came to see that commercial prosperity was in the public interest, but expressed his concern about its social impact in a 1784 letter to Benjamin Harrison (Washington, *Writings*, xxvii, 474). Nevertheless, the number of American corporations grew from seven in 1780 to 335 by 1800. By 1795 the infant republic could boast of twenty-one banks as against none prior to 1776 (J. S. Davis, 22; Henretta and Nobles, 211). In addition, men like John Witherspoon wrote in support of credit as an economic keystone, while William Findley endorsed the importance of personal wealth during the 1785–86 fight over the Bank of North America (Crowley, 152–54). Beyond this, the *American Mercury* of 13 August 1787 counseled that "manufactures will promote industry, and industry contributes to good health, virtue, riches and population" (Morgan, "Puritan Ethic and American Revolution," 37). Tench Coxe was particularly vociferous in his promotion of industrialization as early as 1787 when he described the potential of both machinery and factories (L. Marx, 152–54). Hamilton's *Report on the Subject of Manufactures* in 1791 stressed the same points (ibid., 167–68), while Matthew Carey's *American Museum* urged that factory growth would give work to the "industrious poor" (Jensen, 223–24). Jefferson, on the other hand, used his *Notes on the State of Virginia* (1786) to argue that manufacturing be confined to Europe. Still, the the nail factory he maintained on his plantation in the 1790s had such a massive output that it required a statewide distribution system. Only in an 1816 letter to Benjamin Austin did Jefferson reluctantly accept the inevitable (Jefferson, 157–58; L. Marx, 146; Bender, 22–23). But in the America of his time 84 percent were still "directly engaged" in agriculture (Henretta and Nobles, 222–23), and as Adam Seybert noted in 1818, commerce seemed more attractive than industry (Bruchey, *Enterprise*, 144).

The springboard for the emergence of a powerful market economy and its wealth-seeking values was the great commercial boom of the late eighteenth century. New York merchants who had enjoyed a leisurely and comfortable lifestyle now used their talents to exploit the China trade. Ships from Salem and Nantucket profited from Pacific whaling and the spice trade of the East Indies, while the wars of the French Revolution from 1793 to 1815 gave American shipowners a chance to profit from the carrying trade and food supply to the belligerents. This commercial boom saw American exports explode from $20.2 in 1790 to $108.3 million in 1807. Men like Girard and Astor won the fortunes that enabled them to expand in new directions, while Moses Brown of Providence used his commercial gains to build the foundation of the American textile industry. But despite these individual successes in the "premarket" world of the 1815, the culture of the land continued to vie with the culture of the market. The Pennsylvania Dutch and southern cotton farmers both sought profitable sales for their products, but did not cross "the cultural divide into the pursuit of wealth." But the more typical Yankees of southeastern New England so accepted the new mercantile orientation that an Amherst schoolgirl noticed how "generally avaricious" people had become. By the advent of the Jacksonian era acceptance of the market economy and its hallmarks of success and enterprise had become widespread. Unhappily an increasing number of the workshop and factory operatives found the new regime relegated them to the status of semiskilled wage-workers (Sellers, 22–23, 10, 16, 19) who had a very limited participation in the new success culture.

For blacks in post-Revolutionary America the situation offered even less hope. In 1790 most of the 750,000 free and slave blacks were concentrated in the South. Virginia headed the list of states with 304,000, while the South as a whole had 641,691 slaves and some 32,048 free blacks. Of the Northern states, blacks were concentrated in New York (25,000), New Jersey (14,000), and Pennsylvania (10,000). But slavery was not growing north of the Mason-Dixon line, and some 14,000 or 28 percent of the blacks in this area lived as free women and men. This was probably attributable to the influence of antislavery organizations and the more liberal values of the post-Revolutionary era (J. H. Franklin, 97–98). Among the northern blacks who came forward to seize this thin rope of opportunity were men like the successful Massachusetts shipbuilder Paul Cuffe. The National period also witnessed the emergence of the black writer Jupiter Hammon whose work characterized black striving for intellectual freedom, self-respect, and political freedom (ibid., 108–9, 105). Hammon believed that blacks could not elevate themselves without political equality, a situation not unlike that of contemporary disenfranchised Luddites in Britain.

Even more prominent than Cuffe and Hammon was the poet Phillis Wheatley. She was freed by her mistress in 1773 but was only able to publish her first book by going to Britain. Gustavus Vassa, an American black who purchased his own freedom, also used the British route to attack slavery by a petition to Parliament in 1790, while Benjamin Banneker utilized his knowledge of mathematics, astronomy, and engineering to publish a famous series of almanacs between 1791 and 1802. His reputation as a "Black Poor Richard" was ample refutation of the myth that blacks were not capable of intellectual attainment (ibid., 105–7), but this prejudice was too deeply ingrained in the values of white workers, businessmen, and slaveowners north and south to be dispelled by the accomplishments of one talented man. Still, some whites in the North were aware of the political problems faced by blacks. During the Revolutionary War Abigail Adams wrote to her husband about the inconsistency of fighting for freedom from Britain while maintaining black slavery in America. The Pennsylvania Executive Council used the same argument in 1778 in seeking the abolition of slavery. But it was John Adams who was closest to the mark when he observed that slavery in the North would end only because white workers vigorously objected to the cheap competitive labor offered by slaves (Litwack, 6–9, 11). Nevertheless, slavery was not abolished in the North until about 1830. By that time blacks were working on many farms like those in southeastern Pennsylvania, but could also be found in the maritime industries, and the skilled trades (Litwack, 3–5; Oblinger, 98–99). By 1860 Boston alone had 2,000 free blacks in over one hundred different occupations that ranged from engraving to paperhanging. Philadelphia and New York City also saw blacks move into a variety different occupations, but Cincinnati lagged behind (J. H. Franklin, 164).

But this modest progress was diminished by the anger of native white Americans and European immigrants who saw free blacks as economic competitors. Incoming Irish and German

immigrants in southeastern Pennsylvania drove blacks out of
such industries as iron, boots, building, and some craft trades, and
reduced their participation in domestic labor between 1830 and
1860 (Oblinger, 101–3). It was the same in Detroit at the hands of
native Americans and through the auspices of immigrants after
1880 (Katzman, 123; Broom and Glenn, 3). Less surprising was a
similar reaction among Southern workers. In 1847 whites struck
the Tredegar Iron Works in Richmond when blacks were hired in
the mills and furnace areas (Pessen, "Young Republic," 68). Still,
the Saluda textile firm in South Carolina employed ninety-eight
slave workers, but white artisans in the South continued to resist
black participation despite the fact that in cities like Charleston
blacks made up the vast majority of skilled workmen (J. H.
Franklin, 141–42; Frazier, 70, 74). So determined was the resistance
of white workers that the English visitor James William Massie
noted during an 1863 visit to the North that Irish immigrants
"habitually dread the freedom of the Negro, lest he should
become a competitor in the labour market" (Massie, 66, 308).
Added to this on on-the-job prejudice was the virtual segregation
of blacks in the North before 1860. Hotels, schools, steamboats,
railways, and churches kept blacks apart, while racial hostility
was augmented by taunts and epithets that characterized northern
blacks as inferior. To all of this, race riots made life even more
intolerable both for physical attacks and the destruction of black
property. Often, as in the five major riots in Philadelphia between
1832 and 1849, job bias was at the root of the violence. This was
also true of the Columbia, Pennsylvania attack of 1834, although
the Newark riot of 1834 and its counterparts in Pittsburgh in 1834
and Christiana in 1903 seemed to stem from other causes (Litwack, 100–2; Hirsch, 38, L. Baldwin, 305; Roger Lane, 51).

The ability of the blacks to have these grievances remedied in
the North was severely hampered by the limited opportunity to
vote before the passage of the Fifteenth Amendment to the
Constitution in 1870. A British visitor in 1823, John M. Duncan,
noted the "subordination" of emancipated blacks in the North
(Litwack, 15–16), while Theodore Weld told his readers that
English prisoners ate better than Southern slaves, and for that
matter, even better than some paupers and workers (Genovese,
63, 58). But if the answer lay partially in the franchise, states like

Michigan gave only the most reluctant approval to amend their state constitution so blacks could vote. The narrow margin of 54,105 to 50,598 (Katzman, 35, 37) said it all. Clearly, the road to opportunity for blacks still had many waystations. Its progress would be severely limited by the prejudice of white workers, a widespread racism that perceived blacks as inferior, and the legacy of two centuries of slavery that did not prepare freedmen for the world of scientific management.

For white workers, on the other hand, the new industrial regime emerging in the 1820s demanded an "inner discipline" and a new set of work parameters that reduced the independence inherent in their traditional craft status. As part of the new industrial society they owed obedience to their superiors, but were still expected to retain an allegiance to the old virtues of self-reliance, sobriety, and steadfastness. If this was becoming more typical of the Lynn shoemakers (Faler, "1826–1860," 367–68) who labored as outworkers or under masters in ten-footer shacks (Cumbler, *Two Industrial Cities*, 16), it also was a formula well-suited to the first integrated and mechanized American factory that opened in Waltham in 1815. Here standardized output, labor specialization, time-discipline, cost accounting, and the use of machines instead of hand tools set the tone for the larger enterprises that were to follow. Similarly, in the Manayunk area of Philadelphia the independence of the old artisan was lost in the shift to wage labor by the late 1820s. Along with it went his cherished role as a producer, although the republican ideal of an egalitarian world of small producers remained alive. Against even the reality of the transition from artisan to hired hand, some continued to believe Thomas Paine's view that they had "property in [their] own labor" (Shelton, 2–3; Roediger, 43–45).

Somehow the traditional idea of independence continued to linger to the 1850s, if not beyond. Many artisans were still engaged in outwork where they owned their own tools and workplace. In Newark, for example, at least one-third of the jewelers, leatherworkers, and trunkmakers operated in small shops as late as 1840 (Hirsch, 79), while in the factories of the upper Connecticut River valley between 1800 and 1850 the imprecise preindustrial work day could only be replaced by a modern time-discipline in gradual stages. During the 1830s, however, the traditional practice of leaving factory work to harvest crops came under attack by employers in Massachusetts and Connecticut. Workers prized the independence they could retain by having a farm to fall back on in the event of industrial declines (Zonderman, 262–63), but it was a system that could not be maintained in a modern factory setting. By 1841 regular hours were established at the Springfield armory (Brody, *In Labor's Cause*, 26), while the emergence of firms such as the New York Bread Company signalled masters and journeymen alike that dreams of independence were a vanishing vision (Rock, 325). By the 1850s assembly lines could be found in the clock and arms industries, and within the next decade the production of interchangeable parts had become a reality (Zonderman, 9–10; Victor Clark, *Manufactures*, 1:450; Gordon, Edwards, and Reich, 58; Nye, 268; Cochran, *Frontiers of Change*, 97).

Nevertheless, the size and scope of industrial growth to 1860 should not be overstated. While the workforce engaged in non-agricultural pursuits increased from 28% to 41% between 1820 and 1860, and the number of textile spindles reached 100,000 by 1860 (Dublin, *Women*, 5; Victor Clark, *Manufactures*, 1:453), factory growth was more gradual elsewhere except for carpets and the anthracite furnaces and rolling mills of eastern Pennsylvania and western New Jersey (Bruchey, *Enterprise*, 151). Household manufacture did succumb to workshop and factory production, but there was a very uneven transition from shops and mills to large industrial facilities. Philadelphia textile manufacturers, for example, used a combination of traditional artisans, outworkers, and factory employees, while after 1820 the Newark workforce moved through a series of steps from artisanal to shop labor (Bender, 29; Brody, *Labor's Cause*, 23–24). Chandler also noted the uneven develpment of industrialization except in metallurgy and textiles. Some masters simply added more craftsmen to expand production. Shoe and clothing manufacturers, on the other hand, often continued the traditional putting-out system, while other manufacturers used "simple machinery" run by water power prior to the 1840s. In short, there existed an overlapping of old and new work settings that included sweatshops, manufactories, outworking, artisanal shops, and factories (Chandler, *Visible Hand*, 51–53, 76; Laurie and Schmitz, 49–50, 53).

But within this uneven trend toward large businesses there was a growing chorus of praise for factory mechanization during the first half of the nineteenth century. Diverse sources as Moses Brown in 1809, Daniel Webster in an 1838 Senate speech, and a supportive pamphlet in 1855 from the Connecticut State Agricultural Society (Victor Clark, *Manufactures*, 1:432; Siragusa, 70; Prude, 105) added to the acclaim for manufacturing. But for the traditional craftsman it often had negative socioeconomic consequences. Charles Cist, a Cincinnati census taker of 1841 noted the disappearing "workshop of the mechanic," while regimented work in new industries like pork-packing made older artisans wary (Ross, 33–35). Many Philadelphia workers in the 1820s and 1830s were caught in the transition from small-scale operations to larger workshops and factories whose output often depended on distant demand. And as Newark industries moved from the artisanal stage to an industrial level, task simplification, systemization, and mechanization made many craft skills superfluous. As elsewhere, the Newark experience differed by industry, but by 1860 the number of artisans employed in eight crafts studied by Hirsch had dwindled to 38% from 52% in 1826 (Warner, 68; Hirsch, 37, xix). Added to this economic injury was a declining social approval for manual workers. Craftsmen who formerly earned respect by their skill were derided by the *Voice of Industry* in 1848 which advised them to walk in the gutter and live in separate sections of the city (Rorabaugh, *Craft Apprentice*, 134). Nor did the growing number of factory workers enjoy an increasing share of the wealth their industrial labor helped create. While the top 10 percent of American families owned half the country's wealth in 1820, they controlled 60 percent forty years later (Henretta and Nobles, 213). By then American manufacturing had expanded to the third rank among industrial nations (Bruchey, *Enterprise*, 151–52), a point of small consolation to an industrial workforce whose position would soon be diminished by deskilled work and scientific management.

Not surprising in the light of these developments is the emergence of the collective values inherent in unionization. While the first modern union emerged among Philadelphia shoemakers in 1794, isolated job actions could be found as early as 1768. Strikes in Philadelphia (1806) and New York (1810) were defeated by hard times and convictions (Sellers, 25), but by the 1820s new work stoppages occurred in Pawtucket and South Village, Massachusetts in response to wage reductions for status-conscious skilled weavers (Prude, 141–42). In 1830 Lynn, Massachusetts saw the formation of its first union. Walkouts followed in 1835, the 1840s, and culminated in the Great Strike of 1860 which ended any semblance of worker independence in the new world of mechanization and steam power (Brody, *In Labor's Cause*, 20–21). Philadelphia was no different. Between 1830 and 1860 sixty-one trades went on strike because they were losing control over hours and wages and suffering a loss of social status as artisans (Warner, 71–73; Wallace, *Rockdale*, 355–56). Labor unrest was also high in Pittsburgh where workmen imported from England brought strong union traditions with them. Tension continued between 1840 and 1860 in response to wage-cuts and a failure to offer a ten-hour working day in 1848 (Victor Clark, *Manufactures*, 2:87–88; Baldwin, 223–28). A similar story played out in New York City where an unsuccessful 1850 strike was accompanied by violence and anticapitalist thinking (Wilentz, 378, 380–81, 387).

But for the ambitious middle class these issues were of little concern. They continued to wear the nineteenth-century mantle of hard work, and looked for progress and prosperity in a nation where all things seemed possible. The sociologist Henrik Ruitenbeek felt that support for arduous labor had gained strength as people increasingly "internalized the commands and sanctions of the Protestant Ethic." In this temple of middle class values all had to toil so they could "lay up treasure on earth" to prove their worthiness for "admission to heaven" (Ruitenbeek, 48). Nineteenth-century businessmen often massaged their souls with the belief that diligence in the pursuit of profit was a godly mission (W. H. Whyte, *Organization Man*, 16), while their managers sought routinized performance from a labor force that had been conditioned for two centuries to accept "an *internalized* work ethic" (Bendix, 204). Christopher Lasch saw the sanctification of work as a calling that had mellowed into an eighteenth century "Yankee ethic" centered on self-improvement. This outlook approved of work to acquire wealth for its own sake as a precondition of moral and intellectual improvement. But by the nineteenth century this belief had been replaced by a "cult of compulsive industry" devoted to success as an end itself (Lasch, *Narcissism*, 111–14). Gutman, however, observed continual resistance to the work ethic as "deeply ingrained in the nation's social fabric," while Bernstein and Rodgers claimed that devotion to strenuous labor in the nineteenth century was the province of self-employed and high-discretion workers (Gutman, *Work, Culture, and Society*, 4; P. Bernstein, "Work Ethic," 19–24; Rodgers, *Work Ethic*, xi–xiii). For Rodgers, the work ethic was confined to the "simple but dynamic world that intervened between the manors and the factories, the distinctive credo of preindustrial capitalism" (Rodgers, *Work Ethic*, xi). But this failed to explain why a 1969 survey found 79 percent of noncollege youth continued to believe that "hard work always pays off" (Yankelovich, *New Morality*, 26, 30–31, 60). It also did not account for the new non-theological motivators that emerged during the three decades after the tumultuous Sixties, inducements that centered on the nature of the work, the ability to develop new skills, open communication, and the relationship of work and family life (Shellenbarger, "Work-Force Study," B1). These strongly suggested that what was really operative outside the time parameters delineated by Rodgers would be better described as a "worth ethic" rather than a work ethic.

Long before this late-twentieth-century trend, however, hard work had received the endorsement of a continuing stream of writers, workers, businessmen, and politicians. This adulation spanned the period from the Era of Good Feeling to the mid-1990s, and included such apologists of diligence as Ralph Waldo Emerson and Charles W. Eliot, President of Harvard. But even among the early mechanics of Baltimore many saw themselves as bulwarks against idleness and the luxury-loving lifestyle of the merchant (Steffen, 85–86). Hard work in a calling received the endorsement of Massachusetts Governor Samuel Adams in 1795 and a quarter century later John Brooks argued that toil improved character, cleared the wilderness, and helped build factories. In 1832 Congressman John Davis added to the clamor by observing that the American worker could best improve his lot by diligent labor. Horace Mann agreed and offered the thought that "we are an industrious and frugal people" (Siragusa, 84), while Samuel Slater wanted only "industrious" people in his mills (Prude, 80). Edward Everett continued the Massachusetts chorus in favor of dedicated labor by claiming that "nature is so ordered, as both to require and encourage men to work" so they can satisfy their material wants. Senator Chaote went beyond this in 1844 when he declared that "labor is the condition—I will not say of our greatness, but—of our being" (Siragusa, 84–85). The Boston railroad magnate John Murray Forbes instructed the guardians of his children to have them brought up in a circle of families that prized labor above luxury (Doerflinger and Rivlin, 66).

That this admonition to labor steadfastly was taken seriously by others can be seen in the concern over excessive labor expressed by Reverend John S. C. Abbott in *Parent's Magazine* of March, 1842. Too many fathers, he felt, were so "eager in the pursuit of business" that they toiled "early and late" and found little time for their children (Cochran, *Business in American Life*, 89). But in an 1844 sermon another minister, Henry Ward Beecher, extolled industry—"plain, rugged, brown-faced, homely clad" and "old fashioned" (Beecher, 28). There is little doubt that the Lynn businessman Benjamin Franklin Newhall imbibed this ratification of labor when he wrote his mother "work I must, and work I would" (Dawley, 34–35). But for those in Lynn who chose not to work, the town fathers resolved to make their time in the poor house a hell on earth. As in England, they drew a distinction between the deserving poor and loafers and were determined to force the lazy to labor out of fear (Faler, *Mechanics and Manufacturers*, 111–13).

Early labor leaders like William Heighton of Philadelphia also urged his fellow artisans to accept hard work and avoid "gaming and frolicking." That industry was prized by many workers can be seen in early-nineteenth-century Pittsburgh where clerks were often on the job at 5 a.m., and many carpenters and bricklayers were heavily engaged an hour later (Pessen, "Young Republic," 71; Baldwin, 268–70). A visiting group of Britons who reported on the New York Exhibition of 1853 praised American workers for their diligence, "regular attendance," and desire to learn new skills (Sawyer, "American System," 378). James Burn, an English hatter who worked in the United States during the Civil War, returned home because of the rigorous pace of work by Americans. He saw Americans as "fireaters" who had "ravenous appetites for labour." One worker even wrote to the Massachusetts

Bureau of Statistics of Labor in 1879 that "hard, untiring labor is necessary for the prosperity and well-being of our country" (Rodgers, *Work Ethic*, 161, 168), and the mill girl-writer Lucy Larcom confided that "surely there must be work to do in heaven since work is the best thing on earth we know" (Larcom, *Poetical Works*, 313). Sarah Hale, a writer of short stories, took a similar tack in her 1838 *Sketches of American Character*: leisure was wasted time because there was so much work to be done (W. R. Taylor, *Cavalier and Yankee*, 136).

Similar messages continued to pour forth during the last half of the nineteenth century. In 1856 Timothy Shay Arthur advanced a log cabin theory that "the most prominent and efficient men are not those who were born to wealth" but those who achieved it by "untiring personal energy" (F. Hunt, 350–51). In the McGuffey reader tale of 1857 entitled "Where There is a Will There is a Way," the hero is praised for his industry and initiative (Minnich, 124), while the Horatio Alger story of *Tom Turner's Legacy* (1890) stressed pride in work and success (Alger, *Tom Turner*, 177). Emerson added his support for labor by noting that "property rushes from the idle and imbecile to the industrious, brave, and persevering" (Rischin, 41). To which Longfellow noted in his "Ladder of St. Augustine" that great men did not reach their goals with "sudden flight," but "while their companions slept, were toiling upward in the night" (Longfellow, *Poetical Works*, 238). In his poem on "Work," Lowell attacked those who "stand with arms akimbo," and went on to say that "no man is born into the world whose work is not born with him" (Morris, *American Worker*, 145). Yet another literary light, William M. Thayer, pressed his readers to accept hard labor, for the importance of character included "industry, perseverance, and patience" (Thayer, *Ethics of Success*, 17).

Arguments on behalf of diligent labor also emanated from such diverse press sources as the business journalist Matthew Hale Smith and an 1886 Durham, North Carolina newspaper which claimed that in Durham "everybody works" and "everybody is busy" (M. H. Smith, 541; J. D. Hall et al., 24). Russell Sage, writing for Hearst press in 1903, praised work as "the strongest habit that I have and the only habit that I would find impossible to break" (Wyllie, 43). To which the self-help publicist Marden added that the greatest genius "is the genius for downright hard work, persistent drudgery" (Marden, 27). Not to be shy Horace G. Burt, President of the Union Pacific Railroad, argued that getting ahead, a key message of the time, was a combination of "application" and persistent labor (Rodgers, *Work Ethic*, 37). Elbert Hubbard's *A Message to Garcia* (1899) followed a slightly different path by emphasizing the importance of self-discipline, of getting the job done without supervision (Hubbard, 9–16). And by 1908 the banker Henry Clews saw America as a land of opportunity for those who combined ability with effort (Clews, 559).

Added to these many voices on behalf of energetic effort were the endorsements of William Graham Sumner and the Populist Party platform of 1892. Support for diligence also came from the socialist leader John Spargo and Henry George (Rodgers, *Work Ethic*, 211–12, 215), but the reformer John Gregory drew a distinction between those who wanted to work and those who fled from it. In lines reminiscent of both Elizabethan and late twentieth century concerns on this matter, Gregory argued in the 10 November 1887 issue of *The Independent* that society had a responsibility only to those who really sought a job (Yellowitz, 33). Andrew Carnegie recommended that vagabonds and idlers be placed in state-sponsored workhouses for they were no more than "social lepers" who might infect others (Carnegie, *Gospel of Wealth*, 63). This thought was shared by many in late nineteenth century America who believed that poverty was the result of laziness. Hard work was the road to success and independence, and for all who were healthy, society offered the "prescription" of industriousness (Wright and Fowler, 102).

Endorsements of hard work as a societal good continued to flow from all ranks of society through the twenties. Henry Ford saw work as the only road to salvation, and offered his five dollar a day wage in 1914 to give workers an "opportunity to do better" (Jardim, 181; Marquis, 152–53). Coolidge, on the other hand, believed success was directly related to "the amount of hard work put into it" (Coolidge, 171). The Cincinnati minister Frank Stevenson even suggested that work was the key ingredient "to make us satisfied with life" (Stevenson, *Gospel of Work*, 8), while mill worker Mary Thompson reflected: "It's just in the Bible that people is [sic] supposed to make their living by the sweat of their brow." And while not all her co-workers agreed (J. D. Hall et al., 124–25), many rural migrants to the Carolina mill towns of the twenties shared her perspective (I. Bernstein, *Turbulent Years*, 6–7). In their *Middletown* study during the mid-twenties, the Lynds found that work was valued more for its "instrumental aspect" rather than any "intrinsic satisfaction." This is what kept the town "working so hard" (Lynd and Lynd, 73, 80–81). Yet some inner pleasure must have been drawn from hard work by the industrious Italian immigrants depicted by Ignazio Silone in the thirties when they boasted of "the industry of us Italians" whose labor "founded towns and cities" (Silone, 214).

More typical was the great stress on work by A. C. Bedford, a prominent Standard Oil executive of the twenties. He told employees that work was more important than love, learning, religion, and patriotism, for none of these could exist without toil. "Industry," he stated, "is the fundamental basis of civilization" and its "high office" was to "train men to productive effort." The manufacturer H. C. Atkins (1926) strongly opposed the five day week for fear it would elevate leisure above work, a view shared a year later by National Association of Manufacturer's President John E. Edgerton (Prothro, 67, 6–8).

Even in the early days of the Great Depression (August 1930) when work was virtually unobtainable Henry Ford made the same point (Ford and Crowther, 19). By 1932 when unemployment was close to its nadir Ford saw it as little more than leisure on a mass scale (Mowry, 69), while investment counselor Roger Babson concluded that hard work was "coming back into vogue" (A. Shaw, 25). By March of 1933 unemployment peaked at almost 25 percent of the labor force. Thereafter, the volume of praise for work declined even as its availability disappeared. Only the onset of World War II wiped out the last remnant of pre-war unemployment, and by 1948 Norman Vincent Peale could advise his readers to "give your job your best; work hard, slight nothing" (Peale, *Confident Living*, 69). A decade later Galbraith concluded that "older attitudes" make us "gravely suspicious" of those who "expend less than the maximum effort" (Galbraith, *Affluent Society*, 336). And a Yankelovich survey of youth in 1969 suggested that such values were still in vogue when it showed that 79 percent of the noncollege respondents agreed with the idea that "hard work always pays off." Yet by 1973 he found that only 56 percent clung to that view. Among collegiate youth the numbers were less affirmative (Yankelovich, *New Morality*, 26, 30–31, 60).

In addition to the powerful influence of the Sixties, other voices began to question the ancient acceptance of hard work as an unmitigated good. E. F. Schumacher (1977) called for "good work" rather than hard work, and advocated "work that ennobles the product as it ennobles the producer" (Schumacher, 63). Shortly after, the psychologist Mara Spiegel questioned the age-old dedication to diligence, since many who followed this formula did not see their best efforts rewarded with the brass ring of success (*World of Work Report* 3. 9 [September, 1978]: 76). And sociologist Bennett Berger believed that work had lost "much of its moral content" and had become just a job (Bennett Berger, 29). Arnold Deutsch saw the deemphasis on work as the end of its status as a "quasi-religion." Those who approached it with the old fervor, he argued in 1979, would be viewed as little more than workaholics. "Never before," Deutsch noted, "have so many asked so much for doing so little" (Deutsch, 57).

The important Yankelovich and Immerwahr survey of 1983 added substance to these statements. It found that only 25% of American workers delivered their best efforts at work, yet 52% professed an "inner need" to do their best. And 62% said people "do not work as hard today as they did five or ten years ago" (Yankelovich and Immerwahr, 21, 27, 19). Clearly new motivators were at work. By the Nineties talk of labor for heavenly reward or as a sure route to success had faded away. Respondents to the 1993 "National Study of the Changing Workforce" now spoke of very different work values such as open communicaton, the relation of work to family life, and the nature of the job. The concept of hard work as a good in itself or as a character-building device was gone. More important was the content of work and a desire to master new skills (Shellenbarger, "Work-Force Study," B1). For the nineties empowerment at work seemed to be the new frontier of opportunity, but this was questioned by Lasch who saw a society that commended getting ahead and devalued the traditional goals of "competence, energy, and devotion" (Lasch, *Elites*, 78–79).

The emphasis on hard work that characterized the work values of most Americans after 1815 flowed from beliefs tinged with optimism and replete with notions of opportunity and individualism. Rapid industrialization, construction of a vast canal and rail complex, and the first telegraph and telephone systems fed this American commitment to the idea of progress. It was an outlook that gained strength from the emergence of a public school system and a westward expansion that pushed America to the shores of the Pacific. While this motivation to accomplish was partially generated by the optimism of the the Era of Good Feeling, the idea of progress was given further impetus by a national fervor that led many Americans to see the superiority of the new world over the old, and to view their future through the prism of the Monroe Doctrine and the cult of Manifest Destiny. In short, there was faith that American democracy was an beacon to the world (Ekirch, 34–37, 73, 134).

This idea of a progressive America was strengthened by the leverage of a fluid social structure. A visiting group from Britain in 1853 noted the absence of class and craft lines, and saw possibilities of upward elevation that were less likely to occur at home (Sawyer, "American System," 376–77). The American Revolution, of course, had first begun the process of levelling class lines. Men like Nathaniel Greene and Roger Sherman were able to advance themselves from blacksmith and shoemaker to honored general and able political leader (Rorabaugh, *Craft Apprentice*, 23–24). In place of the old social rigidities, individualism and the "competitive pursuit of wealth" combined to foster a "market revolution." It led the entrepreneurial-minded Fourteenth Congress of December 1815 to see "equal rights as liberating the enterprise of free men to create a rich and powerful United States" (Sellers, 5, 70). The Baltimore editor Hezekiah Niles conveyed this spirit of progress when he exulted that "everywhere the sound of the axe is heard opening the forest to the sun. . . . [O]ur cities and towns rise up as by magic. . . . [T]he busy hum of ten thousand wheels fills our seaports" (ibid., 71). Progress seemed to loom in every vista, and many believed it was our Manifest Destiny to become a "transcontinental agricultural republic" that would include Texas, Mexico, Cuba, and Canada (Rorabaugh, *Craft Apprentice*, 57–58).

Foreign visitors were amazed at the intensity with which Americans approached work and business. They were both fascinated and appalled by the American dedication to get ahead, and were aghast over what appeared to be a crass effort at social mobility and money-making (Chevalier, 262, 267–68; Sawyer, "France," 11–14, 17-19; Grund, 202; De Tocqueville, 1:51; Lundén, 1; Marryat, 43; Trollope, 121). But Americans of the 1820s and 1830s believed getting rich was an attainable reality. It was conveyed in Albert Gallatin's exhortation that "the energy of this nation is not to be controlled; it is at present exclusively applied to the acquisition of wealth" (Cochran, *Business in American Life*, 61).

How then were these early-nineteenth-century values of progress, diligence, and enterprise reenforced so they became part of the popular culture? More than a small share of the credit could be traced to a widely read children's literature that created a context for the adulation of self-made men, and lent support for belief in opportunity and success. Leading the parade were the stories of Maria Edgeworth which were brought from England around 1796. This worthy successor to Franklin also published her famous *Parent's Assistant*, a volume so popular that new editions were still flowing from the presses a century later. In her "Idleness and Industry" Edgeworth demonstrated the virtues of the industrious boy over the lazy lad. To this important British influence on the work values of young Americans, Samuel Goodrich added the importance of earnest labor, duty, and responsbility. He also used his "I'd Be a Butterfly" (1833) to observe that "it is by industry and study alone, that men become great and esteemed." In 1838 the Congregationist minister, Jacob Abbott, wrote a guide for parents which was meant to be read by children. *Rollo at Work* stressed the value of diligence, perseverance, and the systematic work habits needed to succeed in adulthood. Exertion and self-denial completed a belief pattern (Rodgers, *Work Ethic*, 129–32) aimed primarily at the middle class (Cawelti, 104). A year later Reverend John Hersey offered his *Advice to Christian Parents* in which he urged children be taught the great value of time so they would "avoid the sluggard's bed." The minister Lyman Beecher sent out a similar success message in his *Addresses to Young Men* in 1849: diligence is the way of those who would do well (Cochran, *Business in American Life*, 90). Soon thereafter William T. Adams began to publish his Oliver Optic stories, a far more exciting series than the sermonettes of Edgeworth and Abbott. *The Boat Club* of 1854 was in the old tradition of character-building in which young men learned discipline under the eye of a benevolent father. But as Adams continued the series the boys won fame on their own. His 1866 book entitled *Work and Win* again pushed forward young heroes who were "industrious, useful, and reliable" (Rodgers, *Work Ethic*, 136–38).

Much more influential were the Horatio Alger stories. Unlike Abbott, Alger did not stress religiosity but wrote of poor boys who rose or fell on their own merits. His books urged youths to strive for success, for upward mobility was within the grasp of all (Cawelti, 104–6). In *Strive and Succeed* Alger showed how poor lads could become self-made men by effort and perseverance (Alger, *Strive and Succeed*, 68–69). To these virtues Alger added achievement (Alger, *Herbert Carter's Legacy*, 322). Beyond the influence of Alger and his colleagues was the impact of the elementary school literature which employed the well-known themes of hard work, material gain, and success (Elson, 246–48). But most influential were the long-lived and widely circulated McGuffey readers. These were printed in huge numbers from about 1836 to 1900, and offered millions of school children a formula for success through hard labor: "Work, work, my boy, be not afraid; Look labor boldly in the face" (Wyllie, 42). William Wirt, a former attorney-general, reenforced this theme in his McGuffey tract on "No Excellence Without Labor" (Minnich, 314), while the story "Industry a Treasury" extolled diligent effort over fortune-seeking (Lindberg, 105–6). Self-discipline, another recurrent message, was profiled in "The Poor Boy," a lad with no time to lose who efficiently coupled learning in school with labor at home. This control of time and self was the opportunity key that would unlock the vistas of a better life (ibid., 41–42).

Thrift, however, could not be ignored. In "Waste Not, Want Not," a story borrowed from Maria Edgeworth, the frugal boy won out. The McGuffey readers also pushed the lessons of perseverance and self-reliance in "Try, Try Again" and "The Lark and the Farmer" (Minnich, 107–10, 34). "Emulation," on the other hand, praised competition, and urged its readers to avoid the curse of envy (Lindberg, 162). Underlying the entire McGuffey message was the belief in opportunity. Everything seemed possible for those who strived to achieve. Low estate was but a temporary impediment (Nye, 12–13, 383), and all things were possible for people of good character. Even within the positive parameters of an optimistic age, making money in itself was not enough. The McGuffey readers also laid out a message that all had a responsibility to help the less fortunate, a key character ethic that weakened as the nineteenth century progressed. With sales that approached 120,000,000, these books reached about half the school children in nineteenth-century America (Huber, 23–25), and had an influence that cannot be underestimated.

In addition to the books devoted to the indoctrination of the young, a belief system that combined the concepts of opportunity, enterprise, and success ran like a thread through the writing of nineteenth-century opinion-makers. Early New England entre- preneurs like Samuel Slater, Moses Brown, Francis Lowell, and John Murray Forbes helped elevate enterprise to an honorable calling (Doerflinger and Rivlin, 88–89, 65–69; Victor Clark, *Manu- factures*, 1:451), while an anonymous writer of 1835 exulted that "the spirit of enterprise" turned the wilderness around Lowell "into a busy, enterprising and prosperous city" (Bender, 76). Not to be outdone, the editor Hezekiah Niles described his country- men as devoted to "the almost universal ambition to get forward" (Chevalier, x).

Craftsmen were not exempt from this desire. The successful New York sailmaker, Stephen Allen, was both entreprenueurial and competitive, and while few of his associates got rich, the spirit of the time whetted the appetites of many others (Rock, 152–53, 177; Bridenbaugh, *Colonial Craftsmen*, 165). Later in the nineteenth century technically-skilled machine builders in Newark, Paterson, and Lynn were able to rise above their former station. In Phila- delphia the hatter Charles Oakford succeeded in moving up, while the tailor Edward Fox and the cabinetmaker Henry Weil prospered in New York City.

This attachment to the idea of upward mobility remained quite strong in the Philadelphia of 1860. Here some 3,600 "artisan shops" collectively made up 58 percent of the city's industrial firms. It was a far cry from the probable 100 percent that existed two to three generations earlier (Blumin, 74–75), and suggested the overall position of artisans had worsened by 1860 despite the favorable entrepreneurial climate (N. Ware, 26). However, in both Philadelphia and Poughkeepsie there was a "modest mobility" between manual and nonmanual areas. Gottlieb Vollmer of Phila-delphia, a former cabinet maker, had become a prosperous manu-facturer by the early 1860s (Blumin, 121, 70). In nearby Rockdale, cotton mill operatives could become carders or boss-weavers (Wallace, *Rockdale*, 386–87), and master-printer H. H. K. Elliott of Philadelphia told his associates to remember that many wealthy employers had started out as mechanics (Laurie, 358–59). Pough-keepsie artisans also enjoyed considerable upward mobility between 1850 and 1880 (Blumin, 120), while during the same period in Newburyport, Massachusetts improvement could be seen *within* the working class. Few got rich like Joseph Greenough and Stephen Fowle, but many who listened to the lectures of Russell Conwell did see enough improvement to be optimistic (Thernstrom, 114, 161–65, 213, 223). Late-nineteenth-century rail employees found ways to advance (Licht, 147, 49), as did black, Polish, and Italian immigrants who came to Pittsburgh around 1917 (Bodnar, Simon, and Weber, 35, 36, 42). For most employees, however, the concept of upward mobility was a dream of the middle class, a point under-scored by a study of industrial leaders of the 1870s which showed that only 8 percent had a working-class background (Gregory and Neu, 202).

For blacks during the century after Appomattox opportunity proved to be elusive. When Lincoln issued the Emancipation Proclamation in 1863 about 5 million blacks lived in the old union. Of these half a million were free. But when the Civil War ended blacks were ill-equipped to make their way. Despite the fact that the Thirteenth, Fourteenth, and Fifteenth Amendments to the Constitution gave them citizenship, many former slaves were not able to close the educational and economic gap. The meagre efforts of the Freedmen's Bureau did little to help ex-slaves make the transition to an industrial society. Blacks were also held back by two key court decisions: *Plessy v. Ferguson* (1896), which enshrined segregation by its "separate but equal" doctrine, and *Williams v. Mississippi* (1898), which took away their voting rights in that state. Lynchings were commonplace, and although they peaked during the 1880s and 1890s, caused blacks to live in fear (Broom and Glenn, 3, 5, 7). Race riots in the North also under-mined the black effort to live in freedom and improve their eco-nomic position. These had occurred in St. Paul, Cincinnati, and

Toledo during the Civil War, and were compounded by major attacks in Detroit in March 1863 by Irish workers who feared black job competition. Most ferocious were the New York City draft riots against blacks and abolitionists in July 1863. Similar attacks occurred in Brooklyn, Boston, Troy, and Buffalo (Katzman, 45). After the turn of the century additional riots occurred in Philadelphia, Springfield, Ohio, Greencastle, Indiana, and even in Lincoln's Springfield, Illinois in 1908 (J. H. Franklin, 314–19). By any measure this was not an environment of opportunity. Nevertheless, black leaders like Frederick Douglas and W. E. B. DuBois continued to press for equal rights, and by 1909 the middle-class-oriented NAACP emerged to push for better schools and improved pay in jobs open to blacks. But it was not until World War II that a black middle class began to emerge as part of an integrated workforce (Broom and Glenn, 46-48).

A closer look at how blacks fared in several Northern cities up to the 1930s suggests that while there were some upward openings the future was not blessed with opportunity. In Newark blacks were pushed out of the skilled crafts by white immigrants from Europe even before the Civil War (Hirsch, 37–38). Philadelphia presented black workers with a similar situation. British, Irish, and German workers who arrived in the 1840s and 1850s found a favorable haven, but in 1847 less than one-half of one percent of the city's blacks could find work despite Philadelphia's expanding steel, iron, and machine tool industries. Blacks were also driven from even unskilled jobs, denied apprenticeships, and prevented from practicing the skills many already had. It was a pattern that continued between 1850 and 1880 despite continuing economic expansion. Beyond this, differences in pay, status, and work environment helped the new German and Irish immigrants ascend the socioeconomic scale (Hershberg, Burstein, et al., 470, 473). To make matters worse the 1850 United States census showed that the number of blacks in such relatively high-paying jobs as hod carrier and stevedore had dropped from 5 percent of the workforce to only 1 percent (Hershberg, "Free Blacks," 375–76). And while some black entrepreneurs like Colonel John McKee, Reverend Joshua Eddy, William Still, and James Forten, Sr. did well in the city of Brotherly Love (Lane, 98, 101–5), there were few "bootstraps" for blacks who sought upward avenues (Hershberg,

Burstein, et al., 470). Even during the extremely rapid industrial expansion from 1865 to 1900 blacks could not break into the more lucrative newer occupations that included sheet metal workers, boilermakers, locomotive engineers, and streetcar conductors. In addition, blacks were kept out of most skilled and semi-skilled factory jobs, and by the mid-1890s 80 percent over the age of twenty-one worked as laborers or servants (Lane, 63, 71). Things did not improve between 1900 and 1930. As new white collar occupations became available in the professional and service areas, blacks ran into the barriers of outright discrimination, limited education, and language problems. By 1930, 43.4 percent of Philadelphia blacks were in domestic or personal service, but only 2.4 percent in professional occupations (Hershberg, Burstein, et al., 474–75; DuBois, 337–39).

The picture in Detroit before the 1930s was similar. Blacks had come to Detroit in the nineteenth century in search of economic opportunity and political freedom. But unlike the British Luddites and Chartists who sought the ballot in a class-oriented society that was less wedded to striving and success, blacks saw the opportunities of a relatively open frontier and the chance to make their influence felt. Men like D. Augustus Starker and Charles R. Roxborough tried to improve the political position of blacks, while Peter Cooper and George DeBaptiste emerged as two celebrated success stories (Katzman, 14–15). Despite this, most blacks living in the Detroit of 1860 were in personal service, unskilled labor, or semi-skilled jobs. They remained politically conscious even after winning the right to vote in 1870 (ibid., 31, 3–4), but endured severe attacks by Irish immigrants in March, 1863 who feared black job competition. As in Philadelphia, blacks were kept at the bottom of the economic ladder by the continuous stream of European immigrants who came between 1880 and 1920. And while blacks also came in large numbers between 1870 and 1900, their hopes were not realized. Even in the 1930s with the favorable climate of the New Deal and the emergence of a fairly friendly union in the CIO, blacks still had to contend with the fears of white workers who saw them as competitors in the market place.

Pittsburgh, on the other hand, presented a somewhat brighter picture for the many blacks who migrated north. Blacks sensed the possibilities of social improvement and occupational opportunity, and was no surprise that their numbers grew by 350 percent during the three decades between 1890 and 1920 (Bodnar, Simon, and Weber, 35–36, 30; Myrdal, 193–97). Between 1900 and 1930 both Southern-born and Northern-born Pittsburgh blacks did relatively well as almost one-third experienced some upward mobility. This reflected "high aspirations" and a "willingness to take risks" (Bodnar, Simon, and Weber, 140–41, 250).

Initially, Cleveland also appeared to present greater hope for blacks who migrated to the shore of Lake Erie. Blacks made up only 1.9% of the population in 1900, but with the Great Migration (1915–40) from the South, it rose to 4.3% in 1920 and 8.0% ten years later. As elsewhere, blacks found that even in the reasonably favorable climate of Cleveland they remained anchored in the Gehenna of the unskilled. There were, as elsewhere, success stories that typified what blacks might accomplish in a setting of open opportunity: George Peake became a sizable landowner and inventor, while Madison Tully emerged as a political leader and contractor who supervised an integrated workforce. Even in 1915 the black community in Cleveland could boast of a large number of professionals (especially lawyers) despite their small absolute numbers. Still, by 1910 opportunity in factory employment was declining for most blacks despite the vast economic expansion in Cleveland and elsewhere. Employers believed blacks were better suited to agriculture, and noted that they often lacked industrial skills. In addition, most AFL unions excluded blacks in practice even when their constitutions did not. And when blacks were finally hired in large numbers in the unskilled categories it was only because the economic demands during World War I made them an indispensable reserve army (Kusmer, 219, 10–11, 18–19, 81, 67–68).

Perhaps the most difficult problem facing blacks who sought a better life by leaving the South both before and during the Great Migration (Myrdal, 196–97) was the implacable opposition of unions. The AFL under Gompers concentrated on the improvement of wages and working conditions, and despite the leadership's position that all were welcome, most kept blacks at bay. In Philadelphia, a few blacks broke into the Typographers Union, and a much larger number were admitted by the cigarmakers, Gompers' own bastion. But the International Longshoremen's Association used force to stop black entry (DuBois, 228, 335). By 1900 only 30,000 blacks were union members, 10,000 of whom were craft members. In fact, 39 of the 82 AFL affiliates had no black members, and more than a few had charters excluding blacks. This sometimes forced blacks into the role of strikebreakers which led white workers to see them as tools of anti-union bosses. But testimony to the white fear of blacks as economic threats was Gompers' 1905 statement at Minneapolis that "Caucasians" would not let their living standards be dragged down by "negroes, Chinamen, Japs, or any others" (J. R. Green,*World of Worker*, 98). So bad did it get that in 1894 the *Christian Recorder*, the official paper of the African Methodist Episcopal Church, asked the British union leader John Burns for help in getting the white-only clauses removed from AFL constitutions (Lane, 69).

As bad as things were, the United Mine Workers proved to be an exception. Its leader, John Mitchell, welcomed blacks in large numbers and used them along with British and Irish organizers in the soft-coal fields of the South. But the 1917 AFL refused to pass resolutions against racial discrimination and denied that union leaders had any responsibility for the July 1917 race riots in East St. Louis, Illinois. Its resolution favoring the acceptance of black members was thus seen as meaningless by W. E. B. Dubois (J. R. Green, *World of Worker*, 51, 98).

To these problems was added the issue of respectability. Reuben Forker, a key Trenton, New Jersey labor leader, argued that unions wanted only "clean looking citizens" who were "respectable." In practice this meant blacks and Italian immigrants were to be excluded (Cumbler, *Trenton*, 37–43). The issue of respectablility also arose in Cleveland where blacks were blocked from entering craft unions. The Cleveland Paperhangers' Union made it clear they did not want close "personal contact" with black co-workers. This was echoed by the Parquet Floor Layers: not only would their white patrons object to black workmen, but union members would lose status (Kusmer, 69–70; 74).

But for black workers who survived shunning by those worried about respectability, the horrid years of the Great Depression offered some hope of future improvement. This came with the establishment of the CIO in 1936. Under men like John L. Lewis and Walter Reuther the CIO went beyond the AFL's emphasis on the organization of craft workers and began to build strong unions among the industrial workers in steel, autos, and rubber. They were willing to enlist blacks, and by 1940 the auto industry had 20,740 in its ranks. But this was done with muted enthusiasm because of the vigorous opposition of many white workers. The ILGWU (International Ladies' Garment Workers Union) also opened its doors, but since few blacks were employed in making women's clothes, it was of little help. Much more important was the black entry into the longshoremen's union so that by 1940 they made up 30 percent of the membership (J. H. Franklin, 399–401; Meier and Rudwick, 27–28). A further step forward came in 1941 when A. Philip Randolph, head of the Brotherhood of Sleeping Car Porters, threatened a march on Washington unless job discrimination in defense industries ceased. It led President Roosevelt to issue Executive Order 8802 which required that defense contracts contain nondiscrimination clauses. He also set up a Committee on Fair Employment Practices to monitor the working of the executive order, but while both actions provided a bit of help, they did little to quell the anger of white workers (Galenson, 57). As blacks continued to press against the prevailing bias in hiring and promotion, racial tensions exploded into the June 1943 Detroit race riots (Meier and Rudwick, 106–7, 109). In Philadelphia, the hiring of over 68,000 blacks by March 1944 introduced similar tensions. When eight blacks were actually hired as motormen trainees by the Philadelphia Transportation Company in August, 1944, a walkout of white workers occurred despite the CIO's support of the training program. Only by calling out the army was Roosevelt able to end the strike (Bontemps and Conroy, 311–13).

Despite these serious problems, black employment in defense industries grew from 3% to 8% between 1942 and 1944. And while even CIO unions in 1947 were reluctant to organize blacks in their Operation Dixie (J. R. Green, World of Worker, 193), some overall improvement in the economic status of minorities was evident: while only 8.5% of blacks were in white collar or skilled jobs in 1940, it had risen to 20% by 1960. This whetted the sense of what might be achieved. As two researchers put it: "Success is a companion to a discovery of the possible and an increase in aspiration" (Broom and Glenn, 105). The bell of opportunity rang again in May 1954 when the *Brown* decision outlawed segregated schools as "inherently unequal" (J. H. Franklin, 409). But despite the wide industrial and white collar experience blacks gained during the war years, blacks remained skeptical about unions. Their leadership continued to speak for civil rights and against bias on the job, but blacks continued to find a less than open door when they attempted to enter apprenticeship programs (A. Blum, 640). Blacks did move into some intermediate level positions vacated by whites who had moved into higher-level jobs, but they were still underrepresented in skilled positions and white-collar jobs. In addition, by 1959 blacks remained concentrated in lower-paying work, and black unemployment remained high (Broom and Glenn, 109–11, 113–16). Much more time and effort would need to be expended before blacks would view America as an opportunity society. And in this quest during the 1970s and 1980s they would continue to find some unions among their most determined opponents before the Supreme Court.

For white Americans upward mobility in both the nineteenth and twentieth cenutries held more hopeful prospects. The Lancaster, Pennsylvania *Examiner and Herald* of 1835 found "want of enterprise" was "as strange as it is unnatural" (Henretta, "Study of Social Mobility," 171). Henry Barnard, the eminent educator, wrote a catechism for working class children urging thrift as the way to accumulate enough capital to insure success (Diamond, *American Businessman*, 140), but never explained how this could be done on the meager wages paid their parents. Nevertheless, the chance to move up was heralded by Emerson who urged that the "doors of opportunity" should be opened "to talent and virtue," a message strongly endorsed by Russell Conwell over 6,000 times in his "Acres of Diamonds" speech between 1870 and 1920 (Rischin, 41; Conwell, *Diamonds*, 2, 17; Conwell, *New Day*, 9). Phineas Barnum, John D. Rockefeller, and Henry Clews also portrayed an America of boundless opportunity (Barnum, *Money-Getting*, 7; Rockefeller, 368–72; Clews, 1001, 1004). This message was repeated during the twenties by Julius Barnes, president of the U.S. Chamber of Commerce (Prothro, 26), and was reenforced by the *Charlotte Observer* on 24 May 1937 in connection with the death of Rockefeller (Diamond, *American Businessman*, 140, 129). In 1940, however, James B. Conant, president of Harvard, put a new twist on the opportunity ethic. He urged that the public school system offered the best vehicle for moving up in the world, and believed "social mobility through education" was the American way to achieve a "classless society" (Conant, 600, 602, 598). Some three decades later Nixon used his Labor Day address of 1971 to address the issue of upward mobility. In it he praised American workers for making the country a "citadel of individual freedom and of opportunity" (*New York Times*, 7 September 1971, 14).

Opportunity, of course, was clearly evident in the era of enterprise that followed. It could be seen in the efforts of Ray Kroc at McDonalds and Sam Walton of Wal Mart. In areas of high technology Bill Gates of Microsoft and Andrew Grove at Intel used their ability to both enrich themselves and create jobs for thousands of talented people. Opportunity also was seized by entrepreneurs in health care (Columbia/HCA Healthcare), bio-technology (Chiron), computer communications (Cisco Systems) and fast food (Boston Chicken) (Serwer, 42–59). Companies such as Xerox created "skunk works" within their bureaucratic struc-ture so that their scientific personnel would be free to experiment and develop new ideas. It offered opportunity *within* the cor-poration, and enabled employees who were not able to take the financial and psychological risk of entrepreneurship a chance to grow in work. For those with drive and education America continued to be an open frontier.

Implicit in the themes of progress, opportunity, and enter-prise was the American aspiration for success. Two centuries of commercial enterprise and the existence of a secularized work ethic already had created a climate favorable to the idea of self-improvement. Franklin's maxims and Emerson's ideas on self-reliance lent additional prestige to the older concept of success. But during the last three decades of the nineteenth century com-petition, initiative, and aggressiveness took precedence over the traditional success virtues of work, thrift, and honesty. The old balance between economic and moral values had been weakened, and for a growing number the quest for wealth became the watch-word of the Gilded Age. Industrialization, secularism, and a scientfic world view offered a platform for the success virtues of tough competition, inititative, and even aggressiveness. Beyond this, self-help emerged as a prominent theme, and lingered into the twentieth century as an inspirational force. Added to this amalgam was the belief of some clergymen who equated the successful with the blessed, and led ministers like William Lawrence to proclaim that "Godliness was in league with riches." A half century later Norman Vincent Peale departed from the traditional Protestant emphasis on piety and work and offered his many readers a religious rationale for success (Cawelti, 4–6, 168– 169; Bruchey, *Roots*, 195; P. Miller, *American Puritans*, 172; W. Lawrence, 287).

Those who rationalized the drive for success often argued that initiative and hard work not only enriched the enterprising but created opportunities for the unemployed. They believed in the reality of success, and felt the door was open to all who wanted to get ahead. Failure was clearly a matter of character (Cawelti, 173). Many like Robert Winthrop in 1856 upheld Franklin as the personification of "triumphant success," and a few years later Thayer saw Franklin's "energy, industry, integrity, and perseverance" as appropriate guidelines for the nation's youth (Wyllie, 14; Thayer, *Printer Boy*, 256,). For Emerson, the successful man made things happen. He was orderly, timely, and could plan for the future (Cawelti, 88). The politician Lewis Cass equated success with the desire to "acquire riches, or honor, or power" (Rogin, 207), while Nicholas Biddle described Stephen Girard as a man who did well because of his "industry, exertions, and enterprise" (Diamond, *American Businessman*, 7). Beyond this, the McGuffey readers urged perseverance as a success formula in "Try, Try, Again" (Minnich, 110). Within this desire to move up there was a widespread public "passion for acquisition," a theme underscored by Pastor William Ellery Channing in 1842. This may have inspired Moses Yale Beach to satisfy the enormous interest in success and the successful by publishing a directory of New Yorkers worth $100,000. By 1845 a similar compendium came off the press for Philadelphians (Baida, 78-79). Clearly, the desire to do well struck a responsive chord, and success remained a goal that continued to entice the many even as it remained within the grasp of the few.

Some nineteenth-century supporters of success saw its highest realization as achievement in commerce. Under the title "Success in Life," an 1853 edition of *Harper's New Monthly Magazine* urged parents to instill the idea of "getting on" in their children. Success, in this sense, meant doing well in business, and men of affairs became models for the young (Bruchey, *Enterprise*, 195; Wyllie, 9). By 1867 Horace Greeley was speaking to capacity audiences in New York City as he delivered his message on *Success in Business* (Wyllie, 122). Two decades later Andrew Carnegie noted that the success of the few was "essential for the future progress of the race." Such advancement was but "a simple matter of honest work, ability, and concentration" (Carnegie, "Wealth," 659; Carnegie, "Business," 205). The journalist Edward Bok told young men that the route to the top in business was carrying out the wishes of the boss. If this was coupled with the example of successful men plus hard work, promotion was sure to follow (Bok, "Young Man," 731; Bok, *Success*, 100). Benjamin Wood elaborated on this advice by urging aspiring businessmen to do thoroughly "what others do indifferently" (Wood, *Successful Man*, 59), while Horatio Alger repeated his now-familiar theme that striving would enable boys to replace poverty with wealth (Alger, *Strive and Succeed*, 68).

Beyond the emphasis on hard work, perseverance, and character (Owen, 160; Wyllie, 45; Ruoff, 200), the late-nineteenth-century advocates of success added a Darwinian potion to the old mix. William Graham Sumner saw poverty as part of a struggle for existence. In this context, only strenuous effort offered opportunity. To Sumner, centuries of evolution had demonstrated the relationship of progress and economic success (Keller and Davie, 1:109; Hofstadter, *Social Darwinism*, 60–61). In this impersonal arena, every individual had to work out "his personal destiny" amidst a struggle in which only the strongest would endure (Sumner, 34–35). Herbert Spencer offered similar advice to businessmen of the Gilded Age to which Nicholas Murray Butler of Columbia University added that "nature's cure for most social and political diseases is better than man's" (Trachtenberg, 81). Popular Darwinists like John Fiske even saw "evolution as God's benevolent plan for human progress" (Cawelti, 173), while C. R. Henderson suggested that "competitive commercial life is not a flowery bed of ease, but a battlefield where the 'struggle for existence' is defining the industrially 'fittest to survive'" (Henderson, *Theorists*, 385). Both Elbert Hubbard and Andrew Carnegie added their voices to the Darwinian choir (Hubbard, 14; Carnegie, "Wealth," 655–66) in the belief that only the free play of economic forces would ensure success.

Those who rhapsodized on behalf of success in nineteenth century America repeatedly pointed to the model of the self-made man. Henry Clay probably first used the term in an 1832 speech in the U.S. Senate, and left his countrymen a model of success that was repeatedly recommended throughout the nineteenth century. Those who lauded the self-made man believed the key to success lay within each person. Everyone was in charge of their own destiny, and could succeed if they worked diligently. Ministers like Henry Ward Beecher saw self-help as the cure for poverty, (Mallory, 2:31; Cawelti, 52–53; Bruchey, *Enterprise*, 195), and Franklin, Girard, Astor, and Vanderbilt were held up as models for the multitude. All could move up in America, argued the Whig politician Robert Winthrop, even those who worked in mill or farm (Siragusa, 94). It was an optimistic creed by those who were willing to sacrifice in the present and live for the future, a belief system that endorsed patience, thrift, and discipline as conditioners of the new American hero.

All of this thrived in the optimistic atmosphere of America's vast nineteenth century industrial expansion. Employment in cotton goods doubled between 1840 and 1870, while those working on the mushrooming railroad system saw their numbers grow from a few thousand to 154,000 during the same period. In addition, the number working in the boot and shoe industry expanded by 500%, and when added to a vast urbanization between 1860 and 1910, depicted a rapidly expanding economy (Gordon, Edwards, and Reich, 80; Briggs, *Victorian Cities*, 74; Bendix, 254–255). And, at least until the nineties, the western frontier offered some opportunity to both immigrants and those who found meager offerings elsewhere.

Given this scenario of optimism and a belief in progress, it was easy to understand the continuous emphasis on success by dint of personal achievement. Newspapers, books, interviews, speeches, and literature abounded with praise for the successful who had made it their own (Bruchey, *Roots*, 196). The emergence of some sixty millionaires by 1840 lent credence to the belief that upward mobility was the province of those who relied on their own efforts, and the successes of Robert Oliver, Stephen Girard, and John Jacob Astor offered visible "proof" that all could climb the mountain (Bruchey, *Enterprise*, 147; Sellers, 238–39). Samuel

Slater and his associates in western Massachusetts and Benjamin Franklin Newhall in Lynn were lesser known but additional proofs that self-made men were a reality (Prude, 62–63, 60; Dawley, 33, 37) In fact, C. Wright Mills noted that 43 percent of business leaders born between 1820 and 1849 had fathers whose origins were "lower" or "lower middle class" (Mills, "American Business Elite," 20–44).

If early examples like Andrew Jackson (Ward, 168, 258) were not sufficient, self-made men continued to be extolled in the literature of the 1850s by Timothy Arthur, Charles Seymour, and Calvin Colton (Wyllie, 19; Cawelti, page facing title page). The novels of Mrs. E. Southworth in the 1860s and James McCabe's 1871 volume on self-made men continued to laud those who demonstrated that in an open society people of talent could rise to the top (Cawelti, 127–28, 41). More interesting was how many Paterson, New Jersey employees who "started their careers as workers" were able to elevate themselves between 1830 and 1880 (Gutman, *Work Culture, and Society*, 220–21). In a speech to graduates of a business college in 1869 James Garfield sent out the same success message, and was himself dubbed a self-made man by Rutherford Hayes (Garfield, 13–14; T. H. Williams, 278). Needless to say many of the Horatio Alger stories urged that success could be achieved by self-help (Alger, *Jed*, 50), while at the turn of the century George Lorimer and Edward Bok suggested the scenario of self-sacrifice and hard work (Cawelti, 176–77; Bok, *Success*, 100).

But after the turn of the century the cult of the self-made man went the way of a once-beckoning frontier and a pre-industrial America that had offered a reasonable hope of advancement. By 1922 the businessman Bruce Barton showed a clear preference for educated managers rather than untutored individuals who rose from the ranks (Wyllie, 168–69). Nevertheless, distant echoes of the old ideal lingered. Even in the early thirties businessmen continued to believe that even "average" men could pull themselves up if they worked hard (Taussig and Joslyn, 299–300), but by December 1947 *Advertising Age* was still seeking a new Horatio Alger to inspire young Americans with the spirit of enterprise. Hope continued for the reemergence of self-made men as the American Schools and Colleges Association continued to offer Horatio Alger awards to such prominent businessmen as Benjamin Fairless of U.S. Steel (Cawelti, 101–2). Richard Nixon also played the theme of self-reliance as late as 1971 (*New York Times,* 7 September 1971, 14), while a 1980 Wall Street Journal/Gallup survey of 282 executives continued to reveal adherence to the belief in self-reliance as a way to the top (F. Allen, "Bosses," 33).

That much of this reflected the views of successful businessmen or their sympathetic publicists puts this reverence for self-made men in a context that excluded most industrial workers by the 1880s. If the promise of success was little more than a dull thud for the industrial helots who were expected to obey authority and provide the sinews for the brave new world of Taylorism, Russell Sage offered the ambitious middle and upper classes the traditional maxims for advancement in 1903: work hard and avoid liquor and loose women (Wyllie, 43, 47). To this Calvinistic offering, Rockefeller added the old theme of perseverance. The banker Henry Clews believed merit was "the supreme and only qualification essential to success" (Rockefeller, 369; Clews, 559), while Russell Conwell proclaimed that "it is your duty to get rich" (Conwell, *Diamonds,* 18–19). But to these elements success advocates like Frederic Van Rennsalaer Dey now added the importance of will and "scientifically controllable inner energies." In his *The Magic Story,* he used biography and parable to show readers how to grab the brass ring (Cawelti, 176). The more influential George Lorimer of the *Saturday Evening Post* urged that will-power, good interpersonal relations, and self-confidence were ingredients that had to be added to the traditional work ethic if one wished to scale the success pyramid (Lasch, *Narcissism,* 114). Other popular magazines such as *Success, Colliers,* and *American* also showered an expectant middle class with variations on the theme of success (Cawelti, 176–77), and on the 200th anniversary of Franklin's birth in 1906 the city of Boston published his still very popular maxims on how to do well in business (Wyllie, 125). Visiting British writers like Anthony Trollope and W. L. George both noted a broad "optimism" and a devotion to a "religion of utility." These led Americans to work for success with a zeal that impelled George to observe that "America is a great country for a young man to get born in" (Nevins, 223, 338, 340).

These efforts to condition the middle class were supplemented by the ideas of the New Thought movement. Inspired by

Phineas Quimby (1802–66), who believed illness could be cured by a proper mental approach, Prentice Mulford wrote a series of pamphlets urging that business success could be fostered by appropriate use of the mind. Mulford argued that "to think success brings success" (Baida, 245–46). Emerson's admonition to "nerve us with incessant affirmatives" offered additional encouragement to those who believed that an appropriate mental outlook led to success, and clearly anticipated Peale's "positive thinking" (Cawelti, 92). Even more influential in the New Thought movement was the success literature of Elizabeth Towne. She offered the view that wealth could be attained if people could cultivate a "*wealthy* attitude of mind." To be successful, Towne added, it would be necessary to "wash away all those nagging fears by flooding your mind with self-confident assertions" (Bendix, 260–61; Huber, 174). Ralph Waldo Trine's *In Tune with the Infinite* (1897) gave the New Thought literature additional popularity as did Orison Swett Marden's *Success* magazine and some thirty of his books. Marden made the switch from the old character ethic he had stressed in the 1890s to the belief that mental power was the path to a mercantile nirvana. For Marden the way to wealth was simplicity itself: "Change the thought, change the Man." Confidence itself was a guarantor of success. Needed was a counter to negative thinking, "a self-treatment" in which each person convinced themselves that "God made you for success, not failure." As late as 1922 Marden used his *Prosperity: How to Attract It* to argue that "prosperity and abundance" was "a mental law." He also told his readers that "only by thinking abundance can you realize the abundant, prosperous life that is your birthright." To this advice Marden added that "if you would attract success, keep you mind saturated with the success idea" (Huber, 145, 171, 156, 166; Baida, 246–47; Rodgers, *Work Ethic*, 38).

This emphasis on positive thinking was reenforced by Emile Coué in the early twenties. In his *Self-Mastery Through Conscious Autosuggestion* written in 1922 Coué indicated that the power of the mind could confer the will to get things done. He believed that "if you persuade yourself that you can do a certain thing, provided this thing be *possible*, you will do it however difficult it may be." To which he added "man is what he thinks" (Coué, 12, 40). Even during the midst of the Great Depression in 1931–32 the visiting British writer, Mary Agnes Hamilton, noted the American penchant for "abounding material success," of "rising," and "making good." She noted that both parents and the educational system pushed the young to accept these values (Nevins, 455–56). Five years later Dale Carnegie told his audience that success required not only hard work but a mental attitude that enabled a person to enjoy their work (Dale Carnegie, 67). Positive thinking as a precondition of success was given an additional boost in 1937 through the writings of Napoleon Hill. In his *Think and Grow Rich*, Hill suggested that "riches begin with a state of mind," and stated that "you can never have riches in great quantitities unless you can work yourself into a white heat of *desire* for money" (Napoleon Hill, 27, 37). Not to be outdone by Hill, Claude Bristol published his *Magic of Believing* (1948) in which he told the faithful that "you are the product of your own thought," that "thought is the original source of all wealth." To this he added that you must "*feel* and *think* yourself successful" (Bristol, 29, 75–76, 63).

But most influential of all who believed mind power was the vehicle of success was Norman Vincent Peale. His millions of readers were told that success was dependent on an "optimistic mind pattern." They were instructed to "believe in your own God-released powers," and told to "mentally visualize and affirm and reaffirm your assets and keep your thoughts on them." If this were done it was possible to "rise out of any difficulty" (Peale, *Positive Thinking*, 22–23). In 1956 Hornell Hart, a professor of sociology, also jumped on the bandwagon of mind power as a key element in individual success. Hart differed from his mind-oriented predecessors by suggesting that "autoconditioning" (self-hypnosis) alone was not enough, that success also required basic ability and education (Hart, 143). In the mid-1970s psychiatric specialists like Lazarus and Fay continued the old theme with a new twist. Each person was the master of their own destiny, and positive change was within the grasp of anyone who could overcome the negative outlook of hopelessness (Lazarus and Fay, 116–17). By 1981 Robert McKain returned to the Peale refrain that success could be achieved with the help of a "positive mental attitude." To this he appended the need to have a good self-image, and in a statement reminiscent of Coué, urged his readers to "get excited about your possibilities" (McKain, 18–19). In the 1990s the hucksters of success continued to advocate a determined mental attitude as a pre-requisite to advancement. Notable among them was the motivational "expert" Brian Tracy who was convinced that nothing was beyond the reach of an individual if they put their mind to it. But he warned that success could not be achieved overnight, and might take from five to seven years. The key was to "create" opportunities. Precisely how this was done required attendance at one of Tracy's seminars where you could learn "to build yourself to the point where you are successful" (Parets, A1–A2).

But if a positive frame of mind did not yield great wealth, those who drank at the fountain of success could rely on the numerous self-help books that pointed to personal magnetism as a way to "influence and dominate others." Here the new hero was the aggressive John Graham of Lorimer's "Letters from a Self-Made Merchant to His Son." Gone was the old Protestant virtue of hard work found in Enos Hitchcock's *The Farmer's Friend* or the Christian-oriented self-improvement of Timothy Arthur. Now "laws" of personal magnetism led Orison Swett Marden to suggest the use of mental power as a way to develop a success-oriented personality. In his *Masterful Personality* (1921) Marden even suggested that "YOU CAN COMPEL PEOPLE TO LIKE YOU. . . . It's the smile that boosts you up the ladder" (Cawelti, 183–84; Baida, 251). By 1924 the advertising executive Bruce Barton was using Christ as a example of the personal magnetism needed by all who wished to move up in the world (Barton, 24). Two years later the publisher B. C. Forbes took a more secular path by suggesting that "success in business . . . . is simply the art of pleasing" (Forbes, 75).

These messages were not lost on the later advocates of personality as a vehicle to earthly reward. In 1936 Carnegie published his best-selling *How to Win Friends and Influence People*, a book that offered an avenue to success by showing the reader how to be liked. It was essential, said Carnegie, to get other people to do what you wanted by being persuasive and gratifying their ego. To do this "you have to use showmanship," or you will be passed over in the game of getting to the top (Dale Carnegie, 15–16, 196–97, 166). By the early fifties Riesman and his colleagues identified "other-directed" types who sought the approval of their peers as a "source of direction." They observed a trend toward behavioral conformity through sensitivity, a desire to fit in, please others, and manage personal relations. Less important was the old "psycho-logical gyroscope" that family and society had implanted so "inner directed" individuals could be guided toward life goals. Now the mass media and the popular culture reenforced a trend toward a "friendship" system (Riesman, Glazer, and Denney, 32–38) through which the ambitious middle class could find ways to navigate the route to success.

But this was of little consequence to blue-collar America. Despite almost two centuries of exposure to the clarion call of success and the importance of personality, the children of blue collar America had lesser opportunity to gain entry into the pro-fessional or corporate world. Despite the GI Bill, only a minority had the collegiate credentials that served as an entry ticket to the corporate world of the fifties. Few had parents who could find them a comfortable place in their business, and, of necessity, "advancement" was confined to a quest for increased consump-tion (Chinoy, 112; Packard, 311). Only after the development of a body of behavioral research and company experimentation during the sixties and seventies was it recognized that their talents could be unleashed by employee development and partici-pative management.

But beyond the emphasis on personality and positive thinking as paths to success, a more generalized support for getting ahead continued to intrigue Americans between the twenties and the nineties. As we have seen, the success theme had become the play-thing of the business community during the 1920s. Andre Siegfried referred to it as "the mysticism of success" (F. L. Allen, *Only Yester-day*, 147), while Marden's *Success Fundamentals* (1920) extolled the successful businessman as a model whose achievements provided employment to thousands of workmen. Yet businessmen like Arthur Reynolds sounded more like a person of the 1990s in his desire "to *accomplish* something" rather than concentrate on how much money he could make (Lundén, 13, 135). Roger Babson, on the other hand, offered a six-point formula to achieve success that centered on great men as models, but cautioned that "success is a spiritual quality" that cannot be measured in monetary terms (Babson, *Success*, 11–33, 76). The oil industry executive A. C. Bedford believed that those who were productive had earned their wealth (Prothro, 69). Not to be outdone, the multimillionaire chairman of the Democratic National Committee published an article in the *Ladies Home Journal* of October, 1929 entitled "Everybody Ought to be Rich" (Mowry, 65). Shortly thereafter the Great Depression struck.

In the field of literature, Peter Kyne's *The Go-Getter* (1922) reflected the prevalent success theme. Sheldon Wills' story on "Graysons, Unlimited" noted the importance of hard work and thrift to the hero's success, while Booth Tarkington's 1927 novel *The Plutocrat* depicted successful businessmen in heroic terms. Still, attacks on the "gospel of success" in Sinclair Lewis' *Babbitt* and the lampooning of business types by H. L. Mencken did not go unnoticed (Lundén, 9–11). It may have led John Edgerton, president of the National Association of Manufacturers, to note that success was threatened by the envy of the unfit (Prothro, 51). But the advent of the Great Depression saw the optimistic literature of the Twenties displaced by labor novels and books like *Studs Lonigan* where the hero seeks work that does not exist (I. Bernstein, *Caring Society*, 208–09).

By the late 1940s, however, Peale began to toll the bells of "religious faith" so his followers could eliminate all self-doubt. "Remind yourself that God is with you and nothing can defeat you," he counseled. To which Peale added that the boulevard to success required an emphasis on your assets so that "your inner powers will reassert themselves and, with the help of God, lift you from defeat to victory" (Peale, *Confident Living*, 55; Peale, *Positive Thinking*, 25, 23). By 1959 Vance Packard questioned the cost of success if upward mobility was blocked by a situation beyond individual control. To which Rosabeth Moss Kanter added twenty years later that many had come to believe that material rewards might have too high a price if purchased at the cost of family, friends, and community. She suggested that many now came to see that work had a larger meaning than the traditional concept of success. For a new generation it now reflected a desire for challenge and growth through meaningful labor. Within these parameters the old success values of advancement and accumulation had not slipped away, but they were now encumbered by the nonmaterial aspirations (Packard, 294; Kanter, "Work in a New America," 58, 53) that reflected values that had surfaced in the sixties. A 1979 survey of 1,851 men by Gail Sheehy noted that while they continued to be "programmed for upward mobility" and had a "rigid success ethic" learned from their fathers, this was coupled with a demand for personal growth and a balance between work and life (Sheehy, 25–27).

But there were other voices as well. A 1980 survey of 782 chief executives found a "strong consensus" that "inner" character was the key to success. The traditional values of hard work and self-reliance were also stressed (F. Allen, "Bosses," 33), and suggested a divergence of values between managers and employees. Its findings were underscored by an 1980 analysis of Wall Street's top brokers, men who worked night and day in "the image of Horatio Alger" (Nevans, 44). At the same time, Robert Ringer and Michael Korda saw success as the province of those who looked after themselves. In the zero-sum world they portrayed one player's gain had to be another's loss (Baida, 336–37). Clearly success had a diversity of meanings, but among employees the trend toward challenge, participation, and time for family was unmistakable.

A 1992 survey tended to reenforce this point. This study of 500 employees between the ages of 21 and 29 showed that 33% saw "a rich family life" as the highest measure of success. Twenty-one percent believed that financial success was important, and 16% sought "a rich spiritual life." Most important was the fact that 43% remained "very optimistic about their prospects" (Deutschman, 46, 48, 42). A year later research by the Families and Work Institute indicated that 52% saw the importance of personal satisfaction in doing a good job. Earning the respect or recognition of others was endorsed by 30%, while job advancement was seen as a token of success by only 22% (Shellenbarger, "Work-Force Study," B1). From these surveys plus the earlier work of Yankelovich, Sheehy, and Kanter, success in the 1990s had come to include a set of aspirations not known in America prior to the sixties. These desires for recognition and fulfillment could in part be traced to the human relations movement of the 1920s, but more significantly to the human resources trend that emerged in the 1960s. It is through an analysis of these two periods that we will be able to observe how an emerging body of behavioral research revealed the basic work aspirations of Americans, and at the same time, displaced the influence of ministers, writers, politicians, and businessmen.

Part III
Work as Self-Fulfillment

Chapter 8

THE HUMAN RELATIONS MOVEMENT

A second important *discontinuity* in cultural orientations to work emerged in the 1930s. This new configuration of work values, Work as Self-Fulfillment (c. 1930s–present), was a sharp break with both the ministerial outlooks of Bucer and Zwingli and the Tayloristic perspective of the period we have called Work as Alienation and Opportunity (c. 1730s–1930s). Work as a Sign of Salvation (c. 1450–1730s) now aroused only a miniscule minority. But the opportunity offered workers during the two centuries after 1730 was of continuing importance, and vied for their attention along side the alienated labor of new factory world. How managers tried to turn aside the alienation engendered by repetitious and rationalized labor constituted a continuous struggle on the long road to Work as Self-Fulfillment. Only with the emergence of welfare capitalism and the Human Relations and Human Resources Movements would Taylorism be challenged and modified in the late twentieth century. Taken together, these three initiatives formed the foundation for the world of Work as Self-Fulfillment. It proved to be a sharp *discontinuity* with past eras, and ushered in a matrix of new work values. By the late sixties a growing number of employees took the unusual view that they were stakeholders in their jobs. They wanted work that tested their ability and offered some independence. Supervisors were expected to communicate and become resource people in facilities that no longer smacked of scientific management. If not all of this could be fulfilled with the speed of light, it still served as the mantra of an expectant generation.

Beyond this, the *four continuities* of hard work, opportunity, job insecurity, and the issue of the deserving and undeserving poor retained an on-going importance in the optimistic universe of fulfillment. From the sixties they would be augmented by a series of new aspirations and challenges that included a more prominent role for women and blacks in the world of work. These included the desire for a better balance between the demands of work and family in the context of flexible scheduling, home work, and employer-sponsored child care. They also embraced the Afro-American desire for access to education and employment that would offer them the vistas of opportunity so long enjoyed by whites.

Of the *four continuities* that flowed into the age of self-fulfillment, the belief in hard work retained its old flavor even as it underwent a subtle change. Some have called this a shift to a "worth ethic" because it elevated employee aspirations to a level never seen between the end of the feudal era and the beginning of a post-industrial society. Employees needed more "interaction," said Louis O' Leary of AT & T in 1979. They still had the old-fashioned work ethic, but wanted to be involved in decision-making (Kleinfield, 32). If they were to work diligently in the competitive world of the late twentieth century, workers required meaningful jobs, some autonomy, and feedback (Oldham, 8–9). The old Lutheran emphasis on working hard as a sign of salvation had been transmuted to a desire for employment that would stretch individual creativity. Employees now saw themselves almost as "sacred shrines," but this "faint echo" of the theological past now carried with it the overlay of secular striving.

In this age of new yearnings the quest for opportunity continued with great energy as a *second continuity*. Entrepreneurs found the gates to success open and started hundreds of enterprises in computing, biotechnology, health care, and telecommunications. New names like Oracle, Comcast, America-Online, Netscape, Sybase, and U.S. Heathcare graced the pages of business and created opportunity for thousands of professional employees. It was a world that would have made Girard, Astor, and Carnegie comfortable, and reflected a long tradition that could be traced to Jakob Fugger and Jacques Coeur.

Unfortunately, insecure employment remained as the *third important continuity* in the history of work values. Despite the emergence of many new businesses and a generally expanding economy, the half century after the end of the Second World War offered more than a few serious recessions. Unemployment hit 7% in 1957, stayed high in 1961–62, and rose to 9% in 1975. Downturns in 1981–82 and 1990–91 added to the continuing problem of job insecurity. To all of this was added a wave of restructuring, downsizing, and mergers that saw Fortune 500 companies drop 4,400,000 workers between 1979 and 1992 (Barnet, 47–48). If this was different in character from the Panic of 1819 which probably threw half a million out of work (Sellers, 137, 23–25), its results were similar. In both cases the emotional and economic turmoil of being detached from the workforce was severe. People were supposed to work. Any separation from that activity engendered a loss of self-esteem which only added to the negative overlay of want.

The *fourth continuity* involved the issue surrounding the deserving and undeserving poor. Help to those who would work if they could emerged in the Tudor era with the enactment of the Poor Law of 1601. This legislation codified a community obligation to help the unemployed, sick, and aged, but the feeling against non-working vagabonds and vagrants persisted. Colonial Americans drew on these Tudor values. Jefferson himself noted that from Savannah to Portsmouth "vagabonds without visible property or vocation, are placed in work houses, where they are well clothed, fed, lodged, and made to labor" (Smith and Zeitz, 18). These workhouses were seldom the positive setting described by our third president. They were designed to be harsh and thus make work a preferable alternative. Nevertheless, as late as 1884 New England had 600 workhouses (Piven and Cloward, 46–47). Aid to the deserving poor continued to be a local responsibility as poverty was equated with idleness (Bremner, 16–17). Only with the advent of the Great Depression did Wisconsin pass the first unemployment insurance act in 1932 (Schlesinger, *New Deal*, 301–2). This was followed by the Aid to Dependent Children program in 1935, but in the Tudor tradition, was designed for those truly in need (Marmor, 26). Only with the coming of the Great Society programs in the sixties did help for the deserving poor win federal support. Some thirty years later, however, this helping net had been so widely cast that 40 percent of all women who went on welfare before age twenty-five were there ten years later (Horowitz,

"Ending Welfare," A1). Such data led critics to argue that the old distinction between the deserving and undeserving poor had become irrelevant. They believed that by the nineties assistance had become an entitlement which supported those who would work if they could along with an undeserving core who saw life on the dole as a pleasant continuity.

Given these continuities and discontinuities in work values that stretched across the ages, the focus must now be turned to the role of welfare capitalism and the Human Relations Movement as key points of entry to the age of self-fulfillment (c. 1930s–present). In essence, these initiatives were a response to the values of Taylor, Fayol, and Weber who stressed control and coordination of the new semi-skilled factory workforce. Most of these men and women had nothing to offer but their labor. Their future was firmly fixed in a factory civilization regulated by mechanization and a division of labor. It was a world in which better pay formed the outer limits of aspiration.

In this new Tayloristic setting, the production of standardized ware under the supervision of managerial hierarchies became the norm (Rischin, 7–8; Bellamy, 165). To produce efficiently, factories squeezed out skilled workers and initiated a process that led to a "homogenization" of labor. More and more the worker was separated from his craft and left in a limbo of alienation. Craft workers who had been an important component of the American economy in the 1860s were largely supplanted by semi-skilled brethren some sixty years later (Dawley, 93–94; Dubofsky, 4–5; Yellowitz, 39). By the 1890s there was no longer an open frontier to absorb the unemployed or those who found factory work incompatible with their higher hopes (F. J. Turner, *Frontier*, 1–3, 37). Even the old religious homilies in praise of diligence failed to rouse factory operatives from their bleak surroundings and repetitious labor. The Reverend Frank Stevenson of Cincinnati could invoke John 5.17 in praise of labor ("My Father worketh hitherto, and I work") (Stevenson, 6), but in a 1914 debate with Frederick Taylor an unknown machinist noted

We don't want to work as fast as we think it's comfortable for us to work. We haven't come into existence for the purpose of seeing how great a task we can

perform through a lifetime. We are trying to regulate
our work so as to make it an auxiliary to our lives.
(Rodgers, *Work Ethic*, 168)

What then, was the nature of the Tayloristic system that
raised such fundamental objections among American workers?
Perhaps the most important concern was the systematic element
that predated Taylor himself. Earlier in the nineteenth century the
emerging engineers and managers saw that plant size and com-
plexity required a broad step away from the traditional "rule of
thumb" operations. Administration could no longer be impro-
vised, and cost accounting plus inventory control had to be instituted to insure greater control over the manufacturing process.
And while "incentive wages" would be paid to acquire an efficient
and compliant workforce, all of this was done at the cost of worker
and foreman autonomy (Nelson, *Managers and Workers*, 48–50, 58;
Doerflinger and Rivlin, 99; R. H. Parker, *Management Accounting*,
23–25).

Taylor built on this foundation of systematic management. In
1911 he attacked the old method of personal administration, and
urged managers to take the lead in the use of standardized production methods. To do this he suggested the adoption of the best
tools and "working conditions," time and motion studies, and
"enforced" cooperation to insure that "faster work can be assured."
Managers were to train each operative and provide a road map for
the navigation for each day's effort. Taylor anticipated worker
resistance to such rationalization, but believed his system would
work if employees were given "extra pay" for submitting to
"rigid standardization" and onerous labor (Taylor, *Principles*, 6–7,
37, 39, 83, 117–18). To Taylor, workers were economic men. Money
in exchange for a speedy regime of piece work was the new
industrial bargain, and "high pay for success" its watchword
(Taylor, *Shop Management*, 64).

But Taylorites did not anticipate worker suspicion that speed-
ups would follow improved productivity Gompers himself
rebutted Taylor's view that employees were guilty of "soldiering,"
while the president of the International Association of Machinists
argued in a circular letter of 1911 that scientific management
would deprive his constituents of their skills (Haber, 67–69). So

serious was union opposition to Taylorism that it led to walkouts at the federal arsenals in Watertown, Massachusetts and Rock Island, a strike in Worcester in 1915, and serious tensions at Amoskeag in the 1920s (Rodgers, *Work Ethic*, 166–67; Rosenzweig, 23, 25–26; Hareven, 138–39).

Taylor and his colleagues also overlooked the deadening effect of a division of labor (Wells, 93), while emphasizing the merits of standardization, specialization, and synchronization (Jenks, 436). Efficiency became the byword of scientific management, and led to an exposition on its behalf in New York City in April 1914 (Haber, 60–61). But even Taylor told a congressional committee in 1912 that "the whole subject of time study is only an approximation" (Nelson, *Managers and Workers*, 58), and urged labor and management to place less emphasis on how profits were to be divided and more on the production of a surplus (Urwick and Brech, 1:35). But neither Taylor nor his colleagues understood the group dynamics and social needs of industrial operatives. These oversights attracted the attention of human relations proponents during the three and a half decades after the Hawthorne experiments were initiated, and opened a new chapter in the evolution of twentieth century work values.

One year after the death of Frederick Taylor in 1915, Henri Fayol published his influential *General and Industrial Management*. Like Taylor, he placed the new managerial elite in the forefront of all business activity. Managers had to organize, plan, command, coordinate, and control (Fayol, 97–110). Within these key functions Fayol suggested fourteen universal principles of management which included the division of labor plus a centralized and hierarchical organizational structure that left all decision-making in administrative hands (ibid., 19–42). Fayol hoped to "eliminate the human factor" in management, but acknowledged that a "responsible administrator" would find this difficult (Urwick and Brech, 1:43).

To the ideas and values of Taylor and Fayol, Max Weber offered the additional prescription of bureaucracy. Weber's concern with organizational structure led him to believe that bureaucrats, those middle-level managers who carried out policy rather than made it, offered business and government many advantages. Among the more significant were "precision, speed, unambiguity, knowledge of the files, continuity, discretion, strict subordination" and a "reduction of friction." Bureaucracy, he alleged, rids a company of "love, hatred, and all purely personal, irrational, and emotional elements which escape calculation." What it offered the new industrial society was order, system, uniformity, consistency, and rationality. All of this would be available in a framework of impersonality and strict rules that elevated competence and eliminated favoritism (Gerth and Mills, 214–216). That Weber was addressing an interested audience could be seen by the rapidly growing ratio of administrative to production employees in the United States. In 1899 it was but 7.7%, but by 1947 it had risen to 21.6% (Bendix, 214).

Taken together, Taylor, Fayol, and Weber won the attention of many managers during the twentieth century. While there were differences in their approaches to organizational efficiency, a commonality of values emerged around managerial domination, rationality, uniformity, and systematic effort. To a considerable extent, the human element was set aside despite statements to the contrary by Weber and Taylor. In this new universe men and machines became factors of production. Their efficient use resulted in a "social" loss of craft (Aitken, 225), and introduced a "technological determinism" that relegated cultural and social factors to a peripheral position (L. Davis, "Job Design," 70). Taylor never foresaw how his system could be "catastrophic to . . . dignity" (Herzberg, 35), nor could he know that workers would continue to stymie the time-study engineers with contrived slowdowns (Matthewson, 68). Nevertheless, Taylorism spread rapidly during the twenties and thirties (Riegel, 118) despite the growing influence of human relations theorists. Firms such as General Electric came under the influence of Charles Bedaux's Tayloristic approaches, while the economist W. C. Mitchell spoke with respect of a system that has "applied intelligence to the day's work" (Montgomery, *House of Labor*, 440; Faulkner, 607). Tayloristic values also received the endorsement of Hugo Munsterberg, an important industrial psychologist who shared the physical-economic thrust of scientific management (Munsterberg, 308–9; E. A. Locke, 1300).

How subordinate groups responded to these ideas and the emergence of Fordism between 1910 and 1914 offered a clue to some of the shortcomings of rationalization and mass production.

In the new Ford facilities such as Highland Park the introduction of "progressive assembly" required hiring thousands of semi-skilled operatives. Many were immigrant peasants from Southern and Eastern Europe who lacked both a craft tradition or industrial experience, and brought with them many preindustrial work values including high absenteeism and turnover, lateness, and output restriction. To deal with these problems Ford established the five dollar day for eight hours of work, a pay scale far higher than that paid by most manufacturers in January 1914. This was clearly an incentive to get foreign workers, blacks, and "substandard men" (those who were blind, deaf, tubercular, or epileptic) to accept the repetitive and demanding labor of the assembly line (Meyer, 5–6; Flink, 85).

The Fordist Sociological Department also intruded on the private lives of many workers in order to acculturate them to the American values it believed were an essential component of good factory discipline. Along with the new Taylorist technology that robbed work of its intellectual content, it was a clear attempt to create a new kind of industrial worker, a "trained gorilla" who Gramsci believed would endure repetitive and measured labor for good pay (Gramsci, 277, 308–10). This infamous department tried to break up ethnic groupings and loyalties, lent aid to churches for their conservative outlook, supported anti-liquor laws, and demanded domestic cleanliness and efficiency (Green, *World of Worker*, 109–10). Codes of behavior were also established for married and single workers, all for the purpose of ultimately improving efficiency on the assembly line. Married men, for example, were to live with their families, provide a good home atmosphere, and be thrifty. That these attempts to mold foreign workers to the values Ford believed were essential to be a good worker and good American had less than great success can be seen by a turnover rate of 370 percent in 1913 (Meyer, 117–18, 83; Gramsci, 311–12).

Clearly, Ford workers saw these high-paying positions as little more than a job. Even a Ford manager like John R. Lee noted discipline problems among younger workers who were loathe to become interchangeable parts in a new industrial universe designed by Ford and Taylor. Passive resistance also emerged via secretly communicated signals dubbed the "Ford whisper" or

"Fordization of the face," and soldiering was openly advocated by union organizers from the Industrial Workers of the World (IWW). For now, satisfaction was reduced to a paycheck, and the old Protestant Ethic became a forgotten work value (Meyer, 92–93; Flink, 87–88).

Nevertheless, Taylorism continued to be a major industrial value system throughout the course of the twentieth century. During the 1940s Alford added to the field by suggesting that close supervision of small groups led to greater efficiency (Alford, *Production Handbook*, 1333). Later in that decade British and American research into ergonomics led to increased knowledge of man-machine relationships and a field that eventually was called human factors (Murrell, *Men and Machines*, 12), although its human side seemed to be less salient than its technical thrust.

Even more significant were the changes in scientific management that were apparent by the early eighties. By this time modern technical systems frequently absorbed the fractionated tasks of old-style scientific management. Tasks could now be programmed and automated, and abstractions often superceded concrete objects. Now it was important that a better educated industrial workforce be able to read and interpret computer printouts, dials, and meters so that machines and throughput processes were directed correctly. In the new industrial world, the Tayloristic emphasis on repetitive labor with material objects was bypassed for a more professional workforce whose cognitive skills enabled them to control complex work processes (L. Davis, "Individuals and Organizations," 11–13). Still, Taylor would not have been disappointed in the workplace of the nineties. He would have salivated over the worker-imposed scientific management system at the NUMMI (New United Motor Manufacturing, Inc.) plant in Fremont, California (Adler, 102–3), and would have applauded the poultry processing lines from Delaware to Texas (Horwitz, 1A, 8A, 9A). Taylor would have been at home at the food preparation tables of McDonald's and at American Airlines' reservations desks where a modern system of scientific management restricted autonomy and kept the skill-level low (Garson, *Electronic Sweatshop*, 165-66). Thus, despite the opposition against rationality and control by the human relations school and the later Human Resources Movement, some citadels of the old faith survived. By the nineties, however, a far larger number of firms had come to view employees as assets whose development merited a higher level of participation, communication, and autonomy.

What, then, was responsible for the emergence of the Human Relations Movement as a direct challenge to scientific management? While the concept of human relations did not gain notoriety until the 1920s, its origins in welfare capitalism had late-nineteenth-century roots. At this juncture businesses were faced with huge economic losses because of an extremely poor labor-management relations climate. Between 1880 and 1900, for example, almost 23,000 strikes occurred in 117,000 different firms. Violence often accompanied these industrial actions. The result was a considerable cost in both money and poor public relations. Managers were also aware of the harmful effects of high absenteeism and turnover, insobriety, sabotage, and a less than sterling work effort. Taken together, these problems led more enlightened businessmen to seek some amelioration of the situation through the medium of welfare capitalism (Brandes, 1–2).

As an early phase of the human relations movement, welfare capitalism offered employees a variety of benefits which were neither required by law nor needed to improve productivity (ibid., 4–6). Men like George Pullman, Harold McCormick, John H. Patterson, William Proctor, Henry Heinz, and G. Harry Lester used profit sharing, improved pay, medical aid, sick benefits, housing, libraries, restaurants, and club houses to improve the lives of their workers. Some such as Heinz and William Filene even hired welfare secretaries to deal with grievances, check on absentees, hire, fire, and offer counseling. Pullman and Lester (the predecessor of Endicott Johnson) even built model cities for their workers (Zahavi, 1–3; Nelson, *Managers and Workers*, 102, 106–8; Brody, *Industrial America*, 49–50; Brandes, 12; Haber, 18–19).

But the basic thrust of welfare capitalism went beyond employee self-improvement and concentrated on winning the loyalty and cooperation of the workforce (Nelson, *Managers and Workers*, 101). Above all, control was to remain in the hands of management. This became clear when unionization made an appearance at Endicott Johnson despite the benefits of welfare work. The company fought and destroyed the nascent union in 1896 (Zahavi, 13), an action repeated at National Cash Register in 1901 despite that firm's leadership in both welfare capitalism and early personnel management (Nelson, *Managers and Workers*, 109). Even the paternalistic Amoskeag Manufacturing Company was hit by a United Textile Workers strike in 1919 (Hareven and Langenbach, 24). Clearly, welfare work alone was not achieving what some of its business advocates had predicted. In addition, while many corporations continued to support welfare work within the National Civic Federation after its formation in 1901, the strategy was designed to win worker cooperation for managerial initiatives. Many firms threw their efforts behind an open shop campaign to fight increased unionization even as they embraced some aspects of welfare capitalism. What most managers still prized above all other things was loyalty and compliance (Dubofsky, 86–88; Montgomery, *House of Labor*, 274–75). Workers were still seen in a physical-economic context in which directed labor was traded for a paycheck.

Along with the Personnel Management Movement, welfare capitalism had its heyday in the twenties. International Harvester had joined the ranks of the paternalistic with a pension plan as early as 1911, while Sears, Roebuck under Julius Rosenwald offered a profit-sharing plan in 1916 (Hicks, 42–43; Worthy, 151). Colorado Fuel and Iron crafted the highly publicized Rockefeller Plan in 1915 which gave employees a modest level of representation so they could voice their grievances. But Rockefeller's key aim was to win employee "cooperation." Despite his many forward-looking benefit programs, the Colorado workforce voted for a union during the first free election in 1933 (I. Bernstein, *Lean Years*, 164–66; Bruchey, *Enterprise*, 417).

These plans did little to influence labor turnover in other industries, and during World War I that number reached 8 percent *per month*. Militant unions proved to be another obstacle during the war years (Levitan and Johnson, 153), and led some managers to counter with yellow-dog contracts, strikebreakers, and blacklisting. Immigrant labor, mechanized factories, and adherence to the open shop philosophy of the "American Plan" were also used by employers to fight unionization and maintain control over their employees (Galambos and Pratt, 79; I. Bernstein, *Lean Years*, 147). Some managers continued to employ welfarism to counter growing union strength that reached 4 million members in 1920.

So great was the expansion of welfare capitalism that a survey of 1,500 firms in 1926 found that 80% had at least one form of welfarism. 50% had "comprehensive programs," and some 4 million employees worked in firms that had some form of welfare capitalism (Brandes, 6–8, 27–28, 32). Sensitivity to public opinion also played a part in the expansion of welfarism in the twenties. Influential business leaders like Elbert Gary of U.S. Steel and George W. Perkins of J. P. Morgan worried about earlier muckraker assaults and government investigations, while in 1929 a director of the U.S. Chamber of Commerce said there had been "an enormous change" in management attitudes during the twenties (Brody, *Industrial America*, 51–52, 48).

Nevertheless, welfare capitalism lost much of its momentum during the later 1920s. Despite its good human relations, workers saw it as manna from above, and acceptance suggested they could not provide these benefits for themselves. From the managerial perspective, workers appeared unappreciative. When added to the effects of the Great Depression, many employers decided to reduce or eliminate their welfare programs (Brandes, 142–43). What survived contained the seeds of current fringe benefit programs (Witte, 355). But welfare capitalism as a tool to secure a cooperative and well-behaved workforce had failed. Chester Barnard said as much at a 1935 management conference when he urged that welfarism would not "do much to develop the individual or foster the will to collaborate" (Barnard, *Organization and Management*, 13). But it should not be overlooked that during the Great Depression firms such as U.S. Steel, Goodyear, General Electric, Bethlehem Steel, International Harvester, and Standard Oil of New Jersey helped their unemployed operatives with loans, food, and programs to spread the work (Brody, *Industrial America*, 67–69). It may have done little to motivate their workers in better times, but in the gloomy decade of a depression that left 25 percent of the labor force unemployed in early 1933 it was a humanitarian gesture of some significance.

Also important as a forerunner of the human relations movement was the trend toward a modern system of personnel management. Its origin occurred at the National Cash Register Company (NCR) after the strike and lockout of 1901 had led to the defeat of the union. John H. Patterson, NCR's president, appointed

Charles U. Carpenter to improve the situation by organizing a Personnel Department. The new department was given authority to handle grievances and discharges, and was made responsible for safety and sanitary work conditions. It kept management abreast of pending labor legislation and court decisions and trained supervisors. As a result, the power of foremen was substantially reduced. Management won more direct control over its workforce, although the price was often paid in declining loyalty and morale. In many companies the result was an impersonal labor-management relationship that became the norm in an age of growing rationality and systemization. Still, the NCR model became a forerunner of the Personnel Management Movement of the World War I era and the 1920s (Nelson, *Taylor*, 17–18; Nelson, *Managers and Workers*, 101).

The Personnel Management Movement was strengthened by a series of important interventions during the Progressive Era. Industrial psychologists such as Hugo Munsterberg and Walter Scott Dill were now using psychology to address the issues of worker satisfaction and efficiency. Labor economists John R. Commons and Robert Hoxie published widely on the role of unions, the economic basis of labor problems, and government intervention to solve labor-management differences. Forward-looking businessmen instituted welfare programs, and even Taylor saw his scientific management as a pathway to the solution of labor tensions. Union leaders, however, increasingly looked to collective bargaining as a tool, while civic organizations, Quakers, Socialists, and government commissions all kept labor problems in the forefront of the public mind (B. Kaufman, *Industrial Relations*, 8). Despite these efforts, labor unrest and high turnover plagued American industry during World War I. The traditional "drive system" that gave foremen the right to hire and fire and engage in extremely close supervision now came into question. Union strength and support from a friendly Wilson Administration also caused employers to re-evaluate their practices. Employment managers now began to displace foremen in such roles as training, hiring, and firing, and instituted the use of intelligence testing and job analysis. Their numbers grew to over 4,000 by 1920 (B. Kaufman, *Industrial Relations*, 9; Nelson, *Taylor*, 200–201).

By the early twenties it was clear that a growing number of firms had accepted the idea that high turnover was a sign of employee dissatisfaction. Whether it reflected an unwillingness to perpetuate the "drudgery of modern repetitive factory work" (Slichter, "Labor Turnover Problem," 337, 343) or the influence of Rockefeller's human relations approach that looked to "coopera- tion" between employers and workers (I. Bernstein, *Lean Years*, 164–66; Gordon, Edwards, and Reich, 180), more and more com- panies came to rely on personnel management that stressed "the human factor in production." These new personnel or labor rela- tions departments emphasized the fair and dignified treatment of workers, industrial safety, welfare programs, and workmen's compensation (Witte, 356–57). A cadre of new industrial relations experts like Clarence Hicks and Arthur H. Young emerged along with expert groups such as Industrial Relations Counselors, Inc. (Brody, *Industrial America*, 53). Increasingly, workers were viewed "as a variable factor in the efficiency of an organization," and good employee relations became a paramount goal of personnel departments (Levitan and Johnson, 153–54).

By the second half of the twenties, however, the Personnel Management Movement became a trend that accompanied and abetted the growing trend toward human relations in industry. One of its most important manifestations was the immense inter- viewing effort at Hawthorne that began in 1928 and involved over 21,000 employees. The program was the earliest "to get human data" on such a large scale, and suggested the importance of listening to employee concerns. Paying attention was the pathway to good results (Roethlisberger, 16, 19).

Even during the turbulent thirties personnel management continued to play a significant role. While the proportion of firms employing 250 or more that had personnel offices was 25% in 1920, it grew to 64% by 1935 (Bruchey, *Enterprise*, 461). Many were now needed to handle grievance procedures that were more common in the contracts won by industrial unions in the Thirties. They also had to deal with new seniority systems, and the growth of restrictions on employer hiring and firing (I. Bernstein, *Turbu- lent Years*, 775–76; Slichter, *Union Policies*, 105–7). Personnel depart- ments also had an important role in getting good results from workers, a view endorsed by the National Industrial Conference Board in 1931 (Brody, *Industrial America*, 13). Chester Barnard enlarged on this point in 1935 when he told a management conference that the "development of the individual is to be a central consideration in all personnel work." This, he noted, should be honest, and "not merely as a matter of tactics, nor . . . a matter of industrial efficiency" (Barnard, *Organization and Management*, 8–9).

Running like a thread through the values of both welfare capitalism and the Personnel Management Movement was the idea of worker cooperation with management. It became a key element in the value structure of the Human Relations Movement, and permeated the ideas of many engineers and managers (Jenks, 437) including Taylor (Taylor, *Principles*, 26) and the Gilbreths (W. F. Whyte et al., *Money and Motivation*, 5). During the 1920s many businessmen such as Rockefeller underscored the need for labor-management cooperation, but the greatest booster of cooperative industrialism during the New Era of the twenties was Herbert Hoover (I. Bernstein, *Lean Years*, 164–66; Brandes, 28). Hoover envisaged a cooperative world of work based on "areas of common interest," and looked to "cooperation and good will among groups" as practical outcomes (Wilbur and Hyde, 44–45). He believed the business world was "moving strongly toward cooperation" through which he had "great hopes that we can . . . gain in indivduality, equality of opportunity, and an enlarged field for initiative" (Hoover, 44; Warren, 35). Hoover looked to an "associative state" in which private groups would cooperative to further mutual agendas. In this way industrial relations would be harmonized and living standards improved. But many felt his "associationalism" had an undemocratic ring, and some workers saw it as a shield for business (Hawley, "Hoover," 138–40, 117).

More influential in the long run were the ideas of Mary Parker Follett. Like many others during this era, she saw the study of human relations as a way of helping people "interact and coact better." She demeaned the thirst for power in itself as "coercive control," and looked for a cooperative industrial setting that emphasized "coactive control." Follett urged that "we need a technique of human relations based on the preservation of the integrity of the individual" (Follett, xi–xiii). She looked to the functional cooperation of all employees as a group. Most important was the development of a cooperative spirit to accomplish "what the law of the situation" requires. Final authority by managers, Follett urged, was an "illusion" that was disappearing

(Urwick and Brech, 1:52–54). She believed that "arbitrary command" ignored the desire of others to have an element of freedom in their working lives. It was fallacious to believe that only managers wanted to do the job right, "that the worker has to be goaded" to perform properly. But if managers felt compelled to retain control it could only decrease the sense of worker "responsibility" (P. Graham, *Follett*, 125). Elton Mayo, the "father" of human relations, also stressed the importance of cooperation in work. He noted that in one of the Hawthorne experiments (1924–32), the Relay Assembly Test Room, the researchers actively sought "the cooperation of the workers." The six, Mayo stated, "became a team" and as such offered its spontaneous cooperation (Mayo, *Social Problems*, 72).

In 1928 Herbert Feis reported on such collaboration at Proctor and Gamble where "cooperation between workers and management" was based on "a recognition of the worker's needs and desires." This common effort, he believed, would lead to an improved efficiency which would yield greater material gains for all (Feis, 2). In the same year Charles Schwab of Bethlehem Steel told a group of engineers that industry's key task was the "management of men on a human basis" (Brody, *Industrial America*, 53). This philosophy of cooperation was reiterated in 1929 by a Chamber of Commerce official (Brody, *Steelworkers*, 149), but in all three cases no mention was made of greater worker participation or responsibility. Managers were still in the business of seeking cooperative if not compliant operatives. The rewards to be had were limited to the material, although good human relationships received an increasing volume of praise.

Chester Barnard, then president of New Jersey Bell, made this point effectively in 1935. Managers had to see workers as more than a "market or contract commodity." Instead they needed to regard them as persons who had a "stake" in the business (Barnard, *Organization and Management*, 20). Barnard saw "an organization as a *system of cooperative activities*" and believed that the "*willingness* of persons to contribute efforts to the cooperative system is indispensable" (Barnard, *Executive*, 75, 83). A *Management Review* article of 1937 returned to the more prevalent view that workers wanted to be regarded "not as servants, but as cooperators." If employees were treated badly their morale would fall and poor work would follow (Bendix, 294). The Training Within Industries (TWI) program established by the U.S. government in 1940 also emphasized the importance of good human relations to elicit the cooperation of the workforce (Robinson and Schroeder, 37, 42). During 1941 Clarence Hicks lent his prestige to the concept of a cooperative relationship between managers and the managed. He attacked "autocratic methods" as ineffective and believed they lowered worker morale and efficiency (Hicks, 67, 77). In the same year Mayo worried lest "collaboration . . . be left to chance." Management had to take the lead to avoid suspicion or hostility (Roethlisberger, xxi–xxii).

In 1944 this formula was endorsed by Eric Johnston, president of the U.S. Chamber of Commerce (Johnston, 11). But a more important turn in management thinking was expressed four years later by Alexander Heron of Crown Zellerbach, who noted how important it was for the average employee to have a chance "to share in the task of thinking." Pay and security were not to be set aside, but "organized consultation" had to accompany good working relationships. Seeking employee cooperation in itself was not enough. The fundamental need was for more "bottom-up management" in which employees were involved in both planning and thinking (Heron, 172–75). He anticipated many of the fundamental tenets of the Human Resources Movement in suggesting a level of participation that went beyond morale surveys and group dynamics that so transfixed the advocates of human relations. Heron also understood that people wanted to feel both useful and important in the workplace. In this very important sense he readily accepted the prevailing idea of cooperation, but appended an appeal that employees be regarded as valuable human resources whose minds were more valuable than their muscles. Heron was clearly ahead of his time. The industrial world of the late forties was still trying to digest the changes suggested by the advocates of human relations. It might accept cooperation and a continuation of personnel management, but the jump to employees as thinking assets was a distant dream.

Nevertheless, the evolution of the Human Relations Movement did contain nutrients needed by the Human Resources Movement that emerged in the sixties. Gellerman saw American moralism as the source of human relations values. It affected the conscience of American managers during the twenties (Gellerman, 16), and led men like Rockefeller to emphasize the importance of Christian principles as the surest route to a "harmony of interests." In 1927 ten leading executives endorsed the importance of "the human element in industry" (I. Bernstein, *Lean Years*, 164–65), but their belief that the good morale would lead to better productivity was not challenged until later in the century (Thurman, 260–61). More important was the role of human relations as an antidote to values of scientific management. In 1920 Ordway Tead and Henry Metcalf were already advocating that the new personnel officers apply "the administration of human relations in industry." Two years later Gordon S. Watkins attacked Taylorism and suggested the need to "evaluate the human elements in production and distribution." Books by Edward L. Thorndike and Sam Lewisohn emphasized the nonmonetary rewards that might motivate workers, and offered the portrait of workers as social men to counter the Tayloristic notion they were motivated by money alone (B. Kaufman, *Industrial Relations*, 24–26). In addition, the importance of social relationships on the job was recognized by Elton Mayo during his studies at a Philadelphia textile mill in 1923–24 (Mayo, *Social Problems*, 67). It also showed up in the research of other Philadelphia firms by Anne Bezanson in 1925 (Bezanson 165–66).

But it was the ideas of Mayo in particular that gave the Human Relations Movement its greatest impetus. Taken together with books by T. N. Whitehead and Roethlisberger and Dickson on the Hawthorne experiments, they propelled human relations to a position where the behavioral assumptions of Taylorism no longer went unquestioned. Beginning with his work in a Philadelphia textile mill, Mayo noted how consultation with workers on the scheduling of rest periods helped transform them from a "horde of 'solitaries' into a social group." He observed that "efficiency experts" had never placed much credence in what workers thought or said, and saw operatives as economic entities whose opinions reflected the ideas of a disorganized "rabble." In this modified work situation, however, Mayo observed that production rose by 80 percent during the next five months. Turnover decreased by 5–6 percent, and absenteeism dropped on Mondays and Fridays (Mayo, *Social Problems*, 65–67). Despite this modest level of success, Mayo still worried about the separation of work and family life. Work was no longer supported by a social community and easily led to anomie, a "planlessness of living" that was characterized by insecurity and normlessness (Mayo, *Human Problems*, 130, 136). Perhaps Mayo saw a partial solution in the Hawthorne research, for it was here that employees found work group attachment a source of social strength and a first glimpse at "self-determination" (ibid., 73).

The Hawthorne studies which followed from 1924 to 1932 provided the fundamental body of research that propelled the human relations movement for the next thirty years. They were initiated by the well-known Illumination experiments in 1924 at the Hawthorne Works of AT & T's Western Electric plant near Chicago. In these experiments lighting in the experimental room was increased, held constant, and decreased. In all cases output went up (Landsberger, 7). This raised questions about the prevailing belief that there was a connection between physical conditions and productivity (Roethlisberger and Dickson, 9–11, 14–18). Later investigators even spoke of a "Hawthorne effect." They suggested that paying attention to employees altered their behavior, because special treatment and increased status singled them out as special (Blumberg, 15–16; Mosteller, 115). Some managers began to believe that "attitudes and sentiments" were also involved, that employee motives and behavior had to be studied (Whitehead, 99). Later social scientists like Robert L. Kahn suggested that later research found the "Hawthorne effect" was "not unvarying or even dependable." The key to the Illumination Experiments was that the young women involved had a real chance to participate, "to alter their work roles in content, duration, pace, rewards and relationship to conventional authority. There was, in short, a genuine transfer of power." Kahn concluded that "real participation has real effects" (Kahn, 52–53, 59, 61). But beyond the boundaries of the experiment there remained strong managerial resistance to power-sharing.

A second phase of Hawthorne was the important Relay Assembly Test Room experiments. Done in two phases betweeen April 1927 and July 1932, the researchers changed several of the physical conditions of work in line with the prevailing belief (as in the earlier Illumination experiment) that these alone would have an effect on productivity. But as Whitehead noted, "nothing of the sort occurred." The rest pauses, changes in hours worked, and the light lunches "were constant reminders of the important relations that the Relay Test group enjoyed with Management itself and with what might be described as these girls' public." Whitehead continued: "Almost always, the social significance of a change in physical conditions far outweighed the importance of its immediate suitability as a working environment." Of primary importance was the "improved relations" between management and its workforce (Whitehead, 241). Roethlisberger and Dickson noted that this improvement was related to the fact that the operators were "consulted about changes to be made." In several instances, the experimenters even dispensed with ideas that met with the disapproval of the work group. Beyond this, the operators were "questioned sympathetically" about their reactions. The results led investigators to conclude that wage incentives, hours, and other conditions of work were important, but only as part of a "total situation." Included in this "total situation" was the appearance of an informal organization. It was this invisible entity that provided a network of personal and working relationships that could bring satisfaction to its members and a level of output that pleased management (Roethlisberger and Dickson, 181, 185, 561). It strongly suggested "the importance of employee attitudes and sentiments." Indeed, the reasearchers came to believe that the "meaning of a change is likely to be as important, if not more so, than the change itself" (Roethlisberger, 15). Clearly, each worker felt she had been elevated "to the status of a chosen collaborator" (Whitehead, 104).

A later social scientist even suggested that factories produced more than goods, that within their economic environment they served a social function that could offer satisfaction and involvement as key supplements to a paycheck (J. A. C. Brown, 70–72). Above all, getting the cooperation of the workers was a crucial objective. Mayo noted that the absence of "coercion from above" and the ability to participate "freely" welded six individuals into a team that "gave itself wholeheartedly and spontaneously to cooperation in the experiment" (Mayo, *Social Problems*, 72). The same women who were irked with the traditional supervisors before the experiment readily accepted close observation inside the Relay Test room because "they themselves could feel a sense of participation"

(Urwick and Brech, 3:48). This feeling also emerged in the later Hawthorne Interview Program (1928–30) where employees appreciated "being recognized as individuals who had valuable comments to make" (ibid., 3:112). Nevertheless, while the immediate effect of the changed conditions led to improved "morale," Whitehead believed "that the effect wears off with time" (Whitehead, 241).

The subsequent Bank Wiring Observation phase of Hawthorne from November 1931 to May 1932 involved fourteen male workers from three "occupational groups" (wiremen, soldermen, and inspectors). These employees exhibited a set of work "sentiments" that conditioned the group not to work too slowly for fear of being dubbed a "chiseler." On the other hand, group norms dictated that only a "rate buster" would exert excessive effort. Moreover, the social code forbade any worker from offering adverse comments about a co-worker to the supervisor, and required worker-inspectors not to be too "officious." To be accepted into the work group, operatives had "to act in accordance with these social standards" (Roethlisberger, 22), and accept the team "concept of a day's work" as a norm. By an informal consensus, this was limited to two "equipments" per day. Workers who tried to produce more (Roethlisberger and Dickson, 412, 415–16) were struck physically ("binged") or subjected to name-calling such as "speed king" or "slave." It was a pressure few could resist. Observers were quick to conclude that "the worker is a social animal" (Roethlisberger, 81–82, 26, 22) which alerted a few contemporary managers to pay attention to informal groups that could exercise a powerful control over work behavior (Urwick and Brech, 3:74). But it did not prevent the banking of work during succeeding decades by printers, locomotive firemen, and painters who even placed restrictions on the width of paint brushes (Berg, 30).

But because the Hawthorne experiments suggested such a novel way of analyzing the values that motivated factory workers, it elicited a wide spectrum of interpretation. Clearly, its underlying work values were a sharp departure from the Tayloristic emphasis on workers as economic men. The Hawthorne studies did not offer evidence that financial rewards were unimportant, but they suggested that a "failure to treat workers as human beings" could result in "low morale" and unresponsive behavior

(Bendix, 294). The contemporary management authority Mary Follett noted how important "mutual influence" was "when people work together" (P. Graham, *Follett*, xvi), while British researchers Warr and Wall saw this emphasis on good human relations at work as a way to achieve "more effective operation" (Warr and Wall, 32). But in the mid-1980s British observer Michael Rose questioned some of Mayo's approaches. Mayo, he noted, worked for a goal that would integrate managerial and worker obligations as a moral imperative, but paid insufficient attention as to how they might increase production. Rose also believed that Mayo did not fully perceive the competitive nature of the marketplace. Workers in this environment might be induced to work more effectively by improved pay and a less fragmented division of labor. But he conceded that the Human Relations Movement altered employee expectations about how they should be treated. The dissemination of its ideas through management literature and education led many employers to modify the way in which they interpreted their roles, or at least how they felt they could express them in public (Rose, 116–17, 121).

On the other hand, Richard Walton believed that Hawthorne led to the realization that work was a social system in contrast to the mechanistic approach of scientific managers. But he asserted that the "human factors" that may have improved productivity were seen by the researchers as means rather than ends. Later experiments in the 1970s at Kalmar, Sweden and Topeka included "a more explicit concern for improving the quality of working life as well as productivity" (Walton, "Hawthorne," 122). Fred Fiedler asserted that Hawthorne led to a "new era" in industrial relations, and suggested alternative managerial styles and the importance of group dynamics. To a greater degree, managers were encouraged to act as counselors and facilitators rather than task masters (Fiedler, 207). But contemporaries such as Mayo emphasized the value of "working teams" (Mayo, *Social Problems*, 69), while C. Canby Balderston supported the concept of group incentives (Balderston, 1–2, 28–29). Despite the wide variety of criticisms that emerged (Landsberger, 30–31; Carey, 403–6; Franke and Kaul, 625, 636–38), Hawthorne was a turning point. Over the succeeding decades a growing number of managers began to reassess their work values. More and more gradually modified their negative behavioral assumptions about workers, and came to see the importance of group dynamics and social aspects of employment as possible avenues to improved productivity. Taylorism was under challenge, but most managers were still too strongly tied to the tenets of efficiency to see employees in terms of the sentiments and interactions suggested by human relations advocates. Despite this, the human relations researchers began the long and laborious process that gradually shifted the eyes of managers to possibilities beyond Taylorism.

The emphasis on group dynamics that permeated Hawthorne was taken up by Kurt Lewin during the thirties and forties. Along with Rensis Likert, Lewin studied the motivation of individuals and groups who were influenced by the contextual factors of the workplace, and saw groups as agents of change. In industry and elsewhere they had a great capacity to "unfreeze" a static situation, move along the process of change, and then "freeze" the new status quo. "Group decision," he believed, was "a process of social management" (K. Lewin, "Group Decision," 299–300). Along with John French, he conducted additional research that led both men to conclude that autocratic managers needed retraining to modify behavior that often spawned aggressive responses (Lewin, Lippett, and White, "Aggressive Behavior," 298–99; French, 235–37). In a another study done under Lewin's direction, participation and involvement of the work group seemed to lead to goals employees could accept. This was in contrast to the ordained objectives of management that permeated more directive work environments. In this experiment, the closely supervised control group showed little improvement in productivity, and led Lewin to conclude that to modify the ingrained values of employees it was necessary to change the culture. If this could be achieved, the group could be changed as a group, and in turn, detach individual members from strongly held beliefs that impeded work progress (J. A. C. Brown, 182–84).

While most managers did not fully grasp the significance of Lewin's research with groups during the thirties and forties, the the basic human relations concepts did gain a bit of ground. Even as early as 1929 the Deputy Director of the Taylor Society conceded that employee cooperation was a critical element in industrial efficiency (Friedmann, *Industrial Society*, 293–94). A few years later

Mary Follett offered a paper called "The Giving of Orders" in which she urged managers to worry less about "how to get control of people" and more about how all working together "can get control of a situation." Follett went on to urge "that we can never wholly separate the human from the mechanical." This, she suggested, "bound up together" the study of human relations and the daily operating procedures of business. Autocratic leadership, Follett asserted, was "the theory of the past" and would not be found in our "best-managed industries." Like Lewin, she strongly believed in "the development of group responsibility," but in her own time was not accorded the recognition of a Taylor or Gilbreth (P. Graham, *Follett*, 130, 27, 165, 195, 4).

More influential in the thirties was Chester Barnard. Like Follett, Lewin, and the Hawthorne researchers, the president of New Jersey Bell believed "enlarged participation" was crucial. It gave workers a "feeling of importance" because they were now part of a "cooperative effort." Leaning on Mayo and Follett, Barnard told his fellow managers that informal groups existed in most organizations. They constituted an "invisible government" that was a necessary part of the formal administrative structure. It was a grouping that could help or hinder the work of a company and merited the attention of all administrators. Above all, he urged executives to focus on the individual worker, to appreciate his life experience, and adjust the social conditions of the workplace accordingly (Barnard, *Executive*, 146–48; Barnard, *Organization and Management*, 7). Roethlisberger underscored this point in his 1941 book on *Management and Morale* and again in a 1950 speech. Employers would stand or fall on how effectively they dealt with the "human situations" in their firms. Treating employees well, he argued, might even outweigh good pay (Roethlisberger, 194; McNair, 325–26). The industrial relations specialist Clarence Hicks went beyond this. Too much of American industry was still run on an "autocratic basis," he said in 1941, and while it is often successful, "is neither logical nor consonant with the rights of individuals in a free country" (Hicks, 66). Four years later Sam Lewisohn, past president of Miami Copper Company, attacked the view that an "interest in human relations" would be a sign of "weakness in an executive." He urged that "wide-awake industrial executives" now place as much stress on "human relationships" as they did on production (Lewisohn, 41–42).

It was Sears, Roebuck, however, that probably made more headway in human relations than most other firms. With the help of W. Lloyd Warner and Burleigh Grimes, assessments of employee morale as well as "trends in employee attitudes" were undertaken. Of the 12,000 respondents to a 1948 survey, 95 percent said they preferred to work at Sears over any other firm. A later 1950 survey noted that employee satisfaction was heightened by Sears' flat organizational structure, profit sharing, employee benefits, and the quality of supervision (Worthy, 158–59). Undoubtedly, more than a little satisfaction came from Sears' decentralized structure that encouraged worker responsibility and initiative (Hoslett, 318). Its president, Robert E. Wood, contributed to this emphasis on individual initiative by urging that employees be given "some voice in the affairs of the organization" (Emmet and Jeuck, 371). James Worthy of Sears' Personnel Department went beyond this in a 1951 speech. Workers, he believed, would never play a key role in their company unless managers permitted a "creative relationship with work." This meant that Taylorism had to be revisited, that managers could no longer deal with the human problems of their employees in a mechanistic way (Friedmann, *Anatomy of Work*, 34–35). At Crown Zellerbach Alexander Heron was even more blunt: we cannot expect "a team spirit" among employees if we "keep on telling them that their function is to work and ours is to think" (Heron, 85).

Elsewhere there were small signs of forward movement. During the forties job enlargement as a partial antidote to Taylorism was introduced at IBM, Maytag, Sears, Roebuck, Detroit Edison, and Colonial Insurance (Blumberg, 67; Friedmann, *Anatomy of Work*, 44–45, 49–52). The 1941 Yankee City studies of Warner and Lunt continued the analysis of "group aspects of social behavior." To understand "human relations in action", these social scientists believed it was vital to know "the place the worker occupies" in the larger factory context. Like Mayo, they rejected "a merely economic logic of production," for such a path would only swell opposition "at a lower level" (Warner and Lunt, 1–3, 11–14). Eight years later Reynolds and Shister's work in a mid-sized New England city suggested that having some independence and control was an important element in job satisfaction (Reynolds and Shister, 4–5, 7). A 1947 poll also noted the importance of job challenge. And while 54% of all factory workers found their work interesting, it was a relatively small number compared to the 92% of professionals and executives. The survey also noted that only 39.9% of factory operatives believed hard work would help them advance, in contrast to the 58.3% of managers and professionals (Heron, 71–72).

In the America of the forties the ideas of Peter Drucker emerged as an important catalyst that went beyond the prevailing human relations emphasis. He argued that there was a "problem of dignity and fulfillment" in American industry, a situation that could not be turned around by focussing on pay and promotion alone. Drucker believed that employees needed a psychological connection with their work if their commitment was to be won. But if getting ahead was to be society's paramount work value, only a minority would ever achieve a sense of accomplishment. Most important was the need for the workplace to go beyond the values of "the market society" whose Calvinist bent refused to concern itself "with the great majority . . . not elected to be saved." He asserted that the very "survival of our basic beliefs" depended on the corporation's ability "to carry the burden of our dreams," and suggested employees had to be given a chance "to show what they can do" (Drucker, *Concept*, 129–31, 179, 123, 134–35, 36; Drucker, *New Society*, 6).

During the fifties George Homans and William F. Whyte made additional contributions to the Human Relations Movement. Like his predecessors, Homans stresssed the diminishing returns industry could expect if it continued to stress a repetitive division of labor based on financial reward alone. Also important was "pleasant companionship, prestige, connection with an important business, and, not least, the sheer interest of the job." To Homans, the importance of cohesive work groups was decisive (Homans, 102, 401-2, 112, 95-97). In line with Homans' thinking, William F. Whyte also studied sentiments, interaction, and worker activities. He noted how crucial it was for management to understand the values workers brought to the workplace. These sentiments could affect employee attitudes toward management and were not be ignored. Whyte criticized managers who equated men and machines as the passive agents of profit. For machines, managers could switch on the electricity, but for workers "money takes the place of electricity." Whyte continued by urging that pay might bring about better results if it was awarded by groups that established their own "norms or standards of behavior." Above all managers had to see that "the factory was a social system." They had to appreciate that such a system was based on the "mutual dependence" of people, and needed to develop an organizational structure and work processes that reflected this reality (W. F. Whyte, *Men and Work*, 41–43; W. F. Whyte, *Money and Motivation*, 3, 210–13, 218).

Two surveys in the fifties tended to support some of the suggestions made by the human relations school. The study conducted by Robert Dubin in 1952–53 in three Midwestern plants found that "work and the workplace *are not* central life interests." Only 24 percent of the workers surveyed could be classified as "job oriented." They saw factory life in instrumental terms, and preferred social interaction or other activity outside the workplace. Dubin saw the worker desire for "intimate human relationships" as something to be sought after working hours. And in a clear jab at the human relations experts, he asserted that "all the communication effort and group dynamics in the world will not alter the basic drift in our society away from a central life interest in work" (Dubin, "Industrial Workers'," 54, 60, 68, 70).

A second research effort of importance was the nationwide Morse-Weiss study on the meaning of work. It surveyed 401 men in September 1953, and provided results that varied by occupational category. Managers placed a higher value on salary than workers in the professions, crafts, or trades who stressed job content. But unskilled workers tended to emphasize pay, while service employees valued congenial co-workers. If this were looked at on the basis of class, the survey found that middle class workers looked to job interest as a source of satisfaction. Few working class respondents shared this perspective. In that group 71 percent felt it was important to keep occupied, and did not see accomplishment in the same light as their middle-class counterparts. But work did give meaning to the lives of most of these employees. Some gained a sense of self-respect, enjoyment, good health, and a feeling of attachment to an activity that kept them interested or at least occupied. A majority even said they would continue to labor even if there was no economic pressure to do so.

In addition, the 80 percent level of job satisfaction suggested that "most individuals accommodate themselves to their chances and possibilities in life and in general do not maintain, as conscious aspirations, chances and opportunities not within their scope to realize" (Morse and Weiss, 195–97, 192–93, 198). It was this relatively low level of employment horizons that would change from the sixties onward.

By the late fifties the Human Relations Movement had run its course. Malcolm McNair of Harvard agreed that its thrust for the respect of the dignity of the individual was important, but felt that "too much emphasis on human relations encourages people to feel sorry for themselves," avoid responsibility and "find excuses for failure" (McNair, 324–25, 327). Even advocates like Whyte came to believe that human relations training programs yielded few results. It was necessary to look beyond the "narrow" base of interpersonal relations and consider the impact of technology, culture, work flow, managerial personality, and the nature of the organization (W. F. Whyte, *Man and Organization*, 5, 11–14). Mills viewed the absence of discussion on power as a fundamental weakness of human relations thinking, and criticized its displacement by an overemphasis on status (Mills,"Contributions of Sociology," 212–13; A. W. Green, *Sociology*, 242).

On the other hand, McGregor saw much naivete in the thinking of human relations advocates. In their desire to move managers from a "hard" to a "soft" approach, they failed to see that removing controls was not a viable alternative to authoritarian management. There was no direct connection between employee satisfaction and productivity and progress did not always flow from the "elimination of dissatisfaction, disagreement, or even open conflict" (McGregor, 46). This perspective clearly influenced many managers in the fifties to look more closely at "organizational and structural influences" on employer-employee relations and less in the human relations direction that underscored "face-to-face relations in small group settings" (B. Kaufman, *Industrial Relations*, 120). But if "persuasion and participation" were now "displacing authoritarian methods of management" as Lester suggested in 1958 (Lester, 39–40), the studies of Raymond Miles were not as hopeful. Miles felt that participative structures set up by managers were done only as a way "of improving subordinate morale and satisfaction." His research indicated that managers were not particularly hopeful that participative practices would lead to better performance, that even their emphasis on human relations was but "a lubricant which oils away resistance to formal authority." In short, administrators were quite willing to use human relations as a method to improve performance and maintain their control. But for themselves, they preferred a human resources approach through which *their* superiors would "recognize and make full use of their currently wasted talents" (Miles, 154, 148–50). What they wanted for themselves they were unwilling to give to subordinates.

By the early sixties the Human Relations Movement was increasingly seen as a fad of the past. Some critics even viewed it as somewhat simplistic (Williams, 13), while others were concerned that human relations strategies hoodwinked employees by giving them the impression they were making decisions. It impelled observers like Ellul to denounce human relations because it led the worker "to accept his slavery" in a context that subordinated "human spontaneity to the mathematical calculations of technicians" (Ellul, 354–56). But despite these criticisms, the Human Relations Movement was an important step forward. Its emphasis on interpersonal relations, group dynamics, and employee morale may not in themselves have contributed to improved performance or employee challenge. But they helped humanize the workplace and paved the way for the human resources approach that saw workers as talented individuals who merited attention and development.

Chapter 9

THE HUMAN RESOURCES MOVEMENT

While the human relations advocates helped sensitize managers to the need for better interpersonal relations, morale, and group dynamics, it was but the first step on the long road to viewing workers as valued resources. During the fifties it was still common to design manufacturing jobs around such traditional criteria as specialization, work simplification, and minimal training times. In line with the existing Tayloristic outlook, planning and coordination were handled at more rarefied levels. This eliminated employees from most creative roles, and tended to degrade their motivation (Davis, Canter, and Hoffman, "Job Design Criteria," 21–22). Such practices in auto assembly led to rules laid down by time-study experts, while management tried to appease workers through the usual human relations formula of a pleasant workplace, good medical facilities, and a nearby canteen.

But workers were not taken in by these contextual changes. What many wanted was work content that made a difference (Guest, "Assembly–Line Worker," 496–501). Moreover, most managers did not understand how repetitive labor often led to high turnover and absenteeism. Nor was the apathy and dissatisfaction that frequently followed of great importance to executive mind of the fifties (Walker and Guest, 115–22). In a mid-fifties study of auto workers, Chinoy found they spoke wistfully about escape from the assembly line to start a business of their own. But despite the public rhetoric about opportunity and success most realized that advancement within the plant or union was limited. Many confined their hopes to less deadening labor off the line or turned to consumerism to replace a loss of independence on the job (Chinoy, 82–83, 71, xii-xv). What resulted was a sharp cleavage between management and workers, a we-they division that led workers to seek help from foremen who would stand up to management in matters like reasonable line-pacing (A. Turner, "Foreman," 382–85). A 1973 study of 180 assembly-line workers by Guest found that little had changed from his 1952 anaylsis of the GM facility at Framingham, Massachusetts: estrangement from their job led many workers to absent themselves or leave. Many workers in auto plants came to believe that "you need a strong back and a weak mind to work here" (Al Nash, "Job Satisfaction," 66–67). It was not surprising that Orzack's 1959 study found that only 24 percent of industrial workers saw work as a "central life interest." Many even resorted to "factory games" to avoid boring work. By contrast, 79 percent of the nurses interviewed saw work as a key element in their lives. That nursing offered more challenge and control probably had a great deal to do with the very different work values held by professionals in general (Orzack, 75; Bennett Berger, 33–36). This situation led Erich Fromm to question the overall danger of an industrial world oriented to mass production. To avoid making robots of workers he suggested the "active and responsible participation" of employees. He saw them as potential "co-managers" (Fromm, 313) who could enrich their jobs even as they enriched their company. Walter Buckingham, on the other hand, believed automated work would emerge as an avenue of increased worker control. It required greater skills and provided work that gave employees the status and dignity that elevated their efforts beyond earning a livelihood (Buckingham, 100). More influential were the ideas of Douglas McGregor. Writing in 1960, he suggested that both the needs of the individual and those of the firm had to recognized. To implement this "principle of integration" managers had to set aside their existing negative assumptions about human behavior. In short, they needed to drop a Theory X approach that viewed workers as lazy practitioners who had to be pushed for performance. Managers also had to avoid seeing their employees as irresponsible individuals who were content to leave decisions to their supervisors in exchange for pay. Through his Theory Y McGregor urged managers to accept a series of positive behavioral assumptions that were more likely to win employee commitment. Giving workers more responsibility and an opportunity for self-direction could make workplaces the creative enclaves of the future instead of the controlled cells of the past. If this were done, organizations would be able to enlist a fuller measure of worker support for the achievement of organizational objectives (McGregor, 47–50, 34–35). Rensis Likert took a similar approach. Only if employees had "a high sense of involvement" would they identify with company goals and avoid alienation (Likert, 98). Friedmann also urged greater employee participation so that "an unbridgeable psychological gulf" with management could be avoided (Friedmann, *Anatomy of Work*, 156). Herzberg, on the other hand, stressed the particular motivators that led to improved performance, intrinsic factors that centered on the content of work rather than its context. To do this managers had to cultivate the creative "Abraham" side of their workers by designing jobs that offered responsibility, recognition, and achievement (Herzberg, 188–89, 98).

The issue was joined in the early sixties. Would American managers continue their well-established philosophy of control, or could they hone off its sharper edges in favor of a more participative leadership style? It was a question that could not be answered solely within an industrial context, for they were confronted by a series of deep societal changes that racked America during the sixties and early seventies. Most important as a challenge to traditional work values was the decline of the old authority structure. Protests against the Vietnam War brought governmental authority into question, while the Civil Rights Movement questioned the old power structure in the South and demanded a societal change that would improve the socioeconomic position of Afro-Americans. The corporate world was confronted by an environmental movement that sprung from the pen of Rachael Carson, while college students used sit-ins to win influence over curriculum, faculty, and governance. It was a decade in which the feminist movement became a reality, and Dr. Spock's advocacy of permissive child-rearing became an article of faith in millions of middle-class homes. Hair, clothes, and personal uncleanliness emerged as symbols of revolt against society, corporate technocracy, and authority in general. Taken together it formed a "counter culture" that questioned "nation, party, corporation . . . [and] socioeconomic system," and constituted an attack on "the regime of experts" who used the affluence created by technology "to charm conformity" from a willing populace. Needed was a revolt against the "gigantic technological mechanism" that kept society in thrall. For a generation that came to question all authority their answer lay in "community" and "participative democracy" (Roszak, 54–55, 9).

For those in America who led the attack on traditional authority there was less than a compelling interest in competition and advancement. Their values centered on a "rampant individualism" that led activists to believe they were more than their job. What followed was the enshrinement of swift gratification (Howard and Wilson, 33) as an eleventh commandment. But with this came a desire for fulfillment in work and a lesser willingness to accept close supervision (Zimpel, 10–12, 122). In fact a *Work in America Institute* report indicated that by the early 1980s many younger workers accepted managerial authority with considerable reservation. Wanted was more autonomy on the job (Rosow and Zager, 23). Relegated to a lesser position in the new pantheon of work values was the organization man (W. H. Whyte, *Organization Man*, 6). In the brave new world of the counter-culture nothing could be further from nirvana.

Kenneth Keniston reflected this new outlook on work with great accuracy. He believed that "too few jobs challenge the heart, imagination, or spirit." Instead, they required employees to subordinate these to "the cognitive requirements" of work, a situation whose psychological weight often left labor without meaning. In short, Keniston urged that work had to include the rational, but not to the extent that it suppressed individuality (Keniston, 266). Looking back on this in 1974, Brigitte Berger suggested that the trend toward meaningful work was "legitimized" rather than caused by the cultural revolution of the sixties (Brigitte Berger, 56), while Thomas J. Watson of IBM argued that technological change had to be implemented with human considerations in mind (T. J. Watson, 299). Ellul worried that unless individuals had more control over their work and life they would be "smoothed out, like a pair of pants under a steam iron" (Ellul, 411). It is little wonder that a *Fortune*-Yankelovich survey of January 1969 on basic values showed that over two-thirds of both noncollege and college students wanted work that was more than just a job (Maher and Piersol, 16–17). Clark Kerr also believed these turbulent times would lead to a demand for "good jobs" that gave employees greater control and went beyond collective bargaining. This was particularly relevant for white collar workers who made up half the workforce by 1978. In addition, Kerr saw a displacement of the work ethic-oriented "old breed" worker by a growing "new breed" who would extend themselves only if work had meaning and challenge (Kerr, xi–xii). Richard Walton noted the same desires for challenge, but believed that the pervasive new social forces suggested worker demand for changes to grow and learn in work that had some intrinsic interest. Employees wanted the opportunity to use some initiative, and were less tolerant of hierarchy and status differentials (Walton, "Innovative Restructuring of Work," 147–48).

Money and benefits now motivated workers to a lesser degree, for they were seen as givens rather than part of the reward structure for performance. Unless workers felt a sense of participation, had meaningful jobs, and were accorded some responsibility there would be a "holding back" of effort (Yankelovich, "Today's Workers," 68). In the words of one West Coast manager "young workers seem to be more loyal to a lifestyle or a type of work than they are to a company" (*U.S. News and World Report*, 3 September 1979, 36). They also were "less tolerant of contradictions that exist between their raised expectations and prevailing realities either on or off the job" (Freedman, 14). Despite all of this, two Gallup polls in 1971 and 1979 revealed job satisfaction at 84% and 81% respectively (L. Wood, 13), and may be explained in part by increasing managerial recognition that employees could be effective contributors capable of self-direction and useful participation. If so, the ideas of Herzberg, Robert Ford, J. R. Maher, Walton, and others clearly helped give the Human Resources Movement a push forward (Miles, 151–52; E. A. Locke, 1299–1300), although the number of companies involved was still modest.

Behind the social tides of the sixties and early seventies lay a series of socioeconomic changes that gave the Human Resources Movement additional propulsion. Most important was the emergence of an increasingly well-educated workforce. Between 1959 and 1977 the percentage of high school graduates in the workforce rose from 32% to 42%, while the number of college graduates in this category jumped from 10% to 18%. Even more significant was

growth in the median years of education of the American workforce which leaped from only 8.7 years in 1940 to 12.7 in 1980
(Yankelovich and Immerwahr, 2, 15). This, in turn, led to a pro-
fessionalization of the labor force. By 1977 the number of professionals had grown by 97% as compared to 1958, while managers
and administrators experienced a 42% increase during the same
time frame (Zuboff, "Work Ethic," 167). Or put another way, there
was a decided trend toward white collar employment, a category
in which the worker had greater discretion over commitment to
the job. In 1920 only 25% held white collar jobs, but by 1981 the
number reached 53% (Yankelovich and Immerwahr, 14). America
had become a "post-industrial society" in which service jobs
became increasingly important. In this changed setting "cooperation and reciprocity rather than coordination and hierarchy" held
sway (Bell, 148–49). This trend continued throughout the eighties
when 18 million positions were created in the service sector (Lester
Thurow, "Nightly Business Report" [TV], 22 December 1993). It
was this expansion of educated employees who added fuel on the
fires of self-fulfillment.

   These very different employees and the work values that
motivated them took deep root during the 1970s. Their new conception of success placed greater reliance on "expression, satisfaction, [and] actualization," but far less emphasis on "keeping up
with the Joneses." They saw greater value in creativity, time with
friends, and interesting work. Yet these men and women believed
that many employers stifled their desires by controlling management systems and bureaucracy (Yankelovich, "Meaning of Work,"
25–26, 35). Forty percent of those surveyed in 1974 were even
willing to take some economic risks to enhance their quality of life
(Yankelovich, "Turbulence," 81–87). In short, these "new breed"
workers were preoccupied with aspirations that centered on their
individual requirements—a need for self-esteem, a desire for identity, and a job that offered participation and self-respect (Yankelovich, "Psychological Contracts, 47, 50). These men and women
wanted to make shorter "more one-sided commitments" to their
organizations but viewed employers as "more obligated to them"
(Kanter, *Changing Shape of Work*, 5). By 1977 Yankelovich estimated
that 52 percent of Americans subscribed to "new breed" work
values. Losing force were the old values that mandated men find

their identity in work even if it conflicted with personal desires. Also weakening was the view that women should stay at home and avoid paid work if they could afford to do so (Yankelovich, "New Breed," 9–10).

These new "inner-directed" employees clearly placed their personal wants and aspirations above those of employers. Work schedules, personal conduct, and business priorities all had to be filtered through their screen of self-fulfillment (Sinetar, 752). That life had to be "more than a grim economic chore" (Yankelovich, "New Rules," 39) was reflected in the 1977 General Mills Survey on personal values. It showed that 67% of parents and 87% of university students subscribed to the concept of "self-fulfillment," while 62% of the parents and only 43% of the students looked favorably on hard work (Caplow, et al., 391). By comparison, the Yankelovich surveys on the belief that "hard work always pays off" showed that 58% of the public accepted this statement in 1968, but only 36% in 1981 (Yankelovich and Immerwahr, 17). Interestingly enough, workers surveyed in the mid-seventies placed friendly and helpful co-workers at the top of their list of job requirements. Yet a similar 70% that subscribed to this also endorsed interesting employment as a coveted work value (Yankelovich, *New Morality*, 104). Nevertheless, Yankelovich was only able to find 15% of those surveyed in 1979 in the category of "go-getters." These under-35 money-motivated and ambitious workers were clearly a minority, but they were supplemented by an additional 19% of over-35 employees who were dedicated to their jobs and wanted to contribute (Yankelovich, "Today's Workers," 63–65).

But for the "new breed" there was a different watchword: "the less they [gave] to the job, the more they seem[ed] to demand" (Yankelovich, "Psychological Contracts," 47). It is not surprising, therefore, that a 1979 study of 17,000 high school seniors suggested that the best places to work were those that offered "the least external control." Still, 75% of both the college and non-college youth surveyed agreed that they expected work "to be a very central part of my life" (Bachman and Johnson, 82, 80). Of more concern was the 1979 finding that only 13% of all workers found their jobs "meaningful and more important to them than leisure-time pursuits" (Yankelovich, "Today's Workers," 61), a number that grew to 39% according to a 1995 Roper Starch World-wide study (*Wall Street Journal*, 26 September 1995, A1). A survey of American managers earlier in the decade found a deep concern over an eroding work ethic (Rose, 65–66), while Amitai Etzioni worried about the emergence of a "siesta society" (*U.S. News and World Report*, 14 April 1980, 54).

These trends continued into the eighties and nineties. A 1982 survey of 1,460 managers indicated they wanted applicants who had initiative and were willing to accept responsibility, things they tended to associate with the traditional work ethic (Schmidt and Posner, 9, 33). But an AT & T study of managerial recruits published the same year led researchers to conclude these employees wanted more than an "interesting job." They also sought employment that would give them "emotional sustenance from peers with no heavy commitment to the organization." They were not inclined to assume leadership, and had a disdain for following others (Howard and Wilson, 38).

A national survey published in 1983 shed additional light on why some American workers had less than a stellar commitment to their companies. Respondents stated that they strongly preferred to work with people who treated them with respect. Of equally high importance was a demand for interesting work, recognition for a job well done, and a chance to develop skills. They wanted managers who at least considered their ideas, and placed considerable value on being well-informed in matters that affected them (Yankelovich and Immerwahr, 22–23). However, 75% did not think their managers knew how to motivate employees, and almost the same number felt there was no pay differential for diligence. Other results were even more eye-opening. Only 23% indicated they were working at their full potential, while 44% said they did what was necessary to hold their jobs. In short, there was far less than a maximum "discretionary effort" (ibid., 28, 2, 25, 18). Clearly, employees were looking for what social scientists called a quality of working life. It embraced a chance to develop one's capacity, and offered an opportunity to advance. Additionally, it conferred more control over work, and had both a collaborative management style and an environment of open communication (Walton, "Criteria for Quality of Working Life," 1:91–97; Walton, "Alienation," 231; A. Nash, "Job Satisfaction," 63, 76; Glaser, *Worklife Improvements*, 3–4).

But most important was a distinction social scientists now drew between job satisfaction and performance. Job satisfaction, so high in all post-1945 surveys, did not necessarily lead to good performance. More and more organizational objectives centered on work challenge to improve both motivation and productivity. If these brought satisfaction in their wake so much the better, but more attention was now placed on results.

As discouraging as some of the Yankelovich-Immerwahr (1983) results were for American workers, they appeared far better when compared to responses from British employees. When asked if they could offer an endorsement of the work ethic, 52% of Americans responded favorably to only 21% on the part of their British counterparts. Only 21% of Americans felt a limited commitment to their work or saw it as no more than a financial necessity; 48% of British respondents felt this way, while 54% in West Germany agreed (Yankelovich and Immerwahr, 21).

By the 1990s the parameters of the Human Resources Movement were firmly established. A *Fortune* magazine survey of five hundred 21- to 29-year-old employees found that 70% felt it very important to work with people "you like," a result not unlike a mid-seventies survey (Deutschman, 54; Yankelovich, *New Morality*, 104). Some 40% believed that in comparison to their parents it was easier to find enjoyment and accomplishment in work; 47% found no difference in this category (Deutschman, 44). Research on the values of the 18–29 age group by the Roper organization in 1993 found that interesting work was seen as a key part of the good life by 69% (the same as pay) as compared to 75% in 1978. But far fewer felt they had both good pay and challenging work, and more in this group sought satisfaction from family and friends (Otten, B1). Another 1993 study of 2,958 wage and salaried employees by the Families and Work Institute found that 52% equated success with the satisfaction of doing a good job. Thirty percent looked for respect and recognition, while only 21% saw good income as a sign of doing well. Important was the finding that women who sensed a lesser chance for advancement had decreased loyalty and commitment to the job (Shellenbarger, "Work-Force Study," B1, B8). And because 46% of the entire U.S. workforce was female in 1992 and almost 60% of married women were working in May 1993 (*Wall Street Journal*, 21 June 1993, R4; Feldstein, A14), this was no small problem.

Putting these ideas on worker responsibility and challenge into practice became increasingly common in corporate America during the last quarter century. Considerable impetus came from abroad, particularly the sociotechnical approaches of the Tavistock Institute coal mine studies in England (Trist and Bamforth, 3–38), the Norwegian experiments of Einar Thorsrud (Thorsrud, Sorensen, and Gustavsen, 422), and the participative practices of Swedish firms such as Volvo under Pehr Gyllenhammar (P. Bernstein, "Volvo," 87–95). Not to be overlooked was the quality circle concept that flourished in Japan in the early sixties (Glaser, *Worklife Improvements*, 183) and surfaced in Britain with more success by the nineties. Taken as a group, these foreign attempts to use semi-autonomous work groups and participative managerial practices had considerable influence in North America during the 1970s and thereafter.

In the United States these ideas were often translated in work redesigned to challenge employees. Jobs, Robert Dubin argued, had to be fashioned to fit people rather than make them adapt to a given technology or work process (Dubin, "Work in Modern Society," 9). Louis Davis looked to organizational design that emphasized "cooperation and responsive adaptation" in which "composite self-directing work groups" had participative roles. It was also vital that employees be given enough authority to do their jobs and, true to the human resource philosophy, have the opportunity for "continued development" (L. Davis, "Sociotechnical Systems," 324). To do this managers had to think of jobs as part of a sociotechnical system in which the social and technical elements together formed the context of work (L. Davis, "Job Design," 92). In this context worker motivation required a restructuring of work through job enrichment, sociotechnical systems design, or even job rotation. Evidence that these strategies could work came out of the successful work redesign effort at the General Foods plant in Topeka, Kansas in the early 1970s (W. Skinner, 217; Hackman, 98–104). These points were underscored in a later 1975 survey reported by Cherrington. Workers were now looking for the intrinsic rewards inherent in their labor, a desire for the three R's of modern work—responsibility, recognition, and respect. (Cherrington, 44). The Renwick and Lawler study of the late seventies underscored these work values: employees wanted some control over workplace decisions, some flexibility in working time, and interesting jobs (Renwick and Lawler, 53, 57). A 1977 survey indicated that many felt under-utilized in relation to their relatively high educational levels (Quinn and Staines, 300), and were willing to offer less than a full measure of devotion to unresponsive managers. In fact, a Gallup survey in April 1972 indicated that 57 percent of the "total public" said they could produce more if they tried (Berg, 29–30, 34). In the late seventies a University of Michigan survey found that 27 percent of all American workers were so ashamed of the quality of the things they were producing "that they would not want to buy them themselves" (Yankelovich, "New Rules," 78).

Underscoring this negative outlook was the findings of a 1979 study by M. R. Cooper and his colleagues. Based on 175,000 worker responses from surveys conducted since 1950, the researchers found a decided "hierarchy gap" between managers and their clerical and hourly workers. While managerial levels of job satis-faction remained relatively high on matters such as advancement, good communication, and respect, clerical and hourly workers suggested far less happiness in these areas. They were displeased with the relative lack of fairness by management and often found them unresponsive. Pay was not a central concern, but employees wanted what managers were perceived to have—a chance to achieve, be challenged, and win recognition for work well done (M. R. Cooper, 117–18, 123–24).

Despite these concerns many innovative workplace experi-ments were tried in an attempt to accommodate to the new work values. Among the more notable was that of General Foods. Employees at the existing Gaines Pet Food Plant at Kankakee, Illinois exhibited a series of problems which concerned managers, particularly "employee indifference and inattention." There was considerable waste at the plant, and shutdowns were not un-known. Employees often worked only part of each day, and some sabotage had been detected. These problems led General Foods to begin thinking about a new facility as early as 1968, but inter-estingly, less emphasis was placed on improving the situation at Kankakee. Instead a new Gaines pet food facility was built at Topeka, Kansas, a "greenfield" experiment in which new moti-vational methods would be tried. Self-managed work groups became Topeka's centerpiece. These 7 to 14 person teams were given considerable independence which allowed them to make group decisions by consensus. Teams were given responsibilty for maintenance of high quality standards, and jobs were designed so that each had some aspects of planning, problem-solving, or liasion work with others. For each new skill learned, team members were given a pay increase. This rewarded employee growth and learning and promoted the formation of multiskilled work groups. Managers at Topeka became facilitative leaders responsible for team development unlike traditional supervisiors who seldom deviated from a philosphy of control and direction (Walton, "Alienation," 74–75). All of this was done under the guidance of Lyman D. Ketchum despite the resistance of other top managers at General Foods (Ketchum, 2–3). Comparisons between Kankakee and Topeka in 1974 showed that the old facility was turning out .75 tons of pet food per worker, while Topeka produced 4.17 (Schrank, 126). In addition, after only eighteen months of operation in June 1972 Topeka had an overhead 33 percent lower than that of Kankakee (Walton, "Alienation," 77). Other savings at Topeka amounted to about one million dollars annually, while turnover ranged from only 0.8% to 1.4% (Walton, "Old Dog," 42). By 1981 the new plant manager reported that productivity had increased in every year but one (Simon, 7). Two years later the president of General Foods, Philip L. Smith, pointed to Topeka as a facility where worker control was based on giving them more responsibility (Rukeyser, 14C).

Many other major corporations introduced programs that emphasized employee participation, less bureaucracy, and decentralized authority. Dana Corporation, a maker of auto parts, saw its "humanistic management" lead to a doubling of productivity between 1972 and 1979 (*Forbes*, 19 March 1979, 4–5). Motorola's concentration on job enrichment, the use of self-contained work groups, and the redesign of production lines all improved employee motivation. Its chairman, Robert Galvin, also noted that employees were more committed to their job when they were given control over their work (R. Hill, 12, 15). Experiments among production workers at the Harwood Company between 1957 and 1972 also showed the value of participative groups. Based on these Marrow argued that in the seventies American industry was "overmanaged and overcontrolled," and that workers would strike back if this situation was not rectified (Marrow, 35).

Worker sabotage on the Vega line at the GM Lordstown, Ohio plant in the early 1970s was evidence of how serious this problem could be among younger workers (ibid., 35). In addition, friction between workers at AT & T and the Communication Workers of America in the late seventies led the union to dub 15 June 1979 "job pressures day." This tension plus the on-going dialogue with the union finally led AT & T to establish a Work Relationship Unit under Rex Reed to enlarge employee involvement (*Business Week*, 25 June 1979, 91, 96). Eaton Corporation inaugurated a more extensive participative program at thirteen plants which involved 5,000 workers between 1968 and 1975. Employees joined in weekly staff meetings, conducted business with staff on the shop floor, and attended meetings on planning, production, and process engineering. Results varied, but at the new plants absenteeism dropped to a range of 0.5–3.0% instead of 6–8% at traditional facilities. Turnover declined sharply to only 4% at the newer plants compared to a rate that sometimes approached 60% at traditional workplaces (Scobel, 137–39). One cautionary note crept in, however. In the successful Rushton Mining Company experiments at Osceola Mills, Pennsylvania during the early 1970s, the researchers came to believe that the personal work values of the president was the key element in the participative equation (Goodman and Lawler, 149, 164). If this indicated that employee involvement as a concept was difficult to institutionalize, then the diffusion of the Human Resources Movement faced serious limitations. To this day it is remains a concern of some magnitude.

Despite these doubts American businesses continued to move in the direction of employee involvement. Often, it took a situation that had national dimensions before some action followed. A case in point was the well-publicized strike at the General Motors assembly plant in Lordstown, Ohio in March 1972. The problems at Lordstown included not only noise, heat, and pollution, but monotonous work assignments that bored the young workforce. One 1972 worker felt the jobs offered little challenge to an educated labor force (*Worker Alienation, 1972*, 10, 12) that had an average 13.2 years of schooling in 1975. The assembly line moved at a phenomenal 101 cars per hour and was recognized as the fastest in the world. This gave operatives only thirty-six seconds to complete a task before repeating it. And while automation and work simplification did help some operatives, it deprived others of pride in their work. It is little wonder that this situation led to slowdowns, stoppages, and finally a twenty-two day strike in March 1972. Some 130,000 Vegas had to be recalled by GM at considerable cost, and the firm had to deal with 15,000 grievances that were filed prior to the strike. Alienation from the Tayloristic work was undoubtedly one of the major causes of the walkout, but it was not until management ran an attitude survey just after the strike that it learned of the distrust and antagonism that was rampant in its workforce. To its credit, the organization instituted a new communications program to keep employees informed about sales, inventory, and production schedules, but it made few efforts to solicit employee ideas (Garson, "Luddites," 68; Salpukas, N34; Lee and Grix, 21–23). A visit to Lordstown by the author in November 1979 found the situation almost unchanged. While the managers had made a genuine effort to improve communications, job enrichment was not as yet on the front burner. Lordstown may have been a marvel of coordination, but the author observed that several Sunbird assemblers let cars pass without doing their job. By 1982, however, Serrin reported that the older Lordstown workers had mellowed with age and were sobered by the declining auto market. Managers finally allowed some employee involvement, and slowed the line pacing to 42-44 seconds per job (Serrin, 1–2).

The events that occurred at Lordstown undoubtedly facilitated the quality of working life pact between GM and the United Auto Workers (UAW) in 1973. Led by Irving Bluestone of the UAW and George Morris of GM, a general agreement was developed (Bluestone, "Work Humanization," 173). But in practice its implementation was dependent on the outlook of the individual plant manager, and was not institutionalized as part of a GM outlook. Nevertheless, an important venture was attempted at the Tarrytown, New York assembly plant under the direction of Sidney Rubenstein. It was a sincere attempt to inculcate trust between UAW Local 664 represented by Ray Calore and the plant manager, Bill Slachta. The agreement reached in 1973 gave workers some responsibity and induced supervisors to consider employee ideas.

That some progress was made in the ensuing years was noted by the author during a November 1978 conference at the Tarrytown facility. During these sessions one worker observed that Tarrytown was no longer a place where workers felt managers "paid for our hands and feet and chopped off our head." Now, based on a careful training program for both workers and supervisors plus much improved communication, the program was expanded to include 3,800 workers. It led to a reduction in absenteeism from over 7% in 1972 to only 2.5% in 1976. Only thirty-two grievances were on the books at the end of 1978 in contrast to 2,000 seven years earlier. And most important, Tarrytown rose from one of GM's worst assembly plants to one of the highest rated of eighteen facilities (Guest, "Quality of Work Life," 77, 79, 85). Clearly, both climate and productivity had improved. As a GM human resource executive told the November 1978 GM-UAW conference at Tarrytown, it was vital to "treat people as human beings and all other things will fall in place." The author also heard union leader Irving Bluestone confirm that the old GM view of workers had changed. No longer would supervisors crow that "I am the boss and you are the horse." This new attitude led to increased worker participation. Instead of being a battleground, manager Gus Beirne noted that now "a lot of good ideas come forward" (GM-UAW Quality of Work Life Conference, Tarrytown, N.Y., 9 November 1978; *Time*, 5 May 1980, 87). But with a change in management in the early eighties, the participative phase at Tarrytown faded. According to Dutch Landen of GM, training in QWL did not lead to entry into employee participation teams such as those at Fisher Body Detroit (D. Jenkins, 15). Change, it would seem, had always been plant manager-dependent at GM, and with shifts in management, it often became an encapsulated event rather than an institutionalized fact. Despite this, Japanese competition forced GM to make some definitive steps toward team-based participation in plants other than Tarrytown.

While it would be impossible to catalog the many efforts to increase employee involvement during the eighties and nineties, work at numerous facilities served to illustrate the continuity of the trend. GM's use of self-managed work teams at its Warren, Ohio Packard Electric Division plant involved Local 717 in all major manpower decisions ("Pioneering Pact," *Business Week*, 31

December 1984, 48–49). Its joint venture with Toyota at the New United Motor Manufacturing (NUMMI) facility in Fremont, California gave self-directed groups considerable control over their labor. The plant did employ many of the standardized and repetitive jobs that other workplaces had jettisoned, but team members now held the stop-watches. A no-layoff policy reenforced the team culture which allowed workers considerable latitude in defining work methods and standards (Adler, 102–3; Adler and Cole, 86). Even more ambitious was GM's venture at its new Saturn plant in Spring Hill, Tennessee. As part of the 1985 pact to charter the facility, both GM and the UAW agreed that all Saturn decisions had to be hammered out by consensus. New hires had to be approved jointly, while union members also participated in choosing suppliers, dealers and ad agencies ("Here Comes GM's Saturn," *Business Week*, 9 April 1990, 57, 59). Beyond this, participative teams became an integral part of the Spring Hill work effort. Adversarial relationships so common at other GM facilities, said one member of the pedal team (accelerators, brakes, and clutches), was simply absent at Saturn (Raimy, 18–21).

Change also came to the GM's Rochester Products factory in the mid-eighties. Layoffs of 1,800 seemed to have awakened both workers and managers who then faced a choice of cooperation or extinction. What followed was training in team development, consensus decision-making, and how to improve on competitor products. In addition, Employee Involvement Groups (EIG) were used to identify and solve workplace problems. By 1985 there were thirty-two active EIGs (Interviews with GM employees from Rochester Products, 1982–87). Similar progress was made at the Saginaw Vanguard plant where workers and managers established "a real team feeling" (GM Bets an Arm and a Leg on a People-Free Plant," *Business Week*, 12 September 1988, 72–73). In this light the GM *Beliefs and Values* statement that stressed employees as "full partners in the business" became more credible (*Beliefs and Values*, General Motors Corporation, September 1990).

General Electric also made great strides in employee involvement from 1981 to the present under CEO Jack Welch. Since his elevation to the top post at GE Welch has made delegation down the line a cardinal point of belief at General Electric. Under Welch the traditional foreman fast became a relic of the past. At GE's locomotive diesel engine plant in Grove City, Pennsylvania, for example, the 600 hourly workers use self-managed teams to improve output. They were assisted by five "nonsupervisor salaried workers," rather than old-line foremen (J. R. Norman, *Forbes*, 10 October 1994, 91). At its GE Capital unit Senior Vice-President David Ekedahl used a "Work-out Process" to "unlock the creativity" of his employees. It involved open forums to elicit employee ideas, and obligated managers to follow up suggestions ("Participative Organizations Demand a New Breed of Leader," *Work in America* [June, 1993], 3; N. Tichy, 118). At GE's Louisville, Kentucky refrigerator, dishwasher, and range manufacturing unit, the use of teams saved GE $29 million in reduced supervisory and training costs. So successful was this venture that teams were planned for the entire plant by October of 1994 ("GE Management and IUEW Team Up to Save 7,000 Jobs in Louisville," *Work in America* [May, 1993], 4). There was little doubt that when Welch said "we've got to take out the boss element" he meant it (T. A. Stewart, "GE Keeps Those Ideas Coming," *Fortune*, 12 August 1991, 41).

Efforts to involve employees continued to proliferate during the last two decades of the century. Xerox Corporation was among the leaders in seeking employee cooperation in the improvement of product quality (Xerox Corporation, *NAMD News*, March 1981, 1). It was joined by Sherwin-Williams at its Richmond, Kentucky plant, Harman International in Bolivar, Tennessee, Jones and Laughlin at Aliquippa, Pennsylvania, and the Honeywell Torpedo '83 program (Poza and Markus, 3–25; Macy, 41–43; Casner-Lotto, 9–10; *World of Work Report* [April, 1984], 3). All stressed worker participation and the use of teams to improve manufacturing operations and provide a basis for employee involvement. In addition, Champion International introduced participative management at its new Quinnesec Pulp Mill when it opened on Michigan's Upper Peninsula in 1984. Peer involvement in hiring, tasks grouped in "job families," and training in collaborative skills, team building, and conflict resolution" were made a part of the new culture (*Work in America* [June 1988], 2). Chrysler also introduced the use of teams at its Jefferson North plant in Detroit. Employee ideas were invited *before* its new Grand Cherokee was launched in the early nineties (D. Levin, "Graying Factory," 6F). Ford also launched a program that emphasized cooperation and involvement to over-come deep worker suspicion at its Walton Hills, Ohio stamping mill. It was so successful that labor and overhead costs were cut by an average 3.2 percent each year between 1985 and 1992 (Templin, 1).

Many other firms carried the Human Resources Movement into the nineties. Employee empowerment at Chaparral Steel took a great leap forward between 1988 and 1991. CEO Gordon Forward emphasized that Chaparral was "a learning organization," and needed to involve its workforce in getting new products to market at low cost. Chaparral flattened its hierarchy so that only two levels remained between the CEO and operators in the rolling mill. Workers came to "feel ownership in the system" and a desire to "continuously solve problems" (Leonard-Barton, 23, 26). No less devoted to teamwork was the new AT & T organization under CEO Robert Allen. Allen invited union members to sit on planning committees at both the plant and corporate level, and helped move both the Communication Workers of America and the company away from old confrontational positions (D. Kirk-patrick, 55–56, 64, 66). Alcoa also made considerable progress along the road to employee involvement. Under CEO Paul O'Neill quality became a communal rallying point, and "enablers" were used to help managers and employees introduce better communi-cation and a broad-based involvement (Kolesar, 146, 155–56). Even Perdue Farms, Inc. began the process of worker involvement in decision-making. Under James Perdue employee ideas helped reduce carpal tunnel syndrome among food preparers by reshaping knives and adjusting work stations to the height of the employee (Barmash, F7). BMW also chose to use self-directed work teams in its new Spartanburg, South Carolina plant. Here multiskilled workers worked independently so they could switch jobs when the need arose (D. Levin, "BMW," F5). Amoco's CEO, H. L. Fuller also pushed the idea of empowerment. He cut many layers of management (*New York Times*, 12 July 1992, 8F) and sought to change the culture by improved communication.

But despite these beginnings serious difficulties remained. Many managers could not make the courage jump and relinquish some control. In concept they might agree with what had worked the GM-Toyota NUMMI venture or even laud the 30–40 percent productivity increase participative management helped achieve at Proctor and Gamble. But their traditional managerial style kept many from giving employees the responsibility and authority needed in the modern cooperative workplace (Donna Brown, 42). As late as 1993 self-directing teams at Hewlett-Packard ran into some difficulties with managers who could not forego an element of control (Joseph Weber, 218–19). During the same year at Bausch and Lomb half of the twenty managers taught to be team leaders had to be reassigned because they could not escape the old command and control culture. Group results are now used as an incentive to get all to work as a team (A. L. Stern, F5). The same problem surfaced in Zuboff's investigation of the technically advanced "Piney Wood" plant. Here managers even delayed the introduction of new technology so they could retain control. The idea of creating responsible and participative employees—"smart people"— was viewed as a direct threat to managerial power (Zuboff, *Smart Machine*, 251). At the end of 1993 a similar problem was reported at Kraft Foods. Here teams shared common goals and had "integrated duties," but problems occurred when supervisors insisted on making all assessments and rewarding individuals (B. Kelley, 28–30). This subtle problem of talking teamwork but basing rewards on individual performance was not only inconsistent but self-defeating. In this type of setting people quickly recognized the need to stand out as individuals (B. P. Noble, F21), as the author discovered in July 1994 while speaking with an accountant who worked for a nationally known firm in Columbus, Ohio. In this organization teamwork was touted as the hallmark of its style, but performance reviews and rewards were made on the basis of individual accomplishment. This employee quickly adapted to the real work values of the firm and did everything possible to highlight her individual achievements.

Greater insight into this problem may be gotten from a 1993 Accountemps survey of 150 executives who worked for some of the largest U.S. firms. Of these managers 59% rated money as the thing that motivated employees most, while only 26% ascribed this to personal satisfaction with work (M. Woods, 4). But a 1992 study of what *workers* wanted from their job suggested far different results. Interesting work was ranked as very important by 78% who responded, while high income drew a favorable response from

56%. In addition, being able to work independently was seen as a desirable feature by 64% of the respondents (Caggiano, 101). Clearly, there was a gulf between managerial and employee perceptions.

Leonard Greenhalgh saw the problem in the socialization of middle managers. During their entire career organizations led them to believe that "their job is to control those under them." Some companies may have added cooperation and teamwork to the evaluation system, but it was competitive skills that were really valued (Raub and Driscoll, 8F). So despite the many and varied human resource proposals since the early 1970s more than a few managers could not or would not make the participatory jump. This may prove to be particularly damaging in an technically advanced organization where a learning environment is crucial in dealing with short product life-cycles on the outside and fluid working relationships on the inside. In these settings commitment to the job has become a *sine qua non*. To succeed, companies must move toward a value system that utilizes people to their full potential (Zuboff, *Smart Machine*, 390, 414).

A survey of 553 global firms by the Boston Consulting Group found that the most successful were those that fostered "cooperation among employees." The differences between American and foreign companies could be found "in how people work together, how decisions get made and how leadership is practiced" (J. Lublin, A2). It pointed to the need for an organizational value system that supported career development and personal fulfillment. Without these, employers "will have an increasing number of unmotivated and ultimately unproductive workers" (Schein, 9). In an age of brutal competition, companies wedded to the philosophy of control will have satisfied managers but reluctant employees. Unless they retrain existing managers and seek new candidates from younger entrants to the labor force, their firms will lose the fine edge of creativity needed for survival. Companies can have control or cooperation. But unless the internal emphasis is on teamwork and the external thrust is on competition, their ability to survive in a global economy will be compromised.

Chapter 10

OLD CHALLENGES AND NEW ASPIRATIONS

In reflecting on the evolution of work values since the time of Martin Luther, it is clear that the old theological context had faded by the early eighteenth century. Both Luther and Calvin praised hard work, but always in the context of the calling. Calvin made it clear that those who worked steadfastly in their vocation did so for the glory of God and not for personal gain (Fullerton, 13). This was the message Increase Mather (1639–1723) took to the New World when he warned that all labor was to be done with the Lord in mind (Middlekauff, 170). The Reverend John Higginson even reminded the General Court of Massachusetts in 1663 that *"New-England is originally* a plantation of Religion, not a Plantation of Trade" (Bruchey, *Colonial Merchant*, 112).

But by the 1730s Congregationists, Quakers, and Anglicans all were singing the praises of profitable diligence. It heralded the successor world of alienation and opportunity, and formed the *first discontinuity* in work values by encouraging hard work as an avenue to advancement. This was a meaningful message for the eighteenth-century merchants like Thomas Hancock, and had a favorable resonance within the rising middle class of nineteenth-century America. But for factory laborers of the 1840s and after, it did not speak to a division of labor that made craft workers increasingly obsolete. Work was denuded of meaning, and pride in product was replaced by the controls of scientific management. Few of these operatives could appreciate the advice of Franklin or Horatio Alger who urged that opportunity was at hand for those who would work, save, and persevere. Nor could they relate to the message that nothing was beyond the grasp of the go-getter, that one only had to strive in order to grab the brass ring.

That this did not reflect reality for the new semi-skilled factory workers was not perceived until the 1880s. Only then did a small but influential group of managers see the need to win the support of their employees if they were to maximize output. Between 1905 and 1915 one scholar identified forty "progressive firms" where managers tried to avoid labor conflict by offering a wide range of benefits to their employees. And to the consternation of Frederick Taylor, the National Civic Federation even formed a welfare department in 1904 to spread the good news (Nelson, *Managers and Workers*, 115; Nelson, *Taylor*, 19). Collectively, these initiatives came to be known as welfare capitalism. They heralded the faint beginning of the *second discontinuity* in modern work values, and together with the later and more significant Human Relations and Human Resources Movements, constituted the period of Work as Self-Fulfillment.

By the late 1920s welfare capitalism had lost its momentum. Of increasing influence was the emerging Human Relations Movement (1930s–60) under Elton Mayo and Mary Parker Follett. Like the earlier proponents of welfare capitalism, their goal was to win the "cooperation" of employees. But there was a subtle new thrust that included good communication and a measure of employee involvement. Business leaders such as James Worthy of Sears, Roebuck also tried to win the support of employees through a modicum of consultation and huge doses of dignity. But by 1960 the Human Relations Movement had run its course without offering substantial results. Good personal relations had failed to improve output. Now it was time to test the thesis that if employees were treated as valuable human resources they would respond with a commitment that was lacking in earlier ages. It was to be the true measure of work as self-fulfillment.

During the last four decades of the twentieth century both social scientists and managers directed a vast array of projects designed to address the new aspirations of employees. They continually emphasized employee empowerment so that the inner commitment of workers could be tapped. Many managers such as those at Harley-Davidson had difficulty in making the tradeoff of control for commitment. Others at Westinghouse found their niche in "self-administering teams" that reduced the layers of management and enabled the firm to redeploy its workforce to meet changing project demands (Bruzzese, 21–22). At Milwaukee Electric Tool Company in Jackson, Mississippi self-directed work teams took charge of inventory control, quality, and on-time delivery. They were made responsible for the final product and were given additional pay for increasing their skill level. These moves toward treating employees as valued human resources improved productivity by 65 percent (CNBC Broadcast, 24 October 1995, 11:30 a.m.). But many managers still found it difficult to yield control. They failed to perceive that new information technology had made employees more self-contained and less needful of close monitoring. More hopeful was the emergence of a "post-heroic leadership" that provided a broad vision within which employees could work as independent entities. It was this type of nineties leadership that Levi Strauss provided at its Murphy, North Carolina facility. Instead of a culture dependent on "barking orders," the factory was converted to a gain-sharing system in which pay was tied to plant performance. Worker teams were trained to do thirty-six tasks instead of the normal one or two, and won a major voice in running the facility (Huey, 42). Whether these attempts to address the new aspirations of workers would become the norm of the future or be doomed as encapsulated exceptions of an idealistic experiment will determine the ultimate success of the Human Resources Movement.

What, then, happened to the *old challenges* of hard work, opportunity, job insecurity, and the issue of the deserving and undeserving poor? These were the key *continuities* that flowed across the five centuries after the Reformation. Their contemporary status would reveal a great deal about the current outlook on work values. It would also suggest that the mix of these challenges require the need to address the problems of unemployment and poverty even as opportunity and diligence are given the enduring support of society.

Of these *continuities* the belief in hard work remained a constant over the centuries. But within this value system the meaning of hard work changed. In the shift from a world dependent on agriculture to a factory universe, workers had to be "molded" to meet the rationalized expectations of industry. This socialization was a rite of passage that inculcated in the new operatives "the qualities of discipline, orderliness, and punctuality to a degree unknown in most other cultures." Work was now infused with an inner drive that pushed aside the less regimented traditions of an agricultural past. Society had produced a new "social character" (Ruitenbeek, 25) who now was induced to work in the mills of Lynn and Philadelphia. By the end of the nineteenth century the new factory hand had become an alienated laborer, the human residue of a deskilled industrial world. Hard work paid off only in consumption. Not until well into the twentieth century did diligence take on a more positive overtone. Only then did the proponents of welfare capitalism and Human Relations see the importance of winning worker cooperation. It was not a humanitarian gesture to make hard work more palatable, but an attempt to seek improved productivity by treating employees as means rather than ends. Still, the work ethic was perceived positively by 79% of noncollege respondents as late as 1969, although this number fell to 56% four years later. But even in these surveys a majority did not believe that adherence to the work ethic would lead to economic or psychological rewards (Yankelovich, *New Morality*, 26, 30–31, 60). By 1982 some 52 percent of American respondents indicated a commitment to the work ethic. But most important, the number was even higher among those holding high-discretion jobs. It was a key finding that underscored the importance of giving employees at all levels as much autonomy as they could handle, and suggested that adherence to hard work could now be framed as a "worth ethic." But in an analysis that was reminiscent of why many came to America after 1607, Rosabeth Moss Kanter suggested that commitment to the work ethic was really a "mobility ethic" to insure a better future for one's family (Kanter, "Work in a New America," 57). More recently, a 1993 Gallup poll found that all age groups surveyed believed that people could progress through hard work. Favorable percentages ranged from 63% to 69% (*Fortune*, 21 February 1994, 24). And when one researcher in December of 1994 asked individuals if they would continue to work if enough money was inherited to live well, 80% opted to stay employed (Dumaine, "Why Do We Work," 196). Clearly, most Americans continued to believe the Chinese proverb that "idleness is the holiday of fools."

Beyond the continuity that framed the American commitment to hard work was their adherence to the belief in opportunity. This *second continuity* surfaced in seventeenth-century America when the promise of land and freedom drew millions across the treacherous Atlantic (Wertenbaker, 184). Farmers and artisans often became indentured servants for as many as seven years so they could pay for their passage and seek a better life for themselves and their children (Cochran, *Business in American Life,* 13). So great was the pull that from 1640 to 1699 some 69 percent of the total natural increase of the English population emigrated to America. And from 1695 to 1801 emigration to America still accounted for 20 percent of England's natural increase (Wrigley and Schofield, 175).

To this must be added the American belief in progress that permeated the nineteenth century. It could be seen in a letter Jefferson wrote to a friend in 1818 (Ekirch, 32) and the comments of the French visitor Michel Chevalier in 1835 (Chevalier, 262). It was no less visible in the April, 1857 edition of *Harper's New Monthly Magazine* where the editor lauded the progress of industrialization as an advance that would help the poor (Yellowitz, 10–11). The continued belief in opportunity beckoned 8 million immigrants to the United States from 1870 to 1890. In most cases they now came less for land and more because of "livelihood-hunger." The flood continued, and between 1903 and 1914 over 800,000 immigrants arrived annually. In 1907, however, over 1,285,000 came, while 1913 saw a peak of 1,387,000 (Schnapper, 181, 290; P. Taft, 169). So great was the pull of opportunity that in 1907–08 between 49% and 59% of all workers in the various branches of metal manufacturing were foreign-born. For textiles it ranged from 57% to 72%, while the number was an astounding 82% in clothing (Nelson, *Managers and Workers,* 80). In most cases the pay was poor, but these new Americans saw their work as a stepping-stone to a better future. It was, in short, a progress ethic.

Writing in 1922 Herbert Hoover continued voice the belief in opportunity as the great "ideal of American individualism" (Hoover, 8–9). Opportunity was also the magnet that drew migrants to the great cities. An analysis of over one hundred American novels by George Dunlap in 1934 found that many moved to urban settings "hoping to find there more favorable surroundings or enlarged opportunities" (Dunlap, 11). A decade later the president of the U.S. Chamber of Commerce, Eric Johnston, repeated the old theme: "The two essentials in the American pattern of life and thought are *freedom and opportunity*. These were the values for which men and women of many nations, races, tongues, and cultures uprooted themselves to come to America" (E. Johnston, 243). During the fifties and sixties entrepreneurs made the most of their opportunities as companies like Hewlett-Packard and Texas Instruments became major players in transistors and semiconductors. Ray Kroc franchised his first McDonald's in 1955, while Holiday Inns, Aamco (auto repairs), and H & R Block grew from small beginnings (Galambos and Pratt, 175–76). Richard Nixon echoed a now-familiar tradition in a Labor Day address in 1971 when he lauded the American worker who helped make "this land the citadel of individual freedom and . . . opportunity" (*New York Times*, 7 September 1971, 14), while Ronald Reagan maintained this traditional commitment to the concept of opportunity in his 1980 speech accepting the Republican nomination for president (*New York Times*, 18 July 1980, A8). In the world of business entrepreneurs like Bill Gates of Microsoft and Andrew Grove of Intel exemplified the ideal in practice. And among the better-known theologians, Norman Vincent Peale could proclaim in 1990 that "one must believe in the country which affords opportunity, and be a believer in opportunity itself" (Peale, *Power of Positive Living*, 23).

Rosabeth Moss Kanter, however, looked at opportunity from the vantage point of the employee. Her research led her to conclude that the day-to-day comfort of job satisfaction was no substitute for the possibility of growth in work, for progress through development. This, she believed, was the true source of opportunity (Kanter, *Men and Women of the Corporation*, 161). A more recent study by K. I. Miller and P. R. Monge led them to a similar conclusion: the most satisfying aspect of opportunity is not the actual choice that an employee makes among a range of options, but the perception that the opportunity to make that choice is actually available. Another researcher, P. Muchinsky, believed that opportunity was "the great satisfier" in our culture (Schneider, Gunnarson, and Wheeler, 54, 65). Perhaps it is this sense of opportunity that energized so many young people to start their own businesses rather than work for others. A February 1995 Opinion Research Corporation poll found that 54 percent of those between

18 and 34 years of age were extremely or very interested in developing their own business. A study by Paul Reynolds of Marquette University found that 10 percent of Americans between the ages of 25 and 34 were actively engaged in beginning a new venture, triple the number for any other age group. Reynolds estimates the number actually trying to start an enterprise of some type at about seven million persons (Randall Lane, 102).

It is this sense of opportunity that continued to attract so many immigrants to the United States. Millions have braved the deserts of the southwest and the border patrols along the Rio Grande to seek a better life, while boatloads of political and economic refugees from Cuba and Haiti sought freedom and opportunity in Florida and the cities of the east coast. Likewise Asians from Taiwan, the PRC, India, and Pakistan have come to America in the hope of creating a better future for their families. Among all of these recent immigrants the old opportunity ethic has continued to flourish. Not all of them have risen into the middle class, but they continue to strive for an improved tomorrow.

For Afro-Americans the belief in opportunity was tightly constrained by three centuries of slavery, race riots, and job discrimination. They did not leave the shores of West Africa for opportunity, but were forcibly removed by slave traders who saw profit in their passage. As unwilling immigrants of the past, slaves of the South, and the victims of Jim Crow legislation in the aftermath of Reconstruction there were few avenues of upward mobility. Only through their struggle for better jobs in defense industries during World War II and the *Brown* decision in the mid-fifties were the doors of opportunity opened slightly. Their efforts gained some momentum after affirmative action became a reality in 1965, and were helped by leaders like Jesse Jackson who spoke eloquently of the virtues of hard work, discipline, and individual responsibility (*New York Times*, 4 March 1979, 38). By 1995 black men and women held 9% of the middle management jobs, but white men continued to hold 97% of the top managerial positions in Fortune 1000 industrial corporations (Kilborn, "Women and Minorities," A22; G. Craig, 6A). Despite these small improvements, the vast majority of blacks had to seek employment on a more modest level. Liberal black Professor William T. Wilson of the University of Chicago, a presidential adviser in 1995, made a series of suggestions that went beyond the affirmative action programs he viewed with some suspicion. Schools, he believed, had to emphasize language skills as the pathway to economic advancement in the growing service sector. He pointed out that employees with poor work attitudes were not wanted, and advocated that some young black males who desired independence in work and could not do well in routinized service sector employment be counseled into construction and long-haul trucking. Wilson also noted that inner-city youths often mistook the best jobs as those with the highest pay. Job counselors needed to help them see that getting a firm start was often the fastest way to good pay. Finally, for those with few skills he advocated subsized public transportation to the suburbs where job opportunities were often available ("Battleground Chicago," *Newsweek*, 3 April 1995, 33).

To this must be added the *third important continuity*, the endless quest for job security. Uncertainty of employment was the pervasive curse of the ages. It struck with suddenness and left the unemployed with the baggage of emotional turmoil and economic distress. With the appearance of an unpredictable market economy during the mid-fifteenth century, unemployment drove thousands to workhouses and welfare and created a climate of uncertainty within the thrust of opportunity.

As early as the sixteenth century it was clear that the fluctuations of the new global market place were causing turmoil in the English textile industry. Changes in distant demand caused considerable unemployment in 1528, 1551, and 1586. Within a domestic system that was dependent on faraway markets for profits and consistent work, craftsmen were turned into employees (Garraty, 32; R. Davis, *Atlantic Economies*, 21; Youings, 280). By the 1590s a combination of plague, poor harvests, population growth and great unemployment led policy makers to pass the Elizabethan Poor Laws. From this point, the public tax base became a source of support for the destitute and unemployed (Youings, 255, 270–71, 277–78). Nevertheless, the problem of job security continued without respite in Stuart England. Between 1603 and 1688 seven depressions or recessions wracked the English labor force to be followed by five additional convulsions from 1696 and 1710 (Hill, *Century of Revolution*, 321).

Job insecurity in colonial America also caused stress and privation despite the abundance of land. As early as 1685 Boston was compelled to establish a workhouse for the unemployed (Bridenbaugh, *Cities in the Wilderness*, 82). This was supplemented by "out relief" of goods and money (Smith and Zeitz, 15–16), but workhouses continued to proliferate in the nineteenth century and could be found as late as 1929 (Piven and Cloward, 48). During the eighteenth century trade fluctuations, currency depreciation, and a tide of poor immigrants contributed to poverty and unemployment (R. Morris, *Government and Labor*, 47, 11–12). Colonial Philadelphia, for example, was plagued by business cycles, seasonal problems, and illness that drove many to the workhouse. Suffering was particularly bad during two decades between 1763 and 1783 (B. G. Smith, "Laboring Philadelphians, 201–2).

Things did not improve as the old subsistence economy was gradually superceded by the new boom-and-bust "money economy." In particular, the Panic of 1819 struck hard at urban wage-earners. Some 75 percent were reportedly unemployed in Philadelphia. Baltimore and New York City each had an estimated 50,000 unemployed, while the national total may have reached 500,000. Many paupers were forced to flee to their families in the countryside, while skilled artisans were not exempt from the first of the many cyclical downturns that were to follow (Sellers, 137, 23–25). A second depression hit during 1837–39 that left one-third of the workers in New York City without work. Many New England mills either closed or ran part-time, and between 1839 and 1843 wages dropped 30–50 percent (N. Ware, 26–27). So great was the problem that Luddism surfaced in both Philadelphia and various New England mill towns (Shelton, 116–17; Zonderman, 47–48). To add to the misery, deskilling of the workforce (Hirsch, 22–23) made the craftsmen of yore replaceable factors of production.

Panics and depressions followed with appalling regularity in 1857, 1873, 1893, 1907, and 1921. The ultimate blow occurred during the Great Depression of 1929–41 when unemployment hit a high of 24.9 percent in early 1933 (I. Bernstein, *Lean Years*, 17–18). Only the advent of World War II ended the misery of the thirties. After 1945, however, postwar downturns continued to plague the industrial scene in 1957, 1974–75, 1981–82 and 1990–91. But one element changed in recent years. The traditional blue-collar unemployed were joined by waves of white-collar brethren. Altogether, American businesses dropped 4.4 million employees between 1979 and 1992. Increased use of temporaries, automation, and restructuring contributed to a general sense of job insecurity despite a gain of 15 million new jobs from 1982 to 1988. Most of these new jobs were in the service sector, while employment in the higher-paying manufacturing area dropped by 1.6 million after 1989 (Barnet, 47–48).

Job insecurity remained high in the early nineties. A survey of 1,100 adult Americans for *Time*/CNN in November, 1993 found 66 percent felt job security had declined over the past two years. Fifty-three percent believed it was a long-term problem, and 54 percent felt it would be more difficult to find a new job if one was fired. These findings were not surprising in the light of well-publicized layoffs of 1,850,000 between 1990 and 1993 ("Jobs in an Age of Insecurity," *Time*, 22 November 1993, 35, 37–38) despite the overall gain of jobs during this period and thereafter. Firms as diverse as Jostens Learning Corporation, AT & T, and Alliant Techsystems, Inc. reported considerable stress and fear among those who survived layoffs (*Wall Street Journal*, 6 December 1993, 1). And in a University of Michigan study of 12,600 persons ages 51 through 61 almost 50 percent feared they would be dropped in the coming year although many were not far from retirement (*AARP Bulletin* [September 1993], 15).

Most enlightening was a research study on job security by Cognetics, Inc. of Cambridge, Massachusetts which based its conclusions on an analysis of U.S. firms in its *Corporate Almanac* of 1994. The survey indicated that despite a growing economy that was creating 200,000 jobs monthly in early 1994, about 30 percent of all existing jobs in 1989 had disappeared by 1993. Two-thirds were due to plant or office closings. Layoffs were spread over large and small firms and were to be found in all regions. Hiring, on the other hand, was concentrated in a small number of fast-growing companies which it called "gazelles." Of these "gazelles," 250,000 just 3% of all firms it followed, created 70% of all "net new jobs." Still, Cognetics believed that the turmoil of the 1990–91 recession was not as severe as that in 1975 because many firms had already downsized and did not have to drop additional personnel (*Fortune*, 30 May 1994, 28).

Other problems involving job security were more subtle. These involved what one writer called the contingency workforce which included part-timers, temps, and the self-employed. According to the Bureau of Labor Statistics, a record 6.4 million of the 21 million part-timers in 1993 said they wanted full-time positions. Temporary workers also quadrupled between 1980 and the second quarter of 1993 from 400,000 to 1.6 million (Fierman, "Contingency Work Force," 31, 33). All of this suggests that the desire for full-time employment by many contingency workers is not likely to be fulfilled, for many businesses have discovered that hiring such employees enabled them to avoid costly benefit packages.

Beyond this was the question of employee loyalty during an age of job insecurity. Indicative of lesser loyalty to employers were the results of the Families and Work Institute Survey of 1993. This study of 3,381 workers over a five-year period showed that employees were far more committed to their personal goals than those of their employer. But employees who had greater control over their work exhibited less burnout and greater support for their firms. Supportive supervisors and a good social climate also yielded greater "on the job loyalty and initiative" (Sulit, 26–27).

Still, the national wave of restructuring and downsizing was exacting a price. Professor C. K. Pralahad of the University of Michigan noted dropping morale at many businesses and argued that "if you want continuous motivation and an energized company, you have to have some implicit guarantee that pink slips are a last resort. Loyalty is reciprocal" (Holusha, D1). Paul Osterman of MIT's Sloan School of Management added that "it's very hard to empower the labor force while laying so many people off" (*Fortune*, 18 April 1994, 28; *Investor's Business Daily*, 12 July 1993, 4). This concern was given additional confirmation by a survey of over 1,000 factories by Maryellen Kelley and Bennett Harrison. After studying employee involvement in these firms they found that massive layoffs undercut the trust needed to sustain employee loyalty (Donna Brown, "Participative Management," 44–45). William Rothwell of Pennsylvania State University was convinced that many workers "jump ship" because of the work overload that often follows downsizing. There is also the question of just how much loyalty temporary replacements are willing to offer (*Investor's Business Daily*, 14 February 1994, 4). But even in this fluid world where labor might be viewed as a "disposable commodity," it is not likely that businesses will give up immediate bottom-line gain for the possible benefits of long-term employment. For better or worse "contingent labor" is here to stay (Harrison and Bluestone, 13).

To meet the desire for stable employment some have suggested a shorter work week so that employment could be spread over a wider base. In this sense Richard Barnet looked at jobs as instruments to enhance life, living, and leisure. A shorter week would thus encourage the "healthy notion that a job is not the whole of life" (Barnet, 51–52). In a 1995 publication Jeremy Rifkin saw a thirty hour week as the panacea that could lead to job sharing and a reduction in much of the stress of modern life. Businessmen gave this idea little support, since it would place them at a competitive disadvantage with many foreign firms (Rifkin, 58). Nevertheless, the four-day 33-hour week is getting serious consideration in France where unemployment in recent years has often been above 10 percent. This French proposal would supposedly increase employment by 2 million and reduce unemployment and welfare benefits. However, Daniel Hamermesh of the University of Texas sees its productivity assumptions as "wing-and-a-prayer economics" (Passell, D2). Given the current climate and the fact that the average workweek in the United States has dropped from 38.1 hours per week in 1981 (Levitan and Johnson, 57) to 34.9 for employees in the private sector in January 1995 (manufacturing was 42.2) (*Monthly Labor Review* [March 1995], 89), legislative change to support a shorter work week does not appear to be imminent.

A more useful way to deal with the continuing problem of job security is the need to understand the nature of today's market. From the perspective of the mid-nineties it seems evident that the American economy has made the transition from "mass labor" to "elite labor." Taken together, the computer revolution, automation, and reengineering have wrought tremendous changes in the manufacturing sector. Today only 17% of American workers are engaged here compared to 33% in 1950, but productivity has jumped by 35% from 1979 to 1992. In the service sector, technical and mangerial changes could eliminate as many as 700,000 positions in banking as the number of such insitutions drops by about

25 percent due to continuing consolidation. As demonstrated by the separation of 50,000 employees at the Sears' merchandising division alone in 1993, retail jobs were not immune from downsizing. New technology has also put secretarial labor at risk. However, more optimistic scenarios reveal that service sector employment as a whole has almost tripled betweeen 1900 and 1990, while retail trade has leaped from 0.5% of the population to 17.8% during that time frame (Rifkin, 54–55, 59).

What, then, does this suggest as a way of dealing with job insecurity? Most important is the need to remain marketable by maintaining an appropriate skill and knowledge base. Computer literacy, the three R's, and apprenticeship training are essential for those who are not college-bound. For those who have opted for professional career tracks there will be a need for "constant retraining" to avoid technological obsolescence (Kilborn, "Job Security," 1). In addition, knowledge workers will need the foresight to seek out new job opportunities before short product-life cycles, restructuring, and obsolescence overtake them. They will need to look to a career path in prospect and not wait for the grim reaper of unemployment to provide them with the impetus to change. In a market economy job security will never be a realistic goal. No amount of hard work, dedication, and loyalty will overcome the cold hand of rationality if people must be laid off. To be prepared by continuous learning and a mind set that "nothing is forever" is the best defense. Franklin's observation best sums the need to be educated and vigilant: "The Bird that sits, is easily shot" (L. Labaree, *Franklin*, 7:83).

Even more contentious was the continuing public debate over work and welfare, an extension of the old controversy that differentiated the deserving and undeserving poor. It formed the *fourth continuity* in the history of work values, and without doubt, the most quarrelsome. Since the eighties the debate on work and welfare had become particularly passionate because of its attachment to new values of entitlement. This concept suggested that the unemployed and poor had a right to public assistance, and constituted a complete departure from Anglo-American values that had been in place since the Elizabethan era. A closer look at this four-hundred-year tradition of public assistance will clarify why the entitlement controversy has become so bitter.

To begin, it would not be unfair to say that sixteenth-century England was a particularly inhospitable haven for the unemployed. Both ministers and laymen demanded the poor be kept in labor. A London minister, Richard Stock (c. 1569–1627) was typical: "it benefits the giver to have them labor; it benefits the commonweal to suffer no drones, nor to nourish any in idleness; it benefits the poor themselves" (Hill, *Society and Puritanism*, 268). Most important was the Tudor admonition that only the deserving poor be helped. Only those who would work if it were available deserved community support (George and George, *Protestant Mind*, 154–59; Youings, 279). But it was not until the Elizabethan poor laws were codified in 1601 (after the devastating recession of the 1590s during which many almost starved) that the community fully acknowledged a responsibility to care for those who were poor, sick, unemployed, or encumbered by more children than they could support. To help, each parish was obligated to tax its citizens through a poor rate. Beggars were to be returned to their home parish for support, and materials were provided so the unemployed could be put to work (Bridenbaugh, *Vexed and Troubled Englishmen*, 382; Ashley, 88; Garraty, 33). Given the depth of the economic decline in the 1590s it was clear that state action was needed to handle poverty on such a scale. For the first time the crown "seriously entered the field of social welfare" (L. B. Smith, 228).

Colonial Americans drew heavily on Tudor work values. An article of faith was the distinction they drew between the deserving and undeserving poor. Widows, infants, aged, and disabled persons deserved the support of the community, but the able-bodied who could labor and did not were cast into the category of undeserving wretches. To support them by taxing the diligent was believed to be a waste of resources that in the end would not change the behavior of those who refused employment (Sachs and Hoogenboom, 83–84). During both the seventeenth and eighteenth centuries colonial Virginia had problems with "idle and disorderly persons, having no visible Estates or Employments" (E. Morgan, *American Slavery*, 238, 339). From 1783 to 1825 New York City officials complained about "Sloathful . . . disobedient, and Stragling Vagabonds" (Mohl, 43). To deal with the problem of the unemployed Boston established a workhouse in 1685, an idea that spread to most of the cities along the Atlantic seaboard during the eighteenth century. During the nineteenth century publicly supported almshouses were designed more to "degrade than reform" their inmates. In addition to the poor, they housed alcoholics, orphans, and the blind and insane. Only in the 1860s did a few states like Ohio appoint permanent inspection boards to oversee administration by local officials. But the prevailing view was that public assistance was to be granted sparingly and under circumstances so abhorrent as to keep most from accepting it (Bremner, 47–49). By 1884 New England alone had 600 almshouses where paupers could get assistance or be assigned to indentured service. Even as late as 1929 the almshouse remained as a refuge for the unemployed and poor, although it was supplemented by pensions for the blind, aged, and widows (Mothers' Aid) by local communities who chose to participate (Piven and Cloward, 46–48). The key to unlocking the labor of the deserving poor, however, was to make the workhouse so unpalatable that outside employment would loom as a desirable alternative.

Of particular interest in the light of today's problems was the Philadelphia welfare crisis of the 1820s. The improvidence of the poor had long been criticized in Philadelphia, but the recession of 1817–20 pushed welfare costs up so high that the Guardians of the Poor were forced to borrow money to pay for mushrooming costs. Citizen concern with paupers, those unworthy poor who could work but refused to do so, spread to Boston, Baltimore, and New York City. New immigrants who were jobless added to the furor. By 1828 new legislation in Pennsylvania permitted Philadelphia to reduce taxes for support of the poor, and created a commission to construct a new almshouse as the primary aid-giver. Those most affected were poor women and children who had been beneficiaries of "outdoor cash aid." This support was to be replaced by residence in the almshouse as soon as it was finished. It was clear that women were the target of the 1828 law: from 1811 to 1829 from 86 to 91 percent of those getting cash relief were females. Two-thirds were sick or disabled single women in the 1814–1815 census, while one-third were mothers (mostly widows) with two to three children to support. Of particular interest concerning the work and welfare debate of the 1990s was the fact that the 1828 Philadelphia legislation ended help for women with illegitimate children, a group that included from 4 to 20 percent of females getting cash assistance between 1814 and 1826. Most important was the negative view of the poor who were viewed as improvident and immoral (P. F. Clement, 152, 154–55, 161–64).

Lynn, Massachusetts also underwent a welfare crisis in the 1820s. One inhabitant who wrote under the name of "Civis" to the *Lynn Mirror* argued that the old distinction between the deserving and undeserving poor had to be drawn more strictly. He believed that many persons who resided in the local poor house lived on a scale better than that of working men. "Civis" advocated that conditions in the poor house be made so severe that they would repel all but those in the most extreme need, and then only those who would work if they could. The Lynn officials did not accept these ideas in 1828. Nevertheless, they now confined almshouse inmates more closely and required them to purchase food from supplies made available at the poor house to insure that no liquor was bought (Faler, *Mechanics and Manufacturers*, 111–13).

The work-welfare dilemma continued to challenge America during the next one hundred sixty years. Recessions and depressions from 1819 to 1990–91 became the unwanted companions of the American worker. Despite these impersonal economic forces that buffeted the unemployed, the belief persisted that many idled employees would not accept work if it were offered. In the 1870s the Philadelphia Society for Organized Charity argued that giving aid to the unemployed "encourages the idle, the shiftless and degraded to live at the public charge rather than earn their own bread" (Garraty, 117). Still, during the 1914–15 recession the New York Association for Improving the Condition of the Poor started a variety of projects to get the destitute back to work (Piven and Cloward, 48n6). But some like the president of the National Association of Manufacturers continued to believe that unemployment was the result of laziness (Mowry, 69). That this myopic view was uttered during the depths of the Great Depression in 1932 suggests that it was so deeply held a belief that it could exclude the reality of an employment rate close to 25 percent. And those who did manage to cling to work during the thirties like Chicago teacher Elsa Ponselle lived with the daily fear of losing their job (T. H. Watkins, 13).

These divergent views were part of the dilemma that would later face policy makers during the three decades after the emergence of the Great Society: along with the consistent suspicion that those on the public dole could find work if they wished to do so was the powerful attachment to the labor force by many who managed to work with some regularity. Less charitable observers saw the split as between those who feared losing their job as compared to those who feared finding a job. The Morse-Weiss study of 1955 spoke of those who found a strong attachment to work. In a study of 401 men who were asked whether they would continue working if they had enough money to live comfortably, 86% of the middle-class and 76% of working-class employees said they would do so (Morse and Weiss, 192, 197). To this must be appended studies in the 1960s by Yankelovich on why many remained wedded to work. He found that the values of the post-1945 period emphasized the "good provider" theme, the bread-winner who worked hard to improve the material condition of his family. In all of this, success continued to have a prominent place in the pantheon of middle-class work values (Yankelovich, "Meaning of Work," 22–25). In itself it was but a continuation of a long American tradition of self-improvement, but in the world of the sixties it was a view that was at variance with the ideals of Great Society policy-makers.

Help for the unemployed and poor through state and national legislation did not begin with the Johnson administration, but could be traced to 1932 legislation by Wisconsin. This law required firms of ten or more workers to pay into a fund that would offer financial assistance to laid-off workers. And since this fit more closely with the traditional American practice of making public assistance a local responsibility, it was an important but not radical departure. Hoover, like Franklin Pierce seventy years earlier (Smith and Zeitz, 33), refused to accept the idea of using federal funds for relief. But when Roosevelt took office in 1933 this changed. He quickly got Congress to establish the Federal Emergency Relief Administration and won an appropriation of $500 million for distribution through state and local agencies. A few months later the Civil Works Administration was put in place as a public works program to alleviate unemployment, and throughout the depression many other programs were used to provide money and jobs for those without work. Hoover and his followers never accepted this expanded federal role. They feared the idea of relief from Washington would destroy the "moral fiber" of Americans and make them less willing to work (Garraty, 212–14). Nevertheless, the enormous pressure of poverty during the Great Depression enabled New Deal policy-makers to win approval for the Aid to Dependent Children (now Aid to Families with Dependent Children or AFDC) program as part of the Social Security Act of 1935. Relief would be distributed by local officials who knew their clients, but in accordance with long established tradition dating back to Tudor England, only the "truly needy" would get assistance (Marmor, 26). Murray argued that this and other New Deal programs such as unemployment insurance had nothing to do with the modern concept of welfare. Rather, they were aimed at helping hard working citizens (the deserving poor) who had lost their job due to economic forces beyond their control or who were too ill or old to work. AFDC in particular had been designed in the thirties for widows with children, but by the late fifties most of the female recipients were single women with children. But despite a rising concern, births to single women in 1960 were only 5.3 percent of the total. When this percentage rose sharply during the next thirty-five years, the new lifestyle violated middle-class conceptions of work and morality and made the concern a heated public issue (Murray, *Losing Ground*, 17–20; Berkowitz and McQuaid, 203–4). By 1979 blacks made up 44% of those getting AFDC. With but 12% of the population, many began to perceive of welfare as a black problem despite the fact that 50% of the recipients were white (Berkowitz, 4).

During the sixties a fundamental change in attitudes toward the poor became evident. Coming out of a period of low inflation and prosperity between 1961 and 1965 during which GNP increased from $520 billion to $685 billion, decisions about social policy and the poor were viewed in an optimistic context by the Johnson Administration (Murray, *Losing Ground*, 25–26). Despite this, Marmor believed that welfare growth did not come from the flood of federal dollars appropriated for Great Society programs, but from other Johnson initiatives that created a cadre of advocates for the poor "who wished to improve the lot of their clientele." Most important were the efforts of workers in Community Action and Legal Services. They worked to inform clients of potential benefits and helped them overcome resistance from state and local welfare offices that worked against "the full implementation of the AFDC program." So successful were these agencies that Marmor suggested AFDC was transformed from a program "that had long been viewed as a form of public gratuity" to one that entailed "welfare rights." Some state legislatures now joined the War on Poverty through increased funding for AFDC (Marmor, 87–88), while AFDC rolls were increased still more through the activities of the National Welfare Rights Organization (NWRO). NWRO offered the view of welfare as a right and mobilized mothers already on public assistance to claim additional benefits. By 1972 it faded from the scene, but what remained according to Mead, was a lesser emphasis on "work enforcement" and a willingness to see "nonworking adults as helpless victims who could not be expected to function" (L. Mead, *New Politics*, 224, 258). Of fundamental importance was the rise of the concept of entitlement. It came forth as a radical departure from the traditional work values of aid to the deserving poor, and as such remained part of a bitter debate on work and welfare until the mid-nineties. Only then would more conservative voices question the concept and demand a return to work as the ultimate objective of help to the deserving poor.

These changes in both values and the programs that followed led to a dramatic growth of the American welfare state. Total expenditures rose from $99.5 billion in 1960 to $519.8 billion in 1987. But within this great increase AFDC, the program generally equated with welfare, did not reach the same levels of expenditure as Medicaid and Food Stamps. In fact, taken as a percentage of GNP, AFDC spending was lower in 1987 than in 1971 although actual dollars disbursed tripled from $6.2 billion to $18.1 billion. Supplemental Security Income (SSI), begun in 1974 by combining federal-state efforts to help special categories of the poor, blind, aged, and disabled, also outpaced allocations for the traditional AFDC welfare program (Marmor, 90–91, 84–85). Put in other terms, AFDC claimed 1.1% of the 1993 federal budget as against 1.5% in 1975, and average monthly cash payments in 1993 dollars actually fell from $542 in 1975 to $376 in 1993 (Cordtz, 25). But since these numbers did not include food stamps, housing assistance, and Medicaid the smaller monthly *cash* payment was only a modest part of total welfare costs. If all levels of government spending are considered, combined welfare costs grew from about $200 billion in 1980 to about $310 billion in 1992 (C. Horowitz, "Ending Welfare," 1; Cordtz, 25).

Also of importance is the fact that one of every seven children is now on AFDC, that 90% of welfare families are headed by a single parent, and that 30% of AFDC's single mothers stay in the program for eight years or longer. And while AFDC is smaller than some other welfare programs, federal and state expenditures still came to $65 billion in 1994 (Sperry, A2). Currently 5% of the total population or 14 million people are receiving some form of welfare assistance (Suskind, A14). In addition, 90% of welfare families are headed by a single parent, generally women (Sperry, A2), while 65% of welfare recipients received aid for eight or more years (Malkin, A1). That welfare is often a long-term situation can be seen from the fact that 40% of all women who go on welfare before the age of twenty-five stay there for over ten years (Horowitz, "Ending Welfare," A1). Looked at from another perspective, only 243,000 children were living with one parent in 1960, but by 1993 the Census Bureau report "Marital Status and Living Arrangements" noted a dramatic increase to 6.3 million. To this must be added that the birthrate for unwed mothers has increased by 70 percent from 1983 to 1993. When these numbers are coupled with the very low median-income level of never-married mothers ($9,272) as compared to divorced mothers with children ($17,014), the plight of unmarried women with children becomes clear (S. Holmes, A1, A8). If looked at in racial terms, long-term recipients (over five years) were 34% black, 23% Hispanic, and 43% white, but those on welfare for two years or less were 65% white. And 72% of the beneficiaries getting assistance for over five years were never married (Dugger, "Iowa Plan," B6). Such data may have led Vedder and Gallaway to conclude that public assistance tends to reduce labor force participation (Vedder and Gallaway, 260).

However one interprets the vast data stream on welfare, some very different ideas on how the system might be made more workable emerged in the eighties. In general, conservatives continued to demand that those on welfare work (Mead, *New Politics*, 6), a continuation of the traditional belief that aid to the deserving poor was justified on a temporary basis. They saw the system as a contributor to poverty and looked for fundamental changes that would push welfare recipients into the workforce. Many seemed concerned that even after spending $5 trillion (in constant 1993 dollars) during the last thirty years over 39 million still lived below the poverty line. Even adjusting for inflation, total 1993 spending for poverty by 75 federal and state programs totalled about $324.3 billion, nine times that of the mid-1960s when the War on Poverty was launched (Horowitz, "Poverty Paradox," A1–A2). Liberals like Marmor countered by noting that the American welfare state was "not primarily directed at the alleviation of poverty." Its principal purpose was to insure workers and their families against common risks. Assistance for destitute individuals and families was provided only if it was perceived as a 'hand up' to self-improvement and productive employment (Marmor, 86). Still, a June, 1994 survey of 600 adults by Yankelovich Partners showed that 84% believed the current welfare system discouraged the poor from seeking employment, and 92% said able-bodied people should labor (Gibbs, 26).

Marmor responded to these points by noting that the increase in "economic incentives produced by the welfare 'reforms' of the 1960s were quite modest," and the "effects of these incentives on behavior were so small that serious social scientists have been unable to detect them after assiduous effort" (Marmor, 112). He noted that non-AFDC programs like food stamps and Medicaid were far more costly than AFDC, the program that the public generally equates with welfare. Rather, says Marmor, the system needs to fill a gap that would give more support to those individuals and couples without children who are not eligible for cash assistance (ibid., 116). James Q. Wilson, on the other hand, noted that while the illegitimacy rate among black women is over twice as high as that for white women, among blacks living in relatively generous welfare-paying states like Idaho, Montana, Maine, and New Hampshire, the illegitimacy rate was low. But in many low-paying states in the Deep South the reverse was true. It led him to ask if there were cultural or noneconomic factors at work which to date have not been understood (J. Q. Wilson, A10). But economic questions continued to intrude. A survey of welfare offices in six large cities including Boston, Washington, D.C., Raleigh, Los Angeles, Atlanta, and Chicago found that welfare benefits from all sources ranged from a low of $14,994 in Atlanta to a high of $19,598 in Boston. These were equivalent to a pre-tax income of $17,646 and $24,792, respectively (Murphy, A1, A2). Given this total benefit package and the limited education and training of many single-mothers on welfare, "making work pay" will be difficult to implement in many communities. This was confirmed by the General Accounting Office (GAO) which indicated that despite a $1.1 billion effort the recent federal jobs program could not move a majority off of welfare during a three-year period. In FY 92 Nebraska had the best record at 31.4%, while Indiana was at the low end with but 2.4% (Horowitz, "Record of Workfare," A1, A2).

Sociologist Christopher Jencks provided a very different perspective. He urged that the best way to get single mothers to work is to permit them to collect AFDC "regardless of how much outside income they get." This would "redefine" AFDC "as a program that ought to provide a single mother with enough income so she can make ends meet if she works, gets child support, or gets help from her boyfriend or family" (Jencks, *Rethinking Social Policy*, 232). Senator Moynihan was also sympathetic to the long-term recipients of assistance who could not escape the clutches of poverty: "There is a difference between people who have some trouble come into their lives and those whose lives are in trouble" (Cordtz, 25). Others such as Charles Murray favored "scrapping the entire federal welfare and income-support structure." He believed that during the past three decades welfare programs created a climate that eroded the old social restraints on illegitimacy. Many poor blacks, Murray urged, saw a better economic alternative in welfare than in taking an entry-level job as the first difficult step away from public assistance (Murray, *Losing Ground*, 227–28, 234, 73–75, 78, 82).

Mead, on the other hand, noted that while conservatives continued to attack "nonwork and crime" and liberals looked for remedies "mainly through benefits," the "focus of politics" has now shifted to "conduct rather than class." Thus, when poverty was equated with nonworking in the seventies and eighties support dropped for change through governmental auspices. The question has shifted to how AFDC can be changed "to minimize dependency" by those who could support themselves by working. For poor blacks, however, there remained the difficulty of taking positions that did not offer "much income or prestige." Blacks,

Mead argued, did this in the past and became parents to many middle-class professionals. But the work ethic of these parents and the courage they showed in the face of Jim Crow laws has not been duplicated by the black youth of today (Mead, *New Politics*, 2–4, 151). There is, Mead continued, a resistance to low pay, memories of a harsh past, and a long-term pessimism that keep the poor "economically passive in a society where other low-skilled people find opportunity." He concluded that "nonwork occurs simply because work is not enforced" (ibid., 12, 134). Mickey Kaus attacked the liberal position more stridently. Despite the fact that liberals wanted to help those on welfare out of "compassion," the public continued to draw a distinction between the "deserving" and "nondeserving" poor. It saw in the welfare poor attributes of "dependence," and worried about the number that have become permanent clients of the welfare state (Kaus, 17–18). Even liberal researchers like Chisman and Pifer have come to accept the necessity of work within the context of a federal umbrella of welfare assistance (Chisman and Pifer, 227–32, 249–50). Workfare rather than welfare would best characterize their position.

But David Ellwood's views of the late Eighties came closest to a liberal program that took notice of changing public values. In his *Poor Support* he worried that past welfare efforts treated only the "symptoms of poverty, not the causes." If solutions were to be reached over time, policies had to be put in place which responded to the fundamental problems of many welfare recipients: "They are poor because they do not have a job, because their wages are too low, because they are trying to raise a child single-handedly, or because they are undergoing some crisis" (Ellwood, *Poor Support*, 6, 9). He now suggested a somewhat different way to deal with the crisis. AFDC would become a "transitional program" to help the poor be self-sufficient, but one that encouraged a move away from rewarding illegitimacy. He urged that welfare beneficiaries would be worse off in a minimum wage job that cost them health and child care assistance, and strongly advocated that pressure be placed on absentee fathers for whatever support they could give. Government had to "make work pay" by providing health benefits and an earned income tax credit. In addition, training and education would provide some of the propulsion needed to move people from welfare to work. Welfare could thus be "replaced by a transitional support system whose duration might vary from eighteen months to three years." One had to go to work after this period was up, or accept a public sector job as a last resort. Work had to become part of the welfare picture, but it was important to "make work pay" by offering support from an earned income tax credit, raising the minimum wage, and making the "child care tax credit refundable" (Ellwood, *Poor Support*, 236–40; *The Economist*, 18 June 1994, 22).

In line with some of Ellwood's ideas, the Family Support Act of 1988 offered more generous child care and working expenses for AFDC recipients who worked. For a few recipients cash benefits were increased, and states were required to seek out absentee fathers for financial support. Some money was included for training and placement programs, but Marmor did not think the bill would reduce the growth of single-parent families. Those who would be helped most would be the working poor and two parent families many of whom would be able to claim an earned income tax credit without a reduction in their AFDC benefits (Marmor, 119–20, 126–27). Even the law's sponsor, Senator Moynihan, believed that in its initial stages only 10 percent of the families covered would become self-supporting (Berkowitz, *America's Welfare State*, 147). Finally, the new law lacked a time limit on welfare, but this point did not attract the attention of the general public until after the 1994 congressional election.

Even before the Republicans took control of both houses of Congress, President Clinton looked to the ideas of David Ellwood as a way to "end welfare as we know it" (DeParle, "Clinton Welfare Bill," A1). Earlier Ellwood noted that Americans did not begrudge help to the aged or disabled, but they did object to welfare for healthy young beneficiaries. He also noted that while the public wanted to help those who are not making it, Americans did not want "to cheapen the efforts of those who are struggling hard just to get by." There was, Ellwood believed, support for those with little income, but a concern that they would not work if pressure to do so was insufficient. In short, the public only wanted to help those in need if they strived to help themselves (Ellwood, *Poor Support*, 5–6). In raising this "security-work conundrum," Ellwood noted that "no one seriously disputes [the] proposition" that if people are given public assistance there is some lessening of pressure on them to take a job. But the system as it exists "penalizes those who try." Only "by making work pay" could society begin to reverse the perverse effects of a welfare system that neither the public nor welfare beneficiaries liked. In line with this thinking, President Clinton sent Congress a bill in June 1994 that he believed would "make work pay" for those "who play by the rules" (ibid., 218, 238, 125). Ellwood, now Assistant Secretary of Health and Human Services, helped draft this legislation. It offered welfare recipients both job training and child care, and toughened child support enforcement by requiring paternity be established. Absent spouses would be tracked across state lines, and states were given the option to deny increased payment to welfare mothers who had additional children. The bill would also require those unemployed after two years to join a government work program at minimum wage. These time limits would not apply to mothers born after 1971. Finally, $400 million would be authorized in grants to fight teen-age pregnancy (DeParle, "Clinton Welfare Bill," A1, A18). Of interest was the negative comments the Clinton bill drew from two liberal senators. Tom Harkin of Iowa attacked the "idea of government jobs for everyone" as "nonsense," while Senator Moynihan saw it as "boob bait for the bubbas." Moynihan also worried that the bill, if implemented, would create an additional 1.5 million government jobs (Sperry, A2).

By contrast, the House Republican bill that was passed in March 1995 placed a cap on welfare spending and the more costly Supplementary Security Income (SSI) program. Limits also were put on housing subsidies and work programs, but in all of these initiatives there would be annual adjustments for inflation and the percentage of people below the poverty line. Those on welfare had to get jobs within two years. This concerned Gary Burtless of the Brookings Institution, who felt the Republicans were far too optimistic about the number of available jobs for which welfare mothers could qualify. In addition, states would receive block grants to use as they saw fit. These would cover eight broad areas including housing, health, employment, training, and food and nutrition. They would replace 300 existing programs that currently disbursed $125 million. Finally, cash payments through AFDC would cease after five years, but beneficiaries would continue to get food stamps and other noncash assistance. Recipients would also have to establish the paternity of children, a requirement that might prove to be difficult since 30 percent of the children currently on AFDC had no such documentation (Horowitz, "Dependency Cycle, A1, A2; Bleakley, A2; Rimer, A1; *Rochester Democrat and Chronicle*, 28 April 1995, 6A).

But at the time of this writing pressure from many governors and senators seemed strong enough to suggest that revisions would be made in the House bill. While the block grant concept will probably stay in any final legislation, it seems almost certain that the Senate will remove many of the restrictions on states in the House bill. It also seems likely that the Senate will drop the provision to terminate assistance to teenage mothers who have additional children while on welfare. States may also be given the authority to run the food stamp and Medicaid programs (Havemann and Vobejda, A8). In addition, the National Governors' Association has taken the position that they cannot meet the requirement that 50% of all welfare beneficiaries be at work by 2003. They also have opposed "the wholesale elimination of Federal services to legal immigrants" which they believe would result from the House bill, and have asked the Senate to reject House bill provisions that would cut off assistance to many disabled children on SSI. The governors also took exception to House initiatives that would end AFDC benefits to unmarried teen-age mothers and for additional aid to those mothers if they had more children while on welfare. Finally, the governors urged the Senate to leave time limits on welfare to the states rather than have a rigid five-year constraint imposed on them. They also sought a contingency fund to help states pay for welfare programs if they were affected by recessions (Pear, "Governors' Draft," A22). What seems possible is that the final compromise on welfare between Congress and the president will return welfare responsibilities to the states and provide funding through block grants (Verhovek, B10). In this sense, it would move the administration of public assistance back to a more local level in line with traditional practice since the Elizabethan Poor Law of 1601. At this writing in January 1996, however, President Clinton vetoed the legislation that finally passed Congress.

Despite this stalemate in Washington, many states have not waited for Congress and the president to agree on a legislative solution. Ohio, for example, became the twenty-fifth state to get a federal waiver to initiate its own welfare plan. Money that had been paid out in cash and food stamps would be changed to wage supplements. If a welfare client was hired, a private employer would receive 50% of the wage rate from the state during the first year and 25% in year two after which the subsidy would end. Ohio is hoping that former welfare beneficiaries will by then have turned into long-term employees (Seib, "Welfare Reform," A22). Florida and Vermont have approached the problem differently. Following the lead in President Clinton's bill, Florida has placed a two year limit on welfare aid despite the concerns of many case workers. Vermont has required 60 percent of its recipients to agree to a thirty-month time limit as of July 1994 (Suskind, A14), while Iowa's plan involves an actual cutoff of aid if a parent refuses to go to work or take alternative actions to leave the welfare rolls. As of April 1995, it had already removed 881 clients from its list. It also reported that in Dubuque the Visiting Nurse Society found 13 percent of former welfare families they tried to contact had left the state (Dugger, "Iowa Plan," A1, B6).

In New Jersey a new welfare law that went into effect under ex-Governor Florio excluded additional benefits to welfare mothers who had more children. During the first year New Jersey denied additional cash aid to 6,267 children born "to existing AFDC recipients." A legal challenge to this welfare cap was turned down by a Federal district judge in early May 1995 who ruled that the New Jersey law in question had rational goals and did not "constrain the welfare mother's right to bear as many children as she chooses." Some 123,000 welfare mothers still receive AFDC aid, but the number has remained constant since the cap was put in place (Henneberger, A1, A18; Pear, "Judge Upholds Cap on Welfare by New Jersey," A1).

Wisconsin's "Work Not Welfare" approach was initiated by pilot programs in Pierce and Fond Du Lac counties. Able-bodied AFDC recipients must spend the first year on welfare working or training for work, but during the second year must either get a private sector position or work in a government-sponsored community service job. After the second year the job guarantee disappears. Former welfare recipients would then receive no cash assistance for a three-year period. In addition, benefits would be terminated if an individual refused to participate in this program. Exemptions were made for mothers with disabled children or teens needing to finish high school. Governor Thompson has said that he would now want to extend the Pierce and Fond Du Lac pilot programs to other parts of the state. Beyond this, Wisconsin plans to withdraw from the AFDC, the food stamp program, and two state public assistance programs by 1 January 1999. That Wisconsin has had some success in a general sense can be seen by a 27 percent reduction in the welfare caseload since 1987 (Malkin, 1–2; Horowitz, "Ending Welfare," 2; Horowitz, "Dependency Cycle," A2; Verhovek, B10).

California's GAIN (Greater Avenues to Independence) welfare-to-work program was implemented from 1988 to 1990 with mixed results. While it helped 25% of former welfare beneficiaries to work over twenty hours per week, only 2% sought a full-time position. Twenty-seven percent were not working but looking for a job, while 40 percent were not working and not looking for a position (Rimer, B10). With a welfare bill of almost $17 billion, California was trying to restrict aid to teen age mothers and mothers who have children while on welfare. Governor Wilson believes state cuts have saved $9 billion since 1991 (Verhovek, B10).

Michigan took a different approach regarding its General Assistance (GA) program for 80,000 healthy adults in October 1991. The program was initiated to help the state cut a large deficit, a point that seemed to win the approval of most Michigan citizens according to David DeCosse. To see what happened to those who were dropped from this welfare program, a study ("The General Assistance Termination Project") was launched. It was found that 77 percent of former recipients worked either before or while on GA, since they could not make ends meet on welfare aid alone. Two years after the aid was ended, the 43 percent of the beneficiaries who were off of *all* forms of public assistance (not only GA) was "no higher than the number who had managed to get off assistance two years *before* the cutoff" (DeCosse, 30–32).

To the east, the Connecticut legislature approved legislation stipulating a 21-month time limit on welfare beginning 1 January 1996. It would cover 40,000 persons and be phased in over time as officials determined which beneficiaries were actually able to work. This plan needs a federal waiver which was not as yet forthcoming despite a more friendly atmosphere in Congress. If the waiver is received, officials predicted the new law will enable them to place 9,000 welfare recipients in jobs over the next year, and hope to move 40,000 of the state's current 59,000 clients into paid employment by 1999 (Rabinowitz, B4; Verhovek, B10).

What seems most likely at this writing in November 1995 is that leadership on welfare will devolve to the states. To date, thirty states have received permission from the Clinton administration to change their welfare programs. Thirteen states have placed caps on benefits and nineteen are experimenting with time limits. That these approaches may be having some results can be seen by a drop in AFDC recipients from 14.36 million in March 1994 to 13.2 million in August 1995. Whether this is due to new state initiatives, a good economy, or a combination of the two is not clear. But shrinkage in cash payments through federal-state AFDC auspices has occurred (*Rochester Democrat and Chronicle*, 4 November 1995, 3A). Despite these preliminary results, state administrations will have to demonstrate that they can handle the huge sums they would receive in block grants, and will require a bureaucracy that can combine compassion with clear thinking. But states will be able to tailor welfare plans to local work values and their individual economic circumstances. What seems evident is that some form of devolution is coming as states try to work out fifty formulas on how to deal with the old challenge of aid to the deserving and undeserving poor. From an historical perspective this change is a return to the traditional American reliance on local authority to disburse aid to the deserving poor. It is also reminiscent of Franklin Pierce's 1854 refusal to offer federal assistance to the poor because he believed the states and localities were the proper vehicles for such administration (Piven and Cloward, 47). And it reflects the sixteenth-century Lutheran admonitions of Martin Luther and Wenceslaus Linck of Altenburg who drew a distinction between the deserving poor and the itinerant beggars who did the devil's work by resisting employment (Ozment, *Age of Reform*, 266; Ozment, *Protestants*, 72–73).

Another aspect of the *continuity* involving aid to the deserving poor is tied to the current debate on affirmative action (AA). In the public mind, AA is often associated with the age-old question of special assistance to those who have not had economic success. Advocates argue that the preferences associated with AA in education and the labor market are justified by many centuries of discrimination. Opponents counter that after three decades, AA has served its purpose in helping the deserving poor. In any event, AA has become an extension of an ancient debate which pits the needs of those who have been left behind against the belief that a level playing field is now needed in the world of work and learning.

Unlike the work and welfare dilemma which can be traced to Elizabethan England, AA is an American creation whose origins can be traced to the exclusion of blacks from desirable jobs in the antebellum North and in the entire nation after 1865 (DuBois, 228). With the exception of the United Mine Workers (J. R. Green, *World of Worker*, 51) and the Cigarmakers' organization (DuBois, 228) at the turn of the century, unions systematically barred blacks from their ranks. Much of this stemmed from their belief that blacks were inferior, and that their presence lessened the respectability (Cumbler, *Trenton*, 37) skilled unionists desired. Many union members also feared blacks as serious economic competitors. Not until the mid-1930s did the CIO begin to reach out to Afro-Americans who were largely shunned by the craft-oriented AFL (Meier and Rudwick, 27–28). And only when A. Philip Randolph threatened a march on Washington in 1941 unless job discrimination in defense industries ceased did President Roosevelt issue his famous Executive Order 8802 of 1941. This banned all hiring bias on the basis of race in defense industries, and established a Committee on Fair Employment Practices to enforce his executive order. Later, Presidents Truman and Eisenhower issued additional executive orders which extended this anti-discriminatory policy to government contractors (Lynch, 11). But it was not until the 1960s that "a major shift" occurred in the work values that supported the prevailing government policy of racial and ethnic neutrality in hiring, promotion, and university admissions. Much of the change may have been due to urban rioting and the influence of the Kerner Report. There was also a general questioning of authority and established ways of doing business as public opinion seemed to move away from "color-blind justice" to AA (Nieli, ix).

Justification for such a shift came from the fact that blacks were brought to North America "against their will," and then suffered three and a half centuries of slavery, job discrimination, and racism. These wrongs were so serious and of such of long-standing that it became obligatory to give blacks "a unique entitlement" so they could win their fair share of available jobs (Ezorsky, 1). In a study of Philadelphia between 1850 and 1970, Hershberg and his colleagues found the "opportunity structure" for blacks in jobs, housing, and transportation to be poor. For them to rise above this by pulling up their "bootstraps," was a view that ran counter to the situation they faced. Yet many believed that blacks did not have a "uniquely discriminatory past" and thus did not deserve special treatment during the past three decades. Others argued in support of a "last of the immigrants" theory. Blacks, this view contended, were victims of numerous race riots, job discrimination, and continual personal slights. What they now needed to cure these ills was time rather than special legislation. With the passage of years blacks would make progress in upward mobility as did immigrants from Britain, Italy, and Eastern Europe (Hershberg, Burstein, et al., 463). In this view blacks deserved no special attention as the deserving poor. But both of these outlooks ran counter to the exclusion blacks faced in employment during the century after the Civil War. They also ignored the race riots that occurred with frequency in large cities and small, from Detroit and New York on the one hand, to Springfield, Illinois on the other. And finally, they did not take into account the virtual lack of assistance to the newly freed blacks after 1865. Only by the 1960s did changing values and a favorable economic setting give supporters of the Great Society a platform for change.

Accordingly, the Johnson administration did two things that have had a lasting impact. First, they won congressional approval for the 1964 Civil Rights Act. Within this legislation, Title VII empowered the courts to order such "affirmative action as may be appropriate" so that plaintiffs could obtain relief for past discrimination. Second, President Johnson issued Executive Order 11246 in 1965 which required federal contractors to establish AA plans to comply with Title VII. By the late sixties most large firms had such plans which, in turn, were monitored by the Department of Labor's Office of Federal Contract Compliance (Jencks, *Rethinking Social Policy*, 49–50). In 1970 President Nixon amended the earlier Executive Order 11246 of 1965 and added "goals" and "timetables." This was done under Revised Order no. 4 of the Department of Labor's Office of Federal Contract Compliance (*New York Times*, 16 March 1995, A22). An early success in the use of such goals and timetables was the Philadelphia Plan. Under this proposal specific minority goals established in Philadelphia had an effect on the construction industry "throughout the land" (Gould, 339–40).

What followed was a series of Supreme Court decisions that gradually expanded the scope of AA in the seventies. Starting with *Griggs v. Duke Power Company* (1971), the Court held that even neutral employment practices could be seen as discriminatory if they adversely affected minorities and women and could not be justified by "business necessity." In short, if a test given by Duke Power disqualified blacks disproportionately then the employer had to show that it measured an applicant's ability to do the work. The Court ruled that completion of high school or passing a general intelligence test did not "bear a demonstrable relation to successful performance on the jobs for which it is used" (Ezorsky, 124, 39; Glazer, "Racial Quotas," 10). A second case of some importance was that of *Los Angeles Steamfitters Local No. 250* (1972). Here numerical goals were allowed, since the union did not have a single nonwhite member out of a total of over 3,000. In addition, previous "good faith" efforts had resulted in little change (Gould, 322). This was reminiscent of the exclusion of blacks from Trenton unions in the 1920s (Cumbler, *Trenton*, 37–43) and the International Longshoremen's Association in the 1890s (DuBois, 228).

Even more explosive was *Regents of University of California v. Bakke* in 1978. The public context of this decision can be framed by a Gallup Poll of 1977. By an 83 to 10 percent margin respondents said that ability as determined by examination and not preferential treatment to correct past discrimination should be the main consideration in selecting applicants for a job or awarding admission to college (Nieli, 511). Earlier the California Supreme Court had ruled in favor Allan Bakke (Mosk, 164) who had twice been denied admission to the medical school at Davis under the general admission program. But under the special admission program applicants with lower scores than Bakke had been offered places. In this situation, Bakke filed a suit which argued that the special admissions program was in violation of the Civil Rights

Act of 1964 and the U.S. Constitution. The Supreme Court ruled that the special admissions program was not valid, but that in the future race could be used as one factor in the admissions decision (Ezorsky, 132). One observer sympathetic to AA conceded that a white applicant like Bakke might have won admission had there been no AA plan and "the issue of the innocent white victim remains genuine" (Rosenfeld, 171). But Richard Sobol in an *amicus* brief filed for the National Council of Churches of Christ and twenty other organizations argued that the normal strict standard of constitutional review did not apply in *Bakke* since it was "a classification designed to benefit a disadvantaged class in their efforts to overcome the effect of past discrimination" (Sobol, 167). Another proponent of AA, Professor Ronald Dworkin of New York University, felt it was "regrettable when any citizen's [Bakke] expectations are defeated by new programs serving some more general concern." Bakke, he noted, does not share in any collective or individual guilt for the racially unjust practices of the past. "It is not [his] fault that racial justice is now a special need—but he has no right to prevent the most effective measures of securing that justice from being used" (Dworkin, 189).

Of equal importance was *United Steelworkers of America v. Weber* in 1979. A 1974 agreement between the USW and Kaiser Aluminum and Chemical Corporation had been drawn up to eliminate the racial imbalance in the company's almost totally white craft workforce. Under the *voluntary* plan 50 percent of the new openings in craft-training programs would be reserved for blacks. During the first year of the AA program seven blacks and six whites were selected. The most senior black selected had less seniority than some of the white production workers who wished to enter the training program. Brian Weber, one of the white production workers who had been turned down, brought a class-action suit arguing that the Kaiser-USW AA plan violated Title VII of the Civil Rights Act of 1964 (Ezorsky, 122). In a 5–4 decision the Supreme Court upheld the voluntary Kaiser-USW plan which relied on racial quotas to deal with a situation in which only 1.83% of the skilled craftworkers had been black while 39% of the work-force in the plant's geographical area were nonwhite (Rosenfeld, 172–73). The question that remained was similar to that in Bakke: was the decision fair "to innocent parties like Brian Weber?" It also raised two other points of importance. Did the decision suggest a "declining relevance of personal merit and ability?" And would there now be a growing "importance of group or status-based claims?" (M. J. Phillips, 44).

The Court rulings during the eighties presented the picture of a divided body trying to come to grips with "what ought to count as a sufficient constitutional justification for affirmative action." In *Firefighters Local Union No. 1784 v. Stotts* in 1984 the Court ruled against preferential layoffs in public sector employment under terms of a collectively bargained agreement that had a "last hired, first fired" provision. In this case none of the black firefighters to be laid off were seen as victims of discrimination (R. M. Green, "Affirmative Action," 4), but the case was reminiscent of the century-old tensions between blacks and unions (Cumbler, *Trenton*, 37; J. H. Franklin, 399–401). A similar result followed in 1986 when *Wygant v. Jackson Board of Education* was adjudicated (Rosenfeld, 214–15). But in *Johnson v. Transportation Agency, Santa Clara County, California et al.* in 1987 a 6–3 Court decision held that public employers, in addition to private employers, might voluntarily implement AA programs to correct for past discrimination against women. None of the 238 positions in the Transportation Agency "had ever been held by a woman," a point that justified a flexible plan to deal with an unfair situation of long standing (Wermiel, 3). Here the Supreme Court indicated it was willing to allow gender preferences where past practices showed they were warranted. But eighteen months later in *City of Richmond v. Croson* (1989) a 6–3 majority struck down a 30 percent set-aside for black contractors because it violated the Equal Protection clause of the Fourteenth Amendment. "Benign" racial categories that favored one race over another would now be "constitutionally suspect" (Lynch, 15; Greenhouse, A1, A18). What was also at stake were precedents that gave black or Hispanic police or firefighters an edge on examinations (Tolchin, A18). Of considerable importance in the AA debate was another 1989 Court ruling, *Wards Cove Packing Company v. Frank Atonio*. This firm had a largely white work force in skilled jobs, but mostly nonwhite employees in unskilled positions. The facts alone suggested a *prima facie* case against Wards Cove Company by the Court of Appeals, but the Supreme Court overruled them by arguing that an employer with a "racially imbalanced" workforce could be drawn into lengthy and time-consuming litigation to defend the "business necessity" of its hiring procedures. In practical terms it would force employers to institute quotas to avoid drawn-out litigation. Henceforth, as Bork interpreted the ruling, discrimination would have to "be proved rather than assumed" (Bork, 273–74).

More significant were the Court's refusal to hear the *Duquesne Light* and *Birmingham, Alabama Firefighters* cases. In the Birmingham case, the Supreme Court turned down without comment a request by city officials and black fire fighters to reverse a lower court ruling that had invalidated a promotion plan dating back to 1981. That plan had incorporated a 1:1 ratio in promotions until the number of black lieutenants reached 28 percent, the same percentage of the surrounding county's workforce that was black. This target had been reached in 1989, although the case began in 1974 when Birmingham had few black firemen and none in a supervisory capacity (Greenhouse, A14). Earlier the Court had fined a western Pennsylvania power company $425,000 for damages for promoting a black candidate over a more qualified white candidate. Operating under an AA action plan, Duquesne Light Company had denied Frederick Claus a managerial position despite his twenty-nine years of experience and a degree in electrical engineering. At the time only two of eighty-two managers in the division were black ("High Court Sides with Whites in the Workplace," *Rochester Democrat and Chronicle* [from *Los Angeles Times*], 18 April 1995, 1). Taken together, the Supreme Court's unwillingness to review the Birmingham and Pittsburgh decisions represented an setback for affirmative action. Supporters might take some comfort from the comments of Justices Scalia and Thomas who indicated they might be receptive to some kind of nonracial affirmative action (Horowitz, "Affirmative Action," A1).

Given changing public attitudes and the fluidity of Supreme Court decisions it is not surprising that opinion on AA remains sharply divided in 1995. In this situation both whites and blacks have come to see themselves as victims of AA (Jencks, *Rethinking Social Policy*, 58). A telephone poll of 752 adults in late March 1995 revealed that 23% believed blacks were "losing out" because of racial discrimination in the workplace, while 46% saw whites as losers because of AA (Cose, 34). The same *Newsweek* poll indicated that whites opposed AA by a 79–14% margin. Interestingly, minorities favored such preferences by only a 50–46% margin (Fineman, 25).

Supporters of AA, however, continue to believe that any problems it may have caused are outweighed by its public benefits. Professor Paul R. Spickard who himself has lost positions twice because of AA notes that "everything costs something." AA, in his estimation, remains a viable and worthwhile program (Spickard, 108–9). Rosenfeld, on the other hand, believes AA is needed to speed up the process that opens the door to many who have been left behind by the unkind hand of racism (Rosenfeld, 335–36). Krauthammer admits AA is a "breach of justice," but goes on to argue that it is one of the best means to insure "the rapid integration of blacks into American life" (Krauthammer, 148). Ellis Cose notes that while there is an active opposition to AA regarding college admissions, fine athletes and the children of alumni have often been admitted to universities when they were not the most qualified applicants. Likewise veteran's preferences for jobs are not seen as unjust. Critics of AA will have to explain how the elimination of such an approach will help the cause of meritocracy if other preferences remain (Cose, 34).

Those who worry about some aspects of AA cite possible "feelings of self-doubt" that AA might cause among blacks (Jencks, "Affirmative Action," 756; Murray, "Affirmative Racism," 405–6, 408). But those who strongly oppose AA like Charles Murray believe the goal of public policy in this area should be equal opportunity. "Government," says Murray, "cannot identify the worthy, but it can protect a society in which the worthy can identify themselves." He goes on to urge "billions for equal opportunity, not one cent for equal outcome" (Murray, *Losing Ground*, 233–34). In this milieu the fears of angry white men have surfaced. Much of their concern centers on the effects of massive downsizing, technological change, and the layoffs due of global competition (Herbert, A25; Seib, "Angry Males," A16). In this context AA has become politically explosive. It may be that this issue helped account for the 62 percent of the white male vote in the 1994 congressional elections that voted Republican, a result that Howard Fineman says moved many moderate Democrats into an anti-affirmative action stance (Fineman, 25). Even President Clinton told a Democratic audience in Sacramento that "we have to recognize that there is a real problem out there" ("Clinton: Pay Heed to 'Angry White Male,'" *Rochester Democrat and Chronicle* [from Associated Press], 8 April 1995, 10A). And while a recent *USA/Today*/CNN/Gallup Poll showed 55% supported the broad concept of AA, when queried about specifics 67% opposed female and minority scholarships at public universities. In that poll and others, white men proved to be the most implacable opponents of AA (G. Craig, 6A; J. Kaufman, "Affirmative Action," B6).

What, then, should be done? Aside from the polarized positions that AA should be continued without change or set aside quickly, there are few viable options. We can wait to see what the results of Clinton administration's review of AA offers (Herbert, A25), or try modification of AA without racial, ethnic, or gender preferences. Given the Supreme Court's recent decision not to review the Birmingham and Duquesne Light decisions, some have called for this type of "nonracial affirmative action." Others worry that the use of less explosive "economic preferences" could trigger unanticipated outcomes in such areas as mortgage loans (Horowitz, "Affirmative Action," A1–A2). Nathan Glazer, on the other hand, opposes class-based AA and looks to a "voluntary affirmative action" which he believes would be continued in most universities, corporations, and governmental units "even in the absence of federal regulations." Glazer argues that class-based AA might not help blacks as much as proponents believe, because competition for well-paid skilled jobs and public positions would cause them to face applicants from lower income homes who could compete with them equally on the basis of "economic preferences" (Glazer, "Race, Not Class," A12). Senator Dole, on the other hand, favors vigorous enforcement of the anti-discrimination laws and urges that "those who discriminate ought to be punished." And while he attacked federal programs that required goals and timetables (*New York Times*, 16 March 1995, A22), the backlog of cases confronting the Equal Employment Opportunity Commission (EEOC) was a staggering 96,945 in FY 1994. For this it had but 732 investigators compared to 762 in FY 1990 when the EEOC had but 41,987 cases (Yang, 155). If tough enforcement of anti-discrimination laws is the path that might ultimately be chosen, EEOC will have to modify existing procedures and be enlarged to handle the enormous backlog it faces.

In the final analysis, AA is a program whose future is in doubt. It faces a powerful American tradition that has made opportunity a standard fixture of our work values since the colonial era. To modify this belief system by legislation flows against the tide of public values. Only if citizens can be convinced that AA will enable the deserving poor to elevate themselves will there be support for this child of the Great Society.

Beyond the important *old challenges* of hard work, opportunity, job insecurity, and the issue of the deserving poor were several significant *new aspirations* that emerged since the Second World War. Among the most important of these were the new hopes of millions of women who flooded the labor market during the last five decades. What they wanted from work would be important in itself, but because of the sheer numbers involved their expectations drew considerable attention. In 1950, for example, women made up only 29% of the workforce, but by 1990 this number had risen to 46%. It is estimated that this number will grow to 50% by the year 2000 (Trost, B1). A special situation involved married women with children under six: 60% were working in 1991 as against only 19% in 1960 (Shenot, 4). Also interesting was the fact that 55% of women in the workforce in 1992 had children less than three years old. In the case of single parents, those with children under 18 numbered 25% of the women in the labor force (*Wall Street Journal*, 21 June 1993, R4).

So changed were the old work values that by the nineties it had become "increasingly acceptable, perhaps even expected, for mothers to be breadwinners as well as caregivers." Women were marrying later and were able to enter the job market and develop the ties needed to "withstand the pressures of marriage and child rearing" (Hayghe and Bianchi, 26–27). And single women with children had the additional burden of coping alone with the need to earn a living and provide child care. But what was also of more than passing interest was the results of the annual Yankelovich survey published in 1993. For over twenty years Yankelovich had asked women whether they would give up their jobs if they did not need the money. During that period about 30% said they would. In 1989 the number increased to 38%, and by 1991 the number shot up to 56%. It may be that women have adopted the idea that they can follow any path and do so with a clear conscience so long as they can afford it. For females of the Nineties "full-time mothering" has become one of many acceptable choices (Swasy, 1). But a telephone survey done for the *New York Times* and CBS in 1994 found that 86% of teen-age girls between ages 13 and 17 expected to work outside the home after they were married. But boys of that age group had different work values: only 58% of them expected their future wives to seek paid employment (T. Lewin, "Teen-Agers Poll," A1, B7).

Given this setting that drew so many women in the labor force by the mid-nineties, it is also important to recognize the impediments they faced. These included responsibilities that few of their male counterparts accepted. A five-year survey published in 1993 by the Families and Work Institute found that 87% of the female respondents had some daily family responsibility. Seven percent had to deal with elder care, while 18 percent expected to face this problem within the next five years. In addition, 62 percent felt getting good child care was a major concern. Related to these obligations of many female employees was some evidence that employees who had greater control over their time and jobs were more satisfied and had less burnout. These employees planned to stay longer with their current firm (Sulit, 27–28), a clear bonus for companies that leaned to flexible scheduling and employee empowerment. And since 45 percent of all American households were headed by men or women without the presence of another spouse (*Wall Street Journal*, 11 October 1993, B1), the problem of balancing the responsibilities of family and work has become critical. A recent survey by Du Pont Company found that many women (and men) would refuse to relocate or accept positions that required extensive travel (T. Lewin, "Workers of Both Sexes," 25). Nevertheless, this tension between the pulls of family and work may have led many women to jump off the fast track because because the competing demands became too difficult a tightrope to walk. Testimony that suggests how serious this problem might be can be seen by the fact that 50 percent of *Fortune's* list of highly paid women are childless. This, of course, could be due to a variety of other reasons, but the heavy burden of both work and home has forced many women to choose or be subject to continued stress. In line with this point, a Gallup poll of 1993 found that one-third of Americans would accept a 20 percent reduction in salary if they or their spouses could work fewer hours. And a Merck Family Fund study reported in *Working Woman* in August 1995 showed that 28 percent of those surveyed had already made lifestyle changes which reduced their pay (Ehrenreich, 28). But for most women the words of comedienne Lily Tomlin remained pertinent: "If I had known what it would be to have it all, I might have settled for less" (Fierman, "Why Women Still Don't Hit the Top," 40, 54, 58).

Beyond these serious concerns a growing number of women found themselves in need of good elder care. Currently 15–16 percent of the total workforce have some responsibility for an older relative. This number is expected to grow to 22 percent over the next three to four years. Sally Coberly, Aging Specialist for the Washington Business Group on Health, has noted that "as the baby boom moves deeper into middle age, the need for elder-care services will simply explode." By 2005, 37 percent of American workers will be between 40 and 54, the very time period when they will be called upon to take care of older parents (Shellenbarger, "Aging of America," A1, A6). Added to this is the shortage of home health aides. Either the absence or the lateness of an aide can compel an employee to miss work or be tardy (*Wall Street Journal*, 1 June 1994, B1), a situation that can cause both stress and the loss of needed employment.

Some signs of hope can be found in the recent Family and Medical Leave Act of 1993. In January 1995 the Labor Department issued final rules that took effect one month later. Under this law, any company employing fifty or more people over a 75-mile radius must comply. Employees who have put in at least 1,250 hours during the previous year are eligible, and *unpaid* leaves of up to twelve weeks can be taken to care for a child, spouse, parent or oneself. Workers may take this leave for almost any disabling problem, but they may need a doctor's note to support their claim. Leaves do not have to be on consecutive days, and those who take them are entitled to either their old job or an equivalent position. Finally, if employees take twelve weeks of unpaid leave and maintain their health benefits, they can continue to have access to a group health plan for eighteen months if they decide not to return to work and are willing to pay for their insurance (Rowland, F13; Klotz, A 14).

Other signs that companies were aware of the needs of women could be seen in the growing group of family-friendly employers. Notable among them was First Tennessee National under CEO Ralph Horn. Horn did not see work and family as two forces that had to tear employees apart, but looked to programs that met the needs of both. This was accomplished with a group of seven employees responsible for issuance of monthly bank statements who reoriented their work schedules and cut the time needed to produce these statements from eight days to four (*Wall Street Journal*, 1 March 1995, B1). *Working Mother* magazine extended this example to one hundred firms in 1993, a list that included Barnett Banks, Corning, and IBM. Beyond these examples, the use of family leave at Helene Curtis Inc. resulted in a dramatic drop in turnover from 31% to 7% (Shellenbarger, "Working Mothers," A8). Many other firms have also instituted successful programs that address the family-work conundrum. Stride-Rite opened the first corporate child care center as early as 1971. Weyerhauser moved into this area between 1987 and 1993, while GE Silicones began to use flextime, job sharing, and a family leave policy at its Waterford, New York facility when the number of women and minorities in its workforce reached 30 percent in the late eighties (Laabs, 48–49; Haupt, 96–97, 102, 105, 107; Vicki Clark, 148–50). Other firms have agreed to home work so they can hold valued employees. This saved office space and provided for efficient use of computers if those working at home used their equipment during non-office hours. Still, some firms worried about the loss of managerial control, lessened teamwork, and a possible decline in "collective *esprit*" (Leidner, 84), and it is important to observe that 54 percent of the firms surveyed by the Alexander Consulting Group lacked work-family guidelines (*Wall Street Journal*, 11 January 1994, 1). Nevertheless, a recent alliance of major American corporations (Aetna, AT & T, Amoco, etc.) announced a $100 million initiative to improve both child care and elder care.

Also important to families in recent decades was the use of flextime. Beginning in 1967 at the aerospace plant of Messerschmidt-Bolkow-Blohm near Munich, *gleitzeit* or "sliding time" gained in popularity both in Europe and North America (I. Bernstein, *Time and Work*, 6). In its ideal forms, flextime gave workers some control over their time and could facilitate the juggling needed to survive the pulls of work and family. In the United States firms such as Corning instituted flexible work scheduling, job sharing, and work-at-home options after a 1989 employee needs-assessment survey found that employees wanted more control over their time (*Work in America* [June 1992], 3). Even in workaholic Silicon Valley, Sun Microsystems, Tandem Computers, and Hewlett-Packard used many varieties of flextime to help employees deal with the demands of family and work (Shellenbarger, "Work & Family," B1). Still, a question lingered as to how much of this was reality. Work-Family Directions, a Boston consulting firm, found that 85% of the firms surveyed said they had at least one flexible work program, but only 50% had a written policy. Perhaps some of this stemmed from subtle managerial resistance, since flexible schedules were difficult to monitor. Dana Friedman of the Families and Work Institute felt that managers held back because they believed some employees would "abuse the policy." Workers also were reluctant to request such arrangements for fear it might jeopardize their careers (*Wall Street Journal*, 7 September 1993, 1). Also important was the fact that flextime was not well-suited to service or customer-oriented businesses where employees had to be present for a fixed period, a bandwidth. In businesses using project teams flexible hours could be difficult to arrange, since this type of work design required people to be present at the same time (Stroh and Kush, F11). But despite its successes in many quarters flextime was dependent on the outlook of the manager. If there was trust between managers and employees the fear of abuse could be replaced by a willingness to seek a solution that was in accord with the needs of both employer and employee. That such arrangements were of particular importance to women can be traced to the major responsibilities they continued to bear for child and elder care. And while the work values of women in the Nineties incorporated the desire to go as far as their talent would take them, there was the additional need for supportive husbands, assistance with affordable child and elder care, and access to flexible scheduling. But the Bureau of Labor Statistics noted that only 4 percent of employees at medium and large firms had nontraditional hours (*Rochester Democrat and Chronicle*, 27 September 1995, 8B).

Yet another new aspiration that gained impetus in the post-1945 world was the emphasis on career. No longer were baby boomers and those who followed content with a lifetime dedication to a single firm or job. Workers now looked to career development as a lifelong process in prospect. They turned to life script planning and career pathing, and saw their lives in the context of "multiple careers." These changes included mid-life shifts and involved a process of career migration over a lifetime (D. B. Miller, 1-2). It was the antithesis of Luther's doctrine of the *Stand* (station) which required each person to serve God in a fixed occupation so they would not go astray (Althaus, 36, 38). But five centuries later work was no longer a gift of God nor was its dedicated fulfillment an avenue to salvation. For toilers of the late twentieth century, work in a career was a lifetime vision on earth. And the decision to change careers was increasingly a mid-life reassessment that could determine how the remainder of a lifetime would be completed (Sarason et al., 586–87; Schein, 23–24).

But the recent emphasis on career often came into conflict with family needs and led many to seek a balance between work and life. Social scientists have had no small role in framing this new context, and several proposed that a quality work life was tied to a quality existence beyond the job (Van Maanen and Schein, 32). Schein even suggested that careers and life beyond the job did not exist in "isolation" (Schein, 9, 23–24) and could be symbiotic or negatively competitive. However, Juliet Schor, author of the 1992 book *The Overworked American*, believed Americans were firmly attached to hard work so they could pay for increased spending. This inclination has weakened the balance between work and life in favor of a consumption ethic. Schor noted that since 1969 both men and women have worked an average of 138 hours more per year ("All Work and No Play," 12) to support a credit card culture.

Other data also indicate that employees did not want work to intrude on family life. A 1995 study of 6,000 workers in professional and manufacturing positions found that many women and men have made career compromises so they could balance the responsibilities of work and family. In manufacturing, for

example, 45% of women and 39% of men declined to work over-
time. And 47% of women and 41% of male managers and professionals told supervisors they would not accept relocation (T.
Lewin, "Workers of Both Sexes," 25). This suggests that the new
aspiration for a balanced work life has become an integral part of
our work values.

In offering a final reflection on the *continuities* and *discontinuities* that have influenced the origin and development of
American work values, it is essential to focus on the most pervasive
of the continuities, the search for job security. Without work, all
discussion of continuities and discontinuities form an interesting
but meaningless frame of reference. It was work and work alone
that provided a context for all other values. The fulfillment of this
need enabled people to earn their sustinence and retain an attachment to reality. But because of business cycles, global competition,
and the "creative destruction" of capitalism, secure employment
remained the elusive quarry of the ages. From colonial Philadelphia
to the Rust Belt of today the desire for stable employment never
wavered. But despite panics and recessions it cast only a fleeting
cloud over American optimism. It did not diminish the American
inclination for hard work nor did it lessen the search for opportunity. But for many Americans this cheery scenario was blunted by
the history of workhouse and welfare. Until work became a more
assured commodity for the many, the optimism and diligence of
high-discretion workers and managers would remain the treasure
of the few.

To this discussion must be added the effect of the sharp discontinuities that affected American affairs. The Lutheran-Calvinist
message that was transmitted to America posited a world view
that prized work for its otherworldly rewards. Each person had to
function in a fixed calling (*Beruf*) which served as a vehicle to
eternal grace rather than an avenue to worldly abundance. But
despite the support of Hooker and Cotton Mather, the victory of
secularism and industrialism in eighteenth century America
doomed this belief system tied to salvation. It was the first great
discontinuity in the work values of modernity. Now the convictions
of the Philadelphia counting-houses and the workshops of Lynn
sang the earthly praises of opportunity. By the nineteenth century
hope had become the godfather of aspiring Americans. Success

emerged as the *leitmotiv* of the Gilded Age and gathered a believing populace in its bosom until felled by consequences of the Great Depression. So great was this blow that the survivors of this economic holocaust remained tethered to the chains of job insecurity. Only in the sixties did a last *discontinuity* come forth from the rumblings of a counterculture that never experienced the pain of unemployment. This new generation of would-be revolutionaries tilted against authority and saw its nirvana in meaningful work. In the age of self-fulfillment challenge and autonomy became the watchwords of an activist community that would offer its commitment only in a context of lesser control. No, the precepts of Franklin and Horatio Alger had not died. In reality, the miracle of intellectual cryogenics had placed their ideas in hibernation until they could be reincarnated as a "worth ethic" that gave labor meaning even as it produced a profit. The work ethic had not had a stake driven through its heart, but took on a new mantle that would encourage creative work through commitment.

Where, then, does all of this data and speculation about work values lead? Almost two decades ago E. L. Schumacher called for "good work" as the solution. He believed it was "work that ennobles the product as it ennobles the producer." But to know what this meant Schumacher urged that we must first ascertain the rationale for our existence (Schumacher, 63, 56–57). Sigmund Freud, however, viewed work as the touchstone that kept us in contact with reality (Freud, 27n1). Almost a half century later Daniel Bell reached a similar conclusion: "Every society seeks to establish a set of meanings through which people can relate themselves to the world. . . . These meanings are embodied in religion, in culture, and in work" (Bell, *Cultural Contradictions* 146).

In today's age of self-fulfillment workers seem to be looking for meaning in work within themselves rather than in their employment. They almost see the face in the mirror as a "sacred object" whose personal values are paramount. Were it not for the dominance of secular values, it might suggest a distant past when work offered a possible road to salvation. But in the world of the nineties it was more likely a desire for participation and collaboration that enabled people to grow in work even as they earned their bread. Needed today is a generation of managers who are enablers rather than autocrats. They must be men and women who can offer a vision and be willing to share authority. And no less, the world of work requires people that look to employment as more than an instrumental process. Otherwise, as T. S. Eliot has noted we will continue to measure out our lives "with coffee spoons" (T. S. Eliot, "Prufrock," *Complete Poems*, 5).

BIBLIOGRAPHY

INTRODUCTION AND PROLOGUE

Bailyn, Bernard, *The Peopling of British North America* (New York: Vintage Books, 1988).

Bell, Daniel, *The Cultural Contradictions of Capitalism* (New York: Basic Books, 1978).

Bendix, Reinhard, *Work and Authority in Industry. Ideologies of Management in the Course of Industrialization* (Berkeley: University of California Press, 1956).

Bernstein, Paul, "The Work Ethic That Never Was," *The Wharton Magazine*, Vol. 4, no. 3 (Spring, 1980), 19–26.

Bruchey, Stuart W. (ed.), *The Colonial Merchant. Sources and Readings* (New York: Harcourt, Brace, and World, 1966).

Bruchey, Stuart W., *The Roots of American Economic Growth 1607–1861* (New York: Harper and Row, 1965).

Cherrington, David J., *The Work Ethic. Working Values and Values That Work* (New York: AMACOM, 1980).

Chevalier, Michael, *Society, Manners, and Politics in the United States*, ed. John Williams Ward (Ithaca: Cornell University Press, 1961).

Crowley, J. E., *This Sheba Self. The Conceptualization of Economic Life in Eighteenth-Century America* (Baltimore: Johns Hopkins University Press, 1974).

Dorfman, Joseph, *The Economic Mind in American Civilization, 1606–1865.* 5 Vols. (New York: Viking, 1946-1959).

Eisenstadt, S. N., "The Protestant Ethic Thesis in an Analytical and Comparative Framework," in S. N. Eisenstadt (ed.), *The Protestant Ethic and Modernization* (New York: Basic Books, 1988), 3–45.

Genovese, Eugene D., *Roll, Jordan, Roll. The World the Slaves Made* (New York: Vintage Books, 1976).

Green, Robert, *Protestantism and Capitalism. The Weber Thesis and Its Critics* (Boston: D. C. Heath, 1959).

Gutman, Herbert, *Work, Culture, and Society in Industrializing America. Essays in American Working-Class and Social History* (New York: Vintage Books, 1977).

Handlin, Oscar and Lilian, *A Restless People. Americans in Rebellion, 1770–1787* (Garden City, NY: Anchor/Doubleday, 1982).

Huber, Richard M., *The American Idea of Success* (New York: McGraw-Hill, 1971).

Innes, Stephen, *Labor in a New Land: Economy and Society in Seventeenth-Century Springfield* (Princeton: Princeton University Press, 1983).

Lasch, Christopher, *The Culture of Narcissism* (New York: Warner Books, 1979).

Mantoux, Paul, *The Industrial Revolution in the Eighteenth Century* (New York: Harper and Row, 1961).

Marryat, Frederick, *Diary in America*, ed. by Jules Zenger (Bloomington: University of Indiana Press, 1960).

Morris, Richard B., *Government and Labor in Early America* (New York: Columbia University Press, 1946).

Nash, Gary B., "Up from the Bottom in Franklin's Philadelphia," in *The Private Side of American History. Readings in Everyday Life*, ed. by Gary B. Nash (San Diego: Harcourt Brace Jovanovich, 1983), 163–200.

Perkin, Harold, *The Origins of Modern English Society 1780–1880* (London: Routledge and Kegan Paul, 1969).

Riesman, David, Potter, Robert, and Watson, Jeanne, "Sociability, Permissiveness, and Equality," *Psychiatry*, Vol. 23 (1960), 334–336.

Rodgers, Daniel T., "No's to the Grindstone," *New York Times*, April 16, 1980, A 27.

Rodgers, Daniel T., *The Work Ethic in Industrial America, 1850–1920* (Chicago: University of Chicago Press, 1978).

Tawney, R. H., *Religion and the Rise of Capitalism* (New York: Mentor Books, 1954).

Tilgher, Adriano, *Work. What It Has Meant to Men Through the Ages*, trans. by Dorothy Canfield Fisher (New York: Harcourt, Brace, 1930).

Weber, Max, *The Protestant Ethic and the Spirit of Capitalism* (New York: Charles Scribner's Sons, 1958).

Whyte, William H., Jr., *The Organization Man* (New York: Simon and Schuster, 1956).

PART I: WORK AS A SIGN OF SALVATION

Abel, Wilhelm, *Agricultural Fluctuations in Europe from the Thirteenth to the Twentieth Centuries* (New York: St. Martin's Press, 1980).

Albee, George W., "The Protestant Ethic, Sex, and Psychotherapy," *American Psychologist* (February, 1977), 150–161.

Alford, Henry (ed.), *Works*. 6 Vols. (London: Parker, 1839).

Althaus, Paul, *The Ethics of Martin Luther*, trans. by Robert C. Schultz (Philadelphia: Fortress Press, 1972).

Andrews, Charles M., *The Colonial Period of American History. The Settlements*. 2 Vols. (New Haven, Conn.: Yale University Press, 1964).

Arnold, Walter, "How We Came to Live by the Clock," *Wall Street Journal*, November 23, 1983, 28.

Ashley, Maurice, *The People of England. A Short Social and Economic History* (Baton Rouge, LA: Louisiana State University Press,1982).

Aydelotte, F., *Elizabethan Rogues and Vagabonds* (Oxford: Oxford University Press, 1913).

Bailyn, Bernard, *The New England Merchants in the Seventeenth Century* (Cambridge, Mass.: Harvard University Press, 1955).

Bainton, Roland, *Here I Stand. A Life of Martin Luther* (New York: Abington Press, 1950).

Ball, J. N., *Merchants and Merchandise. The Expansion of Trade in Europe 1500–1630* (London: Croom Helm, 1977).

Baron, Hans, "Fifteenth Century Civilisation and the Renaissance," in *The New Cambridge Modern History. The Renaissance 1493–1520*, ed. by G. R. Potter (Cambridge: Cambridge University Press, 1957), 50–75.

Beier, A. L., "Poor Relief in Warwickshire: 1630–1660," *Past and Present*, Vol. 35 (1966), 77–100.

Beier, A. L., "Vagrants and the Social Order in Elizabethan England," *Past and Present*, Vol. 64 (August, 1974), 3–29.

Bernard, Jacques, "Trade and Finance in the Middle Ages 900–1500," *The Fontana History of Europe. The Middle Ages*, ed. by Carlo M. Cipolla (Glasgow: Collins/Fontana, 1972), I, 274–338.

Bernstein, Irving, "Time and Work." Presidential Address, Industrial Relations Research Association, Atlantic City, New Jersey, September 16–18, 1976, IRRA Series, ed. by J. L. Stern and B. Dennis (Madison: IRRA, 1977), 1–8.

Bernstein, Paul, "The Work Ethic That Never Was," *The Wharton Magazine*, Vol. 4, no. 3 (Spring, 1980), 19–26.

Berton, Lee, "Father of Accounting is a Bit of a Stranger to His Own Progeny," *Wall Street Journal*, January 29, 1993, A1, A9.

Bindoff, S. T., *Tudor England* (Baltimore: Penguin, 1961).

Boas, Ralph and Louis, *Cotton Mather. Keeper of the Puritan Conscience* (Hamden, Conn.: Archon Books, 1964).

Boehmer, Heinrich, *Martin Luther: Road to Reformation,* trans. by John W. Doberstein and Theodore G. Tappert (New York: Meridian Books, 1957).

Bouwsma, William J., *John Calvin. A Sixteenth Century Portrait* (New York: Oxford University Press, 1988).

Bradford, William, *History of Plimouth Plantation* (Boston: Wright and Potter, 1899).

Braudel, Fernand, *The Structures of Everyday Life. Civilization and Capitalism 15th to 18th Century* (New York: Harper and Row, 1979).

Braudel, Fernand, *The Wheels of Commerce. Civilization and Capitalism 15th to 18th Century* (New York: Harper and Row, 1979).

Breen, Timothy H., "The Non–Existent Controversy: Puritan and Anglican Attitudes on Work and Wealth, 1600–1640," *Church History,* Vol. 35 (1966), 273–287.

Bridenbaugh, Carl, *Cities in the Wilderness. The First Century of Urban Life in America, 1625–1742* (New York: Alfred Knopf, 1960).

Bridenbaugh, Carl, *Vexed and Troubled Englishmen 1590–1642* (New York: Oxford University Press, 1968).

Briggs, Asa, *A Social History of England* (New York: Viking, 1983).

Brinton, Crane, *The Shaping of Modern Thought* (Englewood Cliffs, N.J.: Prentice-Hall, 1963).

Bruchey, Stuart, *The Colonial Merchant* (New York: Harcourt, Brace and World, 1966).

Bruchey, Stuart, *The Roots of American Economic Growth* (New York: Harper and Row, 1965).

Bushman, Richard L., *From Puritan to Yankee. Character and Social Order in Connecticut, 1690–1765* (Cambridge, Mass.: Harvard University Press, 1967).

Calvin, John, *Institutes of the Christian Religion,* ed. by J.T. Mitchell and trans. by F. L. Battles. 2 Vols. (Philadelphia: Westminster Press, 1960).

Cawelti, John W., *Apostles of the Self-Made Man* (Chicago: University of Chicago Press, 1965).

Cheyney, Edward P., *The Dawn of a New Era 1250–1453* (New York: Harper and Row, 1962).

Cipolla, Carlo M., *Before the Industrial Revolution. European Society and Economy, 1000–1700* (London: Methuen, 1976).

Cipolla, Carlo M., *Clocks and Culture, 1300–1700* (New York: Norton, 1978).

Clark, Sir George, *The Seventeenth Century.* 2nd ed. (New York: Oxford University Press, 1961).

Clark, Peter and Slack, Paul, *English Towns in Transition 1500–1700* (London: Oxford University Press, 1976).

Clarke, Samuel, *A Collection of the Lives of Ten Eminent Divines* (London: William Miller, 1662).

Clarkson, Leslie A., *The Pre-Industrial Economy of England 1500–1750* (New York: Schocken, 1972).

Cochran, Thomas C., *Business in American Life. A History* (New York: McGraw-Hill, 1974).

Cole, Franklin P. (ed.), *Mather Books & Portraits Through Six Early American Generations 1630–1831* (Portland, ME: Casco Printing Company, 1978).

Coleman, D. C., "Labour in the English Economy of the Seventeenth Century," *Economic History Review*, 2nd series, Vol. 8 (1956), 280–295.

Colman, Benjamin, *A Sermon at the Lecture in Boston After Funerals . . .* (Boston: B. Green, 1717).

Cotton, John, *The True Constitution of a Particular Visible Church, Proved by Scripture* (New York: Arno Press, 1972).

Cotton, John, *The Way of Life or, God's Way and Course, in bringing the Soule into, Keeping it in, and carrying it on, in the Wayes of Life and Peace* (London: L. Fawne and S. Gellibrand, 1641).

Coulton, G. G., *Medieval Village, Manor and Monastery* (New York: Harper & Row, 1960).

Crowley, J. E., *This Sheba Self. The Conceptualization of Economic Life in Eighteenth-Century America* (Baltimore:Johns Hopkins University Press, 1974).

Cunningham, W., *The Gospel of Work. Four Lectures on Christian Ethics* (Cambridge: Cambridge University Press, 1902).

Danforth, John, *The Vile Profanations of Prosperity by the Degenerate among the People of God. . . .* (Boston:B.Green,1704).

Davidson, Edward H., *Jonathan Edwards. The Narrative of a Puritan Mind* (Cambridge, Mass.: Harvard University Press, 1968).

Davis, Ralph, "English Foreign Trade, 1660–1700," *Economic History Review*, 2nd series, Vol. 7 (1954), 150–166.

Davis, Ralph, *The Rise of the Atlantic Economies* (Ithaca: Cornell University Press, 1973).

Deane, Phyllis, *The First Industrial Revolution* (London: Cambridge University Press, 1977).

Dickson, P.G.M., *The Financial Revolution in England. A Study in the Development of Public Credit in England, 1688–1756* (London: Macmillan, 1967).

D'Entrèves, A. P. (ed.), *Aquinas. Selected Political Writings* (Oxford: Basil Blackwell, 1965.

DeVries, Jan, *The Economy of Europe in an Age of Crisis, 1660–1750* (Cambridge: Cambridge University Press, 1976).

Dorfman, Joseph, *The Economic Mind in American Civilization 1606–1865*. 5 Vols. (New York: Viking Press, 1946–1959).

Dudley, Edmund, *The Tree of Commonwealth 1509–1510*, ed.by D.M. Brodie (London: Cambridge University Press, 1948).

Eden, Sir Frederick, *The State of the Poor* (London: J. Davis,1797).

Eisenstadt, S. N., "The Protestant Ethic Thesis in an Analytical and Comparative Framework," *The Protestant Ethic and Modernization* ed. by S. N. Eisenstadt. (New York: Basic Books, 1968), 3–45.

Eusden, John G., *Puritans, Lawyers, and Politics in Early Seventeenth Century England* (Hamden, CT: Archon Books, 1968).

Everitt, Alan, "The Marketing of Agricultural Produce," in *The Agrarian History of England and Wales*, Vol. 4, 1500–1640, ed. by Joan Thirsk (London: Cambridge University Press, 1967), 468–473.

Fanfani, Amintore, "Catholicism, Protestantism and Capitalism,"*Protestantism and Capitalism. The Weber Thesis and Its Critics*, ed. by Robert Green. (Boston: D. C. Heath, 1959), 87–93.

Foster, Stephen, *Their Solitary Way. The Puritan Social Elite in the First Century of Settlement in New England* (New Haven: Yale University Press, 1971).

Fromm, Erich, *The Sane Society* (New York: Rinehart, 1955).

Fullerton, Kemper, "Calvinism and Capitalism: An Exploration of the Weber Thesis," *Protestantism and Capitalism. The Weber Thesis and Its Critics*, ed. by Robert Green (Boston: D. C. Heath, 1959), 6–20.

Furniss, E. S., *The Position of the Laborer in the System of Nationalism: A Study in the Labor Theories of the Later English Mercantilists* (Boston: Houghton Mifflin, 1920).

Garraty, John A., *Unemployment in History. Economic Thought and Public Policy* (New York: Harper and Row, 1978).

George, Charles H. and Katherine, "Protestantism and Capitalism in Pre-Revolutionary England," *The Protestant Ethic and Modernization* ed. by S. N. Eisenstadt. (New York: Basic Books, 1968), 155–176.

George, Charles H. and Katherine, *The Protestant Mind of the English Reformation 1570–1640* (Princeton: Princeton University Press, 1961).

Gilmore, Myron P., *The World of Humanism, 1453–1517* (New York: Harper and Row, 1952).

Gimpel, Jean, *The Medieval Machine. The Industrial Revolution in the Middle Ages* (Harmondsworth, Middlesex: Penguin, 1976).

Gough, John W., *The Rise of the Entrepreneur* (New York: Schocken Books, 1969).

Graham, W. Fred, *The Constructive Revolutionary. John Calvin and His Socio-Economic Impact* (Richmond, VA: John Knox Press, 1971).

Green, Robert, *Protestantism and Capitalism. The Weber Thesis and Its Critics* (Boston: D. C. Heath, 1959).

Greene, Jack P., *Pursuits of Happiness. The Social Development of Early Modern British Colonies and the Formation of American Culture* (Chapel Hill: University of North Carolina Press, 1988).

Gutmann, Myron P., *Toward the Modern Economy. Early Industry in Europe 1500–1800* (Philadelphia: Temple University Press, 1988).

Hales, John, *Discourses of the Commonweal of This Realm of England* (Cambridge: At the University Press, 1929).

Haller, William Jr., *The Rise of Puritanism* (New York: Columbia University Press, 1938).

Harrison, J. F. C., *The Common People. A History from the Norman Conquest to the Present* (London: Flamingo, 1984).

Hartwell, Richard M., "Economic Growth in England Before the Industrial Revolution: Some Methodological Issues," *The Journal of Economic History*, Vol. 29, no. 1 (March, 1969), 13–31.

Heaton, Herbert, *The Yorkshire Woollen and Worsted Industries. From the Earliest Times up to the Industrial Revolution*, 2nd ed. (Oxford: Clarendon Press, 1965).

Hibbert, Christopher, *The English. A Social History, 1066–1945* (London: Paladin, 1988).

Hill, Christopher, *Change and Continuity in Seventeenth–Century England* (Cambridge, Mass.: Harvard University Press, 1975).

Hill, Christopher, *Puritanism and Revolution. Studies in the Interpretation of the English Revolution of the 17th Century* (London: Secker and Warburg, 1958).

Hill, Christopher, *Society and Puritanism in Pre-Revolutionary England* (London: Penguin Books, 1991).

Hill, Christopher, *The Century of Revolution 1603–1714* (New York: W. W. Norton, 1961).

Hodges, Graham R., *New York City Cartmen, 1667–1850* (New York: New York University Press, 1986).

Hofstadter, Richard, *Anti–Intellectualism in American Life* (New York: Vintage Press, 1963).

Holborn, Hajo, *A History of Modern Germany: The Reformation* (Princeton: Princeton University Press, 1959).

Holderness, B. A., *Pre-Industrial England: Economy and Society from 1500 to 1750* (London: Dent, 1976).

Hooykas, R., "Science and Reformation," in *The Protestant Ethic and Modernization*, ed. by S. N. Eisenstadt (New York: Basic Books, 1958), 211–239.

Hoskins, W.G., *The Age of Plunder. The England of Henry VIII 1500–1547* (London: Longman, 1976).

Hoskins, W. G., *The Midland Peasant. The Economic and Social History of a Leicestershire Village* (New York: St. Martin's, 1957).

Huber, Richard M., *The American Idea of Success* (New York: McGraw-Hill, 1971).

Hudson, Winthrop S., "Puritanism and the Spirit of Capitalism," *Protestantism and Capitalism. The Weber Thesis and Its Critics*, ed. by Robert Green. (Boston: D. C. Heath, 1959), 56–62.

Hudson, Winthrop S., "The Weber Thesis Reexamined," *Church History*, Vol. 30 (March, 1961), 88–99.

Huppert, George, *After the Black Death. A Social History of Early Modern Europe* (Bloomington: Indiana University Press, 1986).

Hyma, Albert, "The Economic Views of the Protestant Reformers," *Protestantism and Capitalism. The Weber Thesis and Its Critics*, ed. by Robert Green. (Boston: D. C. Heath, 1959), 94–106.

Jones, Whitney R. D., *The Tudor Commonwealth 1529–1559* (London: Athlone Press, 1970).

Jordan, W. K., *Philanthropy in England 1480–1660* (London: Allen and Unwin, 1959).

Kerr, Hugh T. (ed.), *A Compend of Luther's Theology* (Philadelphia: Westminster Press, 1943).

Koenigsberger, H. G. and Mosse, George L., *Europe in the Sixteenth Century* (Singapore: Longman, 1985).

Kriedte, Peter, Medick, Hans, and Schlumbohm, Jurgen, eds., *Industrialization Before Industrialization. Rural Industry in the Genesis of Capitalism* (Cambridge: Cambridge University Press, 1981).

Labaree, Benjamin W., *Colonial Massachusetts. A History* (Millwood, N.Y.: Kraus-Thomson Organization, 1979).

Landes, David, *Revolution in Time. Clocks and the Making of the Modern World* (Cambridge, Mass.: Harvard University Press, 1983).

Langton, J., "Industry and Towns 1500–1730," in *An Historical Geography of England and Wales*, ed. by R. A. Dodgshon and R. A. Butlin (London: Academic Press, 1978), 173–198.

Lasch, Christopher, *The Culture of Narcissism* (New York: Warner Books, 1979).

Laslett, Peter, *The World We Have Lost. England Before the Industrial Revolution*, 3rd ed. (New York: Scribner's, 1984).

LeGoff, Jacques, "Labor Time in the 'Crisis' of the Fourteenth Century: From Medieval to Modern Time," in Jacques LeGoff, *Time, Work and Culture in the Middle Ages* (Chicago: University of Chicago Press, 1980), 43–52.

LeGoff, Jacques, *Time, Work and Culture in the Middle Ages* (Chicago: University of Chicago Press, 1980).

Lemon, James T., "Spatial Order: Households in Local Communities and Regions," in *Colonial British America. Essays in the New History of the Early Modern Era*, ed. by Jack P. Greene and J. R. Pole (Baltimore: Johns Hopkins University Press, 1984), 86–122.

Littell, Franklin, H., "What Calvin Learned at Strassburg," in *The Heritage of John Calvin*, ed. by John H. Bratt (Grand Rapids, Michigan: William B. Eerdmans Publishing Co.,1973), 74–86.

Luther, Martin, *An Open Letter to the Christian Nobility of the German Nation, in Three Treatises*, trans. by C. M. Jacobs (Philadelphia: Fortress Press, 1947).

Lüthy, Herbert, "Once Again: Calvinism and Capitalism," *The Protestant Ethic and Modernization*, ed. by S. N. Eisenstadt. (New York: Basic Books, 1968), 87–108.

Luzzato, Gino, *An Economic History of Italy from the Fall of the Roman Empire to the Beginning of the Sixteenth Century* (London: Routledge and Kegan Paul, 1961).

MacPherson, C. B., *The Political Theory of Possessive Individualism* (Oxford: Clarendon Press, 1962).

Mantoux, Paul, *The Industrial Revolution in the Eighteenth Century* (New York: Harper and Row, 1961).

Marius, Richard, *Luther. A Biography* (Philadelphia: Lippincott,1974).

Marvell, Andrew, "To His Coy Mistress," in *The Oxford Book of Seventeenth Century Verse*, ed. by H. J. C. Grierson and G. Bullough (Oxford: Clarendon Press, 1934).

Mather, Cotton, *Bonifacius. An Essay Upon the Good*, ed. by David Levin (Cambridge, Mass.: Harvard University Press, 1966).

Mather, Cotton, *Small Offers Toward the Service of the Tabernacle in the Wilderness. Four Discourses Accommodated Unto the Designs of Practical Godliness* (Boston: R. Pierce, 1689).

Mather, Cotton, *Sober Sentiments*, funeral sermon produced by the premature and much-lamented death of Mr. Joshua Lamb (Boston: Fleet, 1722).

Mather, Cotton, *Two Brief Discourses, one Directing a Christian in General Calling; another Directing him in his Personal Calling* (Boston: B. Green and J. Allen, 1701).

McNeill, John T., *The History and Character of Calvinism* (London: Oxford University Press, 1954).

Michaelsen, Robert S., "Changes in the Puritan Concept of Calling or Vocation," *New England Quarterly*, Vol. 26 (September, 1953), 315–336.

Middlekauff, Robert, *The Mathers. Three Generations of Puritan Intellectuals 1596–1728* (New York: Oxford University Press, 1971).

Miller, Perry (ed.), *The American Puritans. Their Prose and Poetry* (New York: Doubleday and Company, 1956).

Miller, Perry and Johnson, Thomas H. (eds.), *The Puritans. A Sourcebook of Their Writings* (New York: Harper and Row, 1963).

Mills, C. Wright, *White Collar. The American Middle Classes* (New York: Oxford University Press, 1953).

Minchinton, Walter, "Patterns of Structure and Demand 1500–1750," in *The Fontana Economic History of Europe. The Sixteenth and Seventeenth Centuries*, ed. by Carlo M. Cipolla (Glasgow: Collins/Fontana, 1974), 2:83–176.

Mohl, R. A., *Poverty in New York 1783–1825* (New York: Oxford University Press, 1971).

Mols, Roger, "Population in Europe 1500–1750," in *The Fontana Economic History of Europe. The Sixteenth and Seventeenth Centuries*, ed. by Carlo M. Cipolla (Glasgow: Collins/Fontana, 1974), 2:15–82.

More, Thomas, *Utopia* (Harmondsworth, Middlesex: Penguin, 1965).

Morgan, Edmund S., *American Slavery American Freedom* (New York: W. W. Norton, 1975).

Morgan, Edmund S., *Puritan Political Ideals, 1558–1794* (Indianapolis: Bobbs-Merrill, 1965).

Morgan, Edmund S., "The Puritan Ethic and the American Revolution," *William and Mary Quarterly*, 3rd series, Vol. 24 (October,1967), 3–43.

Morgan, Kenneth O., *The Oxford Illustrated History of England* Oxford: Oxford University Press, 1984).

Morison, Samuel Eliot, *Builders of the Bay Colony* (Boston: Houghton Mifflin, 1930).

Morris, Richard B., *Government and Labor in Early America* (New York: Columbia University Press, 1946).

Mumford, Lewis, *Technics and Civilization* (New York: Harcourt, Brace, 1934).

Mun, Thomas, "England's Treasure by Foreign Trade," in *Early English Tracts on Commerce* [1664], ed. by J. R. McCulloch (Cambridge: Cambridge University Press, 1954).

Murdock, Kenneth B., *Increase Mather. The Foremost American Puritan* (New York: Russell and Russell, 1966).

Nash, Gary, "Poverty and Poor Relief in Pre-Revolutionary Philadelphia," *William and Mary Quarterly*, 3rd series, Vol. 33 (January, 1976), 3–30.

Nash Gary, "Up from the Bottom in Franklin's Philadelphia," in *The Private Side of American History. Readings in Everyday Life*, ed. by Gary Nash (San Diego, California: Harcourt Brace Jovanovich, 1983), 163–200.

Nef, John U., *Cultural Foundations of Industrial Civilization* (Hamden, Conn.: Archon Books, 1974).

Nef, John U., "The Industrial Revolution Reconsidered," *The Journal of Economic History*, Vol. 3, no. 1 (May,1943), 1–31.

Nef, John U., "The Progress of Technology and the Growth of Large–Scale Industry in Great Britain, 1540–1640," *Economic History Review*, Vol. 5 (1934–1935), 3–24.

Nef, John U., *War and Human Progress. An Essay on the Rise of Industrial Civilization* (New York: W. W. Norton, 1950).

Nef, John U., *Western Civilization Since the Renaissance. Peace, War, Industry and the Arts* (New York: Harper and Row, 1963).

Notestein, Wallace, *The English People on the Eve of Colonization* (New York: Harper and Brothers, 1954).

O'Brien, George, *An Essay on the Economic Effects of the Reformation* (New York: Augustus M. Kelley, 1970).

Ogg, David, *England in the Reign of Charles II.* 2 Vols. (London: Oxford University Press, 1962).

Ozment, Steven, *The Age of Reform 1250–1550: An Intellectual and Religious History of Late Medieval and Reformation Europe* (New Haven, Connecticut: Yale University Press, 1980).

Parker, Stanley, *The Future of Work and Leisure* (New York: Praeger, 1971).

Parker, T. H. L., *John Calvin. A Biography* (Philadelphia: Westminster Press, 1975).

Passell, Peter, "A Giant in the Profession Gives a Lift to Economic History," *New York Times*, October 21, 1993, D2.

Pepys, Samuel, *The Diary of Samuel Pepys*, ed. by Henry B. Wheatley. 2 Vols. (New York: Random House, 1946).

Perry, Ralph Barton, *Puritanism and Democracy* (New York: Harper and Row, 1944).

Plucknett, Theodore F. T., *Taswell–Langmead's English Constitutional History from the Teutonic Conquest to the Present Time* (Boston: Houghton Mifflin, 1960).

Postan, Michael, "The Rise of a Money Economy," *Economic History Review*, Vol. 14 (1944), 123–134.

Prothero, G. W. (ed.), *Select Statutes and Other Constitutional Documents Illustrative of the Reigns of Elizabeth I and James I.* 4th ed. (Oxford: Clarendon Press, 1965).

Ribton-Turner, C. J., *A History of Vagrants and Vagrancy, and Beggars and Begging* (London: Chapman and Hall, 1887).

Rischin, Moses (ed.), *The American Gospel of Success* (Chicago: University of Chicago Press, 1965).

Robertson, H.M., "A Criticism of Max Weber and His School," *Protestantism and Capitalism. The Weber Thesis and Its Critics,* ed. by Robert Green. (Boston: D. C. Heath, 1959), 65–86.

Robertson, H. M., *Aspects of the Rise of Economic Individualism. A Criticism of Max Weber and His School* (New York: Augustus M. Kelley, 1970).

Robertson, H. M., "European Economic Developments in the 16th Century." Paper read to Cape Town Senior Seminar, May 18, 1949 in H. M. Robertson, *Aspects of the Rise of Economic Individualism. A Criticism of Max Weber and His School* (New York: Augustus M. Kelley, 1970), 48–49.

Ruitenbeek, Henrik M., *The Individual and the Crowd. A Study of Identity in America* (New York: New American Library, 1964).

Sachs, Williams S. and Hoogenboom, Ari, *The Enterprising Colonials. Society on the Eve of the Revolution* (Chicago: Argonaut, 1965).

Sams, Henry W., "Self–Love and the Doctrine of Work," *Journal of the History of Ideas,* Vol. 4 (1943), 320–332.

Schwartz, Richard B., *Daily Life in Johnson's London* (Madison: University of Wisconsin Press, 1983).

Sée, Henri, "The Contribution of the Puritans to the Evolution of Modern Capitalism," *Protestantism and Capitalism. The Weber Thesis and Its Critics,* ed. by Robert Green (Boston: D. C. Heath, 1959), 62–64.

Sella, Domenico, "European Industries 1500–1700" in *The Fontana Economic History of Europe. The Sixteenth and Seventeenth Centuries,* ed. by Carlo M. Cipolla (Glasgow: Collins/Fontana, 1974), 2:354–426.

Silverman, Kenneth (ed.), *Selected Letters of Cotton Mather* (Baton Rouge: Louisiana State University Press, 1971).

Silverman, Kenneth, *The Life and Times of Cotton Mather* (New York: Harper and Row, 1984).

Slack, Paul A., "Vagrants and Vagrancy in England, 1598–1604," *Economic History Review,* 2nd series, Vol. 27 (1974), 360–379.

Smith, Goldwin, *A Constitutional and Legal History of England* (New York: Charles Scribner's Sons, 1955).

Smith, Lacey Baldwin, *This Realm of England, 1399–1688* (Boston: D. C. Heath, 1966).

Smith, Sir Thomas, *De Republica Anglorum,* ed. by L. Alston (Cambridge: Cambridge University Press, 1906).

Sombart, Werner, *Der Moderne Kapitalismus.* 2 Vols. (Leipzig: Duncker and Humblot, 1902).

Sombart, Werner, "The Role of Religion in the Formation of the Capitalist Spirit," *Protestantism and Capitalism. The Weber Thesis and Its Critics*, ed. by Robert Green. (Boston: D. C. Heath, 1959), 29–38.

Spitz, Lewis W., *The Protestant Reformation, 1517–1559* (New York: Harper and Row, 1985).

Stone, Lawrence, "An Elizabethan Coal Mine," *Economic History Review*, 2nd series, Vol. 3 (1950), 97–106.

Stone, Lawrence, "State Control in Sixteenth-Century England," *Economic History Review*, Vol. 17 (1947), 103–120.

Stone, Lawrence, *The Crisis of the Aristocracy* (London: Oxford University Press, 1965).

Strauss, Eric, *Sir William Petty. Portrait of a Genius* (London: The Bodley Head, 1954).

Swetz, Frank J., *Capitalism and Arithmetic* (La Salle, Illinois: Open Court Publishing Co., 1987).

Tawney, R. H., *Religion and the Rise of Capitalism* (New York: Mentor Books, 1954).

Thomas, Keith, "Work and Leisure in Pre–Industrial Society," *Past and Present*, Vol. 29 (December, 1964), 50–66.

Thirsk, Joan, *Economic Policy and Projects: The Development of a Consumer Society in Early Modern England* (Oxford: Oxford University Press, 1978).

Thompson, E. P., "Time, Work–Discipline, and Industrial Capitalism," *Past and Present*, Vol. 38 (1967), 56–97.

Thrupp, Sylvia L., "Medieval Industry 1000–1500," in *The Fontana Economic History of Europe. The Middle Ages*, ed. by Carlo M. Cipolla (Glasgow: Collins/Fontana, 1972), 1: 221–273.

Tilgher, Adriano, *Work. What It Has Meant to Men Through the Ages*, trans. by Dorothy Canfield Fisher (New York: Harcourt, Brace, 1930).

Trinterud, Leonard J., "The Origins of Puritanism," in Sidney M. Burrell, ed., *The Role of Religion in Modern European History* (New York: Macmillan, 1964), 55–65.

Troeltsch, Ernst, *Protestanism and Progress. A Historical Study of the Relation of Protestantism to the Modern World* (New York: G. P. Putnam's Sons, 1912).

Troeltsch, Ernst, "The Economic Ethic of Calvinism," *Protestantism and Capitalism. The Weber Thesis and Its Critics*, ed. by Robert Green. (Boston: D. C. Heath, 1959). 21–28.

Tucker, G. S. L., "English Pre–Industrial Population Trends," *Economic History Review*, 2nd Series, Vol. 16, no. 2 (December, 1963), 205–218.

Tudor Economic Documents, Being Select Documents Illustrating the Economic and Social History of Tudor England, ed. by R. H. Tawney and Eileen Power. 3 Vols. (London: Longmans, Green,1924).

Walzer, Michael, "Puritanism as a Revolutionary Ideology," in *The Protestant Ethic and Modernization*, ed. by S. N. Eisenstadt. (New York: Basic Books, 1968), 109–134.

Weber, Max, *The Protestant Ethic and the Spirit of Capitalism* (New York: Charles Scribner's Sons, 1958).

Wertenbaker, Thomas Jefferson, *The Puritan Oligarchy. The Founding of American Civilization* (New York: Grosset and Dunlap, 1947).

Westerfield, R. B., *Middlemen in English Business, Particularly Between 1660 and 1760* (New Haven: Yale University Press, 1915).

Wilson, Charles, *England's Apprenticeship 1603–1763* (New York: St. Martin's Press, 1965).

Wright, Louis B., *Middle Class Culture in Elizabethan England* (Ithaca: Cornell University Press, 1958).

Wright, Louis B., *The Cultural Life of the American Colonies 1607–1763* (New York: Harper, 1927).

Wrightson, Keith, *English Society 1580–1680* (New Brunswick, N.J.: Rutgers University Press, 1982).

Wrightson, Keith and Levine, David, *Poverty and Piety in an English Village. Terling 1525–1700* (New York: Academic Press, 1979).

Wrigley, E. A., "The Growth of Population in Eighteenth-Century England: A Conundrum Resolved," *Past and Present*, Vol. 98 (1983), 121–150.

Wyllie, Irwin G., *The Self–Made Man in America. The Myth from Rags to Riches* (New Brunswick, N.J.: Rutgers University Press,1954).

Yelling, J. A., "Agriculture 1500–1730," in *An Historical Geography of England and Wales*, ed. by R. A. Dodgshon and and R. A. Butlin (London: Academic Press, 1978), 151–172.

Youings, Joyce, *Sixteenth–Century England* (London: Penguin, 1984).

Ziff, Larzer, *Puritanism in America. New Culture in a New World* (New York: Viking, 1973).

PART II: WORK AS ALIENATION AND OPPORTUNITY

Abbott, Lyman, "The Ethical Teachings of Jesus: II—Righteousness," *Outlook*, Vol. 94 (March 12, 1910), 576–578.

Aitken, Hugh, G. J., *Taylorism at Watertown Arsenal: Scientific Management in Action, 1908–1915* (Cambridge: Harvard University Press, 1960).

Alger, Horatio, Jr., *Herbert Carter's Legacy or the Inventor's Son* (New York: A. L. Burt Company, n.d.).

Alger, Horatio, Jr., *Jed, the Poorhouse Boy* (Philadelphia: John C. Winston, 1899).

Alger, Horatio, Jr., *Strive and Succeed. Julius or the Store Boy Out West* (New York: Holt, Rinehart and Winston, 1967).

Alger, Horatio, Jr., *Tom Turner's Legacy* (New York: A.L.Burt,1902).

Allen, Frank, "Bosses List Main Strengths, Flaws Determining Potential of Managers," *Wall Street Journal*, November 14, 1980, 33.

Allen, Frederick L., *Only Yesterday. An Informal History of the 1920s* (New York: Harper and Row, 1964).

Andrews, Charles M., *The Colonial Period of American History. The Settlements.* 2 Vols. (New Haven: Yale University Press, 1964).

Anthony, P. D., *The Ideology of Work* (London: Tavistock, 1977).

Appleby, Joyce O., "Value and Society," in *Colonial British America. Essays in the New History of the Early Modern Era*, ed. by Jack P. Greene and J. R. Pole (Baltimore: Johns Hopkins University Press, 1984), 290–316.

Appleby, Joyce O. (ed.), *Materialism and Morality in the American Past: Themes and Sources, 1600–1680* (Reading, Mass.: Addison-Wesley, 1974).

Appleby, Joyce O., "The Social Origins of American Revolutionary Ideology," *Journal of American History*, Vol. 64 (1978), 935–958.

Babson, Roger, *Religion and Business* (New York: Macmillan, 1920).

Babson, Roger, *What is Success?* (New York: Fleming H. Revell,1923).

Bacon, Margaret H., *The Quiet Rebels. The Story of the Quakers in America* (Philadelphia: New Society Publishers, 1985).

Baida, Peter, *Poor Richard's Legacy. American Business Values from Benjamin Franklin to Donald Trump* (New York: William Morrow, 1990).

Bailyn, Bernard, *The New England Merchants in the Seventeenth Century* (Cambridge, Mass.: Harvard University Press, 1955).

Bailyn, Bernard, *The Peopling of British North America* (New York: Vintage, 1988).

Bailyn, Bernard, *Voyagers to the West. A Passage in the Peopling of America on the Eve of the Revolution* (New York: Vintage, 1986).

Baldwin, Leland D., *Pittsburgh: The Story of a City, 1750–1865* (Pittsburgh: University of Pittsburgh Press, 1970).

Barnum, Phineas T., *The Art of Money-Getting* (New York: A. L. Bancroft, 1886).

Barton, Bruce, *The Man in the Book Nobody Knows* (Indianapolis: Bobbs-Merrill, 1959).

Baxter, William T., *The House of Hancock: Business in Boston, 1724–1775* (Cambridge, Mass.: Harvard University Press, 1945).

Beard, Miriam, *A History of Business*. 2 Vols. (Ann Arbor: University of Michigan Press, 1962).

Beecher, Henry Ward, *Lectures to Young Men* (Boston and New York: Saxton and Mills, 1846).

Bender, Thomas, *Toward an Urban Vision. Ideas and Institutions in Nineteenth-Century America* (Baltimore: Johns Hopkins University Press, 1975).

Bendix, Reinhard, *Work and Authority in Industry. Ideologies of Management in the Course of Industrialization* (Berkeley: University of California Press, 1956).

Bensman, David, *The Practice of Solidarity. American Hat Finishers in the Nineteenth Century* (Urbana: University of Illinois Press, 1985).

Bensman, David, "Workers' Control in the Nineteenth Century Hatting Industry," ed. by Herbert G. Gutman and Donald H. Bell, *The New England Working Class and the New Labor History* (Urbana: University of Illinois Press, 1987), 128–136.

Berger, Bennett M., "The Sociology of Leisure: Some Suggestions," in *Work and Leisure*, ed. by Erwin O. Smigel. (New Haven: Yale University Press, 1963), 21–40.

Bernstein, Irving, *A Caring Society. The New Deal, the Worker, and the Great Depression* (Boston: Houghton Mifflin, 1985).

Bernstein, Irving, *Turbulent Years. A History of the American Worker, 1933–1941* (Boston: Houghton Mifflin, 1960).

Bernstein, Paul, "The Work Ethic That Never Was," *The Wharton Magazine*, Vol. 4, no. 3 (Spring, 1980), 19–26.

Beverly, Robert, *The History and Present State of Virginia*, ed. by Louis B. Wright (Chapel Hill: University of North Carolina Press, 1947).

Beynon, Huw, *Working for Ford* (London: Allen Lane, 1973).

Bezanson, Anne, *Four Years of Labor Mobility. A Study of Labor Turnover in a Group of Selected Plants in Philadelphia 1921–1924* (Philadelphia: Industrial Research Department, Wharton School of Finance and Commerce, University of Pennsylvania, 1925).

Bining, Arthur C., *British Regulation of the Colonial Iron Industry* (Philadelphia: University of Pennsylvania Press, 1933).

Bird, Stewart, Georgakas, Dan, and Shaffer, Deborah, *Solidarity Forever. An Oral History of the IWW* (Chicago: Lake View Press, 1985).

Blum, Albert A., "United States," in *International Handbook of Industrial Relations. Contemporary Developments and Research*, ed. by Albert A. Blum (Westport, Conn.: Greenwood Press, 1981), 621–645.

Blumin, Stuart, "Residential and Occupational Mobility in Antebellum Philadelphia," in *Three Centuries of Social Mobility in America*, ed. by Edward Pessen. (Lexington, Mass.: D. C. Heath, 1974), 59–92,

Blumin, Stuart, *The Emergence of the Middle Class. Social Experience in the American City, 1760–1900* (New York: Cambridge University Press, 1989).

Bodnar, John, Simon, Roger, and Weber, Michael P., *Lives of Their Own. Blacks, Italians, and Poles in Pittsburgh 1900–1960* Urbana: University of Illinois Press, 1982).

Bok, Edward, "The Employer and the Young Man," *Cosmopolitan*, Vol. 16 (1894), 731.

Bok, Edward, *The Keys to Success* (Philadelphia: John D. Morris, 1898).

Bontemps, Arna and Conroy, Jack, *Anyplace But Here* (New York: Hill and Wang, 1966).

Boydston, Jeanne, *Home and Work. Housework, Wages, and the Ideology of Labor in the Early Republic* (New York: Oxford University Press, 1990).

Bradford, William, *Of Plymouth Plantation 1620–1647*, ed. by Samuel E. Morison (New York: Alfred Knopf, 1966).

Braithwaite, William C., *The Second Period of Quakerism* (London: Cambridge University Press, 1961).

Brandes, Stuart D., *American Welfare Capitalism, 1880–1940* (Chicago: University of Chicago Press, 1976).

Breen, Timothy H., "An Empire of Goods: The Anglicization of Colonial America, 1690–1776," *Journal of British Studies*, Vol. 25 (October, 1986), 467–499.

Breen, Timothy H., "The Non-Existent Controversy: Puritan and Anglican Attitudes on Work and Wealth, 1600–1640," *Church History*, Vol. 35 (1966), 273–287.

Breen, Timothy H., and Foster, Stephen, "Moving to the New World: The Character of Early Massachusetts Immigration," *William and Mary Quarterly*, 3rd Series, Vol. 30 (1973), 189–222.

Bremner, Robert H., *From the Depths: The Discovery of Poverty in the United States* (New York: New York University Press, 1956).

Bridenbaugh, Carl, *Cities in the Wilderness. The First Century of Urban Life in America 1625–1742* (New York:Alfred Knopf, 1960).

Bridenbaugh, Carl (ed.), *Gentleman's Progress. The Itinerarium of Dr. Alexander Hamilton, 1744* (Chapel Hill: University of North Carolina Press, 1948).

Bridenbaugh, Carl, *The Colonial Craftsman* (New York: New York University Press, 1950).

Bridenbaugh, Carl, *Vexed and Troubled Englishmen 1590–1642* (New York: Oxford University Press, 1968).

Briggs, Asa, *Victorian Cities* (New York: Harper and Row, 1963).

Bristol, Claude M., *The Magic of Believing* (New York: Prentice-Hall, 1948).

Brody, David, *In Labor's Cause: Main Themes on the History of the American Worker* (New York: Oxford University Press, 1993).

Brody, David, *Steelworkers in America: The Nonunion Era* (Cambridge, Mass.: Harvard University Press, 1960).

Brody, David, *Workers in Industrial America. Essays on the Twentieth Century Struggle* (New York: Oxford University Press, 1980).

Broom, Leonard and Glenn, Norval D., *Transformation of the Negro American* (New York: Harper and Row, 1965).

Brown, Richard D., *Modernization. The Transformation of American Life, 1600–1865* (New York: Hill and Wang, 1976).

Bruchey, Stuart W., *Enterprise. The Dynamic Economy of a Free People* (Cambridge: Harvard University Press, 1990).

Bruchey, Stuart W. (ed.), *The Colonial Merchant. Sources and Readings* (New York: Harcourt,Brace, and World, 1966).

Bruchey, Stuart W., *The Roots of American Economic Growth, 1607–1861* (New York: Harper and Row, 1965).

Bucki, Cecilia, "Dilution and Craft Tradition: Munitions Workers in Bridgeport, Connecticut, 1915–19," in *The New England Working Class and the New Labor History*, ed. by Herbert G. Gutman and Donald H. Bell. (Urbana: University of Illinois Press, 1987), 137–156.

Bushman, Richard L., *From Puritan to Yankee. Character and Social Order in Connecticut, 1690–1765* (Cambridge: Harvard University Press, 1967).

Bushman, Richard L., "The Great Awakening in Connecticut, " in *Colonial America. Essays in Politics and Social Development*, ed. by Stanley N. Katz (Boston: Little, Brown, 1971), 297–308.

Butterfield, Lyman, H., Garrett, Wendell and Sprague, Marjorie (eds.), *The Adams Family Correspondence*. 6 Vols. (Cambridge, Mass.: Harvard University Press, 1963–1993).

Butterfield, Lyman, H., *The Adams Papers. Diary and Autobiography of John Adams*. 4 Vols. (Cambridge, Mass.: Harvard University Press, 1961).

Campbell, Mildred, "Social Origins of Some Early Americans," in *Seventeenth Century America. Essays in Colonial History*, ed. by James Morton Smith (Chapel Hill: University of North Carolina Press, 1959), 63–89.

Carnegie, Andrew, "Business," in *The Empire of Business* (New York: Doubleday, Page and Co., 1902).

Carnegie, Andrew, *The Gospel of Wealth and Other Timely Essays* (Garden City, N.Y.: Doubleday and Doran, 1933).

Carnegie, Andrew, "Wealth," *North American Review*, Vol. 148 (June, 1889), 653–664.

Carnegie, Dale, *How to Win Friends and Influence People* (New York: Simon and Schuster, 1936).

Carr, Lois Green and Menard, Russell R., "Immigration and Opportunity: The Freedman in Early Colonial America," in *The Chesapeake in the Seventeenth Century. Essays on Anglo-American Society and Politics*, ed. by Thad W. Tate and David L. Ammerman (New York: W. W. Norton, 1979), 206–242.

Carr, Lois Green and Walsh, Lorena S., "Economic Diversification and Labor Organization in the Chesapeake, 1650–1820," in *Work and Labor in Early America*, ed. by Stephen Innes (Chapel Hill: University of North Carolina Press, 1988), 144–188.

Cawelti, John G., *Apostles of the Self–Made Man* (Chicago: University of Chicago Press, 1965).

Chandler, Alfred D., Jr., *The Visible Hand: The Managerial Revolution in American Business* (Cambridge, Mass.: Harvard University Press, 1977).

Chandler, Alfred D., Jr., and Tedlow, Richard S., *The Coming of Managerial Capitalism* (Homewood, Illinois: Richard Irwin,1985).

Cheney, Lynne, "Hard Work, Once as American as Apple Pie," *Wall Street Journal*, April 6, 1993, A 14.

Chevalier, Michel, *Society, Manners, and Politics in the United States; Letters on North America*, ed. by John William Ward (Ithaca: Cornell University Press, 1961).

Chinoy, Ely, *Automobile Workers and the American Dream* (Boston: Beacon Press, 1965).

Clark, Victor S., *History of Manufactures in the United States*. 3 Vols. (New York: Peter Smith, 1949)

Clarkson, Leslie A., *The Pre-Industrial Economy of England, 1500–1750* (New York: Schocken Books, 1972).

Clawson, Dan, *Bureaucracy and the Labor Process* (New York: Monthly Review Press, 1980).

Clemens, Paul G., *The Atlantic Economy and Colonial Maryland's Eastern Shore: From Tobacco to Grain* (Ithaca: Cornell University Press, 1980).

Clement, Priscilla F., "The Philadelphia Welfare Crisis of the 1820s," *The Pennsylvania Magazine of History and Biography*, Vol. 18 (April, 1981), 150–164.

Clews, Henry, *Fifty Years in Wall Street* (New York: Irving Publishing Company, 1908).

Cochran, Thomas C., *Business in American Life. A History* (New York: McGraw-Hill, 1972).

Cochran, Thomas C., *Frontiers of Change. Early Industrialism in America* (New York: Oxford University Press, 1981).

Cochran, Thomas C., "Business Organization and the Development of an Industrial Discipline," in *Views of American Economic Growth: The Agricultural Era*. 2 Vols., ed. by Thomas C. Cochran and Thomas B. Brewer (New York: McGraw-Hill, 1966), 1:215–227.

Cochran, Thomas C., *200 Years of American Business* (New York: Dell, 1977).

Cochran, Thomas C. and Miller, William, *The Age of Enterprise; a Social History of Industrial America*, rev. ed. (New York: Harper and Row, 1961).

Colman, Benjamin, *A Sermon at the Lecture in Boston after the Funerals . . .* (Boston: Printed by B. Green for Samuel Gerrish and Daniel Henchman, 1717).

Conant, James B., "Education for a Classless Society: The Jeffersonian Tradition," *Atlantic*, Vol. 165 (May, 1940), 593–602.

Conwell, Russell, *Acres of Diamonds* (New York: Harper, 1915).

Conwell, Russell, *The New Day* (Philadelphia: Griffith and Rowland, 1904).

Coolidge, Calvin, *The Autobiography of Calvin Coolidge* (London: Chatto and Windus, 1929).

Corbin, David A., *Life, Work, and Rebellion in the Coal Fields. The Southern West Virginia Miners, 1880–1922* (Urbana: University of Illinois Press, 1981).

Coué, Emile, *Self-Mastery Through Conscious Autosuggestion*, trans. by Archibald Stark Van Orden (New York:Malkan Publishing,1922).

Couvares, Francis G., "The Triumph of Commerce: Class Culture and Mass Culture in Pittsburgh" in *Working-Class America. Essays on Labor, Community and American Society*, ed. by Michael Frisch and Daniel J. Walkowitz. (Urbana: University of Illinois Press, 1983), 123–152.

Crèvecoeur, Hector St. John de, *Sketches of Eighteenth-Century America*, ed. by Henri Bourdin *et al* (New Haven: Yale University Press, 1925).

Crowley, J. E., *This Sheba Self. The Conceptualization of Economic Life in Eighteenth-Century America* (Baltimore: Johns Hopkins University Press, 1974).

Cumbler, John T., *A Social History of Economic Decline. Business, Politics, and Work in Trenton* (New Brunswick, N.J.: Rutgers University Press, 1989).

Cumbler, John T., *Working Class Community in Industrial America. Work, Leisure, and Struggle in Two Industrial Cities, 1880–1930* (Westport, Conn.: Greenwood Press, 1979).

Curtin, Philip D., *The Atlantic Slave Trade: A Census* (Madison: University of Wisconsin Press, 1969).

Dalzell, Robert F., Jr., *Enterprising Elite. The Boston Associates and the World They Made* (New York: W.W. Norton, 1993).

Davidson, Marshall B., *Life in America*, 2nd ed. (Boston: Houghton Mifflin, 1974).

Davis, David Brion, *The Problem of Slavery in Western Culture* (Ithaca: Cornell University Press, 1966).

Davis, J. S., *Essays in the Earlier History of American Corporations* (Cambridge, Mass.: Harvard University Press, 1917).

Davis, Ralph, *The Rise of the Atlantic Economies* (Ithaca: Cornell University Press, 1971).

Dawley, Alan, *Class and Community: The Industrial Revolution in Lynn* (Cambridge, Mass.: Harvard University Press, 1976).

De Tocqueville, Alexis, *Democracy in America*, ed. by Phillips Bradley (New York: Knopf, 1966).

Deutsch, Arnold R., *The Human Resources Revolution* (New York: McGraw-Hill, 1979).

Deutschman, Alan, "The Upbeat Generation," *Fortune*, July 13, 1992, 42–54.

DeVoto, Bernard, *Mark Twain in Eruption. Hitherto Unpublished Pages About Men and Events* (New York: Harper, 1940).

Diamond, Sigmund, "From Organization to Society: Virginia in the Seventeenth Century," in *Colonial America. Essays in Politics and Social Development*, ed. by Stanley N. Katz (Boston: Little, Brown, 1971), 3–31.

Diamond, Sigmund, *The Reputation of the American Businessman* (Cambridge, Mass.: Harvard University Press, 1955).

Diamond, Sigmund, "Values as an Obstacle to Economic Growth: The American Colonies," *Journal of Economic History*, Vol. 27, no.4, (December, 1967), 561–575.

Doerflinger, Thomas M., *A Vigorous Spirit of Enterprise. Merchants and Economic Development in Revolutionary Philadelphia* (Chapel Hill: University of North Carolina Press, 1986).

Doerflinger, Thomas and Rivlin, Jack L., *Risk and Reward. Venture Capital & the Making of America's Great Industries* (New York: Random House, 1987).

Dorfman, Joseph, *The Economic Mind in American Civilization, 1606–1685.* 5 Vols. (New York: Viking Press, 1946–1959).

Dublin, Thomas (ed.), *Farm to Factory: Women's Letters, 1830–1860* (New York: Columbia University Press, 1981).

Dublin, Thomas, *Women at Work: The Transformation of Work and Community in Lowell,Massachusetts, 1826–1860* (New York: Columbia University Press, 1979).

Dubofsky, Melvyn, *Industrialism and the American Worker 1865–1920*. 2nd ed., (Harlan Davidson: Arlington Heights, Illinois, 1985.

DuBois, W. E. B., *The Philadelphia Negro. A Social Study* (New York: Benjamin Blom, 1967).

Duncan, Otis D. and Blau, Peter, "What Determines Occupational Success," in *Three Centuries of Social Mobility in America* (Lexington, Mass.: D. C. Heath, 1974), 284–303.

Dunlap, George A., *The City in the American Novel, 1789–1900* (New York: Russell and Russell, 1965).

Dunn, Richard S., "Servants and Slaves. The Recruitment and Employment of Labor," in *Colonial British America. Essays in the New History of the Early Modern Era*, ed. by Jack P. Greene and J. R. Pole (Baltimore: Johns Hopkins University Press, 1984), 157–194.

Durkheim, Emilé, *Suicide, a Study in Sociology*, trans. by John A. Spaulding and George Simpson (Glencoe, Illinois: Free Press, 1951).

Durkheim, Emilé, *The Division of Labor in Society*, trans. by George Simpson (New York: Free Press of Glencoe, 1964).

Earle, Alice M., *Child Life in Colonial Days* (New York: Macmillan, 1943).

East, Robert A., *Business Enterprise in the American Revolutionary Era* (Gloucester, Mass.: Peter Smith, 1964).

Egnal, Marc, "The Economic Development of the Thirteen Colonies, 1720 to 1775," *William and Mary Quarterly*, 3rd series, Vol. 32, no.2 (April, 1975), 191–222.

Ekirch, Arthur, *The Idea of Progress in America 1815–1860* (New York: Peter Smith, 1951).

Elson, Ruth M., *Guardians of Tradition: American Schoolbooks of the Nineteenth Century* (Lincoln: University of Nebraska Press,1964).

Emerson, Everett (ed.), *Letters from New England: The Massachusetts Bay Colony, 1629–1638* (Amherst, Mass.: University of Massachusetts Press, 1974).

Faler, Paul G., "Cultural Aspects of the Industrial Revolution: Lynn, Massachusetts Shoemakers and Industrial Morality, 1826–1860," *Labor History*, Vol. 15 (1974), 367–394.

Faler, Paul G., *Mechanics and Manufacturers in the Early Industrial Revolution. Lynn, Massachusetts, 1780–1860* (Albany: State University of New York Press, 1981).

Farnie, D. A., "The Commercial Empire of the Atlantic, 1607–1783," *Economic History Review*, 2nd series, Vol. 15, no. 2 (1962) 205–218.

Fayol, Henri, *General and Industrial Management*, trans. by Constance Storrs (London: Pitman, 1949).

Fine, Sidney, *Laissez Faire and the General–Welfare State. A Study of Conflict in American Thought 1865–1901* (Ann Arbor: University of Michigan Press, 1956).

Fleming, Thomas (ed.), *Benjamin Franklin. A Biography in His Own Words* (New York: Harper and Row, 1972).

Fletcher, Stevenson W., *Pennsylvania Agriculture and Country Life* (Harrisburg, Pa.: Pennsylvania Historical and Museum Commission, 1950).

Foner, Philip S. (ed.), *The Factory Girls* (Urbana: University of Illinois Press, 1977).

Forbes, B. C., *Keys to Success: Personal Efficiency* (New York: B. C. Forbes Publishing Co., 1926).

Ford, Henry, "Mass Production," *Enclyclopaedia Britannica*, 14th ed., Vol. 15, 38–41.

Ford, Henry, *My Life and Work* (Garden City, N.Y.: Doubleday, 1923).

Ford, Henry and Crowther, S., "Unemployment or Leisure," *Saturday Evening Post*, Vol. 203 (August, 1930), 19.

Foster, Stephen, *Their Solitary Way. The Puritan Social Ethic in the First Century of Settlement in New England* (New Haven: Yale University Press, 1971).

Franklin, Benjamin, *Autobiography of Benjamin Franklin* (New York: Heritage Press, 1951).

Franklin, John Hope, *From Slavery to Freedom. A History of Negro Americans.* 5th ed. (New York: Knopf, 1980).

Frazier, E. Franklin, *The Negro in the United States.* Rev. ed. (New York: Macmillan, 1957).

Frisch, Michael H. and Walkowitz, Daniel (eds.), *Working-Class America. Essays on Labor, Community, and American Society* (Urbana: University of Illinois Press, 1983).

Furnas, J. C., *The Americans: A Social History of the United States 1587–1914* (New York: Putnam, 1969).

Galambos, Louis, and Pratt, Joseph, *The Rise of the Corporate Commonwealth. United States Business and Public Policy in the 20th Century* (New York: Basic Books, 1988).

Galbraith, John K., *The Affluent Society* (Boston: Houghton Mifflin, 1958).

Galenson, Walter,"The Historical Role of American Trade Unionism," in *Unions in Transition. Entering the Second Century*, ed. by Seymour M. Lipset (San Francisco: ICS Press, 1986), 39–73.

Garfield, James A., *Elements of Success* (Washington: Gibson, 1869).

Garraty, John A., *Unemployment in History. Economic Thought and Public Policy* (New York: Harper and Row, 1978).

Genovese, Eugene, *Roll, Jordan, Roll. The World the Slaves Made* (New York: Vintage Books, 1976).

Gipson, Lawrence H., *The Coming of the Revolution, 1763–1775* (New York: Harper and Row, 1954).

Gordon, David, Edwards, Richard, and Reich, Michael, *Segmented Work, Divided Workers. The Historical Transformation of Labor in the United States* (Cambridge, Mass.: Harvard University Press, 1982).

Grattan, Thomas Colley, *Civilized America*. 2 Vols. (London: Bradbury and Evans, 1859).

Gray, Edward, "Some of the Essentials to Business Success," *Chatauquan*, Vol. 15 (1892), 302–304.

Green, James R., *The World of the Worker. Labor in Twentieth-Century America* (New York: Hill and Wang, 1980).

Greene, Jack P., *Colonies to Nation, 1763–1789* (New York: McGraw-Hill, 1967).

Greene, Jack P., *Pursuits of Happiness. The Social Development of Early Modern British Colonies and the Formation of American Culture* (Chapel Hill: University of North Carolina Press, 1988).

Greene, Jack P. (ed.), *Settlements to Society: 1584–1763* (New York: McGraw-Hill, 1966).

Greene, Jack P., *The American Colonies in the Eighteenth Century, 1689–1763* (New York: Appleton-Century-Crofts, 1969).

Gregory, Frances W. and Neu, Irene D., "The American Industrial Elite in the 1870s: Their Social Origins," in *Essays on the Historical Role of the Entrepreneur*, ed. by William Miller (Cambridge, Mass.: Harvard University Press, 1952), 193–211.

Grund, Francis J., *The Americans in Their Moral, Social, and Political Relations* (Boston: Marsh, Capen & Lyon, 1837).

Gutman, Herbert, *Power & Culture. Essays on the American Working Class*, ed. by Ira Berlin (New York: Pantheon, 1987).

Gutman, Herbert, *Work, Culture, and Society in Industrializing America. Essays in American Working-Class and Social History* (New York: Vintage Books, 1977).

Gutman, Herbert and Bell, Donald H. (eds.), *The New England Working Class and the New Labor History* (Urbana: University of Illinois Press, 1987).

Haber, Samuel, *Efficiency and Uplift. Scientific Management in the Progressive Era* (Chicago: University of Chicago Press, 1964).

Hacker, Louis M., *The Triumph of American Capitalism* (New York: Simon and Schuster, 1940).

Hall, Jacqueline, Leloudis, James, Korstad, Robert, Murphy, Mary, Jones, Lu Ann, and Daly, Christopher B., *Like a Family. The Making of a Southern Cotton Mill World* (New York: W. W. Norton, 1987).

Hammond, John, "Leah and Rachael; or The Two Fruitful Sisters, Virginia and Maryland," in *Narratives of Early Maryland, 1633–1684*, ed. by Clayton Colman Hall (New York: Barnes and Noble, 1967), 277–308.

Handlin, Oscar and Lilian, *A Restless People. Americans in Rebellion, 1770–1787* (Garden City, N.Y.: Anchor Press/Doubleday, 1982).

Hanson, John R., "The Economic Development of the Thirteen Continental Colonies, 1720 to 1775: A Critique," *William and Mary Quarterly*, Vol. 37 (1980), 165–172.

Hart, Hornell, *Autoconditioning. The New Way to a Successful Life* (Englewood Cliffs, N.J.: Prentice-Hall, 1956).

Hawke, David F., *Everyday Life in Early America* (New York: Harper and Row, 1988).

Hawke, David F., *The Colonial Experience* (Indianapolis: Bobbs-Merrill, 1966).

Hawley, Ellis W., "Herbert Hoover, the Commerce Secretariat, and the Vision of an 'Associative State,' 1921–1928," *Journal of American History*, Vol. 61 (June, 1974), 116–140.

Henderson, C. R., "Business Men and Social Theorists," *American Journal of Sociology*, Vol. 1 (1896), 385–397.

Henretta, James A., "Economic Development and the Social Structure of Colonial Boston," *William and Mary Quarterly*, 3rd Series, Vol. 22, no. 1 (January, 1965), 75–92.

Henretta, James A., "Families and Farms: Mentalité in Pre-Industrial America," *William and Mary Quarterly*, 3rd Series, Vol. 35, no. 1 (January, 1978), 3–32.

Henretta, James A., *The Evolution of American Society, 1700–1815: An Interdisciplinary Analysis* (Lexington, Mass.: D.C. Heath, 1973).

Henretta, James A., "The Study of Social Mobility: Ideological Assumptions and Conceptual Bias," *Labor History*, Vol. 18, no. 2 (1977), 166–178.

Henretta, James A., "Wealth and Social Structure," in *Colonial British America. Essays in the New History of the Early Modern Era*, ed. by Jack P. Greene and J. R. Pole (Baltimore: Johns Hopkins University Press, 1984), 262–289.

Henretta, James A. and Nobles, Gregory N., *Evolution and Revolution: American Society, 1600–1820* (Lexington, Mass.: D.C. Heath, 1987).

Hershberg, Theodore, "Free Blacks in Antebellum Philadelphia: A Study of Ex-Slaves, Freeborn, and Socioeconomic Decline," in *Philadelphia. Work, Space, Family, and Group Experience in the 19th Century: Essays Toward an Interdisciplinary History of the City*, ed. by Theodore Hershberg (New York: Oxford University Press, 1981), 368–391.

Hershberg, Theodore (ed.), *Philadelphia. Work, Space, Family, and Group Experience in the 19th Century: Essays Toward an Interdisciplinary History of the City* (New York: Oxford University Press, 1981).

Hershberg, Theodore, Burstein, Alan, Eriksen, Eugene, Greenberg, Stephanie, and Yancey, William, "A Tale of Three Cities: Blacks, Immigrants, and Opportunity in Philadelphia, 1850–1880, 1930, 1970," in *Philadelphia. Work, Space, Family, and Group Experience in the 19th Century: Essays Toward an Interdisciplinary History of the City* (New York: Oxford University Press, 1981, 461–491.

Heyrman, Christine, L., *Commerce and Culture. The Maritime Communities of Colonial Massachusetts, 1690–1750* (New York: W. W. Norton, 1984).

Heyward, Duncan Clinch, *Seed from Madagascar* (Chapel Hill: University of North Carolina Press, 1937).

Hill, Christopher, *Change and Continuity in Seventeenth-Century England* (Cambridge, Mass.: Harvard University Press, 1975).

Hill, Christopher, *Society and Puritanism in Pre-Revolutionary England* (New York: Schocken Books, 1967).

Hill, Napoleon, *Think and Grow Rich* (New York: Crest Books, 1963).

Hirsch, Susan E., *Roots of the American Working Class. The Industrialization of Crafts in Newark, 1800–1860* (Philadelphia: University of Pennsylvania Press, 1978).

Hofstadter, Richard, *Anti-Intellectualism in American Life* (New York: Vintage Books, 1963).

Hofstadter, Richard, *Social Darwinism in American Thought*. Rev. ed. (Boston: Beacon Press, 1955).

Holifield, E. Brooks, *Era of Persuasion; American Thought and Culture, 1521–1680* (Boston: Twayne Publishers, 1989).

Hoover, Herbert, *American Individualism* (New York: Garland, 1979).

Horn, James, "Servant Emigration to the Chesapeake in the Seventeenth Century," in *The Chesapeake in the Seventeenth Century: Essays on Anglo-American Society* (Chapel Hill: University of North Carolina Press, 1979), 51–95.

Hubbard, Elbert, *A Message to Garcia and Thirteen Other Things* (East Aurora, N.Y.: Roycrofters, 1901).

Huber, Richard M., *The American Idea of Success* (New York: McGraw-Hill, 1971).

Hunt, Freeman, *Worth and Wealth* (New York: Stringer and Townsend, 1856).

Innes, Stephen, *Labor in a New Land: Economy and Society in Seventeenth-Century Springfield* (Princeton: Princeton University Press, 1983).

Innes, Stephen (ed.), *Work and Labor in Early America* (Chapel Hill: University of North Carolina Press, 1988).

Isaac, Rhys, "Order and Growth, Authority and Meaning in Colonial New England," *American Historical Review*, Vol. 76 (1971), 728–737.

Isaac, Rhys, *The Transformation of Virginia, 1740–1790* (New York: W. W. Norton, 1982).

James, Bartlett B. and Jameson, J. Franklin (eds.), *Journal of Jasper Danckerts, 1679–1680* (New York: Charles Scribner's Sons, 1913).

James, Sydney V., *A People Among Peoples. Quaker Benevolence in Eighteenth Century America* (Cambridge, Mass.: Harvard University Press, 1963).

Jardim, Anne, *The First Henry Ford: a Study in Personality and Business Leadership* (Cambridge, Mass.: MIT Press, 1970).

Jedrey, Christopher M., *The World of John Cleaveland: Family and Community in Eighteenth-Century New England* (New York: W. W. Norton, 1979).

Jefferson, Thomas, *Notes on the State of Virginia*, ed. by Thomas P. Abernathy (New York: Harper, 1964).

Jefferson, Thomas, *The Papers of Thomas Jefferson*, ed. by Julian Boyd *et al*. 19 Vols. (Princeton: Princeton University Press, 1950–).

Jensen, Merrill, *The New Nation. A History of the United States During the Confederation, 1781–1789* (New York: Vintage,1965).

Jernegan, Marcus W., *The American Colonies 1492–1750. A Study of Their Political, Economic and Social Development* (New York: Frederick Ungar, 1965).

Johnson, Edward, *Johnson's Wonder-Working Providence, 1628–1651*, ed. by J. Franklin Jameson (New York: Barnes and Noble, 1967).

Johnson, James Weldon, *Along This Way. The Autobiography of James Weldon Johnson* (New York: Viking Press, 1933).

Johnston, Eric, *America Unlimited* (Garden City, N.Y.: Doubleday, Doran, 1944).

Jones, Alice Hanson, *Wealth of a Nation to Be: The American Colonies on the Eve of Revolution* (New York: Columbia University Press, 1980).

Jones, Whitney R.D., *The Tudor Commonwealth 1529–1559* (London: Athlone, 1970).

Josephson, Hannah, *The Golden Threads: New England's Mill Girls and Magnates* (New York: Duell, Sloan, and Pearce, 1949).

Kammen, Michael G., *Colonial New York. A History* (New York: Charles Scribner's Sons, 1975).

Kanter, Rosabeth Moss, "Work in a New America," *Daedalus*, Vol. 107 (Winter, 1978), 47–77.

Katz, Sidney N., (ed.), *Colonial America. Essays in Politics and Social Development* (Boston: Little, Brown, 1971).

Katzman, David M., *Before the Ghetto. Black Detroit in the Nineteenth Century* (Urbana: University of Illinois Press,1973).

Keller, Albert G. and Davie, Maurice R. (eds.), *Essays of William Graham Sumner*. 2 Vols. (New Haven: Yale University Press, 1934).

Kern, Stephen, *The Culture of Time and Space 1880–1918* (Cambridge, Mass.: Cambridge University Press, 1983).

Kerr, Clark, Dunlop, John T., Harbison, Frederick H., and Myers, Charles A., *Industrialism and Industrial Man* (Harmondsworth, Middlesex: Penguin, 1962).

Kerridge, Eric, *The Agricultural Revolution* (London: Allen and Unwin, 1967).

Kiefer, Sister Monica, "Early American Childhood in the Middle Atlantic Area," *Pennsylvania Magazine of History and Biography*, Vol. 68 (January, 1944), 3–37.

Kiser, Clyde, V., *Sea Island to City. A Study of St. Helena Islanders in Harlem and Other Urban Centers* (New York: Atheneum, 1969).

Kuhns, Oscar, *The German and Swiss Settlements of Colonial Pennsylvania: A Study of the So-Called Pennsylvania Dutch* (New York: Henry Holt, 1901).

Kulikoff, Allan, *Tobacco and Slaves. The Development of Southern Cultures in the Chesapeake, 1680–1800* (Chapel Hill: University of North Carolina Press, 1986).

Kusmer, Kenneth, *A Ghetto Takes Shape: Black Cleveland,1870–1930* (Urbana: University of Illinois Press, 1976).

Labaree, Benjamin W., *Colonial Massachusetts. A History* (Millwood, New York: KTO Press, 1979).

Labaree, Benjamin W., *Patriots and Partisans: The Merchants of Newburyport 1764–1815* (Cambridge, Mass.: Harvard University Press, 1962).

Labaree, Leonard W. and Bell, Whitfield, J. Jr. (eds.), *The Papers of Benjamin Franklin* (New Haven: Yale University Press, 1959–   ).

Laird, John, *Hume's Philosophy of Human Nature* (London: Methuen, 1932).

Lane, Roger, *William Dorsey's Philadelphia and Ours. On the Past and Future of the Black City in America* (New York: Oxford University Press, 1991).

Larcom, Lucy, *A New England Girlhood* (New York: Corinth, 1961).

Larcom, Lucy, *The Poetical Works of Lucy Larcom* (Boston: Houghton Mifflin, 1885).

Lasch, Christopher, *The Culture of Narcissism* (New York: Warner, 1979).

Lasch, Christopher, *The Revolt of the Elites and the Betrayal of Democracy* (New York: W. W. Norton, 1995).

Laurie, Bruce, "'Nothing on Compulsion': Life Styles of Philadelphia Artisans, 1820–1850," *Labor History*, Vol. 15 (1974), 337–366.

Laurie, Bruce, Hershberg, Theodore and Alter, George, "Immigrants and Industry: The Philadelphia Experience, 1850–1880," in *Philadelphia. Work, Space, Family, and Group Experience in the 19th Century*, ed. by Theodore Hershberg (New York: Oxford University Press, 1981), 93–119.

Laurie, Bruce and Schmitz, Mark, "Manufacture and Productivity: The Making of an Industrial Base, Philadelphia, 1850–1880," in *Philadelphia. Work, Space,*

Family, and Group Experience in the 19th Century, ed. by Theodore Hershberg (New York: Oxford University Press, 1981), 43–92.

Lawrence, William, "The Relation of Wealth to Morals," *World's Work*, Vol. 1 (January, 1901), 286–292.

Lazarus, Arnold A. and Fay, Allen, *I Can If I Want To* (New York: William Morrow, 1975).

Lemon, James T., "Spatial Order: Households in Local Communities and Regions," in *Colonial British America. Essays in the New History of the Early Modern Era*, ed. by Jack P. Greene and J. R. Pole (Baltimore: Johns Hopkins University Press, 1984), 86–122.

Lemon, James T., *The Best Poor Man's Country: A Geographical Study of Southeastern Pennsylvania* (Baltimore: Johns Hopkins University Press, 1972).

Lester, Richard A., *As Unions Mature. An Analysis of the Evolution American Unionism* (Princeton: Princeton University Press, 1958).

Licht, Walter, *Working for the Railroad* (Princeton: Princeton University Press, 1983).

Lindberg, Stanley W. (ed.), *The Annotated McGuffey. Selections from the McGuffey Eclectic Readers, 1836–1920* (New York: Van Nostrand Reinhold, 1976).

Lipset, Seymour M., and Bendix, Reinhard, *Social Mobility in an Industrial Society* (Berkeley: University of California Press, 1967).

Littlefield, Daniel C., "Charleston and Internal Slave Redistribution," *South Carolina Historical Magazine*, Vol. 87 (1986), 93–105.

Litwack, Leon F., *North of Slavery; the Negro in the Free States, 1790–1860* (Chicago: University of Chicago Press, 1961).

Locke, John, *Of Civil Government: Two Treatises* (London: J. M. Dent, 1924).

Longfellow, Henry Wadsworth, *The Complete Poetical Works of Henry Wadsworth Longfellow* (Boston: Houghton Mifflin, 1903).

Lundén, Rolf, *Business and Religion in the American 1920s* (Westport, Conn.: Greenwood Press, 1988).

Lynd, Robert and Helen, *Middletown. A Study in Contemporary American Culture* (New York: Harcourt, Brace,and World, 1959).

Main, Gloria L., *Tobacco Colony: Life in Early Maryland 1650–1720* (Princeton: Princeton University Press, 1982).

Main, Jackson Turner, *Society and Economy in Colonial Connecticut* (Princeton: Princeton University Press, 1985).

Main, Jackson Turner, *The Social Structure of Revolutionary America* (Princeton: Princeton University Press, 1965).

Malcolmson, Robert W., *Life and Labour in England, 1700–1780* (New York: St. Martin's Press, 1981).

Mallory, Daniel (ed.), *The Life and Speeches of Hon. Henry Clay* 2 Vols. (New York: R. P. Bixby and Co., 1844).

Marambaud, Pierre, *William Byrd of Westover 1674–1744* (Charlottesville: University of Virginia Press, 1971).

Marden, Orison S., *The Young Man Entering Business* (New York: T. Y. Crowell, 1903).

Marquis, Samuel S., *Henry Ford, an Interpretation* (Boston: Little, Brown, 1923).

Marryat, Frederick, *Diary in America*, ed. by Jules Zenger (Bloomington, Indiana: University of Indiana Press, 1960).

Martin, John F., *Profits in the Wilderness. Entrepreneurship and the Founding of New England Towns in the Seventeenth Century* (Chapel Hill: University of North Carolina Press, 1991).

Marx, Leo, *The Machine in the Garden. Technology and the Pastoral Ideal in America* (New York: Oxford University Press, 1964).

Massie, James W., *America: The Origin of Her Present Conflict; Her Prospect for the Slave, and Her Claim for Anti-Slavery Sympathy* (London: J. Snow, 1864).

Mather, Cotton, *Bonifacius. An Essay Upon the Good*, ed. by David Levin (Cambridge, Mass.: Harvard University Press, 1966).

Mather, Cotton, *Two Brief Discourses, One Directing a Christian in His General Calling; Another Directing Him in His Personal Calling* (Boston: B. Green and J. Allen, 1701).

Mayo, Lawrence, *John Wentworth, Governor of New Hampshire, 1767–1775* (Cambridge, Mass.: Harvard University Press, 1975).

McCusker, John J. and Menard, Russell R., *The Economy of British North America, 1607–1789* (Chapel Hill: University of North Carolina Press, 1985).

McKain, Robert J., *How to Get to the Top . . . and Stay There* (New York: AMACOM, 1981).

Meier, August and Rudwick, Elliott, *Black Detroit and the Rise of the UAW* (New York: Oxford University Press, 1979).

Meserole, H. T. and Sutton, W. (eds.), *American Literature. Tradition and Innovation* (Lexington, Mass.: D. C. Heath, 1969).

Michaelsen, Robert S., "Changes in the Puritan Concept of the Calling and Vocation," *New England Quarterly*, Vol. 26 (September, 1953), 315–336.

Miller, Perry, *Errand into the Wilderness* (Cambridge: Harvard University Press, 1956).

Miller, Perry (ed.), *The American Puritans. Their Prose and Poetry* (Garden City, N.Y.: Doubleday, 1951).

Miller, Perry, "The Declension of a Bible Commonwealth," *Proceedings of the American Antiquarian Society*, Vol. 51 (1942), 37–94.

Miller, Perry and Johnson, Thomas H. (eds.), *The Puritans. A Sourcebook of Their Writings* (New York: Harper and Row, 1963).

Miller, William (ed.), *Essays on the Historical Role of the Entrepreneur* (Cambridge: Harvard University Press, 1952).

Mills, C. Wright, "The American Business Elite," *Journal of Economic History*, Supplement 5 (December, 1945), 20–44.

Mills, C. Wright, "The Contributions of Sociology to Studies of Industrial Relations," in *Proceedings of the First Annual Meeting of the Industrial Relations Research Association*, December 28–30, 1948, ed. by Milton Derber (Madison, Wisconsin: IRRA, 1948), 199–222.

Minnich, Harvey C. (ed.), *Old Favorites from the McGuffey Readers* (New York: American Book Co., 1936).

Mittleberger, Gottlieb, *Journey to Pennsylvania*, ed. by Oscar Handlin and John Clive (Cambridge, Mass.: Harvard University Press, 1960).

Mohl, R. A., *Poverty in New York: 1783–1825* (New York: Oxford University Press, 1971).

Montgomery, David, *The Fall of the House of Labor. The Workplace, the State, and American Labor Activism, 1865–1925* (New York: Cambridge University Press, 1989).

Montgomery, David, "Workers' Control of Machine Production in the Nineteenth Century," *Labor History*, Vol. 17 (Fall, 1976), 485–509.

Montgomery, David, "The Working Classes of the Pre-Industrial American City, 1780–1830," *Labor History*, Vol. 9 (Winter, 1968), 3–22.

Morgan, Edmund, *American Slavery American Freedom. The Ordeal of Colonial Virginia* (New York: W. W. Norton, 1975).

Morgan, Edmund, "The Labor Problem at Jamestown, 1607–1618," *American Historical Review*, Vol. 76, no.3 (June, 1971), 595–611.

Morgan, Edmund, "The Puritan Ethic and the American Revolution," *William and Mary Quarterly*, 3rd Series, Vol. 24, no. 1 (January, 1967), 3–43.

Morgan, Edmund, *The Puritan Family. Religion and Domestic Relations in Seventeenth-Century New England*. New ed. (New York: Harper and Row, 1966).

Morison, Samuel E., *The Story of the "Old Colony" of New Plymouth, 1620–1692* (New York: Knopf, 1956).

Morison, Samuel E., *The Winthrop Papers 1498–1649*. 5 Vols. (Boston: Massachusetts Historical Society, 1929–1947).

Morris, Richard B., *Government and Labor in Early America* (New York: Columbia University Press, 1946).

Morris, Richard B., *Studies in the History of American Law: With Special Reference to the Seventeenth and Eighteenth Centuries*. 2nd ed. (New York: Octagon Books, 1964).

Morris, Richard B. (ed.), *The American Worker* (Washington, D.C.: Government Printing Office, 1976).

Mowry, George E., *The Urban Nation, 1920–1960* (New York: Hill and Wang, 1965).

Mumford, Lewis, *Technics and Civilization* (New York: Harcourt, Brace, 1934).

Myrdal, Gunnar, *An American Dilemma. The Negro Problem and Modern Democracy* (New York: Harper, 1944).

Namier, Louis B., *England in the Age of the American Revolution* 2nd ed. (New York: St. Martin's Press, 1966).

Nash, Gary, "Poverty and Poor Relief in Pre–Revolutionary Philadelphia," *William and Mary Quarterly*, 3rd series, Vol. 33, (January, 1976), 3–30.

Nash, Gary, "Social Development," in *Colonial British America. Essays in the New History of the Early Modern Era*, ed. by Jack P. Greene and J. R. Pole (Baltimore: Johns Hopkins University Press, 1984), 233–261.

Nash, Gary, *The Urban Crucible. Social Change, Political Consciousness and the Origins of the American Revolution* (Cambridge, Mass.: Harvard University Press, 1979).

Nash, Gary, "Up from the Bottom in Franklin's Philadelphia," in *The Private Side of American History. Readings in Everday Life*, ed. by Gary Nash (San Diego: Harcourt Brace Jovanovich, 1983), 163–200.

Nelson, Daniel, *Frederick W. Taylor and the Rise of Scientific Management* (Madison: University of Wisconsin Press, 1980).

Nelson, Daniel, *Managers and Workers. Origins of the New Factory System in the United States 1880–1920* (Madison: University of Wisconsin Press, 1975).

Nevans, Ronald, "Wall Street's Top Brokers," *Financial World*, August 1, 1980, 44.

Nevins, Allan (ed.), *America Through British Eyes* (New York: Oxford University Press, 1948).

Notestein, Wallace, *The English People on the Eve of Colonization* (New York: Harper, 1954).

Nye, Russell B., *Society and Culture in America 1830–1860* (New York: Harper and Row, 1974).

Oberholzer, Emil, Jr., "The Church in New England Society," in *Seventeenth-Century America. Essays in Colonial History*, ed. by James M. Smith (Chapel Hill: University of North Carolina Press, 1959), 143–165.

Oblinger, Carl D., "Alms for Oblivion: The Making of a Black Underclass in Southeastern Pennsylvania, 1780–1860," in *The Ethnic Experience in Pennsylvania*, ed. by John E. Bodnar (Lewisburg, Pa.: Bucknell University Press, 1973), 94–119.

O'Connor, Harvey, *Mellon's Millions, the Biography of a Fortune. The Life and Times of Andrew D. Mellon* (New York: John Day, 1933).

Owen, William Dale, *Success in Life* (Chicago: Howe Watts, 1878).

Packard, Vance, *The Status Seekers* (New York: Pocket Books,1971).

Parets, Robyn T., "Motivator Brian Tracy," *Investor's Business Daily*, January 20, 1995, A1–A2.

Parker, Robert H., *Management Accounting; an Historical Perspective* (New York: Augustus M. Kelley, 1969).

Peale, Norman Vincent, *A Guide to Confident Living* (New York: Prentice-Hall, 1948).

Peale, Norman Vincent, *The Power of Positive Thinking* (New York: Fawcett Crest, 1963).

Perkins, Edwin J., *The Economy of Colonial America*. 2nd ed. (New York: Columbia University Press, 1988).

Perlman, Selig, *A Theory of the Labor Movement* (New York:Macmillan, 1928).

Perry, Ralph Barton, *Puritanism and Democracy* (New York: Harper and Row, 1944).

Pessen, Edward, "Builders of the Young Republic," in *The American Worker*, ed. by Richard B. Morris (Washington, D.C.: U.S. Government Printing Office, 1976), 56–103.

Pessen, Edward (ed.), *Three Centuries of Social Mobility in America* (Lexington, Mass.: D. C. Heath, 1974).

Pierce, A. D., *Iron in the Pines* (New Brunswick, N.J.: Rutgers University Press, 1957).

Piersen, William D., *Black Legacy. America's Hidden Heritage* (Amherst: University of Massachusetts Press, 1993).

Piven, Frances F. and Cloward, Richard A., *Regulating the Poor. The Functions of Public Welfare* (New York: Pantheon, 1971).

Poe, Edgar Allen, *Complete Tales and Poems of Edgar Allen Poe* (New York: Modern Library, 1938).

Polanyi, Karl, *The Great Transformation. The Political and Economic Origins of Our Time* (Boston: Beacon Press, 1957).

Pomfret, John E., *Colonial New Jersey. A History* (New York: Charles Scribner's Sons, 1973).

Porter, Roy, *English Society in the Eighteenth Century* (Hammondsworth, Middlesex: Penguin, 1982).

Prothero, Iorweth J., *Artisans and Politics in Early Nineteenth-Century London: John Gast and His Times* (Hamden, Conn.: Dawson Publishing, 1978).

314 BIBLIOGRAPHY

Prothro, James, *Dollar Decade: Business Ideas in the 1920s* (Baton Rouge: Louisiana State University Press, 1954).

Prude, Jonathan, *The Coming of Industrial Order. Town and Factory Life in Rural Massachusetts 1810–1860* (Cambridge: Cambridge University Press, 1985).

Rezneck, Samuel, "Depression and American Opinion, 1857–1859," *The Journal of Economic History*, Vol. 2, no. 1 (1942), 1–23.

Rich, E. E., "The Population of Elizabethan England," *Economic History Review*, 2nd series, Vol. 2 (1950), 247–265.

Riesman, David with Glazer, Nathan and Denney, Reuel, *The Lonely Crowd. A Study of the Changing American Character* (Garden City, N.Y.: Doubleday, 1953).

Rischin, Moses (ed.), *The American Gospel of Success* (Chicago: Quadrangle Books, 1965).

Rock, Howard B., *Artisans of the New Republic. The Tradesmen of New York City in the Age of Jefferson* (New York: New York University Press, 1984).

Rockefeller, John D., "John D. Rockefeller on Opportunity in America," *Cosmopolitan*, Vol. 42 (August, 1907), 368–372.

Rodgers, Daniel T., "No's to the Grindstone," *New York Times*, April 16, 1980, A27.

Rodgers, Daniel T., *The Work Ethic in Industrial America 1850–1920* (Chicago: (University of Chicago Press, 1978).

Roediger, David R., *The Wages of Whiteness. Race and the Making of the American Working Class* (London: Verso, 1991).

Rogin, Michael P., *Fathers and Children: Andrew Jackson and the Subjection of the American Indian* (New York: Knopf, 1975).

Rorabaugh, W. J., *The Alcohol Republic. An American Tradition* (New York: Oxford University Press, 1979).

Rorabaugh, W. J., *The Craft Apprentice from Franklin to the Machine Age in America* (New York: Oxford University Press, 1986).

Rosenberg, Nathan, *The American System of Manufactures* (Edinburgh: Edinburgh University Press, 1969).

Rosenzweig, Roy, *Eight Hours for What We Will: Workers and Leisure in an Industrial City, 1870–1920* (New York: Cambridge University Press, 1983).

Ross, Steven J., *Workers on the Edge. Work, Leisure, and Politics in Industrializing Cincinnati 1788–1890* (New York: Columbia Univesity Press, 1985).

Rossiter, Clinton, *Conservatism in America. The Thankless Persuasion*. 2nd ed. (New York: Vintage Books, 1962).

Ruitenbeek, Henrik M., *The Individual and the Crowd. A Study of Identity in America* (New York: New American Library, 1964).

Ruoff, Henry W. (ed.), *Leaders of Men or Types and Principles of Success* (Springfield, Mass.: King-Richardson, 1903).

Sabel, Charles F., *Work and Politics. The Division of Labor in Industry* (Cambridge: Cambridge University Press, 1982).

Sachs, William S. and Hoogenboom, Ari, *The Enterprising Colonials. Society on the Eve of the Revolution* (Chicago: Argonaut,1965).

Salpukas, Agis, "Workers Increasingly Rebel Against Boredom on the Assembly Line," *New York Times*, April 2, 1972, N34.

Sawyer, John E., "The Entrepreneur and the Social Order: France and the United States," in *Men in Business: Essays in the History of Entrepreneurship*, ed. by William Miller (Cambridge, Mass.: Harvard University Press, 1952), 7–22.

Sawyer, John E., "The Social Basis of the American System of Manufacturing," *Journal of Economic History*, Vol. 14 (December, 1954), 361–379.

Schlesinger, Arthur M., Jr., *The Coming of the New Deal* (Boston: Houghton Mifflin, 1959).

Schlesinger, Arthur M., Jr., *The Crisis of the Old Order, 1919–1933* (Boston: Houghton Mifflin, 1957).

Schnapper, M. B., *American Labor* (Washington, D.C.: Public Affairs Press, 1972).

Scott, Emmett J., *Negro Migration During the War* (New York: Oxford University Press, 1920).

Schumacher, E. F., "Good Work," in *Relating Work and Education*, ed. by D. W. Vermilye (San Francisco: Jossey-Bass, 1977), 55–64.

Schumpeter, Joseph A., *Capitalism, Socialism and Democracy*. 6th ed. (London: Unwin, 1987).

Schumpeter, Joseph A., "The Creative Response in Economic History," *Journal of Economic History*, Vol. 7 (1947), 149–159.

Schwind, Arlene P., "The Glassmakers of Early America," in *The Craftsman in Early America*, ed. by Ian M. G. Quimby (New York: W. W. Norton, 1984), 158–189.

Sellers, Charles, *The Market Revolution. Jacksonian America 1815–1846* (New York: Oxford University Press, 1991).

Serwer, Andrew E., "Lessons from America's Fastest Growing Companies," *Fortune*, August 2, 1994, 42–59.

Shalhope, Robert E., *The Roots of Democracy; American Thought and Culture, 1760–1800* (Boston: Twayne, 1990).

Shaw, Albert, "Roger Babson Reflects," *Review of Reviews*, Vol. 85 (May, 1932), 25.

Sheehy, Gail, "Introducing the Postponing Generation. The Truth About Today's Young Man," *Esquire* (October, 1979), 25–33.

Shellenbarger, Sue, "Work-Force Study Finds Loyalty is Weak, Divisions of Race and Gender are Deep," *Wall Street Journal*, September 3, 1993, B1.

Shelton, Cynthia J., *The Mills of Manayunk. Industrialization and Social Conflict in the Philadelphia Region, 1787–1837* (Baltimore: Johns Hopkins University Press, 1986).

Sheridan, Richard B., "The Domestic Economy," in *Colonial British America. Essays in the New History of the Early Modern Era* (Baltimore: Johns Hopkins University Press, 1986), 43–85.

Silone, Ignazio, *Bread and Wine* (New York: Harper, 1937).

Simmons, R. C., *The American Colonies. From Settlement to Independence* (New York: W. W. Norton, 1976).

Siragusa, Carl, *A Mechanical People: Perceptions of the Industrial Order in Massachusetts* (Middleton, Conn.: Wesleyan University Press, 1979).

Slack, Paul A., "Vagrants and Vagrancy in England, 1598–1604," *Economic History Review*, 2nd series, Vol. 27 (1974), 360–379.

Slichter, Sumner H., "The Scope and Nature of the Labor Turnover Problem," *Quarterly Journal of Economics*, Vol. 33 (February, 1920), 329–345.

Slichter, Sumner H., *Union Policies and Industrial Management* (Washington, D.C.: Brookings Institution, 1941).

Smith, Abbott, E., *Colonists in Bondage: White Servitude and Convict Labor in America, 1607–1776* (Chapel Hill: University of North Carolina Press, 1947).

Smith, Adam, *The Wealth of Nations*, ed. by Andrew Skinner (Harmondsworth, Middlesex: Penguin, 1977).

Smith, Billy G., "Death and Life in a Colonial Immigrant City: A Demographic Analysis of Philadelphia," *Journal of Economic History*, Vol. 37 (December, 1977), 863–899.

Smith, Billy G., "The Material Lives of Labouring Philadelphians, 1750–1800," *William and Mary Quarterly*, 3rd series, Vol. 38 (April, 1981), 163–202.

Smith, Matthew Hale, *Twenty Years Among the Bulls and Bears of New York* (Hartford: J. B. Burr, 1875).

Smith, Russell and Zeitz, Dorothy, *American Social Welfare Institutions* (New York: John Wiley, 1970).

Smyth, Albert H. (ed.), *The Writings of Benjamin Franklin*. 10 Vols. (New York: Macmillan, 1907).

Speigel, Mara, *World of Work Report*, 3:no. 9 (September, 1978), 76.

Steffen, Charles G., *The Mechanics of Baltimore. Workers and Politics in the Age of Revolution, 1763–1812* (Urbana: University of Illinois Press, 1984).

Stevenson, Frank H., *The Gospel of Work* (Cincinnati, no publisher noted, 1921).

Stilgoe, John R., *Common Landscape of America 1580 to 1845* (New Haven: Yale University Press, 1982).

Sumner, William Graham, *What Social Classes Owe Each Other* (New York: Harper, 1883).

Taussig, Frank W. and Joslyn, C. S., *American Business Leaders* (New York: Macmillan, 1932).

Taylor, Frederick W., *Shop Management* (New York: Harper, 1912).

Taylor, Frederick W., *The Principles of Scientific Management* (New York: W. W. Norton, 1967).

Taylor, William R., *Cavalier and Yankee. The Old South and American National Character* (New York: George Braziller, 1961).

Terkel, Studs, *Hard Times, an Oral History of the Great Depression* (New York: Pantheon, 1970).

Thayer, William M., *Ethics of Success. A Reader for the Higher Grades of Schools* (Boston: A. M. Thayer, 1893).

Thayer, William M., *The Printer Boy, or, How Ben Franklin Made His Mark: An Example for Youth* (Boston: J. E. Tilton, 1863).

Thernstrom, Stephen, *Poverty and Progress: Social Mobility in a Nineteenth Century City* (Cambridge, Mass.: Harvard University Press, 1964).

Thomas, Keith, "Work and Leisure in Pre-Industrial Society," *Past and Present*, Vol. 29 (December, 1964), 50–66.

Thompson, E. P., "Time, Work-Discipline and Industrial Capitalism," *Past and Present*, Vol. 38 (1967), 56–97.

Trachtenberg, Alan, *The Incorporation of America. Culture & Society in the Gilded Age* (New York: Hill and Wang, 1982).

Trollope, Frances M., *The Domestic Manners of Americans*. Smalley edition (New York: Knopf, 1949).

Tucker, Barbara M., *Samuel Slater and the Origins of the American Textile Industry 1790–1860* (Ithaca: Cornell University Press, 1984).

Turner, Frederick Jackson, *The Frontier in American History* (New York: Holt, Rinehart and Winston, 1962).

Uchitelle, Louis, "The New Faces of U.S. Manufacturing," *New York Times*, July 3, 1994, 1F and 6F.

Van Dyke, Henry, *Essays in Application* (New York: Charles Scribner's Sons, 1905).

Vickers, Daniel, "Working the Fields in a Developing Economy: Essex County, Massachusetts, 1630–1675," in *Work and Labor in Early America*, ed. by Stephen Innes (Chapel Hill: University of North Carolina Press, 1988), 49–69.

Voss, Kim, *The Making of American Exceptionalism. The Knights of Labor and Class Formation in the Nineteenth Century* (Ithaca: Cornell University Press, 1993).

Walkowitz, Daniel J., "Statistics and the Writing of Working Class Culture: A Statistical Portrait of Iron Workers in Troy, New York, 1860–1880," *Labor History*, Vol. 15 (Summer, 1974), 416– 460.

Wallace, Anthony F. C., *Rockdale. The Growth of an American Village in the Early Industrial Revolution* (New York: Knopf, 1978).

Ward, John William, *Andrew Jackson: Symbol for an Age* (New York: Oxford University Press, 1955).

Ware, Caroline, *The Early New England Cotton Manufacture: A Study in Industrial Beginnings* (Boston: Houghton Mifflin, 1931).

Ware, Norman, *The Industrial Worker, 1840–1860. The Reaction of American Industrial Society to the Advance of the Industrial Revolution* (Chicago: Quadrangle Books, 1964).

Warner, Sam Bass, *The Private City: Philadelphia in Three Periods of Its Growth* (Philadelphia:University of Pennsylvania Press, 1968).

Washington, George, *The Writings of George Washington from the Original Manuscript Sources 1745–1799*, ed. by John C. Fitzpatrick. 39 Vols. (Washington, D.C.: U.S. Government Printing Office, 1931–1944).

Watkins, T. H., *The Great Depression. America in the 1930s* (Boston: Little, Brown, 1993).

Weber, Max, *The Protestant Ethic and the Spirit of Capitalism*, trans. by Talcott Parsons (New York: Charles Scribner's Sons, 1958).

Wells, David, *Recent Economic Changes* (New York: Appleton, 1895).

Wenger, J.C., *The Mennonite Church in America* (Scottsdale, Pa.: Herald Press, 1966).

Wertenbaker, Thomas J., *The Puritan Oligarchy. The Founding of American Civilization* (New York: Grosset and Dunlap, 1947).

Whitman, Walt, *Leaves of Grass* (New York: Aventine Press, 1931).

Whyte, William H., Jr., *The Organization Man* (New York: Simon and Schuster, 1956).

Wilbur, Ray L. and Hyde, Arthur M., *The Hoover Policies* (New York: Charles Scribner's Sons, 1937).

Wilentz, Sean, *Chants Democratic. New York City & the Rise of the American Working Class, 1788–1850* (New York: Oxford University Press, 1984).

Williams, Harry T. (ed.), *Hayes: Diary of a President, 1875–1881, Covering the Disputed Election, the End of Reconstruction, and the Beginning of Civil Service* (New York: D. McKay, 1964).

Williamson, Chilton, *American Suffrage: From Property to Democracy, 1760–1860* (Princeton: Princeton University Press, 1960).

Wilson, Woodrow, *The New Freedom* (New York: Doubleday,Page, 1913).

Wood, Benjamin, *The Successful Man of Business*. 2nd ed. (New York: Brentano, 1899).

Wright, Louis B., *The Atlantic Frontier: Colonial American Civilization, 1607–1763* (Ithaca: Cornell University Press,1947).

Wright, Louis B., *The Cultural Life of the American Colonies, 1607–1763* (New York: Harper, 1957).

Wright, Louis B., *The Dream of Prosperity in Colonial America* (New York: New York University Press, 1965).

Wright, Louis B. (ed.), *The Elizabethan's America. A Collection of Early Reports by Englishmen in the New World* (Cambridge: Harvard University Press, 1966).

Wright, Louis B. and Fowler, Elaine W., *Life in the New Nation, 1787–1860* (New York: Capricorn Books, 1974).

Wrigley, E. A. and Schofield, R. S., *The Population History of England, 1541–1871* (Cambridge: Harvard University Press,1981).

Wyllie, Irving G., *The Self Made Man in America. The Myth from Rags to Riches* (New Brunswick: Rutgers University Press, 1954).

Yang, Catherine, "The EEOC: Too Swamped to Shoot Straight," *Business Week*, May 1, 1995, 155.

Yankelovich, Daniel, *The New Morality. A Profile of American Youth in the 70s* (New York: McGraw–Hill, 1974).

Yankelovich, Daniel and Immerwahr, John, *Putting the Work Ethic to Work: A Public Agenda Report on Restoring America's Competitive Vitality* (New York: Public Agenda Foundation of New York,1983).

Yellowitz, Irwin, *Industrialization and the American Labor Movement 1850–1900* (Port Washington, N.Y.: Kennikat Press,1977).

Youings, Joyce, *Sixteenth-Century England* (London: Penguin, 1984).

Zahavi, Gerald, *Workers, Managers, and Welfare Capitalism. The Shoeworkers and Tanners of Endicott Johnson, 1890–1950* (Urbana: University of Illinois Press, 1988).

Ziff, Larzer, *Puritanism in America. New Culture in a New World* (New York: Viking Press, 1973).

Zimpel, Lloyd (ed.), *Man Against Work* (Grand Rapids, Mich.: William B. Eerdmans Publishing Co., 1974).

Zonderman, David A., *Aspirations and Anxieties. New England Workers & the Mechanized Factory System 1815–1850* (New York: Oxford University Press, 1992).

Zuboff, Shoshana, "The Work Ethic and Work Organization," in *The Work Ethic: A Critical Analysis*, ed. by Jack Barbash, Robert J. Lampman, Sar A. Levitan, and Gus Tyler (Madison, Wisconsin: IRRA, 1983).

Zuckerman, Michael, "The Fabrication of Identity," *William and Mary Quarterly*, Vol. 34, no. 2 (April, 1977), 183–214.

PART III: WORK AS SELF-FULFILLMENT

Adler, Paul S., "Time-and-Motion Regained," *Harvard Business Review*, Vol. 71 (January-February, 1993), 97–108.

Adler, Paul S. and Cole, Robert E., "Designed for Learning: A Tale of Two Auto Plants," *Sloan Management Review*, Vol. 34, no. 3 (Spring, 1993), 85–93.

Aitken, Hugh G.J., *Taylorism at Watertown Arsenal: Scientific Management in Action, 1908–1915* (Cambridge, Mass.: Harvard University Press, 1960).

Alford, L. P., *Cost and Production Handbook* (New York: Ronald, 1944).

"All Work and No Play," *Dollars and Sense* (January/February, 1992), 12–15.

Allen, Frank, "Bosses List Main Strengths, Flaws Determining Potential of Managers," *Wall Street Journal*, November 14, 1980, 33.

Althaus, Paul, *The Ethics of Martin Luther*, trans. by Robert C. Schultz (Philadelphia: Fortress Press, 1972).

"A Pioneering Pact Promises Jobs for Life," *Business Week*, December 31, 1984, 48–49.

Ashley, Maurice, *The People of England. A Short Social and Economic History* (Baton Rouge: Louisiana State University Press, 1982).

Bachman, Jerold G. and Johnston, Lloyd D., "The Freshmen, 1979," *Psychology Today*, Vol. 12 (September, 1979), 79–87.

Balderston, C. Canby, *Group Incentives. Some Variations in the Use of Group Bonus Gang Piece Work* (Philadelphia: University of Pennsylvania Press, 1930).

Barmash, Isadore, "The Quieter Style of the New Generation at Perdue Farms," *New York Times*, July 26, 1992, F7.

Barnard, Chester I., *Organization and Management. Selected Papers* (Cambridge, Mass.: Harvard University Press, 1956).

Barnard, Chester I., *The Functions of the Executive* (Cambridge, Mass.: Harvard University Press, 1938).

Barnet, Richard J., "The End of Jobs," *Harper's Magazine* (September, 1993), 47–51.

"Battleground Chicago," *Newsweek*, April 3, 1995, 26–33.

Bass, Bernard and Burger, Philip C., *Assessment of Managers. An International Comparison* (New York: Free Press, 1979).

Beaud, Michel, *A History of Capitalism 1500–1800*, trans. by Tom Dickman and Anny Lefebvre (New York: Monthly Review Press,1983).

Bell, Daniel, *The Cultural Contradictions of Capitalism* (New York: Basic Books, 1978).

Bellamy, Edward, *Looking Backward, 2000–1887* (New York: New American Library, 1960).

Bennett, Amanda, "More and More Women are Staying on the Job Later in Life Than Men," *Wall Street Journal*, September 1, 1994, B1–B2.

Berg, Ivar, "'They Won't Work': the End of the Protestant Ethic and All That," in *Work and the Quality of Life*, ed. by James O'Toole (Cambridge, Mass.: MIT Press, 1974), 27–39.

Berger, Bennett M., "The Sociology of Leisure: Some Suggestions," in *Work and Leisure*, ed. by Erwin O. Smigel (New Haven, Conn.: College and University Press, 1963), 21–40.

Berger, Brigitte, "People Work—the Youth Culture and the Labor Market," *The Public Interest*, Vol. 35 (Spring, 1974), 55–66.

Berkowitz, Edward, *America's Welfare State. From Roosevelt to Reagan* (Baltimore: Johns Hopkins University Press, 1991).

Berkowitz, Edward and McQuaid, Kim, *Creating the Welfare State. The Political Economy of Twentieth-Century Reform*. 2nd ed. (New York: Praeger, 1988).

Bernstein, Irving, *The Lean Years* (Boston: Houghton Mifflin, 1960).

Bernstein, Irving, *Time and Work*. Presidential Address of the Industrial Relations Research Association, Proceedings of the 29th Annual Winter Meeting, Atlantic City, N.J., 16–18 September 1976, ed. by J. L. Stern and B. Dennis (Madison: IRRA, 1977), 1–8.

Bernstein, Irving, *Turbulent Years. A History of the American Worker, 1933–1941* (Boston: Houghton Mifflin, 1941).

Bernstein, Paul, "The Learning Curve at Volvo," *The Columbia Journal of World Business*, Vol. 23, no.4 (Winter, 1988), 87–95.

Bezanson, Anne, *Four Years of Labor Mobility. A Study of Labor Turnover in a Group of Selected Plants in Philadelphia 1921–1924* (Philadelphia: Industrial Research Department, Wharton School of Finance and Commerce, University of Pennsylvania, 1925).

Bleakley, Fred R., "Critics Attack Welfare Proposals," *Wall Street Journal*, February 8, 1995, A2, A5.

Bluestone, Irving, "Creating a New World of Work," *International Labour Review*, Vol. 115, no. 1 (January, 1977), 1–10.

Bluestone, Irving, "Work Humanization in Practice: What Can Labor Do," in *A Matter of Dignity. Inquiries into the Humanization of Work*, ed. by W. J. Heisler and John W. Houck (Notre Dame, Indiana: University of Notre Dame Press, 1977), 165–178.

Blumberg, Paul, *Industrial Democracy. The Sociology of Participation* (New York: Schocken Books, 1973).

Bok, Derek, "Admitting Success," in *Racial Preferences and Racial Justice. The New Affirmative Action Controversy*, ed. by Russell Nieli (Washington, D.C.: Ethics and Public Policy Center, 1991), 409–414.

Bork, Robert H., "The Supreme Court and Civil Rights," in *Racial Preferences and Racial Justice. The New Affirmative Action Controversy*, ed. by Russell Nieli (Washington, D.C.: Ethics and Public Policy Center, 1991, 269–275.

Brandes, Stuart D., *American Welfare Capitalism, 1880–1940* (Chicago: University of Chicago Press, 1976).

Bremner, Robert H., *From the Depths: The Discovery of Poverty in the United States* (New York: New York University Press, 1956).

Bridenbaugh, Carl, *Cities in the Wilderness. The First Century of Urban Life in America 1625–1742* (New York: Knopf, 1960).

Bridenbaugh, Carl, *Vexed and Troubled Englishmen 1590–1642* (New York: Oxford University Press, 1968).

Bristol, Claude, M., *The Magic of Believing* (New York: Prentice-Hall, 1948).

Brody, David, *Steelworkers in America: The Nonunion Era* (Cambridge: Harvard University Press, 1960).

Brody, David, *Workers in Industrial America. Essays on the Twentieth Century Struggle* (New York: Oxford University Press, 1980).

Brown, Donna, "Why Participative Management Won't Work Here," *Management Review*, Vol. 81 (June, 1992), 42–46.

Brown, J. A. C., *The Social Psychology of Industry* (Harmondsworth, Middlesex: Penguin, 1954).

Bruchey, Stuart, *Enterprise. The Dynamic Economy of a Free People* (Cambridge: Harvard University Press, 1990).

Bruchey, *The Colonial Merchant* (New York: Harcourt, Brace, and World, 1966).

Bruzzese, Anita, "Management Work Teams," *Human Resource Executive* (July, 1994), 21–24.

Buckingham, Walter, *Automation. Its Impact on Business and People* (New York: New American Library, 1961).

Caggiano, C., "What Do Workers Want," *Inc.* (November, 1992), 101.

Caplow, Theodore, Bahr, Howard M., Chadwick, Bruce A., Hill, Reuben, and Williamson, Margaret H., *Middletown Families. Fifty Years of Change and Continuity* (Minneapolis: University of Minnesota Press, 1982).

Carey, Alex, "The Hawthorne Studies: A Radical Criticism," *American Sociological Review*, Vol. 32, no.3 (1967), 403–416.

Casner-Lotto, Jill, "Participation Teams 'Work' at a Jones and Laughlin Plant," *World of Work Report* (February, 1982), 9–10.

Cass, Eugene L. and Zimmer, Frederick G. (eds.), *Men and Work in Society* (New York: Van Nostrand Reinhold Co., 1975).

Chandler, Alfred D., Jr., "The United States: Seedbed of Managerial Capitalism," in *Managerial Hierarchies. Comparative Perspectives on the Rise of Modern Industrial Enterprise*, ed. by Alfred Chandler, Jr. and Herman Daems (Cambridge, Mass.: Harvard University Press, 1980), 1–40.

Cheney, Lynne, "Hard Work, Once as American as Apple Pie," *Wall Street Journal*, April 6, 1993, A14.

Cherrington, David J., *The Work Ethic. Working Values and Values That Work* (New York: AMACOM, 1980).

Chevalier, Michel, *Society, Manners, and Politics in the United States*, ed. by John William Ward (Ithaca: Cornell University Press, 1961).

Chinoy, Eli, *Automobile Workers and the American Dream* (Boston: Beacon Press, 1955).

Chisman, Forrest and Pifer, Alan, *Government for the People. The Federal Social Role: What It Is, What It Should Be* (New York: W. W. Norton, 1987).

Clark, Vicki, "Employers Drive Diversity Efforts at GE Silicones," *Personnel Journal*, Vol. 72 (May, 1993), 148–150, 152–153.

Clement, Priscilla F., "The Philadelphia Welfare Crisis of the 1820s," *The Pennsylvania Magazine of History and Biography*, Vol. 18 (April, 1981), 150–164.

"Clinton: Pay Heed to 'Angry White Male'" *Rochester Democrat and Chronicle* [from Associated Press], April 9, 1995, 1A, 10A.

Coates, Joseph F., Jarratt, Jennifer, and Mahaffie, John B., *Future Work. Seven Critical Forces Reshaping Work and the Work Force in North America* (San Francisco: Jossey-Bass, 1990).

Cochran, Thomas C., *Business in American Life. A History* (New York: McGraw-Hill, 1972).

Cole, Robert E., *Work, Mobility & Participation. A Comparative Study of American and Japanese Industry* (Berkeley: University of California Press, 1979).

Conant, James B., "Education for a Classless Society: The Jeffersonian Tradition," *Atlantic*, Vol. 165 (May, 1940), 593–602.

Cooper, M. R., Morgan, B. S., Foley, P. M., and Kaplan, L. B., "Changing Employee Values: Deepening Discontent," *Harvard Business Review*, Vol. 57 (January-February, 1979), 117–125.

Cordtz, Dan, "Off the Dole," *Financial World*, February 15, 1994, 24–29.

Cose, Ellis, "The Myth of Meritocracy," *Newsweek*, April 3, 1995, 34.

Craig, Gary, "Something Artificial in Way," *Rochester Democrat and Chronicle*, April 3, 1995, 1A, 6A.

Cranny, C. J., Smith, Patricia, C., and Stone, Eugene F., *Job Satisfaction: How People Feel About Their Jobs and How It Affects Their Performance* (New York: Lexington Books, 1992).

Cumbler, John T., *A Social History of Economic Decline. Business, Politics, and Work in Trenton* (New Brunswick, N.J.: Rutgers University Press, 1989).

Dalton, Melville, "The Industrial Rate-Buster: A Characterization," *Applied Anthropology*, Vol. 7 (1948), 5–18.

Dalton, Melville, "Worker Response and Social Background," *The Journal of Political Economy*, Vol. 55 (1947), 323–332.

Davis, Louis E., "Developments in Job Design," in *Personal Goals and Work Design*, ed. by Peter Warr (London: John Wiley, 1976).

Davis, Louis E., "Enhancing the Quality of Working Life: Developments in the United States," *International Labour Review*, Vol. 116, no. 1 (July-August, 1977), 53–65.

Davis, Louis E., "Individuals and the Organization," *California Management Review*, Vol. 22, no. 2 (1980), 5–14.

Davis, Louis E., "Job Design: Overview and Future Direction," *Journal of Contemporary Business*, Vol. 6 (Spring, 1977), 85–102.

Davis, Louis E., "Sociotechnical Systems. The Design of Work and the Quality of Working Life," in *Sociotechnical Systems. A Sourcebook*, ed. by W. A. Pasmore and J. J. Sherwood (La Jolla: California: University Associates, 1978), 322–325.

Davis, Louis E., Canter, Ralph R., and Hoffman, John, "Current Job Design Criteria," *The Journal of Industrial Engineering*, Vol. 6, no. 2 (March-April, 1955), 5–8, 21–23.

Davis, Louis E. and Cherns, Albert (eds.), *The Quality of Working Life*. 2 Vols. (New York: Free Press, 1975).

Davis, Ralph, *The Rise of the Atlantic Economies* (Ithaca: Cornell University Press, 1973).

Dawley, Alan, *Class and Community: The Industrial Revolution in Lynn* (Cambridge: Harvard University Press, 1976).

DeCosse, David E., "When Welfare Ends. A Michigan Study Records the Human Toll," *Ford Foundation Report* (Fall, 1994), 30–32.

DeParle, Jason, "Study Finds that Education Does Not Ease Welfare Rolls," *New York Times*, June 22, 1994, A16.

DeParle, Jason, "The Clinton Welfare Bill Begins Trek in Congress," *New York Times*, July 15, 1994, A1, A8.

Deutschman, Alan, "The Upbeat Generation," *Fortune*, July 13, 1992, 42–54.

Doerflinger, Thomas and Rivlin, Jack L., *Risk and Reward. Venture Capital & the Making of America's Great Industries* (New York: Random House, 1987).

Drucker, Peter F., *The Concept of the Corporation* (New York: John Day, 1946).

Drucker, Peter F., *The New Society. The Anatomy of the Industrial Order* (New York: Harper, 1949).

Dubin, Robert, "Industrial Workers' Worlds: A Study of the 'Central Life Interests' of Industrial Workers," in *Work and Leisure*, ed. by Erwin O. Smigel (New Haven: College and University Press, 1963), 53–72.

Dubin, Robert, "Work in Modern Society," in *Handbook of Work, Organization, and Society*, ed. by Robert Dubin (Chicago: Rand McNally, 1976), 5–35.

Dubofsky, Melvyn, *Industrialism and the American Worker 1865–1920*. 2nd ed. (Arlington Heights, Illinois: Harlan Davidson 1985).

Dubois, W. E. B., *The Philadelphia Negro. A Social Study* (New York: Benjamin Blom, 1967).

Dugger, Celia W., "Exodus over Welfare Cuts? Researchers Say It Isn't So," *New York Times*, May 1, 1995, A1, B4.

Dugger, Celia W., "Iowa Plan Tries to Cut Off Cash," *New York Times*, April 7, 1995, A1, B6.

Dumaine, Brian, "Mr. Learning Organization," *Fortune*, October 17, 1994, 147–157.

Dumaine, Brian, "Why Do We Work," *Fortune*, December 26, 1994, 196–204.

Duncan, Otis D. and Blau, Peter, "What Determines Occupational Success," in *Three Centuries of Social Mobility in America*, ed. by Edward Pessen (Lexington, Mass.: D. C. Heath, 1974), 284–303.

Dunlap, George A., *The City in the American Novel, 1789–1900* (New York: Russell and Russell, 1965).

Durkheim, Émile, *Suicide, a Study in Sociology*, trans. by John A. Spaulding and George Simpson (Glencoe, Illinois: Free Press, 1951).

Dworkin, Ronald, "Are Quotas Unfair," in *Racial Preferences and Racial Justice. The New Affirmative Action Controversy*, ed. by Russell Nieli (Washington, D.C.: Ethics and Public Policy Center, 1991), 175–189.

Ehrenreich, Barbara, "In Search of a Simpler Life," *Working Woman* (December, 1995), 27–29, 62.

Ekirch, Arthur, *The Idea of Progress in America 1815–1860* (New York: Peter Smith, 1951).

Eliot, T. S., "The Love Song of J. Alfred Prufrock," in T. S. Eliot, *The Complete Poems and Plays, 1909–1950* (New York: Harcourt, Brace, 1958).

Ellul, Jacques, *The Technological Society*, trans. by John Wilkinson (New York: Random House, 1964).

Ellwood, David T., *Poor Support: Poverty in the American Family* (New York: Basic Books, 1988).

Emmet, Boris and Jeuck, John E., *Catalogues and Counters: A History of Sears, Roebuck and Company* (Chicago: University of Chicago Press, 1950).

Erikson, Kai and Vallas, Steven P. (eds.), *The Nature of Work. Sociological Perspectives* (New Haven: American Sociological Association Presidential Series and Yale University Press, 1990).

Ezorsky, Gertrude, *Racism and Justice. The Case for Affirmative Action* (Ithaca: Cornell University Press, 1991).

Farnham, Alan, "Holding Firm on Affirmative Action," *Fortune*, March 13, 1989, 87–88.

Faler, Paul G., *Mechanics and Manufacturers in the Early Industrial Revolution. Lynn, Massachusetts, 1780–1860* (Albany: State University of New York Press, 1981).

Faulkner, H. U., *American Economic History* (New York: Harper and Row, 1960).

Fayol, Henri, *General and Industrial Management*, trans. by Constance Storrs (London: Pitman, 1949).

Feder, Barnaby J., "Turnabout Artist on the Loose," *New York Times*, March 24, 1985, 7F.

Feis, Herbert, *Labor Relations. A Study Made in the Proctor and Gamble Company* (New York: Adelphi, 1928).

Feldstein, Martin, "Tax Rates and Human Behavior," *Wall Street Journal*, May 7, 1993, A14.

Fiedler, Fred E., "New Concepts for the Management of Managers," in *Man and Work in Society*, ed. by E. L. Cass and F. G.Zimmer (New York: Van Nostrand, 1975), 207–219.

Fierman, Jaclyn, "The Contingency Work Force," *Fortune*, January 24, 1994, 30–34.

Fierman, Jaclyn, "Why Women Still Don't Hit the Top," *Fortune*, July 30, 1990, 40–62.

Fineman, Howard, "Race and Rage," *Newsweek*, April 3, 1995, 25.

Firestone, David, "New Policy Cuts Numbers on Relief in New York City," *New York Times*, April 19, 1995, A1, B4.

Flink, James J., *The Car Culture* (Cambridge: MIT Press, 1975).

Follett, Mary Parker, *Creative Experience* (New York: Peter Smith, 1951).

Franke, Richard H. and Kaul, James D., "The Hawthorne Experiments: First Statistical Interpretation," *American Sociological Review*, Vol. 43, no. 5 (October, 1978), 623–643.

Freedman, David, *The Contemporary Work Ethic in Industrialised Market Economy Countries* (Geneva: ILO, 1978).

French, John R. P., "Retraining the Autocratic Leader," *Journal of Abnormal and Social Psychology*, Vol. 39 (June, 1944), 224–237.

Freud, Sigmund, *Civilization and Its Discontents*, trans. by James Strachey (New York: W. W. Norton, 1962).

Friedmann, Georges, *Industrial Society. The Emergence of the Human Problems of Automation* (New York: Free Press of Glencoe, 1955).

Friedmann, Georges, *The Anatomy of Work. Labor, Leisure and the Implications of Automation* (New York: Free Press of Glencoe, 1961).

Fromm, Erich, *The Sane Society* (Greenwich, Conn.: Fawcett, 1955).

Fullerton, Kemper, "Calvinism and Capitalism: An Exploration of the Weber Thesis," in *Protestantism and Capitalism. The Weber Thesis and Its Critics*, ed. by Robert Green (Boston: D.C. Heath, 1959), 6–20.

Galambos, Louis and Pratt, Joseph, *The Rise of the Corporate Commonwealth. United States Business and Public Policy in the 20th Century* (New York: Basic Books, 1988).

Garraty, John A., *Unemployment in History. Economic Thought and Public Policy* (New York: Harper and Row, 1978).

Garson, Barbara, "Luddites in Lordstown," *Harper's* (June, 1972), 68–73.

Garson, Barbara, *The Electronic Sweatshop. How Computers are Transforming the Office of the Future into the Factory of the Past* (New York: Penguin, 1989).

"GE Management and IUEW Team Up to Save 7,000 Jobs in Louisville," *Work in America*, Vol. 18, no. 5 (May, 1993), 4–5.

Gellerman, Saul, *Motivation and Productivity* (New York:AMACOM,1963).

General Motors Corporation, *Beliefs and Values*, September, 1990. Pamphlet with unnumbered pages.

George, Charles H. and Katherine, *The Protestant Mind of the English Reformation 1570–1640* (Princeton: Princeton University Press, 1961).

Gerth, Hans H. and Mills, C. Wright (trans.), *Max Weber. Essays in Sociology* (New York: Oxford University Press, 1946).

Gibbs, Nancy, "The Vicious Cycle," *Time*, June 20, 1994, 22–33.

Glaser, Edward M., *Productivity Gains Through Worklife Improvements* (New York: Harcourt Brace Jovanovich, 1976).

Glazer, Nathan, "Race, Not Class," *Wall Street Journal*, April 5, 1995, A12.

Glazer, Nathan, "Racial Quotas," in *Racial Preference and Racial Justice. The New Affirmative Action Controversy*, ed. by Russell Nieli (Washington, D.C.: Ethics and Public Policy Center, 1991), 3–27.

"GM Bets an Arm and a Leg on a People-Free Plant," *Business Week*, September 12, 1988, 72–73.

Goodman, Paul S. and Lawler, Edward E., "United States," in *New Forms of Work Organisation* (Geneva: ILO, 1979), 143–173.

Gordon, David M., Edwards, Richard, and Reich, Michael, *Segmented Work, Divided Workers. The Historical Transformation of Labor in the United States* (Cambridge: Cambridge University Press, 1982).

Gould, William B., *Black Workers in White Unions* (Ithaca: Cornell University Press, 1977).

Graham, Pauline (ed.), *Mary Parker Follett—Prophet of Management. A Celebration of Writings from the 1920s* (Boston: Harvard Business School Press, 1995).

Gramsci, Antonio, *Selections from Prison Notebooks of Antonio Gramsci* (New York: International Publishers, 1971).

Green, Arnold, W., *Sociology* (New York: McGraw–Hill, 1952).

Green, James R., *The World of the Worker. Labor in Twentieth-Century America* (New York: Hill and Wang, 1980).

Green, Ronald M., "New Challenges to Affirmative Action," *World of Work Report* (September, 1984), 4–5.

Greenhouse, Linda, "Court Lets Stand Ruling That Found Plan on Bias Unfair," *New York Times*, April 18, 1995, A14.

Greenhouse, Linda, "Signal on Job Rights," *New York Times*, January 25, 1989, A1, A18.

Greenwald, John, "Picking up Speed," *Time*, January 10, 1994, 18–21.

Guest, Robert, "Men and Machines. An Assembly-Line Worker Looks at His Job," *Personnel*, Vol. 32 (May, 1955), 496–503.

Guest, Robert, "Quality of Work Life—Learning from Tarrytown," *Harvard Business Review*, Vol. 57, no.4 (July-August, 1979), 76–87.

Haber, Samuel, *Efficiency and Uplift. Scientific Management in the Progressive Era* (Chicago: University of Chicago Press, 1964).

Hackman, J. Richard, "Work Design," in *Improving Life at Work. Behavioral Science Approaches to Organizational Change*, ed. by J. R. Hackman and J. L. Suttle (Santa Monica: California: Goodyear Publishing, 1977), 96–162.

Hareven, Tamara K., *Family Time and Industrial Time. The Relationship Between the Family and Work in a New England Industrial Community* (Cambridge: Cambridge University Press, 1982).

Hareven, Tamara K. and Langenbach, Ronald, *Amoskeag. Life and Work in an American Factory City* (New York: Pantheon Books, 1978).

Hart, Hornell, *Autoconditioning: The New Way to a Successful Life* (Engelwood Cliffs, N.J.: Prentice-Hall, 1956).

Harrison, Bennett and Bluestone, Barry, *The Great U-Turn. Corporate Restructuring and the Polarizing of America* (New York: Basic Books, 1990).

Haupt, Jennifer, "Employee Action Prompts Management to Respond to Work-and-Family Needs," *Personnel Journal*, Vol. 72 (February, 1993), 96, 98, 100–102, 105, 107.

Havemann, Judith and Vobejda, Barbara, "Senate GOP Welfare Draft Scraps Some Contentious House Rules," *The Washington Post*, April 13, 1995, A8.

Havighurst, Alfred F., *Britain in Transition. The Twentieth Century* (Chicago: University of Chicago Press, 1985).

Hawley, Ellis W., "Herbert Hoover, the Commerce Secretariat, and the Vision of an 'Associative State,' 1921–1928," *Journal of American History*, Vol. 61 (1974), 116–140.

Hayghe, Howard V. and Bianchi, Suzanne M., "Married Mothers' Work Patterns: The Job-Family Compromise," *Monthly Labor Review*, Vol. 117, no. 6 (June, 1994), 24–30.

Henneberger, Melinda, "State Aid is Capped, But to What Effect," *New York Times*, April 11, 1995, A1, A18.

Herbert, Bob, "The Wrong Target," *New York Times*, April 5, 1995, A25.

"Here Comes GM's Saturn," *Business Week*, April 9, 1990, 56–62.

Heron, Alexander, *Why Men Work* (Stanford: Stanford University Press, 1948).

Hershberg, Theodore, Burstein, Alan, Eriksen, Eugene, Greenberg, Stephanie, and Yancey, William, "A Tale of Three Cities: Blacks, Immigrants and Opportunity in Philadelphia, 1850–1880, 1930, 1970," in *Philadelphia. Work, Space, Family, and Group Experience in the 19th Century. Essays Toward an Interdisciplinary History of the City*, ed. by Theodore Hershberg (New York: Oxford University Press, 1981), 461–491.

Herzberg, Frederick, *Work and the Nature of Man* (Cleveland: World Publishing Company, 1966).

Hicks, Clarence J., *My Life in Industrial Relations. Fifty Years in the Growth of a Profession* (New York: Harper, 1941).

"High Court Sides with Whites in Workplace," *Rochester Democrat and Chronicle* [from Los Angeles Times], April 18, 1995, 1.

Hill, Christopher, *Society and Puritanism in Pre-Revolutionary England* (London: Penguin Books, 1991).

Hill, Christopher, *The Century of Revolution, 1603–1714* (New York: W. W. Norton, 1961).

Hill, Roy, "The Relaxed Management Style of a High Technology Company," *International Management*, Vol. 33, no. 3 (March, 1978), 12–15.

Hirsch, Susan E., *Roots of the American Working Class. The Industrialization of Crafts in Newark, 1800–1860* (Philadelphia: University of Pennsylvania Press, 1978).

Hobsbawm, E. J., *Industry and Empire. From 1750 to the Present Day* (Harmondsworth, Middlesex: Penguin, 1969).

Hobsbawm, E. J., "The British Standard of Living, 1790–1850," in *Labouring Men. Studies in the History of Labour* (New York: Basic Books, 1964), 64–104.

Hobsbawm, E. J., "The Tramping Artisan," in *Labouring Men. Studies in the History of Labour* (New York: Basic Books,1964), 34–63.

Hoffman, W. M. and Wyly, T. J. (eds.), *The Work Ethic in Business* (Cambridge, Mass.: Oelgeschlager, Gunn and Hain, 1981).

Holmes, Steven A., "Birthrate for Unwed Women Up 70% Since '83, Study Says," *New York Times*, July 20, 1994, A1, A8.

Holusha, John, "A Profitable Xerox Plans to Cut Staff by 10,000," *New York Times*, December 9, 1993, D1.

Homans, George C., *The Human Group* (New York: Harcourt, Brace and World, 1950).

Hoover, Herbert, *American Individualism* (New York: Garland, 1979).

Horowitz, Carl, "Breaking the Dependency Cycle," *Investor's Business Daily*, December 14, 1994, A1,A2.

Horowitz, Carl, "Ending the Welfare Cycle As We Know It," *Investor's Business Daily*, December 16, 1993, A1, A2.

Horowitz, Carl, "Explaining the Poverty Paradox," *Investor's Business Daily*, December 1, 1994, A1, A2.

Horowitz, Carl, "Need-Based Affirmative Action?" *Investor's Business Daily*, May 5, 1995, A1, A2.

Horowitz, Carl, "The Dismal Record of Workfare," *Investor's Business Daily*, December 21, 1994, A1, A2.

Horwitz, Tony, "9 to Nowhere," *Wall Street Journal*, December 1, 1994, 1A, 8A, 9A.

Hoslet, S. D., *Human Factors in Management*. New ed. (New York: Harper, 1951).

Howard, Ann and Wilson, James A., "Leadership in a Declining Work Ethic," *California Management Review*, Vol. 24 (Summer, 1982), 33–45.

Huey, John, "The New Post–Heroic Leadership," *Fortune*, February 21, 1994, 42–50.

Ichniowski, Casey, "Human Resource Practices and Productive Labor-Management Relations," in *Research Frontiers in Industrial Relations and Human Resources*, ed. by David Lewin et al (Madison, Wisconsin: IRRA, 1992), 239–271.

Jencks, Christopher, "Affirmative Action for Blacks," *The American Behavioral Scientist*, Vol. 28 (July-August, 1985), 731–761.

Jencks, Christopher, *Rethinking Social Policy: Race, Poverty, and the Underclass* (Cambridge, Mass.: Harvard University Press, 1992).

Jenkins, David, "Quality of Working Life: Trends and Directions," in *The Quality of Working Life and the 1980s*, ed. by Harvey Kolodny and Hans Van Beinum (New York: Praeger, 1983), 1–32.

Jenks, Leland H., "Early Phases of the Management Movement," *Administrative Science Quarterly*, Vol. 5 (December, 1960), 421–447.

"Jobs in an Age of Insecurity," *Time*, November 22, 1993, 33–37.

Johnston, Eric, *America Unlimited* (Garden City, N.Y.: Doubleday, Doran, 1944).

Johnston, Lloyd, Bachman, Jerald G., and O'Malley, Patrick M., *Monitoring the Future—1981* (Ann Arbor, Mich.: Institute for Social Research, 1982).

Kahn, Robert L., "In Search of the Hawthorne Effect," in *Man and Work in Society*, ed. by Eugene L. Cass and Frederick G. Zimmer (New York: Van Nostrand Reinhold, 1975), 49–61.

Kanter, Rosabeth Moss, *Men and Women of the Corporation* (New York: Basic Books, 1977).

Kanter, Rosabeth Moss, *The Changing Shape of Work: Psychosocial Trends in America*. Current Issues in Higher Education, 1978, National Conference Series, AAHE (Washington, D.C.:AAHE,1978).

Kanter, Rosabeth Moss, "The New Managerial Work," *Harvard Business Review*, Vol. 67 (November–December, 1989), 85–92.

Kanter, Rosabeth Moss, "Work in a New America," *Daedalus*, Vol. 107 (Winter, 1978), 47–77.

Katzell, Raymond A, Thompson, Donna E., and Guzzo, Richard A., "How Job Satisfaction and Job Performance are and are Not Linked," in *Job Satisfaction: How People Feel About Their Jobs and How It Affects Their Performance*, ed. by C. J. Cranny, Patricia C. Smith, and Eugene F. Stone (New York: Lexington Books, 1992), 195–217.

Kaufman, Bruce E., *The Origins and Evolution of the Field of Industrial Relations in the United States* (Ithaca: Cornell University Press, 1993).

Kaufman, Jonathan, "How Workplaces May Look Without Affirmative Action," *Wall Street Journal*, March 20, 1995, B1, B6.

Kaufman, Robert L., "Looking Forward: Responses to Organizational and Technological Change in an Ultra-High-Technology Firm," in *Research in the*

Sociology of Work, ed. by Richard L. and Ida H. Simpson. 4 Vols. (Greenwich, Conn.: JAI Press, 1988), 4:31–67.

Kaus, Mickey, "Up from Altruism: The Case Against Compassion," *The New Republic*, December 15, 1986, 17–18.

Kelley, Bill, "Measure of Success," *Human Resource Executive*, (December, 1993), 28–30.

Keniston, Kenneth, *The Uncommitted* (New York: Dell, 1960).

Kerr, Clark, "Industrialism with a Human Face," in *Work in a New America. The Decade Ahead*, ed. by Clark Kerr and Jerome Rosow (New York: Van Nostrand Reinhold, 1979), ix–xxvii.

Ketchum, Lyman D., "Innovating Plant Managers are Talking About . . ." International Conference on Quality of Working Life, Toronto, Canada, August 30–September 4, 1981, 1–12.

Kilborn, Peter T., "Job Security Hinges on Skills, Not on Employer for Life," *New York Times*, March 12, 1994, A1, A7.

Kilborn, Peter T., "Women and Minorities Still Face 'Glass Ceiling'," *New York Times*, March 16, 1995, A22.

Kirkpatrick, David, "Could A T & T Rule the World?," *Fortune*, May 17, 1993, 55–66.

Kleinfield, N.R., "A T & T Trying to Lift Morale," *New York Times*, April 14, 1979, 32.

Klotz, Gary, "The High Cost of `Employees' Rights," *Wall Street Journal*, August 3, 1993, A14.

Kolesar, Peter J., "Vision, Values, Milestones: Paul O'Neil Starts Total Quality at Alcoa," *California Management Review*, Vol. 35, no. 3 (Spring, 1993), 133–165.

Krauthammer, Charles, "Why We Need Race Consciousness," in *Racial Preferences and Racial Justice. The New Affirmative Action Controversy*, ed. by Russell Nieli (Washington, D.C.: Ethics and Public Policy Center, 1991), 141–148.

Laabs, Jennifer, J., "Family Issues are a Priority at Stride Rite," *Personnel Journal*, Vol. 72 (July, 1993), 48–49, 51–56.

Labaree, Leonard W. and Bell, Whitfield J. Jr. (eds.), *The Papers of Benjamin Franklin* (New Haven: Yale University Press, 1959–   ).

Lancaster, Hal, "Managing Your Career," *Wall Street Journal*, November 15, 1994, B1.

Landsberger, Henry A., *Hawthorne Revisited* (Ithaca: Cornell University Press, 1958).

Lane, Randall, "Computers are Our Friends," *Forbes*, May 8, 1995, 102–108.

Lazarus, Arnold A. and Fay, Allen, *I Can If I Want to* (New York: William Morrow, 1975).

Lee, Hak C. and Grix, John J., "Communication: An Alternative to Enrichment," *The Personnel Administrator*, Vol. 20 (October, 1975), 20–23.

Leidner, Robin, "Home Work: A Study in the Interaction of Work and Family Organization," in *Research in the Sociology of Work*, ed. by Richard L. and Ida H. Simpson. 4 Vols. (Greenwich, Conn.: JAI Press, 1967–1988), 69–94.

Lenski, Gerhard, *The Religious Factor: A Sociological Study of Religion's Impact on Politics, Economics, and Family Life* (Garden City, N.Y.: Doubleday, 1961).

Leonard, Jonathan, "The Impact of Affirmative Action on Employment," in *Racial Preferences and Racial Justice. The New Affirmative Action Controversy*, ed. by Russell Nieli (Washington, D.C.: Ethics and Public Policy Center, 1991), 493–498.

Leonard-Barton, Dorothy, "The Factory as a Learning Laboratory," *Sloan Management Review*, Vol. 34, no.1 (Fall, 1992), 23–38.

Lester, Richard A., *As Unions Mature: An Analysis of the Evolution of American Unionism* (Princeton: Princeton University Press, 1958).

Levin, Doron P., "The Graying Factory," *New York Times*, February 20, 1994, 6F.

Levin, Doron P., "What BMW Sees in South Carolina," *New York Times*, April 11, 1993, F5.

Levitan, Sar and Johnson, Clifford M., *Second Thoughts on Work* (Kalamazoo, Mich.: W. E. Upjohn Institute for Employment Research, 1982).

Lewin, Kurt, "Studies in Group Decision," in *Group Dynamics*, ed. by Dorwin Cartwright and Alvin Zander (Evanston, Illinois: Row, Peterson, 1953), 287–301.

Lewin, Kurt, Lippitt, Ronald, and White, Ralph K., "Patterns of Aggressive Behavior in Experimentally-Created 'Social Climates'," *The Journal Social Psychology*, Vol. 10 (May,1939), 271–299.

Lewin, Tamar, "Poll of Teen-Agers Finds Boys Prefer Traditional Family," *New York Times*, July 11, 1994, A1, B7.

Lewin, Tamar, "Workers of Both Sexes Make Trade-Offs for Family, Study Shows," *New York Times*, October 29, 1995, A25.

Lewisohn, Sam A., *Human Leadership in Industry. The Challenge of Tomorrow* (New York: Harper, 1945).

Likert, Rensis, *New Patterns of Management* (New York: McGraw-Hill, 1961).

Linden, Dana W., "The Mother of Them All," *Forbes*, January 16,1995, 75–76.

Locke, Edwin A., "The Nature and Causes of Job Satisfaction," in *Handbook of Industrial and Organizational Psychology*, ed. by M. D. Dunnette (Chicago: Rand McNally, 1976), 1297–1349.

Lublin, Jo Ann, "Best Manufacturers Found to Triumph by Fostering Cooperation of Employees," *Wall Street Journal*, July 20, 1993, A2.

Lynch, Frederick R., *Invisible Victims: White Males and the Crisis of Affirmative Action* (New York: Praeger, 1991).

Maccoby, Michael and Terzi, Katherine A., "Character and Work in America," in *Exploring Contradictions: Political Economy in the Corporate State*, ed. by P. Brenner, R. Borosage, and B. Weidner (New York: David McKay, 1974), 116–160.

Maccoby, Michael and Terzi, Katherine A., "What Happened to the Work Ethic," in *The Work Ethic in Business*, ed. by W. Michael Hoffman and Thomas J. Wyly (Cambridge, Mass.: Oelgeschlager, Gunn, and Hain, 1981), 19–58.

Macy, Barry A., "The Quality-of-Worklife Project at Bolivar: An Assessment," *Monthly Labor Review*, Vol. 103 (July, 1980), 41–43.

Maher, John R. and Piersol, D. T., "The Motivation to Work—Outlook for the Future," in *New Perspectives in Job Enrichment*, ed. by John R. Maher (New York: Van Nostrand, 1971), 1–19.

Malkin, Jesse, "Will Wisconsin Workforce Work," *Investor's Business Daily*, December 6, 1993, A1, A2.

Marmor, Theodore R. and Mashaw, Jerry L., *America's Misunderstood Welfare State* (New York: Basic Books, 1990).

Marrow, Alfred J., "Management by Participation," in *Man and Work in Society*, ed. by Eugene L. Cass and Frederick G. Zimmer (New York: Van Nostrand Reinhold, 1975), 33–48.

Matthews, R. C. O., Feinstein, C. H., and Odling-Smee, J. C., *British Economic Growth, 1856–1973* (Stanford: Stanford University Press, 1982).

Matthewson, Stanley B., *Restriction of Output among Unorganized Workers* (New York: Viking, 1931).

Mayo, Elton, *The Human Problems of an Industrial Civilization* (New York: Macmillan, 1933).

Mayo, Elton, *The Social Problems of an Industrial Civilization* (Boston: Graduate School of Business Administration, Harvard University, 1945).

McGregor, Douglas, *The Human Side of Enterprise* (New York: McGraw-Hill, 1960).

McKain, Robert J., *How to Get to the Top . . . and Stay There* (New York: AMACOM, 1981).

McNair, Malcolm P., "A Dissenting Voice on Human Relations in Industry," in *Industrial Man. Businessmen and Business Organizaions*, ed. by W. Lloyd Warner and Norman Martin (New York, Harper, 1959), 323–340.

Mead, Lawrence M., *Beyond Entitlement: The Social Obligations of Citizenship* (New York: Free Press, 1986).

Mead, Lawrence M., *The New Politics of Poverty: The Networking Poor in America* (New York: Basic Books, 1992).

Meier, August and Rudwick, Elliott, *Black Detroit and the Rise of the UAW* (New York: Oxford University Press, 1979).

Meyer, Stephen III, *The Five Dollar Day. Labor Management and Social Control in the Ford Motor Company 1908–1921* (Albany: State University of New York Press, 1981).

Middlekauff, Robert, *The Mathers. Three Generations of Puritan Intellectuals 1596–1728* (New York: Oxford University Press, 1971).

"Midlife Americans Glum About Prospects," *AARP Bulletin* (September, 1993), 15.

Milbank, Dana, "Telephone Sales Reps Do Unrewarding Jobs Few Can Abide," *Wall Street Journal*, September 9, 1993, A1, A10.

Miles, Raymond, "Human Relations or Human Resources?" *Harvard Business Review*, Vol. 43 (July-August, 1965), 148–163.

Miller, Donald B. (ed.), *Career Management. An Annotated Bibliography for the Working Professional* (San Jose, California: American Society for Engineering Education,1975).

Mills, C. Wright, "The Contributions of Sociology to Studies of Industrial Relations," in *Proceedings of the First Annual Meeting of Industrial Relations Research Association* (1948), 199–222.

Mills, Ted, "Work as a Learning Experience," in *Relating Work and Education*, ed. by D. W. Vermilye (San Francisco: Jossey-Bass, 1977), 87–101.

Mohl, R. A., *Poverty in New York: 1783–1825* (New York: Oxford University Press, 1971).

Montgomery, David, *The Fall of the House of Labor. The Workplace, the State, and American Labor Activism, 1865–1925* (Cambridge: Cambridge University Press, 1989).

Moore, Robert, *How to Win the Image Game Everyone is Playing* (New York: Exposition Press, 1970).

Morgan, Edmund S., *American Slavery American Freedom. The Ordeal of Colonial Virginia* (New York: W. W. Norton, 1975).

Morgan, Kenneth O., *The People's Peace. British History 1945–1989* (New York: Oxford University Press, 1990).

Morris, Richard B., *Government and Labor in Early America* (New York: Columbia University Press, 1946).

Morse, Nancy C. and Weiss, Robert S., "The Function and Meaning of Work and the Job," *American Sociological Review* (April, 1955), Vol. 20, no. 2, 191–198.

Mosk, Stanley, "For Bakke," in *Racial Preferences and Racial Justice. The New Affirmative Action Controversy*, ed. by Russell Nieli (Washington, D.C.: Ethics and Public Policy Center, 1991), 159–166.

Mosteller, Frederick, "Nonsampling Errors," in *Encyclopedia of the Social Sciences*, ed. by D. L. Sills (New York: Macmillan Company and Free Press, 1967), 113–132.

Mowry, George W., *The Urban Nation, 1920–1960* (New York: Hill and Wang, 1965).

Munsterberg, Hugo, *Psychology and Industrial Efficiency* (Boston: Houghton Mifflin, 1913).

Murphy, Daniel J., "The Jaws of the Welfare Trap," *Investor's Business Daily*, July 18, 1994, A1–A2.

Murray, Charles, "Affirmative Racism," in *Racial Preferences and Racial Justice. The New Affirmative Action Controversy*, ed. by Russell Nieli (Washington, D.C.: Ethics and Public Policy Center, 1991), 393–408.

Murray, Charles, *Losing Ground: American Social Policy, 1950–1980* (New York: Basic Books, 1984).

Murrell, Hywell, *Men and Machines* (London: Methuen, 1976).

Murrell, Hywell, *Motivation at Work* (London: Methuen, 1976).

Nash, Al, "Job Satisfaction: a Critique," in *Auto Work and Its Discontents*, ed. by B. J. Widrick (Baltimore: Johns Hopkins University Press, 1976), 61–88.

Nelson, Daniel, *Frederick W. Taylor and the Rise of Scientific Management* (Madison: University of Wisconsin Press, 1980).

Nelson, Daniel, *Managers and Workers. Origins of the New Factory System in the United States 1880–1920* (Madison: University of Wisconsin Press, 1975).

Nieli, Russell (ed.), *Racial Preferences and Racial Justice. The New Affirmative Action Controversy* (Washington, D.C.: Ethics and Public Policy Center, 1991).

Nisbet, Lee, "Affirmative Action: A Liberal Program," in *Racial Preferences and Racial Justice. The New Affirmative Action Controversy*, ed. by Russell Nieli (Washington, D.C.: Ethics and Public Policy Center, 1991), 111–118.

Noble, Barbara P., "Questioning Productivity Beliefs," *New York Times*, July 10, 1994, F21.

Norman, James R., "A Very Nimble Elephant," *Forbes*, October 10, 1994, 88–92.

Occupational Outlook Handbook, 1978–1979 edition (Washington, D.C.: U.S. Government Printing Office, 1978).

Oldham, Greg R., "Work Redesign. Enhancing Productivity and the Quality of Working Life," *National Forum* (Spring, 1982), Vol. 62, no. 2, 8–9.

Orzack, Louis H., "Work as a 'Central Life Interest' of Professionals," in *Work and Leisure*, ed. by Erwin O. Smigel (New Haven, Conn.: College and University Press, 1963), 73–84.

O'Toole, James, *Work, Learning, and the American Future* (San Francisco: Jossey-Bass, 1977).

O'Toole, James (Chair), *Work in America. Report of a Special Task Force to the Secretary of Health, Education, and Welfare* (Cambridge: MIT Press, 1973).

Otten, Allen L., "People Patterns," *Wall Street Journal,* September 27, 1993, B1.

Ozment, Steven, *The Age of Reform 1250–1550. An Intellectual and Religious History of Late Medieval and Reformation Europe* (New Haven, Conn.: Yale University Press, 1980).

Ozment, Steven, *Protestants. The Birth of a Revolution* (New York: Doubleday, 1993).

Packard, Vance, *The Status Seekers* (New York: Pocket Books, 1971).

Parets, Robyn, "Motivator Brian Tracy," *Investor's Business Daily,* January 20, 1995, A1–A2.

Parker, Robert H., *Management Accounting; an Historical Perspective* (New York: Augustus M. Kelley, 1969).

"Participative Organizations Demand a New Breed of Leader," *Work in America* (June, 1993), 1–3.

Passell, Peter, "A Four-Day Workweek Plan is Optimistic, Not Realistic," *New York Times,* November 25, 1993, D2.

Peale, Norman Vincent, *The Power of Positive Living* (New York: Fawcett, Crest, 1992).

Pear, Robert, "Governors' Draft Plan Rejects Parts of House Welfare Bill," *New York Times,* April 28, 1995, A22.

Pear, Robert, "Judge Upholds Cap on Welfare by New Jersey," *New York Times,* May 5, 1995, A1, B6.

Perkins, Edwin J., *The Economy of Colonial America* (New York: Columbia University Press, 1988).

Phillips, Michael J., "Paradoxes of Equal Opportunity: 'Voluntary' Racial Preferences and the Weber Case," *Business Horizons* (August, 1980), 41–47.

Piven, Frances F. and Cloward, Richard A., *Regulating the Poor. The Functions of Public Welfare* (New York: Pantheon, 1971).

Pollack, Andrew, "Working Less, and Not Upset," *New York Times,* April 29, 1995, 35–36.

Pollack, Ellen Joan, "Workers Want More Money, But They Also Want to Control Their Own Time," *Wall Street Journal,* November 28, 1995, B1, B13.

Pool, John C. and La Roe, Ross, "Welfare Reform Isn't as Simple as It Seems," *Rochester Democrat and Chronicle,* April 3, 1995, 2.

Poza, Ernesto and Markus, M. Lynne, "Success Story: The Team Approach to Work Restructuring," *Organizational Dynamics,* Vol. 9 (Winter, 1980), 3–25.

Quinn, Robert P. and Staines, Graham L., *The 1977 Quality of Employment Survey* (Ann Arbor, Mich.: Institute for Social Research, 1979).

Rabinowitz, Jonathan, "Hartford Plan Sets Nation's Strictest Time Limit on Welfare," *New York Times*, May 1, 1995, B4.

"Race in the Workplace. Is Affirmative Action Working?," *Business Week*, July 8, 1991, 50, 60–63.

Raimy, Eric, "Hands and Minds," *Human Resource Executive* (August, 1993), 1, 18–21.

Raub, Deborah and Driscoll, Kathleen, "The Sweat of Your Brow," *Rochester Democrat and Chronicle*, October 3, 1993, 8F.

Renwick, Patricia A. and Lawler, Edward E., "What You Really Want From Your Job," *Psychology Today*, Vol. 11 (May, 1978), 53–65.

Reynolds, Lloyd and Shister, Joseph, *Job Horizons. A Study of Job Satisfaction and Labor Mobility* (New York: Harper, 1949).

Richan, Williard C., *Social Service Politics in the United States and Britain* (Philadelphia: Temple University Press, 1981).

Riegel, John W., *Management, Labor, and Technological Change* (Ann Arbor, Mich.: University of Michigan Press, 1942).

Riesman, David with Glazer, Nathan and Denney, Reuel, *The Lonely Crowd. A Study of the Changing American Character* (Garden City, N.Y.: Doubleday, 1953).

Riesman, David, Potter, Robert, and Watson, Jeanne, "Sociability, Permissiveness, and Equality," *Psychiatry*, Vol. 23 (1960), 334–336.

Rifkin, Jeremy, "After Work," *UTNE Reader* (May–June, 1995),53–64.

Rimer, Sara, "Jobs Program Participants: Still Poor and in Need of Aid," *New York Times*, April 10, 1995, A1, B10.

Rischin, Moses, *The American Gospel of Success. Individualism and Beyond* (Chicago: Quadrangle Books, 1965).

Roberts, Sam, "Women's Work: What's New, What Isn't," *New York Times*, April 27, 1995, B6.

Robinson, Alan G. and Schroeder, Dean M., "Training Continuous Improvement and Human Relations: The U.S. TWI Programs and the Japanese Management Style," *California Management Review*, Vol. 35, no. 2 (Winter, 1993), 35–56.

Rodgers, Daniel T., *The Work Ethic in Industrial America, 1850–1920* (Chicago: University of Chicago Press, 1978).

Roethlisberger, F. J., *Management and Morale* (Cambridge, Mass.: Harvard University Press, 1941).

Roethlisberger, F. J. and Dickson, William J., *Management and the Worker* (Cambridge, Mass.: Harvard University Press, 1939).

Rose, Michael, *Re-Working the Work Ethic* (New York: Schocken Books, 1985).

Rosenfeld, Michael, *Affirmative Action and Justice. A Philosophical and Constitutional Inquiry* (New Haven: Yale University Press, 1991).

Rosenzweig, Roy, *Eight Hours for What We Will. Workers & Leisure in an Industrial City, 1870–1920* (Cambridge: Cambridge University Press, 1983).

Rosow, Jerome (ed.), *The Worker and the Job. Coping with Change* (Englewood Cliffs, N.J.: Prentice-Hall, 1974).

Rosow, Jerome and Zager, Robert, *Productivity Through Work Innovations* (New York: Pergamon, 1982).

Roszak, Theodore, *The Making of a Counter-Culture. Reflections on the Technocratic Society and Its Youthful Opposition* (Garden City, N.Y.: Anchor Books, 1969).

Rowland, Mary, "A Clearer Picture of Unpaid Leave," *New York Times*, January 29, 1995, F13.

Ruitenbeek, Henrik M., *The Individual and the Crowd. A Study of Identity in America* (New York: New American Library, 1964).

Rukeyser, Louis, "General Foods Head Says Workers, Not Gadgets, Will Raise Productivity," *Rochester Democrat and Chronicle*, June 25, 1983, 14C.

Sachs, William S. and Hoogenboom, Ari, *The Enterprising Colonials. Society on the Eve of the Revolution* (Chicago: Argonaut,1965).

Sack, Kevin, "Trying to Cut Welfare the Ohio Way," *New York Times*, April 3, 1995, B1–B2.

Salpukas, Agis, "Workers Increasingly Rebel Against Boredom on Assembly Line," *New York Times*, April 2, 1972, N34.

Sarason, S. B. and E. K. and Cowden, P., "Aging and the Nature of Work," *American Psychologist*, Vol. 30 (May, 1975), 584–592.

Saunders, Dero A., "Flashbacks," *Forbes*, January 16, 1995, 125.

Schein, Edgar H., "Career Development: Theoretical and Practical Issues for Organizations," in *Career Planning and Development* (Geneva: ILO, 1976), 9–48.

Schlesinger, Arthur M., Jr., *The Coming of the New Deal* (Boston: Houghton Mifflin, 1959).

Schmidt, Warren H. and Posner, Barry Z., *Managerial Values and Expectations. The Silent Power in Personal and Organizational Life* (New York: AMACOM, 1982).

Schnapper, M. B., *American Labor* (Washington, D.C.: Public Affairs Press, 1972).

Schneider, Benjamin, Gunnarson, Sarah K., and Wheeler, Jill K., "The Role of Opportunity in the Conceptualization and Measurement of Job Satisfaction," in *Job Satisfaction: How People Feel About Their Jobs and How It Affects Their Performance*, ed. by C. J. Cranny, Patricia C. Smith, and Eugene F. Stone (New York: Lexington Books, 1992), 53–68.

Schrank, Robert, "On Ending Worker Alienation: The Gaines Pet Food Plant," in *Humanizing the Workplace*, ed. by Roy Fairfield (Buffalo: Prometheus Books, 1974), 119–140.

Schumacher, E. F., "Good Work," in *Relating Work and Education*, ed. by D. W. Vermilye (San Francisco: Jossey-Bass, 1977), 55–64.

Scobel, Donald N., "Doing Away with the Factory Blues," *Harvard Business Review*. Vol. 53 (November-December, 1975), 132–142.

Seib, Gerald F., "Making Sense of Angry Males and Extremism," *Wall Street Journal*, April 26, 1995, A16.

Seib, Gerald F., "Welfare Reform: Can Washington Let Go," *Wall Street Journal*, March 8, 1995, A22.

Sellers, Charles, *The Market Revolution. Jacksonian America 1815–1846* (New York: Oxford University Press, 1991).

Serrin, William, "Age and U.S. Auto Slump Have Cooled Anger of Lordstown's Militant Workers," *International Herald Tribune*, June 1, 1982, 1–2.

Serwer, Andrew E., "Lessons from America's Fastest Growing Companies," *Fortune*, August 8, 1994, 42–59.

Sheehy, Gail, "Introducing the Postponing Generation. The Truth About Today's Young Men," *Esquire* (October, 1979), 25–33.

Shellenbarger, Sue, "'Best' List for Working Mothers Shows New Faces: Midwest Firms, Oil Giants," *Wall Street Journal*, September 16, 1993, A8.

Shellenbarger, Sue, "How Some Companies Help Their Employees Get a Life," *Wall Street Journal*, November 16, 1994, B1.

Shellenbarger, Sue, "The Aging of America is Making 'Elder Care' a Big Workplace Issue," *Wall Street Journal*, February 16, 1994, A1, A6.

Shellenbarger, Sue, "Work & Family," *Wall Street Journal*, November 18, 1993, B1.

Shellenbarger, Sue, "Work-Force Study Finds Loyalty is Weak, Divisions of Race and Gender are Deep," *Wall Street Journal*, September 3, 1993, B1.

Shelton, Cynthia J., *The Mills of Manayunk. Industrialization and Social Conflict in the Philadelphia Region, 1787–1837* (Baltimore: Johns Hopkins University Press, 1986).

Shenot, Christine, "CEO Briefing on Human Resources," *Investor's Business Daily*, August 31, 1993, 4.

Simon, Herman, *General Foods Topeka. Ten Years Young*. International Conference on the Quality of Working Life, Toronto, Canada, August 31, 1981, 1–8.

Simpson, Richard L. and Ida H. (eds.), *Research in the Sociology of Work*. 4 Vols. (Greenwich, Conn.: JAI Press, 1967–1988).

Sinetar, Marsha, "Management in a New Age: An Exploration of Changing Work Values," *Personnel Journal*, Vol. 59 (September, 1980), 740–755.

Skinner, Wickham, "The Impact of Changing Technology on the Working Environment," in *Work in America. The Decade Ahead*, ed. by Clark Kerr and Jerome M. Rosow (New York: Van Nostrand Reinhold, 1979), 204–230.

Slichter, Sumner H., "The Scope and Nature of the Labor Turnover Problem," *Quarterly Journal of Economics*, Vol. 33 (February, 1920), 329–345.

Slichter, Sumner H., *Union Policies and Industrial Management* (Washington, D.C.: Brookings Institution, 1941).

Smigel, Erwin O. (ed.), *Work and Leisure. A Contemporary Social Problem* (New Haven, Conn.: College and University Press,1963).

Smith, Billy G., "The Material Lives of Laboring Philadelphians, 1750–1800," *William and Mary Quarterly*, 3rd series, Vol. 38, no. 2 (April, 1981), 163–202.

Smith, Lacey Baldwin, *This Realm of England, 1399–1688* (Boston: D. C. Heath, 1966).

Smith, Timothy L., "Work and Human Worth," in *The Nature of Work*, ed. by Alan Kraus (New York: John Wiley, 1972), 23–27.

Smith, Russell E. and Zietz, Dorothy, *American Social Welfare Institutions* (New York: John Wiley, 1970).

Sobol, Richard B., "Against Bakke," in *Racial Preferences and Racial Justice. The New Affirmative Action Controversy*, ed. by Russell Nieli (Washington, D.C.: Ethics and Public Policy Center, 1991), 167–174.

Sowell, Thomas, "Are Quotas Good for Blacks," in *Racial Preferences and Racial Justice. The New Affirmative Action Controversy*, ed. by Russell Nieli (Washington, D.C.: Ethics and Public Policy Center, 1991), 415–428.

Sperry, Paul, "Saving Welfare as We Know It?," *Investor's Business Daily*, July 8, 1994, A1–A2.

Spickard, Paul R., "Why I Believe in Affirmative Action," in *Racial Preferences and Racial Justice. The New Affirmative Action Controversy*, ed. by Russell Nieli (Washington, D.C.: Ethics and Public Policy Center, 1991), 105–109.

Stern, Aimee L., "Managing the Team is Not Always as Easy as It Looks," *New York Times*, July 18, 1993, F5.

Stevenson, Frank H., *The Gospel of Work* (Cincinnati: no publisher noted, 1921).

Stewart, Thomas A., "GE Keeps Those Ideas Coming," *Fortune*, August 12, 1991, 41–49.

Stout, Hilary, "GOP's Welfare Stance Owes a Lot to Prodding from Robert Rector," *Wall Street Journal*, January 23,1995, A1, A10.

Stroh, Linda K. and Kush, Karen S., "Flextime: The Imaginary Innovation," *New York Times*, November 27, 1994, F11.

Sulit, Beth K., "Changing Work Force Dynamics," *Human Resource Executive* (January, 1994), 26–28.

"Survivors of Layoffs Battle Angst, Anger, Hurting Productivity," *Wall Street Journal*, December 6, 1993, 1.

Suskind, Ron, "Florida's Experiment in Time Limit for Welfare Underscores Snares Facing Clinton's Proposal," *Wall Street Journal*, March 28, 1994, A14.

Swasy, Alecia, "Stay-at-Home Moms are Fashionable Again in Many Communities," *Wall Street Journal*, July 23, 1993, A1, A4.

Taft, Philip, "Workers of a New Century," in *The American Worker*, ed. by Richard B. Morris (Washington, D.C.: U.S. Government Printing Office, 1976), 153–199.

Taylor, Frederick Winslow, *Shop Management* (New York: Harper,1912).

Taylor, Frederick Winslow, *The Principles of Scientific Management* (New York: W. W. Norton, 1967).

Templin, Neal, "A Decisive Response to Crisis Brought Ford Enhanced Productivity," *Wall Street Journal*, December 15, 1992, 1A, 8A.

Thomis, Malcolm I., *The Luddites. Machine–Breaking in Regency England* (Hamden, Conn: Archon Books, 1970).

Thompson, E. P., "The Moral Economy of the English Crowd in the Eighteenth Century," *Past and Present*, Vol. 50 (1971),76–136.

Thorsrud, Einar, Sorensen, B. A., and Gustavsen, B., "Sociotechnical Approach to Industrial Democracy in Norway," in *Handbook of Work, Organization, and Society*, ed. by Robert Dubin (Chicago: Rand McNally, 1972), 421–464.

Thurman, J. E., "Job Satisfaction: An International Overview," *International Labour Review*, Vol. 116, no.3 (Novembe-December, 1977), 249–267.

Tichy, Noel M., "Revolutionize Your Company," *Fortune*, December 13, 1993, 114–118.

Tilgher, Adriano, *Work. What It Has Meant to Men Through the Ages* (New York: Arno Press, 1977).

Tolchin, Martin, "Officials in Cities and States Vow to Continue Minority Contractor Programs," *New York Times*, January 25, 1989, A18.

Trist, Eric and Bamforth, K. W., "Social and Psychological Consequences of the Long Wall Method of Coal Getting," *Human Relations*, Vol. 4 (1951), 3–38.

Trost, C., "Firms Heed Women Employees' Needs," *Wall Street Journal*, November 15, 1989, B1.

Turner, Arthur N., "What Makes a `Good' Foreman," *Personnel*, Vol. 32 (March, 1955), 382–392.

Turner, Frederick Jackson, *The Frontier in American History* (New York: Holt, Rinehart and Winston, 1962).

Uchitelle, Louis, "The New Faces of U.S. Manufacturing," *New York Times*, July 3, 1994, 1F, 6F.

Udy, Stanley H., Jr., *Work in Traditional and Modern Society* (Englewood Cliffs, N.J.: Prentice-Hall, 1970).

Urwick, Lyndall and Brech, Edward F. L., *The Making of Scientific Management*. 3 Vols. (London: Management Publications Trust, 1945–1948).

Van Maanen, John and Schein, Edgar H., "Career Development," in *Improving Life at Work*, ed. by J. Richard Hackman and J. Lloyd Suttle (Santa Monica, California: Goodyear Publishing Company), 30–95.

Vedder, Richard and Gallaway, Lowell, *Out of Work. Unemployment and Government in Twentieth Century America* (New York: Holmes and Meier, 1993).

Verhovek, Sam H., "States are Already Providing Glimpse at Welfare's Future," *New York Times*, September 21, 1995, A1,B10.

Walker, Charles R. and Guest, Robert H., *The Man on the Assembly Line* (Cambridge, Mass.: Harvard University Press, 1952).

Walton, Richard E., "Alienation and Innovation in the Workplace," in *Work and the Quality of Life*, ed. by James O'Toole (Cambridge, Mass.: MIT Press, 1974), 227–245.

Walton, Richard E., "Criteria for Quality of Working Life," in *The Quality of Working Life*, ed. by Louis Davis and Albert B. Cherns. 2 Vols. (New York: Free Press, 1975),1:91–104.

Walton, Richard E., "From Hawthorne to Topeka and Kalmar," in *Man and Work in Society*, ed. by Eugene L. Cass and Frederick G. Zimmer (New York: Van Nostrand Reinhold, 1975), 116–134.

Walton, Richard E., "How to Counter Alienation in the Plant," *Harvard Business Review*, Vol. 50 (December, 1972), 70–81.

Walton, Richard E., "Innovative Restructuring of Work," in *The Worker and the Job: Coping with Change*, ed. by Jerome M. Rosow (Englewood Cliffs, N.J.: Prentice–Hall, 1974),145–176.

Walton, Richard E., "Teaching an Old Dog New Tricks," *The Wharton Magazine*, Vol. 2, no. 2 (Winter, 1978), 38–48.

Ware, Norman, *The Industrial Worker, 1840–1860. The Reaction of American Industrial Society to the Advance of the Industrial Revolution* (Chicago: Quadrangle Books, 1964).

Warner, W. Lloyd and Martin, Norman (eds.), *Industrial Man. Businessmen and Business Organizations* (New York: Harper,1959).

Warner, W. Lloyd and Lunt, Paul S., *The Social Life of a Modern Community* (New Haven: Yale University Press, 1941).

Warr, Peter and Wall, Toby, *Work and Well-Being* (Harmondsworth, Middlesex: Penguin, 1975).

Warren, Harris G., *Herbert Hoover and the Great Depression* (New York: W. W. Norton, 1967).

Watkins, T. H., *The Great Depression. America in the 1930s* (Boston: Little, Brown, 1993).

Watson, Thomas J., Jr., "Technological Change," in *Of Men and Machines*, ed. by Arthur O. Lewis, Jr. (New York: E. P. Dutton, 1963), 295–309.

Weber, Joseph, "Letting Go is Hard to Do," *Business Week*, Special Enterprise Issue, 1993, 218–219.

"Welfare Reform in America. You Say You Want a Revolution," *The Economist*, June 18, 1994, 21–22.

Wells, David, *Recent Economic Changes* (New York: Appleton, 1895).

Wermiel, Stephen, "Supreme Court, in 6-3 Vote, Backs Hiring Goals to Correct Sex Bias," *Wall Street Journal*, March 26, 1987, 3, 26.

Wertenbaker, Thomas Jefferson, *The Puritan Oligarchy. The Founding of American Civilization* (New York: Grosset and Dunlap, 1947).

Whitehead, T. N., *The Industrial Worker. A Statistical Study of Human Relations in a Group of Manual Workers* (Cambridge, Mass.: Harvard University Press, 1938).

"Why the Use of Flexible Schedules is Lagging Availability," *Investor's Business Daily*, September 24, 1993, 3.

Whyte, William F., "Human Relations Reconsidered," in *Industrial Man. Businessmen and Business Organizations*, ed. by W. Lloyd Warner and Norman Martin (New York: Harper, 1959), 307–322.

Whyte, William F., *Man and Organization: Three Problems in Human Relations* (Homewood, Illinois: R.D. Irwin, 1959).

Whyte, William F., *Men at Work* (Westport, Conn.: Greenwood Press, 1974).

Whyte, William F., Dalton, M., Roy, D., Sayles, L., Collins, O., Miller, F., Strauss, G., Furstenberg, F. and Bavelas, A., *Money and Motivation: An Analysis of Incentives in Industry* (Westport, Conn.: Greenwood, 1977).

Whyte, William H., Jr., *The Organization Man* (New York: Simon and Schuster, 1956).

Wilbur, Ray L. and Hyde, Arthur M., *The Hoover Policies* (New York: Charles Scribner's Sons, 1937).

Williams, J. Clifton, *Human Behavior in Organizations*. 2nd ed. (Cincinnati: South-Western Publishing, 1982).

Wilson, James Q., "A New Approach to Welfare: Humility," *Wall Street Journal*, December 29, 1994, A10.

Witte, Edwin E., "The Evolution of Managerial Ideas in Industrial Relations," in *Views on U.S. Economic and Business History. Molding the Mixed Enterprise Economy* (Atlanta: Business Publishing Division, College of Business Administration, Georgia State University, 1985) 351–361.

Wood, Leonard A., "Changing Attitudes and the Work Ethic," in *The Work Ethic in Business*, ed. by W. Michael Hoffman and Thomas J. Wyly (Cambridge, Mass.: Oelgeschlager, Gunn and Hain, 1981), 1–17.

Woods, Mike, "CEO Briefing on Management & Leadership," *Investor's Business Daily*, August 9, 1993, 4.

Worker Alienation, 1972. Hearings Before the Subcommittee on Employment, Manpower, and Poverty of the Committee on Labor and Public Welfare, 92nd Congress, 2nd Session, 25–26 July 1972 (Washington, D.C.: U.S. Government Printing Office, 1972).

Worthy, James C., *Shaping an American Institution. Robert E. Wood and Sears, Roebuck* (Urbana: University of Illinois,1984).

Wrigley, E. A. and Schofield, R. S., *The Population History of England, 1541–1871* (Cambridge, Mass.: Harvard University Press, 1981).

Xerox Corporation, *NAMD News* (March, 1981), 1.

Yang, Catherine, "The EEOC: Too Swamped to Shoot Straight," *Business Week*, May 1, 1995, 155.

Yankelovich, Daniel, "New Rules in American Life: Searching for Self-Fulfillment in a World Turned Upside Down," *Psychology Today* (April, 1981), 35–91.

Yankelovich, Daniel, "The Meaning of Work," in *The Worker and the Job. Coping with Change*, ed. by Jerome M. Rosow (Englewood Cliffs, N.J.: Prentice-Hall, 1974), 19–47.

Yankelovich, Daniel, *The New Morality. A Profile of American Youth in the 70s* (New York: McGraw-Hill, 1974).

Yankelovich, Daniel, "The New Psychological Contracts at Work," *Psychology Today* (May, 1978), 46–50.

Yankelovich, Daniel, "Turbulence in the Working World: Angry Workers, Happy Grads," *Psychology Today* (December, 1974), 81–87.

Yankelovich, Daniel, "Work Values, and the New Breed," in *Work in America. The Decade Ahead*, ed. by Jerome M. Rosow (New York: Van Nostrand Reinhold, 1979), 3–26.

Yankelovich, Daniel, "Yankelovich on Today's Workers: We Need New Motivational Tools," *Industry Week*, August 6, 1979, 61–68.

Yankelovich, Daniel and Immerwahr, John, *Putting the Work Ethic to Work* (New York: Public Agenda Foundation, 1983).

Yellowitz, Irwin, *Industrializaion and the American Labor Movement 1850–1900* (Port Washington, N.Y.: Kennikat, 1977).

Youings, Joyce, *Sixteenth-Century England* (London: Penguin,1984).

Zahavi, Gerald, *Workers, Managers, and Welfare Capitalism. The Shoeworkers and Tanners of Endicott Johnson, 1890–1950* (Urbana: University of Illinois Press, 1988).

Zimpel, Lloyd (ed.), *Man Against Work* (Grand Rapids, Michigan: William B. Eerdmans Publishing Co., 1974).

Zonderman, David A., *Aspirations and Anxieties. New England Workers & the Mechanized Factory System 1815–1850* (New York: Oxford University Press, 1992).

Zuboff, Shoshana, *In the Age of the Smart Machine. The Future of Work and Power* (New York: Basic Books, 1988).

Zuboff, Shoshana, "The Work Ethic and Work Organization," in *The Work Ethic: A Critical Analysis*, ed.by Jack Barbash *et al* (Madison, Wisconsin: IRRA, 1983), 153–181.

INDEX

Freedmen's Bureau, 163
freedom dues, 123
French, John, 207
Freud, Sigmund, 279
Frick, Henry, 8
Friedman, Dana, 276
Friedmann, Georges, 217
Frobisher, John, 120
Fromm, Erich, 216
frugality, 133
  Calvinist support of, 55, 67
  See also thrift
Fugger, Jakob, 20, 33, 49, 52, 186
Fuller, H. L., 232

GAIN (Greater Avenues to Independence), 262
gain-sharing, 237
Gallatin, Albert, 160
Gallaway, Lowell, 254
Gantt, Henry L., 8
Garfield, James, 174
Gary, Elbert, 196
Gates, Bill, 7, 20, 170, 240
Gay, Edwin F., 100
"gazelles," 244
Gellerman, Saul, 201-2
gemeine Kasten (general funds for poor), 32
General and Industrial Management (Henri Fayol), 9
general calling, 21, 39, 69, 84, 93, 111-2
General Electric Corporation, 196
  employee involvement, 230-1
General Motors Corporation, 18
  and quality of worklife pact, 228
  George Morris, 228
  Lordstown plant, 18, 227-8
  NUMMI facility, 193, 230, 232
  Rochester factory, 230
  Saginaw plant, 230
  Saturn facility, 230
  Tarrytown plant, 228-9
  Warren factory, 229-230
General Foods Company
  Topeka experiments, 224-6
General Mills Survey (1977), 221
Geneva, 56, 61, 68
  and business world, 64, 66
  Calvinist theocracy, 54-5, 59-60
  Calvin's return to, 53
  Consistory, 55

ordinances for care of poor, 51
suppression of holidays, 85
Venerable Company, 55
George, Henry, 156
George, W. L., 175
GE Silicones, 275
Gilbert, Sir Humphrey, 120
Gilbreth, Frank and Lillian, 8, 199
Girard, Stephen, 5, 16, 20, 112, 129, 146, 186
  and self-help, 173
Glazer, Nathan, 271
gleitzeit (sliding time), 275
  See also flextime
Gompers, Samuel, 166-7, 189
Good News from New-England, 116
"good provider" theme
  Yankelovich on post-1945 values, 251
Goodrich, Samuel
  importance of labor, 160
gospel of work, 88
Gramsci, Antonio, 192
Grand Rebeine (riot) of 1529, 46
Gratian, 33
Great Awakening
  and role of work, 130
Great Depression, 18, 157, 176, 180
  deep unemployment, 243, 251-2, 279
  first unemployment insurance act (Wisconsin), 187
  welfare capitalism, 196
Great Migration
  Afro-American trek northward, 166
  Puritan movement to North America, 87, 119
Great Society, 13, 18, 265, 272
  entitlement programs, 187-8, 251
Greeley, Horace, 172
Green Mountain Boys, 121
  See also Ethan Allen
Green, Robert, 23
Greene, Jack
  and opportunity in colonial America, 117
  poor relief, 139
Greene, Nathaniel, 159
Greenhalgh, Leonard, 234
Greenham, Richard, 71, 73
Greenough, Joseph, 163
Gregory, John, 156
Gresham, Thomas, 20
Grew, Theophilus, 132
Griggs v. Duke Power Company (1971), 266

branded with V under Somerset, 103
colonial America, 136, 138, 187
conny-catchers, 102
dissolution of monasteries, 101
driven to home parishes, 96, 101–2
high in England, 1598–1638, 115
inclination to idleness, 43
in London, 102
Luther on, 19
on roads of England, 104
punishment for, 41
put to hard labor, 51
starvation, 49
to be sent to Virginia, 107, 115–6
Tudor-Stuart antipathy to, 76
Virginia Statute of 1672, 137
See also vagabonds
Vanderbilt, Cornelius, 173
Vassa, Gustabus, 147
Vedder, Richard, 254
Venerable Company (Geneva), 55
Virginia Company, 47
and idleness at Jamestown, 135
Vives, Juan Luis, 50
vocation, 33, 38, 55, 57–9, 70, 83–4, 111
See also Beruf and calling
Voice of the Trumpet (Robert Crowley), 32–3
Vollmer, Gottlieb, 163
Volvo Corporation, 224
Vulgate
and calling, 82

Wadsworth, Benjamin, 132
wage workers (laborers), 64–5
in American colonies, 116
in England, 116
Walker, C. R.
and Guest-Walker study (1952), 11
Wall, Toby, 206
Warr, Peter, 206
Walton, Richard, 11
challenge in work, 219
collaborative management style, 222
Hawthorne experiments, 206
Walton, Sam, 170
Wards Cove Packing Company v. Frank Atonio (1989), 268–9
Warner, W. Lloyd, 209
War on Poverty, 255
Washington Business Group on Health, 274

Washington, George, 124, 145
"Waste Not, Want Not" (Maria Edgeworth and McGuffey readers), 161
Watkins, Gordon S., 202
Watson, Thomas J., 218
Weber, Brian, 267
Weber, Max, 9, 22–3, 188, 190–1
See also Protestant Ethic and Spirit of Capitalism and bureaucracy
Wedgwood, Josiah, 3
Weil, Henry, 162
Welch, Jack
and employee involvement, 230–1
Weld, Theodore, 148
welfare, 12, 247–263
Cotton Mather, 92
Lynn welfare crisis (1820s), 250
Philadelphia welfare crisis (1820s), 249–250
stigma of, 95
work and, 21, 247–263
See also deserving and undeserving poor
welfare capitalism, 17–8, 185, 188, 236, 238
Amoskeag Manufacturing Company, 195
and Great Depression, 196
Endicott Johnson, 194
Henry Heinz, 194
National Cash Register, 144, 194–5
Pullman Company, 144, 194
William Filene, 194
"welfare rights," 253
See also entitlements
Wentworth, John, 128
Westinghouse Corporation, 236
Weyerhauser Corporation, 275
Wharton, Richard, 5, 20, 89–90, 128
Wheatley, Phillis, 147
"Where There is a Will There is a Way"
and support of work, 155
See also McGuffey readers
Whitehead, T. N., 202–4
Whitgift, John, 70
Whyte, William F., 17, 210–1
Whyte, William H., Jr.
The Organization Man, 23
Willard, Samuel
and diligence, 132
and support of wealth, 75
Williams v. Mississippi (1898), 163